Beginning
Information Cards
and Cardspace

From Novice to Professional

Marc Mercuri

Apress®

Beginning Information Cards and CardSpace: From Novice to Professional

Copyright © 2007 by Marc Mercuri

ISBN-13 (paperback): 978-1-59059-807-8

ISBN-13 (electronic): 978-1-4302-0204-2

Printed and bound in the United States of America (POD)

Trademarked names may appear in this book. Rather than use a trademark symbol with every occurrence of a trademarked name, we use the names only in an editorial fashion and to the benefit of the trademark owner, with no intention of infringement of the trademark.

Lead Editor: Jonathan Hassell
Technical Reviewer: Steven Woodward
Editorial Board: Steve Anglin, Ewan Buckingham, Gary Cornell, Jonathan Gennick, Jason Gilmore,
    Jonathan Hassell, Chris Mills, Matthew Moodie, Jeffrey Pepper, Ben Renow-Clarke, Dominic Shakeshaft,
    Matt Wade, Tom Welsh
Project Manager: Beth Christmas
Copy Edit Manager: Nicole Flores
Copy Editor: Kim Wimpsett
Assistant Production Director: Kari Brooks-Copony
Production Editor: Katie Stence
Compositor: Susan Glinert
Proofreader: Elizabeth Berry
Indexer: Becky Hornyak
Artist: April Milne
Cover Designer: Kurt Krames
Manufacturing Director: Tom Debolski

Distributed to the book trade worldwide by Springer-Verlag New York, Inc., 233 Spring Street, 6th Floor, New York, NY 10013. Phone 1-800-SPRINGER, fax 201-348-4505, e-mail orders-ny@springer-sbm.com, or visit http://www.springeronline.com.

For information on translations, please contact Apress directly at 2855 Telegraph Avenue, Suite 600, Berkeley, CA 94705. Phone 510-549-5930, fax 510-549-5939, e-mail info@apress.com, or visit http://www.apress.com.

The source code for this book is available to readers at http://www.apress.com in the Source Code/Download section. You will need to answer questions pertaining to this book in order to successfully download the code.

Contents at a Glance

Contents

Foreword

For all the advances in technology on the Internet over the past 15 years, one thing has remained unchanged—using usernames and passwords to authenticate users to websites in order to access services or restricted content. The idea of a shared secret, known only to the user and service, may be simple, but it's fraught with security challenges and has led to an increase in identity theft and online fraud, which is reaching epidemic proportions. Who hasn't received an email in the past month claiming to be from a major financial institute or e-commerce website? How do we know whether this is the real company or a fraudster trying to steal our passwords in order to wire money out of our bank account into theirs?

Usernames and passwords cause almost as many problems with an enterprise where users may have a dozen different accounts to access different applications or functions in different roles. In addition, a user's identity is trapped within the boundary of the domain. What happens when a user needs to access services being provided by a partner or supplier? Today this problem has solutions, but in many cases the solutions are proprietary and very costly.

The biggest challenge, however, is that this isn't a problem that can just be solved by the major software vendors; it's a problem that needs to be solved at every level—for users, enterprises, governments, and websites. What this problem really needed was a luminary who could help all of us understand at a philosophical level how we should solve this problem and an architectural framework that we could adopt. In mid-2005 Kim Cameron, Microsoft's chief identity architect, started the conversation with the rest of the industry on how we could solve this problem. Through conversations on his blog (www.identityblog.com) he shared his ideas; academics and other thought leaders in the industry discussed them at length. This collective came to be known as the Identity Gang, and it is their input that helped shape not only this vision but also a framework that would allow the negotiation and exchange of identity information. This framework is called the *identity metasystem*, and it describes the interchange between three parties—an identity provider, a subject, and a relying party. The client component of this system is called an *identity selector,* and Microsoft's implementation is Windows CardSpace.

In this book, Marc has provided an excellent introduction to how the identity metasystem works, and he also walks you step by step through the process of developing solutions to participate in changing the way users everywhere deal with identity. Whether you have a website or web service that needs an identity solution, or you have identities that you want to be able to participate in the identity metasystem, this is the place to start.

Steven Woodward
Group Manager, Identity Evangelism
Microsoft Corporation

About the Author

MARC MERCURI is currently employed at Microsoft Corporation, where he is an architect on the DPE Platform Incubation team. His prior role was as a member of the Windows Server Evangelism team, where he worked with Global Fortune 500 customers interested in the early adoption of Windows Communication Foundation, Windows Workflow Foundation, and Windows CardSpace.

Marc has been actively working in the industry for the past 15 years, with a focus on data and systems integration projects in Europe, Latin America, and the United States.

He has served as an architect and in lead roles in both the enterprise and ISV spaces, spanning financial services, the public sector, publishing, hospitality, and retail verticals. Over the course of his career, he has worked on projects that integrated the majority of operating systems (Windows, Unix, Linux, Qnix, DOS, IBM OS/390) and databases (SQL, DB2, Oracle, Sybase, Sybase ASA).

Marc has spoken at numerous conferences and is the coauthor of the books *Windows Communication Foundation: Hands On!* and *Windows Communication Foundation Unleashed!* He has published numerous magazine articles on web services and mobile application development. He is also the author of two popular blogs, http://www.marcmercuri.com and http://www.mashupguy.com.

About the Technical Reviewer

STEVEN WOODWARD spent eight years working in the software industry in the United Kingdom, where he was born and raised, before moving to the United States to work for Microsoft in 1996. During his time at Microsoft he has been a developer and program manager, but he finally settled within Microsoft's Developer and Platform Evangelism group, which works across the industry with partners and customers keen to take advantage of the platform technologies being developed by the Windows division. For the past four years Steve has worked on identity-related technologies and now runs the Identity Evangelism team. For the two last years he has worked with a small group of individuals to help the industry understand the power of the identity metasystem. Having held conversations with many of the world's leading e-commerce and financial services companies, he holds a unique perspective on how this important technology can reshape the Internet into a safer place for the next generation.

Acknowledgments

Authoring a book of this size on your own can be a daunting task. A number of individuals helped—either directly or indirectly—during the research and writing of this book, and I'd like to acknowledge their contributions here.

I'd like to thank Steven Woodward for stepping in and taking over the technical editor role for the book. Steven and I were teammates last year, and I knew he'd provide great feedback, which he did. This is definitely a better book because of his involvement.

I'd also like to thank and acknowledge the contributions of both Chuck Mortimore and Jim Sermsheim. Chuck, well-known for his Firefox identity selector and Java-based relying party, provided feedback and content at several points during the creation of the book. Jim, from Novell's Bandit Project, provided great feedback on Chapter 4, helping update and clarify the current status of some projects in the open source community.

There were a number of folks from Microsoft, both from the product groups and the DPE organization, that I'd like to thank, including Kim Cameron, Steven Woodward, Mike Jones, Bill Barnes, Scott Beaudreau, Charles Fitzgerald, Richard Turner, Nigel Watling, Garrett Serrack, Alberto Arias Maestro, Matt Winkler, and Vittorio Bertocci.

I would also like to thank the team at Apress, particularly Jonathan Hassell, Beth Christmas, Kim Wimpsett, and Katie Stence. They were fantastic to work with, and their editorial skills are unparalleled.

And lastly, and most important, I'd like to thank my wife, Kathryn, who, despite losing me to my writing for far too many nights and weekends and despite my writing back-to-back books, has never stopped being supportive of the project.

Introduction

The Internet was designed without identity in mind. The result is a patchwork of solutions that try to fill the gap, none of them ideal. With cases of identity theft and phishing rising exponentially, something needs to change. With widespread industry agreement on both the Laws of Identity and the concept of an identity metasystem, that change is upon us.

With Microsoft's Windows CardSpace being deployed with the .NET Framework 3.0 and installed by default with Windows Vista, the industry is poised for an "identity big bang."

As someone who works with technologies in the very early phases of development, as well as with customers looking to utilize these technologies, I can see that information cards and Windows CardSpace have the opportunity to truly transform the way that identity is handled on the Internet. There has been a number of great documents made available on the Web that delve into the subject with considerable depth. The challenge is that identity is typically not at the forefront of many technology books today, and going directly to those documents can be a bit daunting.

This book is, as its name implies, for novices and professionals. It's designed to provide an understanding of the concepts, an overview of the projects and technology landscape, and coverage of the technical implementation skills.

From a technical perspective, the book will provide guidance and understanding of how to request, issue, and consume information cards, with specific areas of coverage in the following:

- Adding support for information cards in ASP.NET, PHP, or Java websites

- Using information cards to personalize your websites

- Extending ASP.NET Membership for information card support

- Creating and consuming information card–secured WCF services

- Securing RSS with information cards

- Automating information card issuance with Windows Workflow Foundation

- Working with security token services

Intended Audience

There is a wide audience for this book. Including knowledge about the subject of identity, the laws of identity, the identity metasystem, information cards, and personalization, the content of the book is accessible to everyone.

For the technical chapters, if you are interested in reading the Microsoft technology–focused chapters, you should be knowledgeable in C#. Chapter 13 has examples in PHP and Java, and it is expected that to leverage those chapters you will have an understanding of one or both of the languages.

As mentioned earlier, the book covers a number of technologies to be used in conjunction with information cards and CardSpace, including ASP.NET, ASP.NET membership, Windows Communication Foundation (WCF), Windows Workflow Foundation (WF), and SQL Server Express. The book will contain step-by-step instructions on how to implement the exercise code, and in the case of ASP.NET membership, WCF, and WF, there are sections that provide a basic introduction to those technologies.

The book does not provide a significant amount of coverage of low-level infrastructure implementations. If that's your interest, this may not be the book for you. The reality is that the audience for that is a subset of the overall pool, and there is great documentation on this available today. This book is complementary to that documentation, however, and provides references to specific documents for those looking to go even deeper.

Code Availability

The completed code for all Microsoft technology–focused exercises in this book is available via the Apress website as well as via my blog, http://www.marcmercuri.com.

The sole exception is Chapter 13, which will reside at the URLs of the specific projects mentioned, as identified in the chapter.

How This Book Was Written

I recognize and appreciate your investment in both time and money to read this book and complete the contained exercises. Buying a book on technology is truly an investment in your skill set, and I've taken an approach that I think will make this investment a positive one.

I've established a specific set of guiding rules I focused on when writing the book, as detailed in the following sections, and I think these will help ensure that this book is worth of your time.

Provide Content That Can Be Shared Across the Team

In most teams, there are individuals who look at a project from different perspectives based on their roles and their experience. For whatever reason, most books exclusively target a subset of the roles on the team: business analysts, project managers, junior developers, senior developers, or architects. In my experience, this sometimes causes issues where there are gaps of understanding between people on a team.

When I considered both this and the larger fact that the concepts of identity are not necessarily at the forefront of other technical books, I made a conscious decision to dedicate five chapters to providing information that could be shared across all the roles.

Provide Content on Projects and Code in the Open Source Community and Non-Microsoft Technologies

Having worked in and with enterprise customers for almost 15 years, I am also very much aware that a large percentage of businesses are heterogeneous environments. One of the challenges in this space is that there are a number of different projects from individuals and vendors outside of Microsoft. Chapter 4 of the book is dedicated specifically to identifying the key client-side and server-side projects. In addition to this chapter, which is informational and targeted at all roles, there is a complementary section in Chapter 13 that looks at how to enable the acceptance of information cards in non-Microsoft technologies. This highlights a number of projects and libraries available for adding support to PHP, Java, and Ruby applications, with coverage of code for implementing in PHP and Java.

Go Beyond "Hello, World" and Create Practical Examples

Having invested in a number of books over the years, the books I've appreciated most were those that had practical examples. Your time is valuable, and having you end up with 15 chapters of "Hello, World" exercises is, in my opinion, an insult. When I wrote this book, I did it with a focus on writing examples that would have you build functional utilities or sample applications that would provide a jump-start to your development.

In this book, you'll find many examples of this type—from writing information card–aware ASP.NET controls to workflow activities that automate card issuance to information card–secured RSS services and clients. You'll find your time well spent.

Leverage the Platform

Because the focus of the book is on Microsoft technologies, it was important to focus on how you can leverage information cards and CardSpace on the Microsoft platform—and not just on the technology itself.

The Microsoft platform is incredibly robust, and a great number of technologies are available to you, most at no cost. In this book, you'll use ASP.NET membership, Windows Communication Foundation, Windows Workflow Foundation, SQL Server/SQL Server Express, and the .NET Framework.

If you're not familiar with these technologies, have no fear. This book provides sample exercises and introductions to most of these technologies. For those already familiar, the chapters are designed with no dependencies on the introductory exercises, so you can skip ahead when appropriate.

With this approach, I think you'll find this book provides an acceptable return on investment.

Before You Begin

Before you begin the technical chapters, you'll want to download and install several resources to prepare your system. Microsoft provides the majority of these resources, and I describe them in more detail next.

Installing Internet Information Services

If you do not already have Internet Information Services running on your computer, you will want to install it. You can do this via the Windows Control Panel.

In Windows XP and Windows Service 2003

Follow these steps:

1. Open the Control Panel, and click the Add or Remove Programs icon.

2. Click the Add/Remove Windows Components icon.

3. This will display a dialog box. Click Application Server in the list, and then click the Details button.

4. If the check boxes next to ASP.NET or Internet Information Services (IIS) are not both checked, select them, and then click OK.

5. If Internet Information Services was not installed and you have an existing installation of the .NET Framework 3.0, find the .NET Framework 3.0 in the list of programs in the dialog box, and repair your current installation.

In Windows Vista

Follow these steps:

1. Open the Control Panel, and click the Programs and Settings icon.

2. Click the Turn Windows Features On or Off icon.

3. This will display a dialog box. If the box next to Internet Information Services is not colored blue or checked, click the check box next to it, and click OK.

4. If Internet Information Services was not installed and you have an existing installation of the .NET Framework 3.0, find the .NET Framework 3.0 in the list of programs in the dialog box, and repair your current installation.

Installing the .NET Framework 3.0

If you are using Windows XP SP2 or Windows Server 2003 and do not already have the .NET Framework 3.0 installed, you should install it now.

You can find it on Microsoft's website at the following location:

```
http://www.microsoft.com/downloads/details.aspx?➥
FamilyID=10cc340b-f857-4a14-83f5-25634c3bf043&DisplayLang=en
```

▪**Note** Windows Vista installs the .NET Framework 3.0 by default, so no additional install is required for that operating system.

Installing Visual Studio Extensions for Windows Communication Foundation

This book contains code that uses Windows Communication Foundation (WCF). Currently a separate download will provide tooling support to Visual Studio for WCF.

If you intend to do the WCF-related exercises, you should download and install this from the following location:

```
http://www.microsoft.com/downloads/details.aspx?➥
FamilyID=f54f5537-cc86-4bf5-ae44-f5a1e805680d&DisplayLang=en
```

Installing Visual Studio Extensions for Workflow Foundation

This book contains code that uses Windows Workflow Foundation (WF). Currently a separate download will provide tooling support to Visual Studio for WF.

If you intend to do the WF-related exercises, you should download and install this from the following location:

```
http://www.microsoft.com/downloads/details.aspx?➥
familyid=5D61409E-1FA3-48CF-8023-E8F38E709BA6&displaylang=en
```

Retrieving the Simple-STS Sample

Download and install the Simple-STS sample from the Windows CardSpace community site.

This sample will be used in Chapter 10 and will install and configure a sample certificate for www.fabrikam.com that is used throughout the book.

You can find the Simple-STS sample at the following location:

http://cardspace.netfx3.com/files/folders/samples_rc_1/entry6082.aspx

Download and unzip the file to C:\BeginningCardSpace\SimpleSTS.
Run the setup scripts, setup.bat and setssl.bat, to perform the configuration.

Retrieving the TokenHelper.cs File

As part of most samples, Microsoft provides a sample class called TokenHelper.cs. It's this class that provides functionality to retrieve claims from tokens sent to a website.

Microsoft is actively working on making this and other files available outside of specific demos and with its own installation. Currently, that installation is not yet published; in the interim, you can acquire this file by downloading the website integration sample, which you can find here:

http://cardspace.netfx3.com/files/folders/samples_rc_1/entry7139.aspx

Unzip the file to the directory C:\BeginningCardSpace\temp. Copy the file TokenHelper.cs from the Website\CardSpace\App_Code directory, and paste it into a new directory, C:\BeginningCardSpace\TokenHelper.

CHAPTER 1

■ ■ ■

Introduction

Over the past year, I've spent a significant amount of time working with enterprise customers interested in leveraging the .NET Framework 3.0 in their businesses. Specifically, I've worked with them on architecting systems that leverage Windows Workflow Foundation (WF), Windows Communication Foundation (WCF), and Windows CardSpace.

My focus has been global in scope, with multiple visits throughout the United States and Western Europe. As you might have guessed, I traveled by air for all of these trips, and as I traveled to Boston, New York, Tulsa, London, Paris, and Munich, I encountered many differences—airlines, countries, food, and languages. But there was one commonality on every trip—the need for me to prove my identity.

If you've traveled by plane before, you're familiar with the check-in process. You approach the ticket counter for your airline, and you provide a paper ticket (if you have one) or identify that you have an e-ticket. At that point, the clerk asks you for identification.

If I were to respond with "My name is Marc Mercuri. I live in Washington state in the United States." The response from the clerk would surely be "That's very nice, Mr. Mercuri. Now can you provide some identification?" In this particular situation, my self-assertion of who I am is not acceptable to both the airline and the government of the country I'm in. This particular scenario, like many others we encounter in the real world, requires that we provide some form of documentation that was supplied by someone who the recipient knows, who has an established reputation, and with whom the recipient has an established level of *trust*.

The same is true for a number of scenarios, such as attempting to purchase liquor, obtaining entry to a secured building, or obtaining credit from a financial institution. These types of interactions are of high value and/or of considerable risk. In scenarios where there is risk, value, or a combination of the two associated with a transaction, my identity is less about how I identify myself and really more about what others say about me.

Now, this is not true of all scenarios. If, at a cocktail party, I were to meet you and you asked me who I was, I could respond with "My name is Marc Mercuri. I live in Washington state in the United States." Your reaction would be considerably different from that of the airline employee. You'd likely think I was awkwardly formal for a cocktail party, but aside from that, you would likely accept my self-asserted identity. No risk or value is attached to the introduction. If you think about it, self-asserted identity is valid in a number of everyday scenarios. For example, you're not asked for a government-issued ID when identifying yourself at a dry cleaners or when making a reservation at a restaurant.

If you look at the online world, unless money is involved, websites are primarily based on self-asserted identity. Whether it's your free online email account, your account for your favorite sports website, or comments you make on a blog, your statements of identity are accepted at face value.

This chapter will cover some fundamental topics around identity, such as authentication, authorization, and federation. In addition, you will be introduced to topics such as personalization, the Laws of Identity, the identity metasystem, and Windows CardSpace, all of which are covered in depth in later chapters.

Authentication

Going back to the air travel scenario, why does the clerk at the airline counter trust what someone else says about me more than what I tell her? Well, when I provide certain types of ID, the airline is confident that my claims are authentic because they are made by an authority the airline trusts.

With regard to identity, *authentication* is the process by which an individual or entity is deemed to be who he/she/it is.

One of the acceptable forms of identification for an airline is typically a driver's license. If one looks at the driver's license, it contains several key *claims* about its owner, including name, address, date of birth, gender, height, weight, and eye color. The driver's license also typically contains a photograph.

Now you might think that the authentication occurs when the picture is examined and then compared to the person presenting it. But the claims are not believed just because a picture is present; the claims are considered authentic because they were issued by the state's Department of Motor Vehicles. The license was issued by an organization that the airline has chosen to *trust*.

There is a level of confidence at the airline that the Department of Motor Vehicles has processes in place that authenticate the individual. As you apply for the license in person, the clerks at the Department of Motor Vehicles can validate certain physical claims as authentic—height, gender, approximate age, and so on. For the claims beyond those that can't be seen with the naked eye, the agency depends on the authentication done by other entities that *the Department of Motor Vehicles trusts*.

To authenticate your claims, the Department of Motor Vehicles typically requests up to two types of other forms of identity, such as a birth certificate issued by a hospital or city where you were born that confirms your age, a utility bill that has an address that matches the one on your driver's license application, and so on.

Therefore, for every trip you take on an airline, the airline authenticates your identity based on claims authenticated by a trusted third party, but it actually goes much deeper than that. In reality, a successful interaction is really based upon a *chain of trust.*

As someone who travels quite a bit, I need to withdraw funds from my bank account while away from home. To withdraw funds from this bank account at a physical location from a bank teller, I am required to provide a form of government-issued identification, such as a driver's license. But I rarely have the opportunity to perform a withdrawal from a physical bank location. Instead, I withdraw funds primarily with the assistance of automated teller machines (ATMs).

To utilize these machines, my bank has provided me with a card that has a magnetic stripe. This card contains information about me, typically the information that is visible on the printed card such as my name and account number. When I want to withdraw funds, I insert my card into an ATM, where I am then challenged to present my personal identification number (PIN). In this case, the combination of the presence of the physical card (and the information contained within it) and my knowledge of the PIN is used to authenticate me. This is referred to as *two-factor authentication*.

Authorization

Authentication is typically a prerequisite to authorization. Authentication establishes my identity; *authorization* establishes what resources that identity can access and what actions that identity is allowed to perform.

In the case of air travel, your identity is authenticated with a government-issued ID, it is compared against the information on your plane ticket, and you are then authorized to board the plane and access the seat specified on your ticket.

On most planes, seats are available in what is called the *exit row*. This is a row on the plane located next to the emergency exit. Children are not allowed to sit in this row. If my seat assignment on the plane were for a seat within the exit row, the airline representative would check the claim of age on my driver's license or passport. Because I am older than 18, I would be authorized to sit in this row.

In the exit row scenario, this is an example of authorization based on age. There are many examples of this type of authorization. For example, if I attempt to purchase liquor or cigars in the state of Washington in the United States, the salespeople in each store I visit would request identification and validate I was at least 21 or 18 years of age, respectively.

As I mentioned earlier, I spent a good portion of the past year traveling. As a result, many times I was not home when a shipping company attempted to deliver an order from an online store. As a result, I needed to go to the company's facility to retrieve the package. Now because I was picking up the package at the shipping company's facility, the company needed to guarantee that the package was being delivered to the right party. To validate this, a representative inspected the claims on my driver's license. The combination of name, address, and picture authenticated me, and I was then authorized to receive this specific package.

Thus far, you've learned about authorization based on a form of identification provided by a government agency. There are a number of scenarios where you're given a token by a third party to identify yourself that authorizes you to access a resource from that party.

Let's look at an example of this. If you go to a restaurant or a nightclub, you'll often see a coat check, which provides patrons the opportunity to drop off their coat and retrieve it later in the evening. When you leave your coat, you're typically given a small plastic or other type of token. Although your government-issued identification has a robust number of personalized claims about who you are, this plastic token contains a single claim—a number. A corresponding token with that number is attached to your coat in the coat check closet. At the end of the evening, you present your token to the individual working in the coat check, and that token authorizes you to access the coat that has the same number.

In the preceding examples, the authorization rules have been fairly straightforward, but many times, authorization requires processing a set of business rules. These rules utilize the claims provided on the ID presented. For instance, if I attempt to enter a building at Microsoft, I must present my employee ID. The employee ID is then cross-referenced to determine whether I have access to that particular building on that particular day at that particular time. I might be authorized to access a building from 8 a.m. to 5 p.m. from Monday to Friday, but not at 10 p.m. or on Saturdays.

Authenticating Others

So far, you've seen scenarios where I have been proving my identity to others. But what about others proving their identity to me? In the real world, this is simple enough. If I were to interact with a bank, it would have a physical location, and that location would have a number of physical factors used to validate its authenticity. From signage to ATM machines to branded deposit slips and product literature to employees with name tags to the drive-through teller window—an abundant number of elements can help validate that the entity is indeed what it claims to be. Those physical representations are not, unfortunately, available when engaging with an entity online.

On average, I receive several emails a day from a large online payment company. The email states that there is an issue with my account and that I must go to the website to resolve an issue; for my convenience, a link is provided to the site. Figure 1-1 shows a sample email.

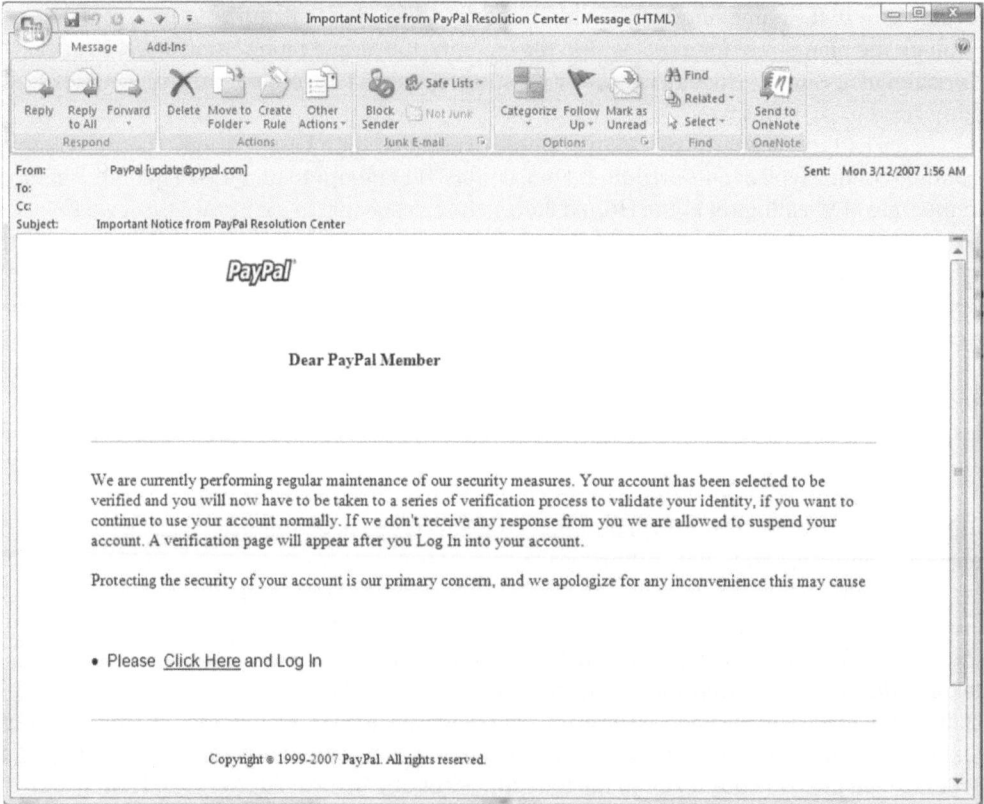

Figure 1-1. *Email from an "online payment site"*

I click the link and am taken to a site that looks identical to the website for the real payment provider, as shown in Figure 1-2. But as you might have guessed, it isn't.

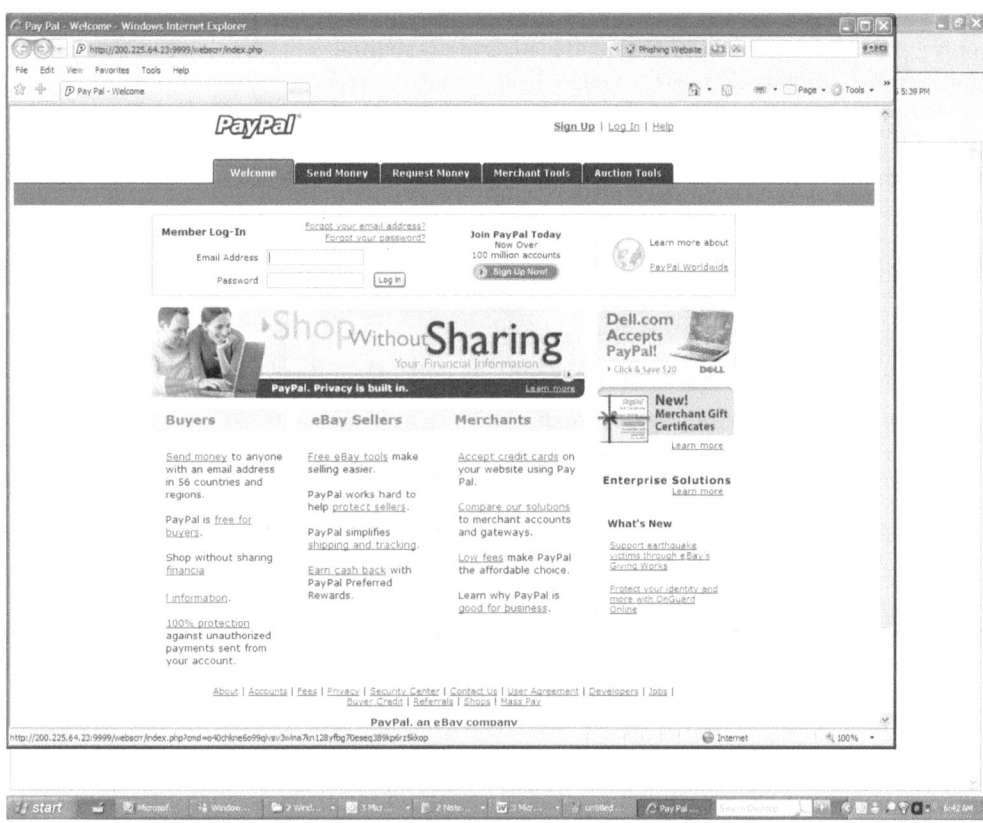

Figure 1-2. *The site at the other end of the link*

The email and site are part of a malicious attempt to gain the information to authenticate to my account on that site. If they managed to steal my identity with their fake site, they could then use my identity on the real one. With this identity, the thief could authenticate to the real site and be authorized to any funds I have in the account.

Note The payment provider the attacker is targeting here is just an example. I also get emails about "my" accounts at many large, well-known banks.

There's an old adage that states, "He who has the gold makes the rules." When it comes to usernames and passwords, the user is attempting to access a resource. That resource is analogous to gold; it's something we desire to access. The site or service, therefore, sets a rule that you must provide both a username and a password to access it. These two data elements are a shared secret with the site.

To prove my identity, I must share these with the site to prove who I am. Unfortunately, the site does not necessarily do the same. As discussed earlier, in the real world if I were to go to a bank, I could discern whether it was indeed a bank by a number of physical factors. This is not the case in an online scenario, and it is fairly trivial to duplicate the look and feel of a third party's website. Because most people use the web page similarities in graphics and layout to verify a site, it increases the likelihood of inadvertently sharing your secret—your username and password combination—with someone other than the real site.

Because of the potential of leveraging this type of attack for financial gain, it has moved beyond hackers to criminal syndicates who steal significant sums from the unsuspecting. This type of attack is called *phishing*, and according to Gartner, these types of attacks are growing at a rate of 1,000 percent per year.

What's worse is that the people perpetrating these attacks know that end users have password fatigue. It's unrealistic that an individual will remember unique usernames and passwords for every site on the Web they visit, and a number of patterns have emerged on how people manage their usernames and passwords.

My colleague Steven Woodward has identified four categories of users:

- Individuals who use a single username and password across all sites

- Individuals who use a pool of several usernames and passwords across all sites

- Individuals who use an attribute of a site to hash a username and password from a standard key

- Individuals who maintain a password-encrypted Microsoft Excel spreadsheet with 100+ usernames and passwords and where they use them

Hackers have recognized the first two patterns and have evolved their attacks such that the fake version of a site will respond that the username/password entered is not valid. In most cases, users of the site will enter another of their username/password pairs. The fake site will continue to collect the username/password pairs until the user enters the same username/password—at which point it redirects the user to the real site. At that point, the criminals behind the fake site have quite possibly stolen all your identities for multiple sites.

In credit card fraud, the consumer has little to no liability for fraudulent purchases made with a stolen credit card. Unfortunately, that is not the case when a criminal logs into your bank account after having authenticated to the site using your username and password. There are numerous cases where individuals have lost tens of thousands of dollars as a result. These cases are becoming well publicized and lowering consumer confidence.

Some application vendors have taken it upon themselves to add protections for customers against these types of attacks. For example, I'm using Microsoft Outlook 2003 and Internet Explorer 7, and these two applications have a number of antiphishing mechanisms that help me identify the site shown in Figure 1-2 as a fake. Outlook initially sent the email to my Junk Mail folder. Within the Junk Mail folder, it turned the link off, and I explicitly had to turn it back on to click it. Internet Explorer 7 identified the site as a phishing site and strongly suggested I not continue. Even after continuing, it turned the address bar in the browser to red indicating a concern about the site. In Outlook 2007, this functionality is extended, such that the URLs are expanded to provide further opportunity to determine whether a link is an attempted phishing attack.

But some people might not be using Outlook; they might be using Lotus Notes. Others might not be using Internet Explorer 7 but instead either an earlier version or another browser such as Opera or Firefox. Although Outlook and Internet Explorer 7 made it difficult to get to this site, this might not be the case in these other scenarios.

So in those cases, someone might make it through to the site unwarned. For the untrained eye, these emails and sites look genuine, and as a result people enter their usernames and passwords.

Although a trained eye can pick up on the signs such as that the email was sent via blind carbon copy (BCC) and that the website is located at an IP address vs. a domain, even the best-trained eyes can be vulnerable. I know of at least one senior person in the identity space who was checking his email late one night, was a bit tired, and fell prey to a phishing attack.

Personalization

Identity can provide more value than just authentication and authorization; it can also provide the means by which to deliver a rich, personalized experience. By allowing an application or website to know certain characteristics of who I am, the site can provide a more one-to-one engagement with me.

Amazon is a recognized leader in the personalization space. Once you've been authenticated and are logged into its website, Amazon utilizes the demographics in your account and combines them with your purchase history to provide a customized experience.

As you can see in Figure 1-3, Amazon has a Marc's Store tab based on what Amazon knows about me—a combination of my expressed and implied identity. Essentially, Amazon has provided me with a personalized store. Because I've purchased several books about identity as research for this book, you can see that the Marc's Store tab consists of a number of books about identity and privacy.

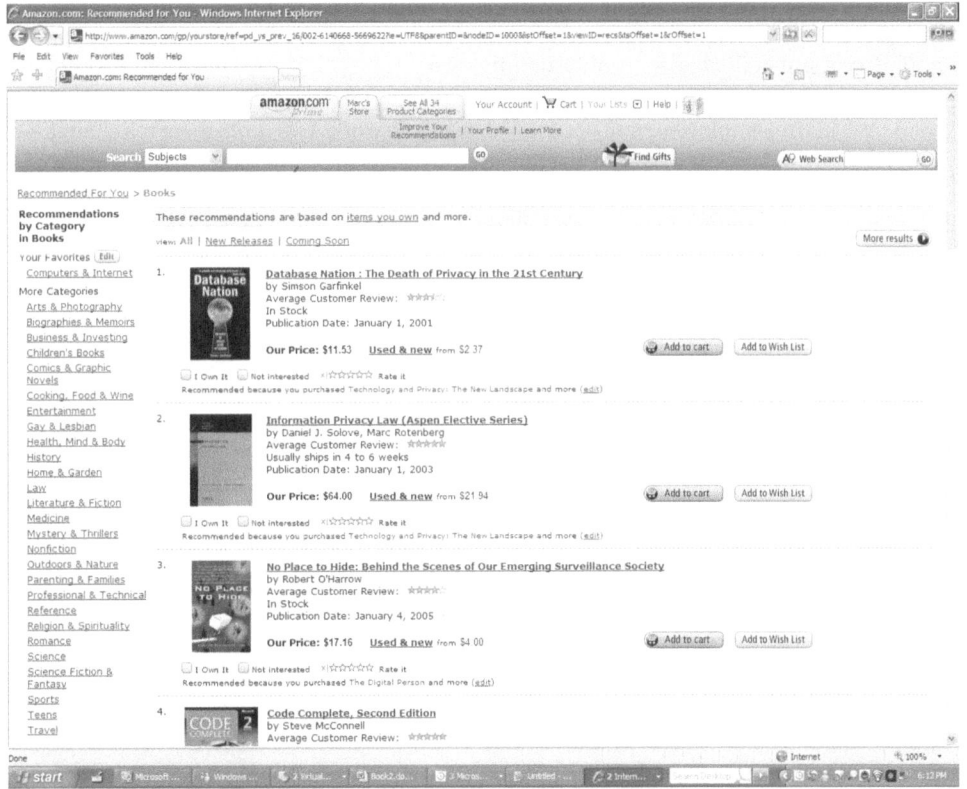

Figure 1-3. *Amazon's "my" store*

Rather than have me peruse a huge online warehouse of books, Amazon has presented just a subset of those it thinks I might be interested in. Historically, this has worked well for both Amazon and me. I've made numerous purchases based on recommendations—and have been happy with the recommended products.

Personalized experiences are most obvious in retail, but they truly span all vertical markets. Regardless of whether you're looking to sell more or make your site "stickier," the ability to personalize a site based on user information can help you get there.

In this book, you'll look at how individuals are doing personalization today and how Windows CardSpace can enable personalization in several scenarios. Also, the book includes a stand-alone project that shows a robust sample that includes personalization as a key piece.

Federation

One of the definitions of the word *federation* is "an organization formed by merging several groups or parties." In reference to identity, federation translates to an ability to share a single identity across multiple sites.

Imagine a business scenario involving a bank and a corporation. If the bank has a partnership with the corporation, there will undoubtedly be an interest in sharing resources between the two companies.

To access these resources, one must be authenticated and authorized. In this particular case, each company maintains identities for its own employees. One option to facilitate access would be to copy the accounts from the bank that needed access to resources at the corporation and place them in the corporation's identity store.

The problem with this scenario is that it requires close communication between the two corporations when an employee event occurs. This scenario works fine, *until* there is a change—a new employee, a change in role for an existing employee, or the termination of an employee.

If there is a change in the bank that occurs and the corporation is not notified—particularly with employee terminations—the corporation is subjected to a level of exposure. A terminated employee with malicious intent could continue to utilize resources at the corporation until such time that the corporation receives a notification from the bank that the employee should no longer have access to the system.

In addition to the challenges of additional risks, this approach also requires a fair amount of time dedicated to setting up and maintaining the identity in two locations by two staffs.

This is not just an issue across businesses but also across applications in a business. For my blog, I use a third-party web hosting company. For my hosting plan, I have one username and password for my administration page, another for the blog itself, a third to access the website statistics, another for my email, and yet another for access to the FTP server. For my one site, I am forced to use five different ID and password pairs. A better solution would be to have a single federated identity that worked across all these different applications.

In the consumer space, I've already established that there's password fatigue. There are distinct benefits to being able to share a single identity across multiple sites.

This book will discuss several approaches to handling federation of identity, including examples using CardSpace.

The Seven Laws of Identity

When looking at a federated identity for consumers, you might be familiar with a service Microsoft began offering a number of years ago, called Passport. Passport was intended to provide the same type of functionality that you saw in the airline travel scenario earlier in the chapter. Specifically, this was to provide a single, trusted identity for an individual that could be used across multiple sites.

Passport was a very successful solution for Microsoft's web properties; however, it was not a runaway success with third parties.

Microsoft has actually spent a fair amount of time looking into what some of the challenges were with the adoption of Passport. Kim Cameron, Microsoft's lead identity architect, looked long and hard at not only this but also why in general people either will accept and use an identity system or will reject it out of hand. He then published his thoughts on his Identity Blog (http://www.identityblog.com), where he discusses identity not just with individuals from Microsoft but with individuals from across the industry, from academics to enterprises and many representatives from the open source community. The distillation of these ideas has come to be known as the Laws of Identity, of which there are seven.

I'll detail the laws in Chapter 3, but here's a complete list:

Law #1: User Control and Consent

Law #2: Minimal Disclosure for a Constrained Use

Law #3: Justifiable Parties

Law #4: Directed Identity

Law #5: Pluralism of Operators and Technologies

Law #6: Human Integration

Law #7: Consistent Experience Across Contexts

One could suggest that Passport did not gain broad adoption amongst third-party sites because it is in conflict with several of the laws. One such conflict is with Law #3, "Justifiable Parties." While looking at Passport adoption, one can see that Microsoft's involvement in a transaction connected to a Microsoft-owned site was considered justified by end users, and Passport, in that instance, was acceptable. Microsoft's involvement (via Passport) in other scenarios on third-party sites, such as in a banking transaction, was not. Another conflict is with Law #5 because there was no pluralism; it was a closed system run by a single entity, Microsoft. One of the benefits of the laws is that they provide a common language to use in identity discussions. One can now say, "This was done to comply with Law #2" or "We can't do that; it violates Law #3."

Note Chapter 3 is dedicated to the Laws of Identity, where I will discuss each of them in more detail.

The Identity Metasystem

Law #5 is "Pluralism of Operators and Technologies." This was one of the challenges that Passport faced. Its implementation was provided by a single operator, Microsoft.

To satisfy Law #5—in other words, to provide a pluralism of operators and technologies—one needs to provide a level of interoperability across platforms, languages, and corporations. In essence, this takes us back to something done in the real world that I discussed earlier—let's revisit the airline scenario.

Specifically, when I check in for a flight, I provide a government-issued ID. This could be a driver's license. In the United States, this allows me to present an identity token provided by more than 50 different identity providers (all the U.S. states, territories, and so on). If I were not a U.S. citizen, I could provide a passport from a host of recognized nations. Although each of the tokens provided by the states or governments might have its own nuances, it complies with standards—whether defined or assumed—that make these tokens readily interoperable.

In the online world, as in the offline world, it is unlikely that there will be a single provider of identity. Instead, there will be a multitude of solutions and operators, as stated in "Microsoft's Vision for an Identity Metasystem":

> *This metasystem, or system of systems, would leverage the strengths of its constituent identity systems, provide interoperability between them, and enable creation of a consistent and straightforward user interface to them all. The resulting improvements in cyberspace would benefit everyone, making the Internet a safer place with the potential to boost e-commerce, combat phishing, and solve other digital identity challenges.*

—"Microsoft's Vision for an Identity Metasystem"

Chapter 3 delves deeper into the identity metasystem, including covering the roles and components contained within it.

Windows CardSpace

If the Laws of Identity provide the guidance and the identity metasystem provides the infrastructure, the next logical piece is an implementation on top of the metasystem.

CardSpace is Microsoft's implementation of a client application for the identity metasystem. It provides a secure, consistent experience for end users that supports the interoperability of the underlying identity metasystem. In essence it acts as an identity selector simplifying the process by which a user selects which identity to use for a specific interaction.

CardSpace ships as part of the .NET Framework 3.0 and can be used in both web applications and with services. In this book, Chapters 5 and 6 are dedicated to utilizing CardSpace in a web application, as well as in services built with WCF.

CardSpace is preinstalled with .NET Framework 3.0 on Windows Vista. It is also available for use on Windows XP Service Pack 2 and Windows Server 2003.

This book focuses on looking at what CardSpace is and where you can use it. In the remainder of the book, I'll explore each of the topics discussed earlier in the chapter and show how the identity metasystem and CardSpace will fundamentally change how identity is handled on the Web.

Summary

As the name of this book implies, the focus is on understanding CardSpace. But to understand CardSpace, it is important to have an understanding of the challenges and opportunities tied to identity.

In this chapter, you learned about the various concepts that are important. You gained an understanding of authorization and authentication and now understand both the challenges (in other words, federation) and the opportunity (in other words, personalization) that are present in the identity space.

In the next chapter, I'll take you on a quick lap around Windows CardSpace. You'll get to see what it is and how it works from hands-on usage.

CHAPTER 2

■■■

A Lap Around CardSpace

Now that I've covered the basics of authentication, authorization, and federation, it's time to dive in and start using CardSpace. In this chapter, you'll take a tour of CardSpace and become familiar with it from a user perspective.

By the conclusion of the chapter, you'll have become familiar with the CardSpace user experience, you'll have created a self-issued card, and you'll have used that card to connect to several sites. And to showcase the interoperability of CardSpace and information cards, one of those sites will be using Windows to access your information card and the other will be using Java.

Getting Started with CardSpace

Before you begin, you'll want to confirm that you have CardSpace installed. The next several sections will identify how to check whether CardSpace is installed and, if not, how to install it on Windows XP SP2, Windows Server 2003, and Windows Vista.

Making Sure You Have CardSpace Installed

The CardSpace identity selector is installed as part of the .NET Framework 3.0. The .NET Framework 3.0 was released with Windows Vista and installed by default. It is available for other operating systems, specifically Windows Server 2003 SP1 and Windows XP SP2. If you are using either of the latter two operation systems, you will need to install the .NET Framework 3.0, which is available via `http://download.microsoft.com`.

To confirm you have Windows CardSpace installed, open the Control Panel and look for the Windows CardSpace icon. If you are using Windows Vista and in the Classic View, it will look like Figure 2-1.

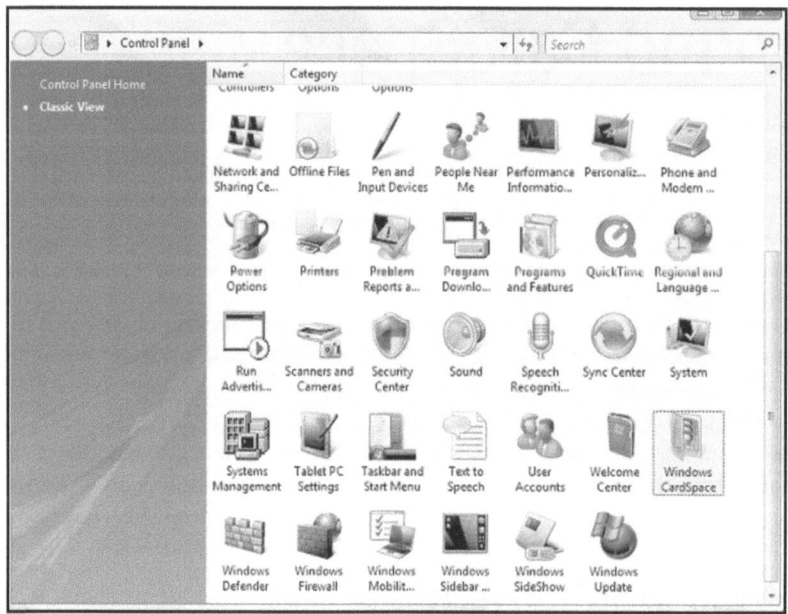

Figure 2-1. *CardSpace inside the Control Panel on Vista (in Classic View)*

If you are using the new view in Windows Vista, you can find it in the User Accounts section, as shown in Figure 2-2.

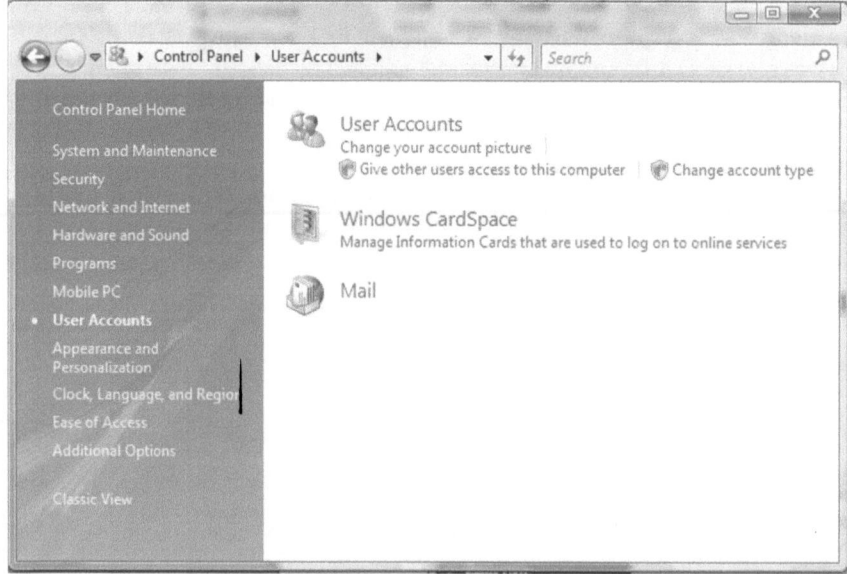

Figure 2-2. *CardSpace inside the Control Panel on Vista (in the new view)*

If you are using Windows XP SP2, you'll find CardSpace in the Control Panel under the User Accounts section, as shown in Figure 2-3.

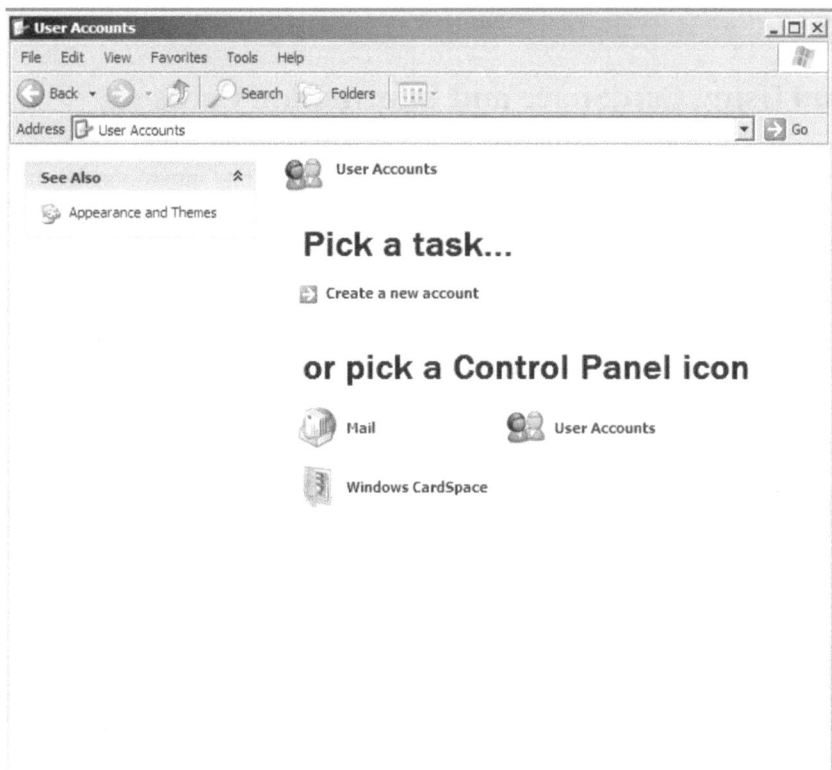

Figure 2-3. *CardSpace inside the Control Panel on Windows XP SP2*

You will also want to confirm that you have a browser that is CardSpace compatible. Internet Explorer 7 supports CardSpace natively and is what will be used in this chapter and for most of this book.

Note CardSpace is not limited solely to Internet Explorer 7 on Windows. Third parties are providing support to integrate CardSpace functionality into applications such as the Firefox browser. Others are incorporating identity selectors that are similar to the identity selector seen in CardSpace. Although the screen shots in this book are focused on usage with Internet Explorer 7, the client-side samples should also work in Firefox 2.0 with an appropriate plug-in for information card support.

■**Note** You can also use CardSpace with Windows Communication Foundation (WCF) to enable CardSpace security on WCF services. This is detailed later in this book, specifically in Chapters 7–9.

Creating and Using CardSpace and Information Cards

Now that you've confirmed that you have CardSpace installed, it's time to create a card and begin using it to access a number of sites. The first site to visit will be Kim Cameron's Identity Blog. Kim is the identity architect at Microsoft who has been a driving force behind the Laws of Identity, the concepts of the identity metasystem, and CardSpace.

His blog is a great source for a vast array of identity information that both Microsoft and the rest of the industry are working on, but particularly for information about CardSpace.

Open your browser, and navigate to http://www.identityblog.com.

In the top-right corner of the home page of his site, you will see the Login link.

Click the Login link, and you will be shown a login screen similar to the one in Figure 2-4.

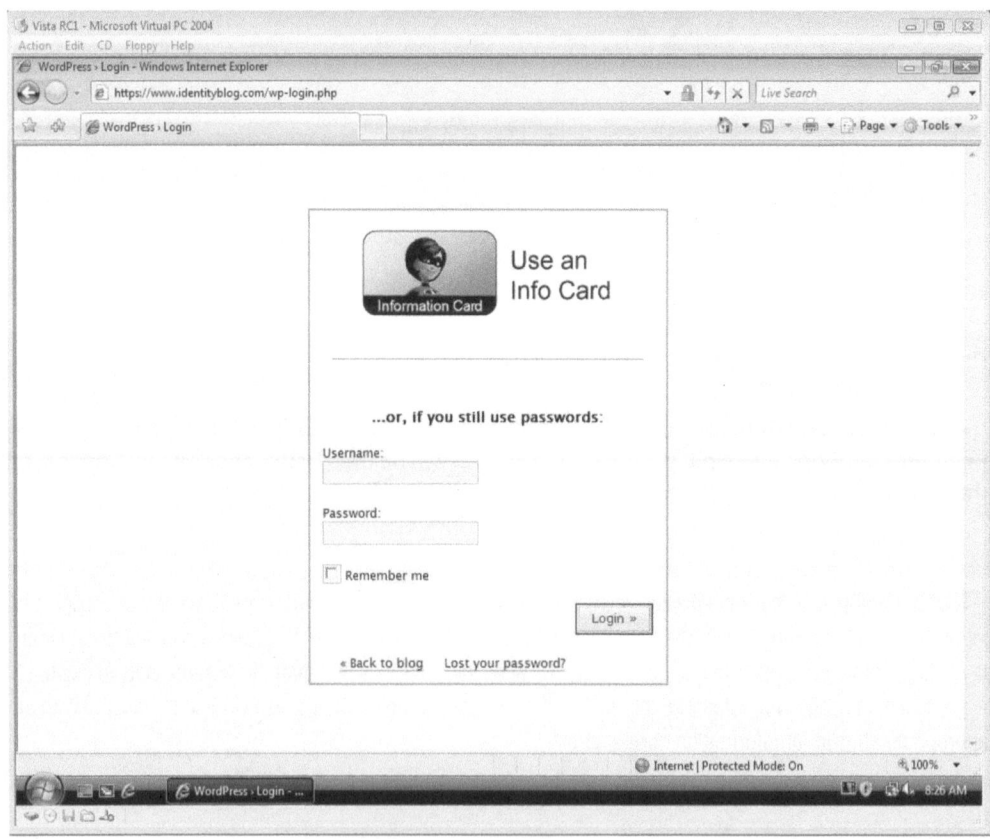

Figure 2-4. *The login screen at Kim Cameron's Identity Blog*

Click the Information Card icon to initiate the CardSpace identity selector.

As I discussed in the previous chapter, Gartner has reported that phishing attacks are growing at a rate of 1,000 percent annually. The common ploy is to send an email that contains a link to a website that looks like the website of an actual site. For users unaware of what to look for that would identify a site as fraudulent, this is a serious issue because it can put their accounts and potentially their finances at risk.

CardSpace tackles this issue head on, as you can see in the screen that is presented first in the identity selector. On this first screen, information about the site is either displayed or readily accessible, as shown in Figure 2-5.

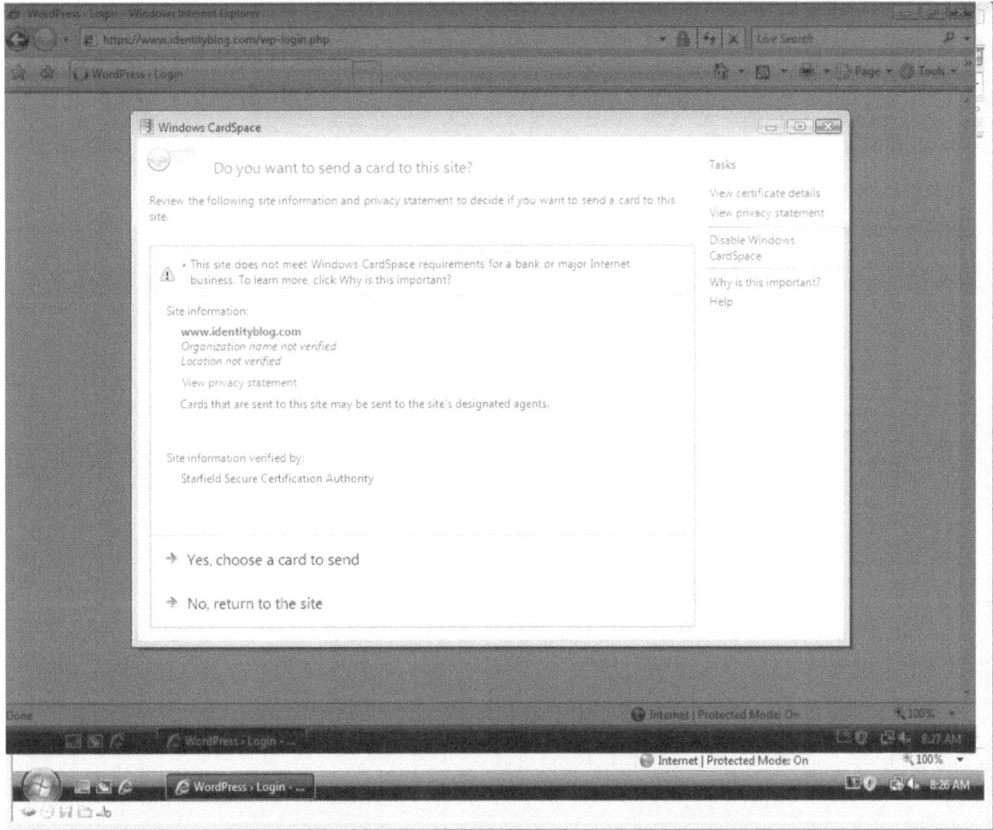

Figure 2-5. *Identifying the site or service requesting your information card*

Note that this screen, known as the Mutual Authentication dialog box, identifies the site information. Immediately, you know that the site requesting this information is http:// www.identityblog.com. You also know that the organization name and the location for this site have not been verified. The site also identifies that cards that are sent to this site might be sent to the site's designated agents.

You are also presented with information about who verified the site—in this case Starfield Secure Certification Authority.

Even with the site address matching the name I would expect, the organization name is not verified and the location is not verified. If this were purporting to be a bank or an online retailer, chances are this is a fake. If I hadn't figured that out on my own, the identity selector would actually display a warning icon and text to that effect.

On the screen shown in Figure 2-5, you're made aware of a number of key pieces of information about the site. If you look under the heading of Tasks, located in the upper-right corner, you'll see you have two opportunities to gather additional information.

Click the task labeled "View certificate details." As is displayed in Figure 2-6, you can see the details of the certificate used on the website, which include the name the certificate was issued to, who the certificate was issued by, the dates the certificate is valid, and that the certificate was created to ensure the identity of a remote computer.

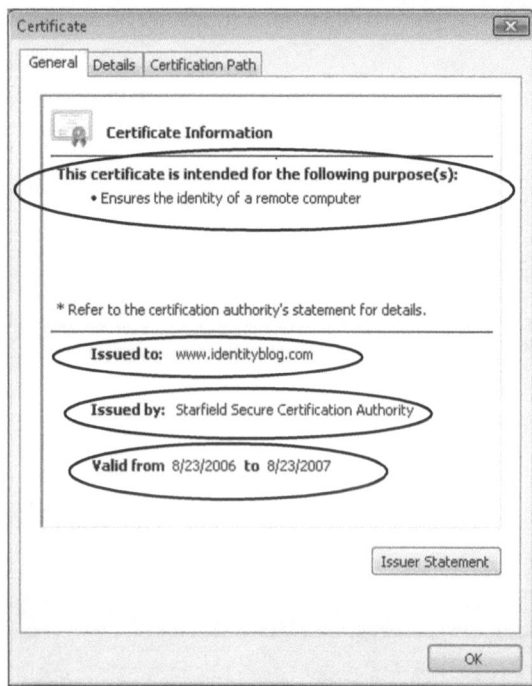

Figure 2-6. *Information about the site's certificate*

Even if a site is valid, it is important to understand what its privacy statement is. The privacy statement will detail what this site will and will not do with the information you provide to it. This information is available by clicking "View privacy statement," which is also under the Tasks heading.

Note You'll see the Mutual Authentication dialog box only on the first visit to a site. On subsequent visits, this information is rechecked, but the dialog box is shown only when the information changes from what you saw on the initial visit.

This is important, because if you somehow are directed to a site that's attempting to phish your information, you'll see the Mutual Authentication dialog box. This is one of the many subtle but powerful features in the CardSpace implementation that helps make the user more aware of potential attacks.

Because this site is a blog and not a bank or a major online site, we'll continue.

Click the back arrow in the identity selector, and then click "Yes, choose a card to send."

This will display the information cards that are on your computer. In addition, you will see an "Add a card" icon that will allow you to add an information card.

If this is the first time you have used CardSpace, your screen should resemble the one in Figure 2-7.

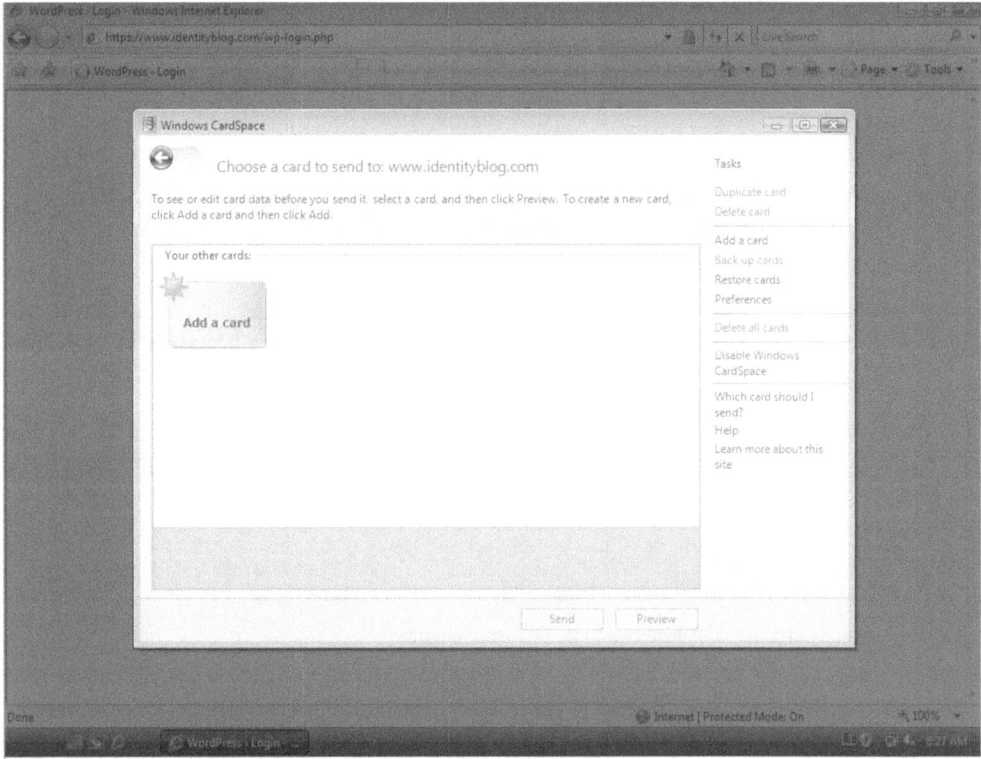

Figure 2-7. *The CardSpace identity selector*

Click the "Add a card" icon, and then click the Add button at the bottom of the identity selector.

This will present you with the option to create a personal card or install a managed card, as shown in Figure 2-8.

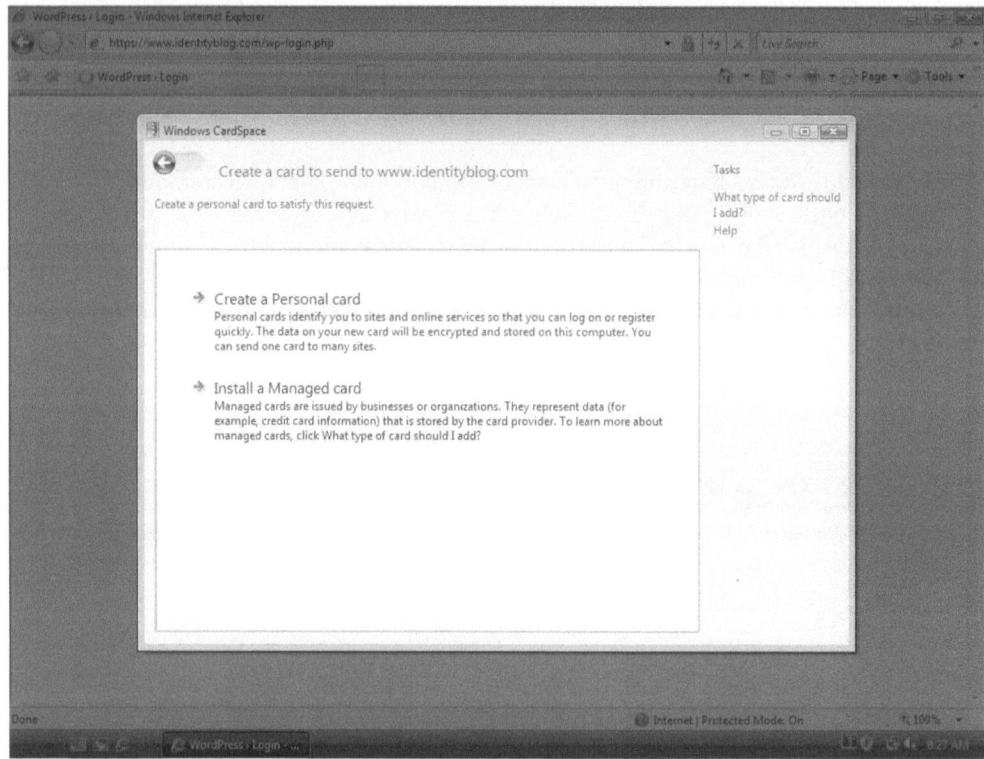

Figure 2-8. *Select the type of card to send.*

A *personal card* is a card that you issue yourself, similar to the real-world equivalent of printing your own business card. In this case, CardSpace on your local machine serves as the identity provider.

■**Note** Personal cards are also referred to as *self-issued* cards.

A *managed card* is a card provided by a third-party identity provider. As with cards that exist in your wallet today, any number of types of companies across many vertical markets can create managed cards. For example, financial institutions, governments, universities, businesses, and organizations are all likely candidates to become identity providers.

For this particular site, a personal card will suffice, so click "Create a Personal card."

This displays the "Edit a new card" dialog box within Windows CardSpace, as shown in Figure 2-9. Here you can provide a name for the card and then the values for a number of values that can be stored inside your information card.

Note The picture you specify for your card is solely for your own use within the CardSpace identity selector.

Sites will typically request and/or require that a user present an information card that contains certain claims. Personal cards contain a number of fields that can contain claims for your name, email address, physical address, phone, gender, date of birth, and website.

None of this information is required for creating a card. The fields populated are determined by you, and you should populate only those fields you feel comfortable sharing with a website or an application that utilizes a CardSpace-secured web service.

Because this card is being created in conjunction with a visit to a website using CardSpace, the fields that are required for *this* website are flagged with an asterisk and in red.

This screen identifies which fields will be sent to the site and which fields will not. When configuring a CardSpace-enabled site or service, you can identify claims as required, and you can also specify that certain claims are optional. Typically a site can do additional personalization with this data (that is, show you sales occurring in your local area based on ZIP code, show you sale items for men's clothes based on gender, and so on).

Note As you can see in Figure 2-9 and as you use CardSpace in other examples, you will continue to see examples of the Laws of Identity. In this case, you can clearly see the laws of "User Control and Consent" and the law of "Minimal Disclosure for a Constrained Use" in play. Here you are releasing only a subset of information associated with the card, and you're doing so only to whom you choose to send it.

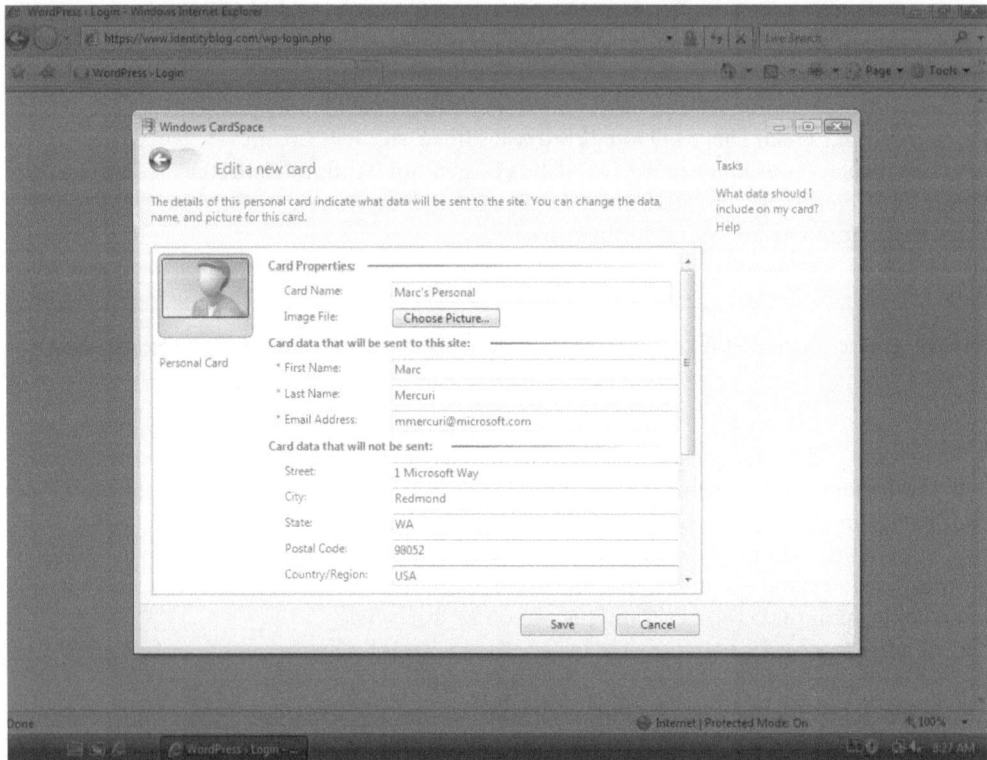

Figure 2-9. *Populating your information card*

Prior to sending your information card to the Identity Blog, you can preview the information that will be sent, as shown in Figure 2-10. Many times, you will already have an existing information card and be presented with this screen. It identifies the data that will be sent, the recent card history for this card, and the date on which it was created.

Click the Send button, and your information card will be sent to this site.

Because you used a personal card, no strongly trusted identity provider is involved. To help authenticate the claims you provided in the personal card, the site sends an email to the email address you entered when creating your personal card.

Check your email at the email address provided, and you'll find an email containing a link from the site. Click the link, and you will be returned to the site. You can now use your information card to log in to this site.

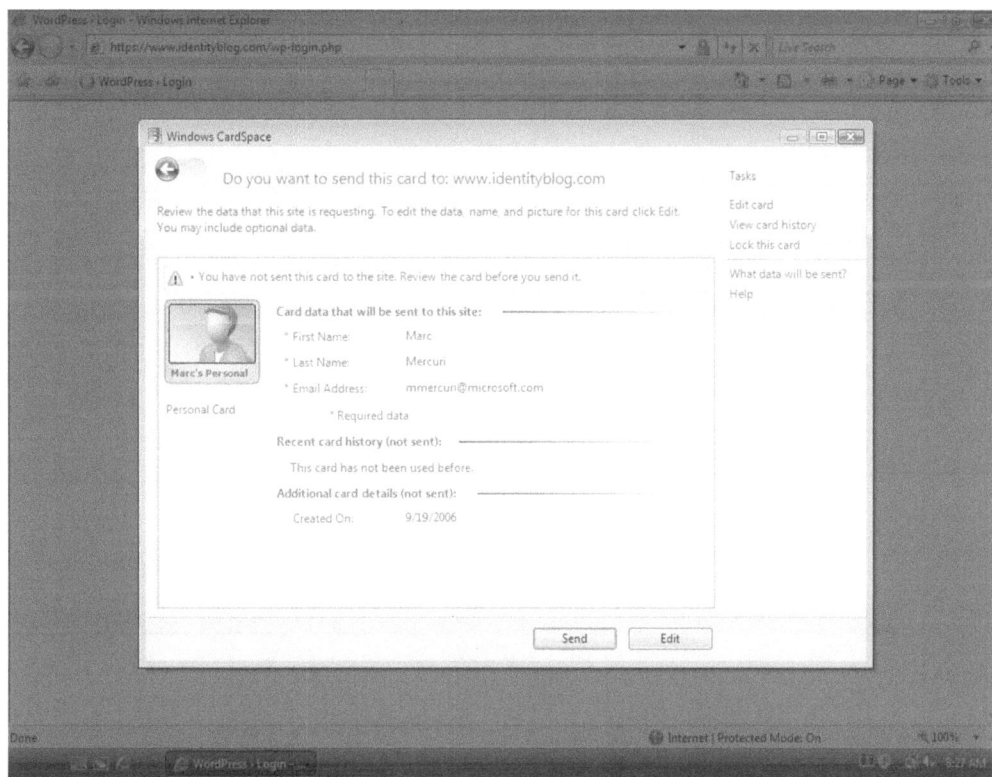

Figure 2-10. *Confirm you want to send a card.*

Using Your Newly Created Card at Another Site

The beauty of information cards and CardSpace is that you can use the same information card across multiple sites.

Now, what you might not have realized is that although the http://www.identityblog.com site is run by someone at Microsoft, to prove the interoperability of information cards, the site is implemented using PHP. In the next example, you will navigate to a third-party site that is not affiliated with Microsoft and that is implemented using Java.

Open your web browser, and navigate to http://www.xmldap.org.

Click the Relying Party link.

You should be presented with the screen shown in Figure 2-11.

Figure 2-11. *The sample relying party provided by* http://www.xmldap.org

Click the Login with an InfoCard icon.

As occurred at the last site, the identity selector will be displayed, and you are presented with the information about the site. The information shown is similar to what you saw in the previous sample.

Click "Yes, choose a card to send."

Select the card you created earlier in the chapter.

As you can see in Figure 2-12, this site requires the claims first name, last name, and email address. You'll also see that your usage of the card at http://www.identityblog.com shows up in the "Recent card history" list.

Unlike the previous exercise, I'll show how to do something different this time: add another level of security to your information card.

If you, for example, are a home user and you share a computer and a login to that computer with several people in your household, you want to ensure that there is another requirement in place that people must fulfill prior to being allowed to use a card.

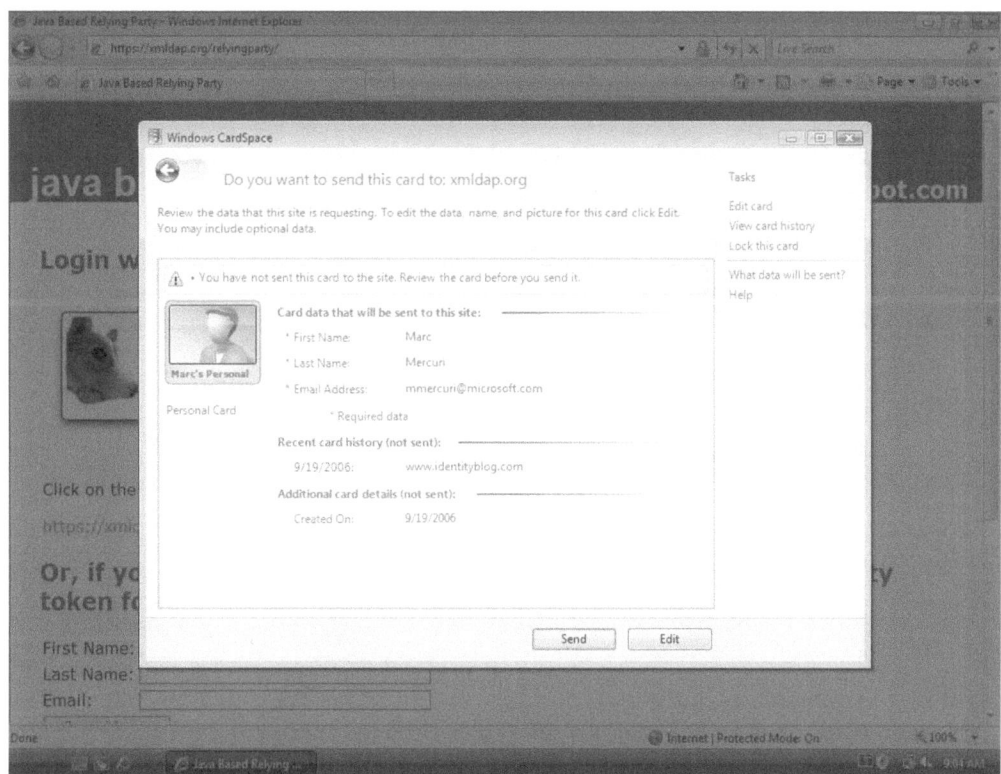

Figure 2-12. *Details about the data to be sent and the information card it's from*

In financial transactions today, this happens quite frequently. My bank provides me with an ATM card, which I can use to withdraw funds. In addition to providing my card, I must also provide a personal identification number (PIN). Credit cards have a similar feature with three- or four-digit security codes.

CardSpace provides the ability to attach a PIN to an information card to secure it.

Under the Tasks heading in the upper right of the identity selector, click "Lock this card."

This will display the dialog box shown in Figure 2-13. In this dialog box, you can identify a PIN to be associated with your card. Anyone wanting to submit this card to a site would first need to provide the PIN.

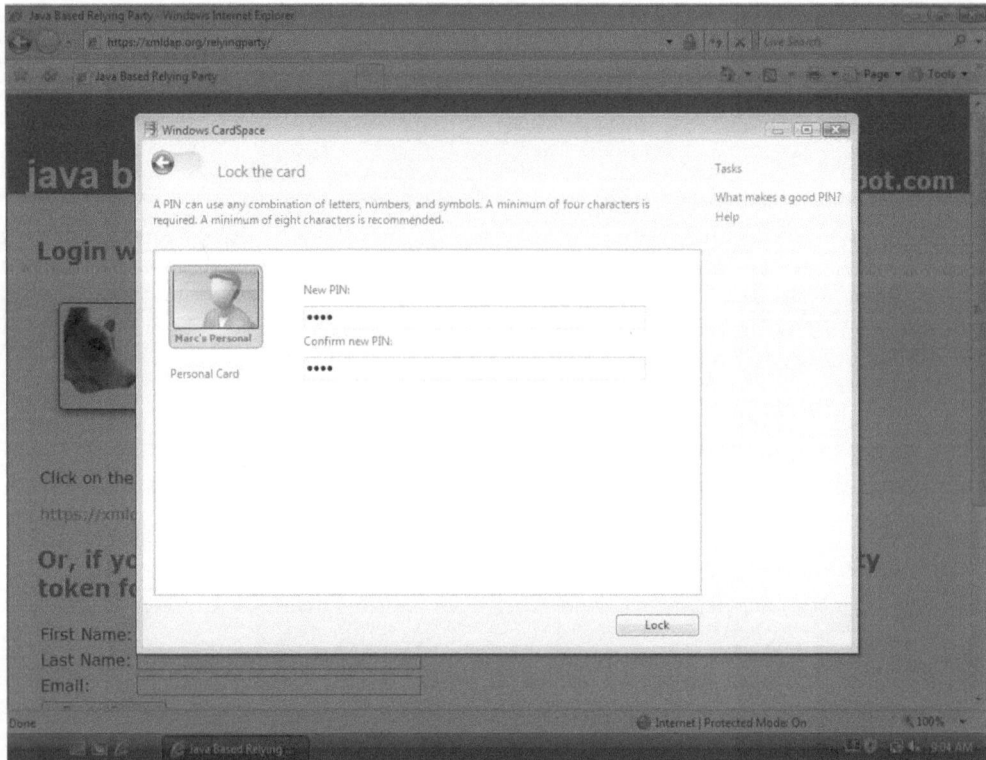

Figure 2-13. *Lock your card with a pin.*

Click the Lock button.

Submit the card to the site.

You will then be presented with the dialog box shown in Figure 2-14. Here you can see the information that was sent, the decrypted token, and the claims that were present on the card.

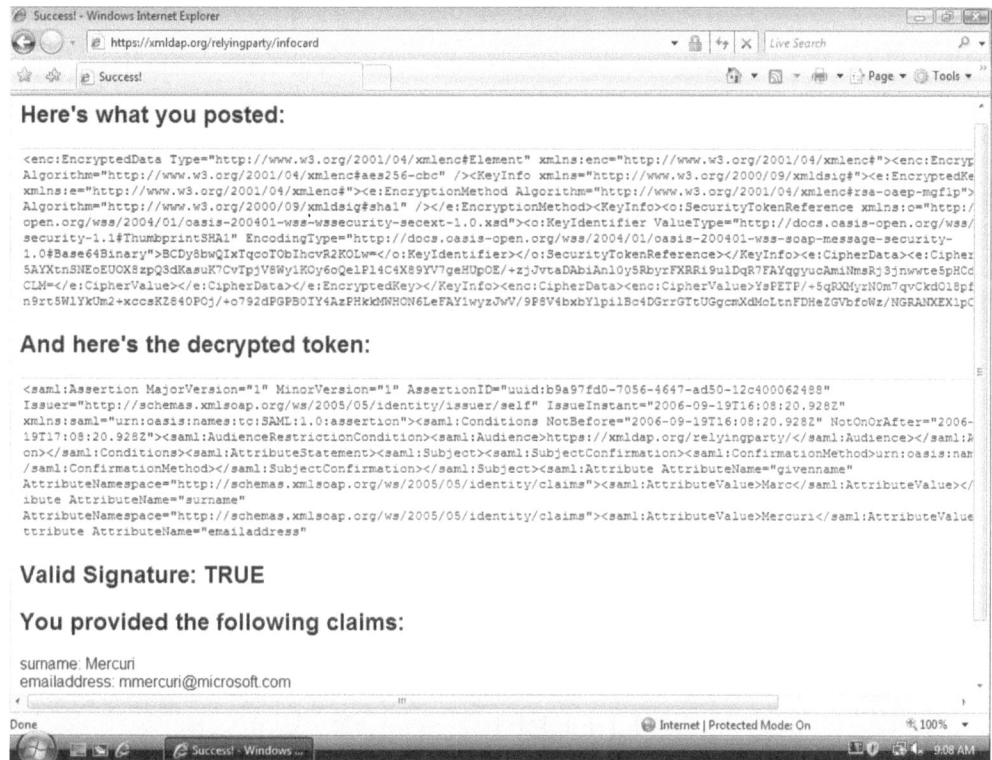

Figure 2-14. *The information received by the relying party from my information card*

Understanding That Personal Cards Are Not Accepted Everywhere

If I attempt to enter Microsoft using my self-issued identity ("Hello, my name is Marc Mercuri. I'm an architect who works here."), I won't get past the reception desk. Entry into Microsoft requires that I provide a card that was issued by the company and contains claims specific to the company.

Sites that request information cards can operate in a similar fashion. In this next exercise, you will navigate to the site of PingIdentity, which is a third party that provides software products and solutions in the identity space.

Open your web browser, and navigate to `https://infocard.pingidentity.com/rpdemo/`. You will be presented with the login screen displayed in Figure 2-15.

Figure 2-15. *A sample portal login from PingIdentity using managed and personal cards*

Here you can see that you have several options to log in to the portal. A user can use a local login (username/password), a self-issued personal card, or a managed card.

Click the Managed InfoCard Login icon.

Each time you choose to send a card to a relying party, the identity selector displays cards for you to choose from. What has not been apparent up to this point in your CardSpace exploration is that CardSpace examines the claims required in the site or service's policies. It then highlights cards that contain the claims required by the site in the identity selector.

In this exercise, you do not have a managed card, so you have no cards that contain the claims required by the site. In addition to no cards being highlighted in the identity selector, there is an informational message displayed in the user interface, "This site requires a managed card that you don't have," as shown in Figure 2-16.

To use this site, you would need to add a managed card that satisfied the site's requirements.

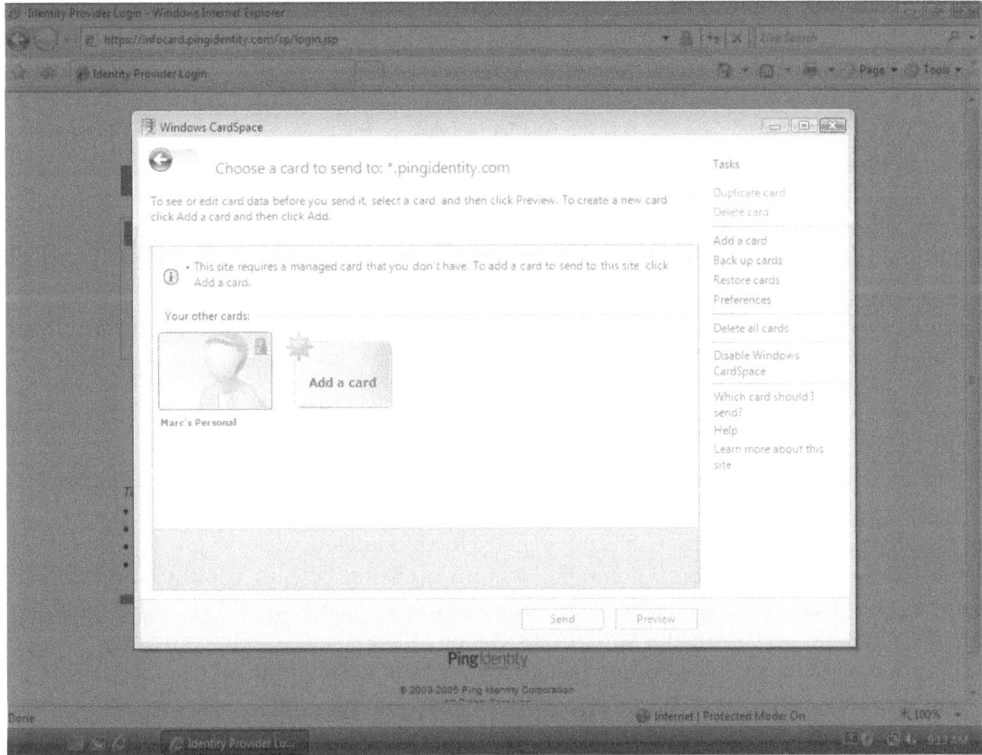

Figure 2-16. *Trying to access a site that requires a managed card without the proper information card*

What Is Going on Behind the Scenes in These Interactions?

At this point, you've created an information card and used it on a couple of websites. But what's really going on behind the scenes when you use an information card?

Revisiting the Airline Counter Scenario

In the previous chapter, you looked at the identity exchange that occurs when you check in for a flight at the airport. There, the focus was on authentication and authorization at a high level. You'll revisit that scenario here to prepare you for the discussion on CardSpace.

When you check in for a flight, you present your ticket to the airline's counter agent. To authenticate you are the person authorized to use the ticket, the agent requests a form of government-issued identification. In most countries, that form of identification must include a picture, your first name, and your last name.

In this case, the counter agent is enforcing the government policies for travel. Those policies dictate that for a person to be authorized to use the resource (in this case a seat on an airplane), they must present identification from an accepted source. The policies also dictate that the form of identification provided must establish certain claims about the person presenting it. Specifically, it must contain a photograph, a first name, and a last name.

The policy also dictates one other important requirement. The token presented must be valid and current. If you were traveling internationally and presented a ticket with an expired driver's license or passport, you would not be given access to the resource regardless of whether the other claims were present and accurate.

In this scenario, a trusted organization is providing an identity token for an individual. There is not just one trusted organization, however, because the airline trusts multiple parties. You can present a passport or a driver's license. The airline will also accept not just U.S.-issued identification but ones from most other countries as well. The only requirements are that the identity provider be both known and trusted, the token is current and valid, and the token contain the claims that are required (photograph, first name, and last name).

Understanding Identity Providers and Relying Parties

The token is being presented by an individual at the airline, which is relying on the identity provided by the government, the identity provider. The airline is the *relying party*. It's relying on the processes the government has put in place to authenticate who you are.

In the real world, there are a number of identity providers beyond just state and federal governments. Open your wallet, and you'll see a number of cards provided by the identity providers you have relationships with. In my wallet, I have several credit cards, a medical insurance card, an auto club card, and various loyalty cards from airlines and hotel chains. The credit card companies, the medical insurance company, the auto club, and the various airlines are all identity providers.

Each of these cards has one or more relying parties. If my car breaks down and I require it to be towed to a service station, I present my auto club card to identify myself and receive authorization for the tow service. Similarly, if I go to the health club, I present my health club ID. For payment, I present my credit cards.

My health club membership is trusted by only a single relying party, the health club itself. My auto club card—like my credit cards—is a federated identity. A number of different businesses have chosen to recognize it and use it to authorize discounts on the purchases of goods and services. A relying party is reliant on the authentication of one or more identity providers.

In the online world, there is a desire to replicate many of the processes that exist in the everyday world. The challenge historically is that the Web was not designed with an identity model. As a result, the gap has been filled by a patchwork of solutions, with the typical model being the not particularly secure use of username and passwords.

CardSpace focuses on solving this problem. Identity interactions in CardSpace occur between a combination of identity providers, relying parties, and the entity attempting to consume the services.

Let's jump right in and take a look at how CardSpace would work in a real scenario.

Looking at Identity Providers and Relying Parties in a Real-World Scenario

In this scenario, you are visiting a website that sells wine. The United States has restrictions in place that limit the purchase of alcoholic beverages. The website would like to accept information cards—issued by a government entity—to validate that a would-be consumer is legally allowed to make purchases.

In this scenario, the identity provider is a government. This government has issued an information card to the citizen, and on that information card is a claim that identifies the citizen's age.

The website is the relying party. The company is relying on the government to properly authenticate your identity prior to issuing you the card.

Figure 2-17 shows the way in which identity is established and accepted using information cards and CardSpace.

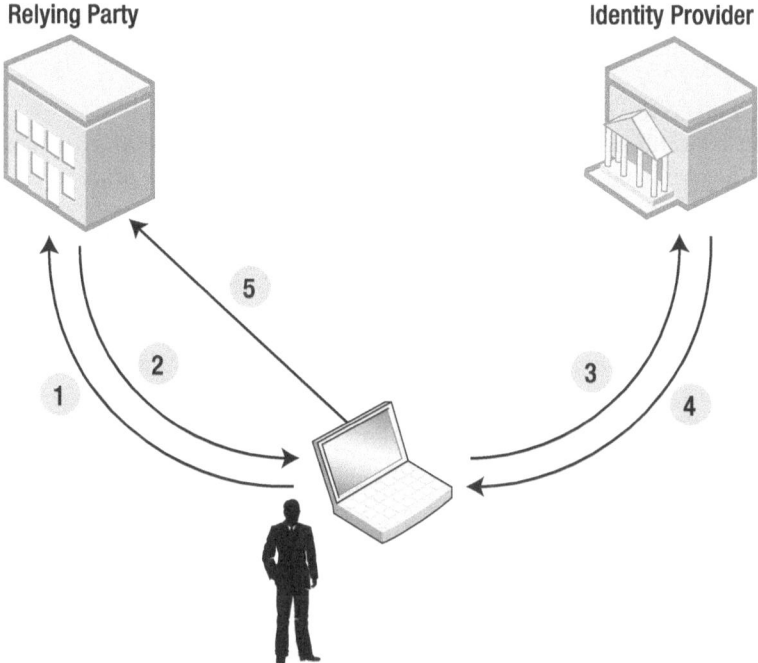

Figure 2-17. *What happens when using CardSpace*

Here's how it breaks down:

1. During checkout, the user clicks the Use My Information Card link.

2. The link triggers a request that returns Contoso Vineyard's policy. The policy includes the names of the claims that it requires, in this case the first name, the last name, the state of residence, and the date of birth. The policy also identifies which identity providers it trusts.

   The policy is received, and the CardSpace identity selector is displayed. This presents a list of the information cards on the user's computer that contains the claims requested in the policy.

3. The user selects the information card they want to use to access the service. The identity provider (the government) for that information card is contacted with a request for a token that contains the specified claims.

4. The token is returned to CardSpace.

5. The token is sent to the relying party, Contoso Vineyards. The relying party validates the token and inspects the claim for date of birth. Because the date of birth indicates you are older than 21 years of age, you are allowed to complete the purchase.

A Closer Look at Some of the Benefits of CardSpace

This chapter has thus far taken you through the use of CardSpace and information cards on real sites. Along the way, I described the actions you could take and the screens through which you navigated. But you might not have noticed some other, subtle elements of the process. The following sections delve into these areas and provide some additional insight.

Passwords

You did not have to use a password once when using information cards. Each information card contains a unique identifier that serves the purpose of what would have traditionally been your username and password.

This eliminates password fatigue for the end user, as well as removes a vector of attack for people who might attempt to phish your information.

Entering Basic Demographic Data at Each Site

Not only did you not use any passwords, but you also didn't need to enter your basic profile information such as name and email address. Information cards contain information about you that you can choose to disclose to websites and services. No longer do you need to enter your basic information every time you visit a new site—you can now simply present your information card.

And because you are in control of what information is shared with each site, you can provide information to each site based on what you personally feel comfortable with.

Note Although you do not need to provide a site with information you are uncomfortable sharing, if you do not feel comfortable providing information a site/service has specified as required, you will not be granted access to the resource.

Separate Desktop

When you were using the identity selector, you likely noticed that the screen behind the identity selector went dark. The identity selector actually is running in a separate private desktop—much like you would see when you press Ctrl+Alt+Delete.

Why is this important? By placing the identity selector on a separate desktop, you make it much more difficult to spoof the identity selector user interface (UI). As a result, this provides an additional barrier to would-be attackers.

Visual Representation of *Your* Cards

If you were approaching your car and you found a wallet, how would you know if it were yours? You would first probably consider whether this wallet looks similar to yours. If it does, you'll likely open the wallet. Once opened, you'll see the cards inside and know fairly quickly whether the wallet is yours. How? Your collection of cards is fairly unique to you. It is extremely unlikely that someone else would have all the same cards in their wallet.

The same is true with CardSpace. Although today you likely have only one card, you'll soon have several. When the identity selector is displayed, you are presented with a selection of *your* information cards. If someone tried to fake the information card interface, the odds of them identifying the cards that you specifically have are remote. Windows CardSpace also provides the user with the ability to associate their own images with the card, making the odds even more remote.

If someone were to attempt this type of attack, you'd be able to visually identify it immediately.

Only the Names of the Claims Live on Your PC

With usernames and passwords, someone could simulate a screen for a bank or a website, and you would enter your username and password. They could collect this information and use it for illegal access to your accounts.

With CardSpace, only the names of claims—for example, the surname, first name, email address—are stored within the information card. The actual data is stored at the identity provider.

Note With a self-issued card, the identity provider is your computer. In that case, the claim data is maintained locally, in a secure store.

If someone were to override all of the other security measures or to physically steal the computer, they would not have access to your personal data.

Summary

In this chapter, you took a tour of the CardSpace user experience. You saw the screens of the CardSpace identity selector in a real-world scenario, created a personal information card, and used that same card to authenticate and gain access to multiple sites.

In the process of doing that, you saw that CardSpace can be utilized with sites hosted on a number of platforms, including ones utilizing operating systems and/or development languages not developed by Microsoft. Finally, you learned the importance of what you didn't see or might not have noticed while using CardSpace and how those hidden items make identity on the Web easier and more friendly—making it easier to use and control your information, as well as hampering would-be phishing attacks.

In the next chapter, you'll learn about the Laws of Identity and the identity metasystem. Both of these subjects are important, because they are what drove the creation of CardSpace and are guiding the next generation of identity on the Web.

CHAPTER 3

■ ■ ■

The Laws of Identity and the Identity Metasystem

When I first joined Microsoft, it was as a principal consultant for Microsoft Consulting Services. For two years, I worked for the company's Caribbean and Central American subsidiary and was based out of the island of Puerto Rico. Although I'd studied Spanish in high school, it had been more than a decade since then. During my time in Puerto Rico, I discovered or relearned a number of Spanish words.

One of those words was *clave*, which is sometimes used to mean "password" and is also translated as "key" (key as in metal object that opens doors). I thought that was an interesting combination. In your everyday life, you likely have a small number of keys that you use to open doors and access resources—one for your home, another for your car, perhaps one for your office, and maybe another for a locker at your health club. That's four keys. Anything more than that, and you'd find it quite cumbersome.

Think about the online world and how many keys you need to maintain—one for each of your email accounts, one for each of the online retailers you deal with, and others for news and entertainment sites you might use. And then there are others for your online banking. And let's not forget the credit card sites.

That's a lot of claves.

You wouldn't carry that many physical keys, and realistically, you won't store that many usernames and passwords. Typically, that number is larger than most individuals can manage. As a result, people often use a set of three to four usernames and passwords, or some people even place the usernames and passwords on Post-it notes attached to their monitors.

The Internet was not designed with identity in mind. It doesn't have any built-in mechanisms so that a site can definitively prove who they are to you or for you to prove your identity to the site. In the absence of this identity layer, a number of different solutions have been created to fill the void. The resulting patchwork creates a world with a number of systems that are effectively in silos. For example, if you have an account with an Internet service provider, you can use that identity to access only the resources of the ISP, but you can't use it when roaming to other sites such as Amazon. If a site such as eBay has a reputation system, your reputation is typically tied to that site and not portable across the Web. Rather than have a small number of identities that travel with them, users are forced to use a large number of site-specific identities. To make that more manageable, users inject their own mechanism of portability, using that subset of three to four pairs of usernames and passwords.

This is obviously not very secure overall—when you introduce the problem of phishing, it becomes exponentially problematic. Phishers can fake a site that matches a common denominator location—for example, one of a country's largest banks or online payment systems—and depending on the complexity of the attack, steal one or more of these username and password pairs. If you use only four username and password pairs, each pair that is stolen gives them the keys to 25 percent of the sites you use. When you see the statistics that phishing is currently growing at a rate of 1,000 percent per year, you probably recognize that this is a problem that needs to be solved expediently.

As our business and supply chains become more and more connected and as online retailing attempts to go the next level, it becomes more and more of a challenge to connect systems and federate identity.

Identity on the Web is a challenge that needs to be addressed now. With the challenges coming from phishing, password fatigue, and the need for federation, growth will be stunted and potentially decrease if identity is not addressed now.

The good news is that as an industry we've been here before. It wasn't all that long ago that there were challenges with networking. There was a time when those writing applications had to make an up-front commitment to a particular networking stack. This lack of interoperability injected costly rewrites if a company needed to move from one stack to another and had the potential to stunt overall growth of connected systems. The industry recognized this was an issue that needed to be solved, and we now use TCP/IP for networking, providing the ability to work with Token Ring, Ethernet, X.25, and Frame Relay. The industry stepped up to the challenge before, and the industry is stepping up to solve the challenge now.

This chapter discusses the lessons learned from past attempts at solving the identity challenge, reviews the laws that were defined based on those lessons learned, and finishes with a review of an identity metasystem based on those laws.

The Laws of Identity

Several attempts were made to resolve the identity problem; the most visible of which was Microsoft's initial approach, Passport. Passport wasn't a failure, but it was by no means a universal success. Passport was—and now as Live ID is—very successful when used for authentication on Microsoft properties such as MSN, but it never had much traction with third-party sites. When one looks back at the challenges Passport had with adoption and then looks at other historical challenges with identity in the digital world, a number of patterns emerge.

On his blog at http://www.identityblog.com, Kim Cameron, an identity architect at Microsoft, has been instrumental in defining, publishing, and engaging in conversation about the key characteristics of what would be necessary for an identity layer to be successful. I use the word *conversation* because these topics have been discussed in the "public square," on his blog. Here, individuals from various backgrounds and platform affinities weighed in on what Cameron referred to as the Laws of Identity. In addition to serving as a guide on which CardSpace's creation was based, you'll find that these laws provide a lingua franca that can be used when discussing identity with other developers or architects. You'll find yourself being able to have conversations where you will reject aspects of a design because it "violates Law #2," or you'll find yourself conversely making architectural decisions to resolve such violations.

The laws are living documents, and they continue to be discussed on Kim Cameron's blog. The following are the laws at the time of this writing, followed by commentary.

Law #1: User Control and Consent

Technical identity systems must reveal information identifying a user only with the user's consent.

For an identity solution to be successful, there has to be user control and consent. This means the user must be made aware of which specific pieces of information are being requested by a site or service and make a conscious decision to provide their data.

If you've read Chapter 2, you've seen that prior to being asked to select an information card, the CardSpace identity selector provides several items to help make sure the decision to consent is an informed one.

Prior to identifying what *claims* are being requested, you are first told who is requesting them. In addition, you are presented with the opportunity to check the certificate of the site or service requesting it. You also have the ability to examine the privacy policy.

You have the opportunity to consent and are in control of who receives your information and what information the relying party will receive. You also have the ability to inspect a display token for a managed card and see what information a third party is releasing about you.

Law #2: Minimal Disclosure for a Constrained Use

The solution that discloses the least amount of identifying information and best limits its use is the most stable long-term solution.

When you provide your driver's license or your passport in the real world, you're providing a physical token that contains multiple claims. If you want to purchase a bottle of wine, the only claims of relevance are your age and perhaps your picture. You do not, however, have a physical token that contains only those claims. Instead, you have to provide one of the physical tokens you do have, and that token contains all of your claims—name, address, height, weight, and so on.

When you think about it, it doesn't make a lot of sense to provide all of this information when only a subset is required. Does the clerk at the all-night liquor store really need to know your address? Of course not. But, because of the limitations of tokens in the physical world, it's something you tolerate. In the physical world, there are no mainstream mechanisms to dynamically show just the claims that are relevant in a particular situation or context. In the digital world, it's actually quite different. It is quite possible to do this.

My self-issued information card contains a number of claims. As you can see in Figure 3-1, the CardSpace identity selector clearly identifies the claims that are being requested. On the site being accessed in Figure 3-1, you can see that the requested fields were first name, last name, and email address. The identity selector presents the end user with the option of agreeing to send a card (and along with it the information requested).

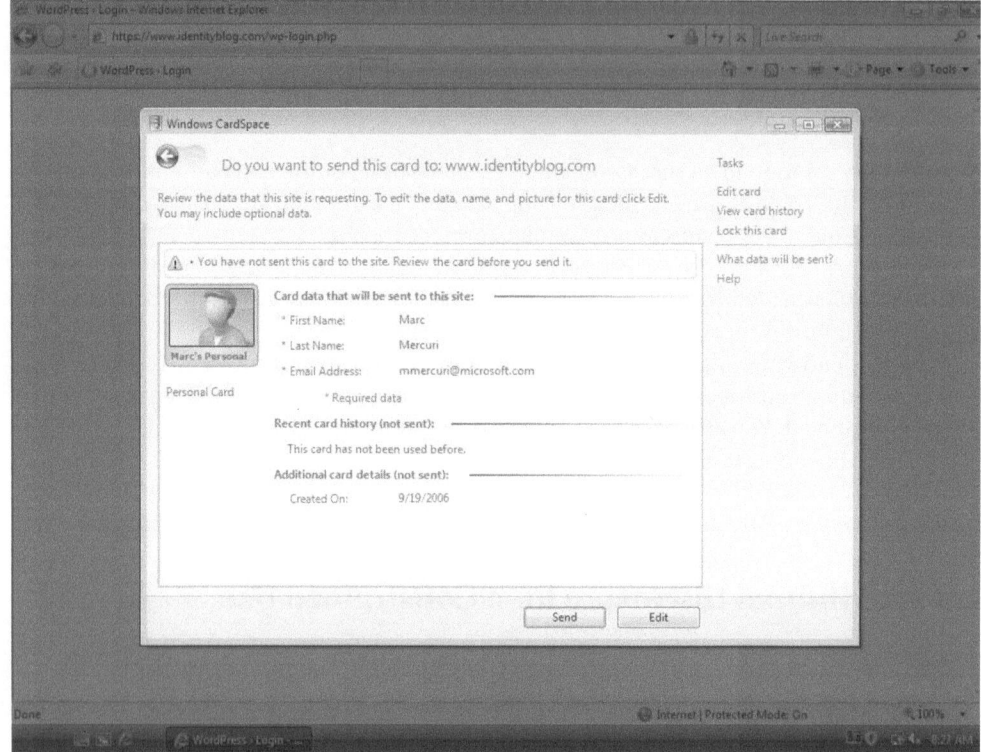

Figure 3-1. *CardSpace identity selector identifies which data is being requested*

This covers the minimal disclosure reflected in the law, but what about "for a constrained use"?

The following is a real story of something that happened to me; I've changed the name of the bank because it's not relevant. When I moved to Redmond, Washington, I decided to buy a house. I consulted with two large financial institutions about a mortgage; let's call them Bank A and Bank B.

During the process of applying for my mortgage, each bank was provided with a mortgage application form. This application contained information by which the bank could check my credit history and determine my credit worthiness.

Now, if there were a white paper called "Prerequisites for Easy Identity Theft," the data collected for the mortgage application would comprise the majority of that paper. The information contained my name, address, date of birth, Social Security number, place of employment, and so on. The information was provided to the bank solely to determine my credit worthiness. The use of this information should have been used for the determination of credit worthiness and for perhaps moving forward to populate parts of my account information with the bank I eventually chose. In the end, Bank A had a lower rate, and I took a mortgage through them. At this point, my relationship with Bank B was complete. One would assume that the right for Bank B to store my data had been withdrawn. I had not provided my data for the bank to use in data mining of potential candidates for future banking opportunities. I did not provide it to the bank to populate a data warehouse of key demographic information on potential borrowers.

You can imagine my surprise when I received a letter from Bank B a year later. I opened it and was very concerned with what was written in it. Bank B had kept my information on file, their data had been compromised, and in the process my Social Security number and identifying information had potentially been exposed to third parties unknown.

At this point, a bank I had chosen *not* to do business with had exposed me to potential identity theft. On my part, there had been an understanding that the information was provided for the constrained use of determining credit worthiness. At the time of my rejection of their services, my data should have been expunged from their systems. Not only did I not get my mortgage from Bank B, but the situation has resulted in a lack of trust in their brand and turned me into a negative advertiser for their services with the resulting story. If you examine the number of high-profile, large-volume identity thefts that have occurred in recent history, many of the stolen records should never have been in the system. Many identity holders were, like me, under the impression that their records were no longer being held. This was because of a natural expectation based on the type and timing of their interaction with the company from which the records were stolen. In some cases, this was based on an unvalidated assumption; in others, it was based on the retention policies of the companies they interacted with.

There are other situations where constrained use becomes important, and you can see this today when filling out profiles or entering contests on websites today. There is typically the "opt out" or "opt in" checkboxes found at the end of the form. These are provided such that your information can be used for other purposes. Sometimes these are for other specific uses, such as contacting you via email with upcoming specials and announcements, and other times these are for less constrained uses, such as allowing partners to contact you.

Note If your business stores personal information, you should evaluate whether you truly need the personal data you're storing and evaluate the security policies in place. These include software security, physical security, and processes and human resources policies. Data theft can many times come from internal employees—either intentionally or accidentally through the misplacement of passwords, laptops, or storage devices containing sensitive information.

One of the more costly operations for a site or service is resetting passwords. As a result, they've introduced self-service mechanisms that allow you to reset your password if you can provide answers to a selected question, such as "What college did you go to?" and "What's the name of your favorite pet?" and so on. If these questions are effectively serving as a makeshift password, such that you can reset your password, you're now using the equivalent of three to four password pairs across multiple sites. Once one site is compromised, it can have the same impacts as a phishing attack.

For an identity layer to be well received, parties should request information on only a "need-to-know" basis and should retain that information on only a "need-to-retain" basis.

Law #3: Justifiable Parties

Digital identity systems must be designed so the disclosure of identifying information is limited to parties having a necessary and justifiable place in a given identity relationship.

This is another area where you can learn a lot from Passport.

If you were buying a book or DVD on Amazon, what justifiable role did Microsoft have in that interaction? None. If you were logging in to check your bank account balance online, what justifiable role did Microsoft have in that interaction? None. If you wanted to buy a bottle of wine online, what justifiable role did Microsoft have in that interaction? None.

When Passport was introduced, I was vice president of software development for a company just outside Boston. We evaluated Passport, and Microsoft not being a justifiable party was one of the key reasons we opted against using it. At the end of the day, we just didn't feel comfortable with it. Outside the software development tools and the operating systems on which software was run, Microsoft was not a company that was part of our business interactions with customers. We couldn't justify that involvement, and as a result, we went another route.

That being said, if an individual was logging on to MSN, Hotmail, MSN Spaces, or any other Microsoft site, did Microsoft have a justifiable role in that interaction? Absolutely. It served a role in the interaction; whether it was as publisher, service provider, and so on, its involvement was crucial to the delivery of the underlying service and content.

Moving beyond Passport, think about other types of tokens from different parties and whether they are justified or appropriate for use in other scenarios.

If you were to go to an online website to purchase wine, should you have to use your corporate-issued token? No. Your company probably has no justifiable reason to be involved in that transaction. However, if you were using that same site and you could receive a discount based on your affiliation with your company, then its inclusion could be justified. You could evaluate the value of their inclusion and consent to include them in the process.

Governments are major issuers of identity in the physical world, and one would imagine this will carry over into the digital world. If you wanted to buy wine from a website, the government would be a justifiable party, even if there wasn't a discount. Why? Because there are laws—issued by the government—that regulate the sale of alcohol. The use of the government ID is justifiable to present proof of age, ensuring the transaction complies with the law.

Law #4: Directed Identity

A universal identity system must support both "omnidirectional" identifiers for use by public entities and "unidirectional" identifiers for use by private entities, thus facilitating discovery while preventing unnecessary release of correlation handles.

If you do online banking or shop online today, you'll notice that the transactions are done using Secure Sockets Layer (SSL). The data between the site and your computer is encrypted. This is done through the use of a certificate. The certificate is attached to a website, and it broadcasts its identity to everyone. You can see who the certificate was issued to, who it was issued by, and the dates the certificate is valid. Here the identity of the website is omnidirectional. The identity is broadcast in public to anyone who uses the site.

Bluetooth and RFID are other examples of omnidirectional identifiers; information is broadcast in public. Here, omnidirectional is a bit more questionable in its appropriateness in different contexts. For RFID, it makes sense for retailers to use this technology with their stock management and supply chains. Although it might make sense for products to broadcast their identity in the context of stock management, it might be less appropriate once the product has been picked up by a shopper. The product doesn't know that it has moved from a palette in a warehouse to a store shelf to a shopping basket. Do you really want to broadcast your purchases to others passing by?

There are other scenarios when you want to have unidirectional identifiers. These are identifiers used between private entities. If you look at your bank statement or your credit card statements, you'll see that you have unique identifiers associated with you for the institution in the form of an account number. If you have multiple accounts, you have unique numbers for each of the accounts. These are unidirectional identifiers.

The text of the law also discusses *correlation handles*, which are identifiers through which someone's identity could be ascertained across different systems. In the United States, your Social Security number is a key correlation handle. It is an identifier used to identify you when you're taking on a new job, when filing taxes, when obtaining credit, and so on. It would be easy to integrate data from any two organizations that had your Social Security number.

With CardSpace, when engaging with a site or service, you may have a single card you use across multiple locations, but for each location, a unique site-specific identifier is created. While using the same information card across multiple sites, each site—at the relying party— would see a different identifier for that card.

Law #5: Pluralism of Operators and Technologies

A universal identity system must channel and enable the interworking of multiple identity technologies run by multiple identity providers.

If you look at the physical world, government-issued passports are quite different. Each country issues its own passports that are good both for identification within their borders and for entry into and identification in foreign countries. The countries that issue passports follow certain standards in the issuance of their passports, and the documents are accepted in most places in the globe.

Passport was actually quite different from government-issued passports. Passport was effectively a closed system. There was one vendor, Microsoft, and one technology, Passport. If another company wanted to serve as an identity provider, there wasn't a mechanism or a set of standards in place that facilitated this. It was the equivalent of only one country providing passports for the world. As you can imagine, it's doubtful that this would be acceptable in the physical world, and it was not in the digital one.

When you move to the digital world, it's even more challenging, because not only do the parties speak different languages (instead of English and Chinese, C# and Java) but there are also different technologies that must get incorporated. The reality is that even if all parties agreed on using the same technology today, undoubtedly an innovation would appear at some point later that would cause some of the participants to begin to stray. By beginning with an assumption that there will be a pluralism of technologies, identity solutions will bypass this rather painful issue.

In addition, and as discussed when looking at justifiable parties, you know that there is a strong inclination to use different identity providers in different contexts.

When I interact with the world—physical or digital—I typically do it in a particular context. In the physical world, there are different versions of me—there's the government version (based on my registered financial and criminal interactions of record), the employee version (based on my performance, skills, position), the family version (husband, wife, parent, daughter), and the hobby version (scuba diver, stamp collector, sky diver). In each of these contexts, I have a means to identify myself—be it a passport, a marriage license, a scuba certification, a club membership, and so on.

In the digital world, I want to be able to identify myself tied to these different contexts, and to do that, I'd typically want to be able to have pluralism of operators to provide me those identities—and just like at a cocktail party, I should be able to provide my own self-issued identity.

Law #6: Human Integration

The universal identity metasystem must define the human user to be a component of the distributed system integrated through unambiguous human-machine communication mechanisms offering protection against identity attacks.

Although much can be done to secure the connections between identity providers, relying parties, and the desktop of the consumer, there is still the challenge of the two feet between the desktop and the user.

A number of things can happen in those two feet that can defeat the most expensive and complex software and hardware security.

The threat of most concern, phishing, attacks at the user interface level. Because there are a patchwork of identity solutions out there and there are changes from site to site, there are no hard expectations of how user interaction should occur. And as a result, some parties exploit this lack of consistency as opportunities to steal information.

Think about password fatigue. Users are requested to use strong passwords. Users have difficulty remembering many of them, so many will write down a password on a Post-it note and affix it to the monitor. Others will use one or a small number of passwords and reuse them across all sites, effectively minimizing the additional security provided through strong passwords.

When defining an identity solution, one must recognize that even with the most expensive and efficient technology in the world, if the aspect of how humans interact with that technology is not properly thought out, it leaves the door open for breaches of security as a result.

Law #7: Consistent Experience Across Contexts

The unifying identity metasystem must guarantee its users a simple, consistent experience while enabling separation of contexts through multiple operators and technologies.

Regardless of the underlying protocols, technologies, and operators, there needs to be a level of consistency and a set of expectations for how identity requests should appear, how the interactions should take place, and what one can expect to occur. These expectations need to be consistent and expected.

The term *experience* here is synonymous with what social engineers refer to as a *ceremony*. Most people use the term *ceremony* in conjunction with a wedding, but here I'm talking about a known interaction pattern. Weddings surely fall into this category, as do a number of more regularly occurring events. When you pass through security at the airport, you will provide your ticket and a form of identity to the employee routing people through the queue. When entering a different country, there is a ceremony where you provide your passport. This ceremony is pretty consistent in most countries in the world. With the large number of travelers crossing borders every day, the consistency of this ceremony helps the system run smoothly, with clear, consistent interactions. The request for and providing of identity tokens in the metasystem is a similar ceremony.

If you're using Internet Explorer, Firefox, or the Safari browser, your experience should be the same. Regardless of whether you're at work or at home, the experience should be the same. Whether you're on Windows or Linux, the experience should be the same. If you're on a desktop, a laptop, or a mobile device, the experience should be the same.

The Identity Metasystem

The following quotes come from the white paper "Visions for an Identity Metasystem" and are very powerful. They're powerful because they succinctly describe how the identity challenge will be solved.

> *Leverage strengths of its constituent identity systems, provide interoperability between them, and enable creation of a consistent and straightforward user interface to them all.*

> *The goals of the identity metasystem are to connect individual identity systems, allowing seamless interoperation between them, to provide applications with a technology-independent representation of identities, and to provide a better, more consistent user experience with all of them. Far from competing with or replacing the identity systems it connects, the metasystem relies on the individual systems to do its work.*

> —"Visions for an Identity Metasystem"

The identity metasystem is a system of systems; instead of a patchwork, you now have a federated network. The network is standards based and is agnostic of platform, location, programming language, or vendor.

Roles in the Identity Metasystem

The identity metasystem has three roles—identity providers, relying parties, and subjects.

Identity Provider

An entity that issues an identity in the form of an information card is referred to as the *identity provider*. Anyone can become an identity provider; there are even mechanisms built into the .NET Framework 3.0 that allow individuals to self-issue information cards.

It is important to note that although anyone could be an identity provider, not every identity provider will be accepted for use in an interaction. If you were to post a comment on a blog, for example, the trust barrier might be fairly low. In this case, most identity providers' cards would be accepted, including any cards you issued yourself. If the scenario was a high-value transaction, such as making a funds transfer or accessing medical records, the risk of accepting a card from a nontrusted source is very high.

Identity providers in the metasystem will map to those in real life—traditional identification providers (the government), payment service providers, financial services providers, clubs and associations, corporations, and individuals. There will also likely be new categories of identity providers that result as part of this open system.

Relying Party

Just as anyone can be an identity provider, anyone can be a relying party. A *relying party* is an entity that requests an identity token that contains specified claims.

They are referred to as a relying party because they rely on a third party, the identity provider, to validate these claims as accurate.

Subject

Identities are associated with a subject. Most often this is an individual, but this can also be a server, device, or other resource.

Claims-Based Identities

At the core of the identity metasystem are claims-based identities. As I've discussed, *claims* are statements about an entity that an identity provider asserts are valid.

For self-issued cards in CardSpace, the following fields are available:

- First Name
- Last Name
- Email
- Street Address
- City
- State
- Postal Code
- Country/Region
- Home Phone
- Other Phone
- Mobile Phone
- Date of Birth
- Gender
- Web Page

Although the most common claims will be from the pool used in the self-issued cards, a claim can be anything. A claim can be specific to an identity provider—for example, a membership number, bank account number, and so on.

Relying parties provide statements of requirements expressed in terms of WS-Policy.

Negotiation

If you have a claim-based identity, the next question is, How does a relying party negotiate to retrieve the information in which it is interested? Relying parties specify the claims they are interested in and whether those claims are required or optional. They also specify the specific type of tokens (X.509, Kerberos, and so on) that they are willing to accept.

Negotiations are conducted using WS-MetadataExchange and WS-SecurityPolicy.

Leveraging Existing Identities and Existing Identity Systems

Because the metasystem is a system of systems, it does not look to compete with or replace existing systems. Rather than a "rip-and-replace" mentality, the focus of the metasystem is on interoperability.

Because a number of different identity solutions and stores are already in place today, this makes it much more realistic for the metasystem to be successful.

Rather than discourage innovation, which tends to happen in a closed system, the focus on interoperability actually fosters innovation.

Security Token Server (STS)

A Security Token Server (STS), as its name implies, is a mechanism through which tokens are processed, tokens are created, and users are authenticated. STSs should also provide support for claims transformation. Chapter 10 covers STSs in more detail.

The WS-Trust protocol provides support for claims transformation.

Claims Transformers

Despite the best intentions, not everyone will use the same grammar to define their claims. In other cases, it might not be desirable or necessary to provide the claim itself; instead, it is something that is established by the claim. In these cases, you would require claims transformers. These would take claims as presented on an information card and transform them to a claim that is understood by the relying party.

A date of birth is a fine example of this. In the United States, if you want to purchase a game for the Xbox 360 that is labeled Mature, you must be older than 17 years of age. Your date of birth is not particularly relevant; the company selling the game merely wants to comply with the law. Its only concern is a "yes" or "no" answer—are you "17 or younger"? A claims transformer could examine the date of birth and transform it to a claim of "17 or younger."

Claims transformers will also change claims from one format to another (that is, to/from SAML). This provides the ability to be extremely agile and provides an opportunity to add both backward- and forward-compatible support into identity systems.

LDAP claims schemas, X.509, Kerberos, and SAML are all examples of different claim types that might be used and/or transformed.

Note You can find Kerberos in Active Directory on the Windows platforms, and it is also available for use in Unix.

Note SAML is a standard used in intercorporate federation scenarios.

The encapsulating protocol used for claims transformation is WS-Trust.

User Experience

A system will be successful only if it is well received by its users. As discussed earlier, the identity metasystem must have a strong focus on user experience. Specifically, that user experience must be easy to understand and consistent in its interactions.

The metasystem is truly user centric in design, where users will be informed of the claims that are being requested, be told the policies in place that detail how the data will be used, and be given the ability to consent—or not—to releasing the information.

The metasystem also employs two-way authentication. Not only will the site authenticate the user, but the user will authenticate the site. This helps solve one of the biggest challenges out there today—phishing.

Identity is consistent, secure, and user centric in the metasystem, making it a more trustworthy and satisfactory experience for the end user.

The Microsoft Road Map for the Identity Metasystem

Microsoft has a road map for providing support for Windows CardSpace. Support takes place in the client, on the server, in the tools, and in the browser.

CardSpace on the Client

The .NET Framework 3.0 was delivered with Windows Vista and Office 2007, and Windows CardSpace was delivered as part of that. In addition, CardSpace is available as a free download for Windows XP SP2 and Windows Server 2003 SP1.

The user-facing support for CardSpace on the client consists of two main components—the identity selector and the simple self-issued identity provider.

CardSpace Identity Selector

The CardSpace identity selector provides the user experience for the identity metasystem. It is within the identity selector that the claims being requested are displayed and the cards the user has available are displayed; in addition, there are access points to view policies, create self-issued cards, apply PINs to cards, and so on.

The identity selector appears in a separate, private desktop to avoid spoofing and various phishing-like attacks.

Note I should point out that unlike cards issued by a third-party identity provider, the data for claims in self-issued cards is stored locally. CardSpace provides a secure store for this information.

CardSpace Simple Self-issued Identity Provider

The .NET Framework 3.0 also installs support for the simple self-issued identity provider. This identity provider includes a personal security token server that generates SAML tokens containing the information to be sent to the relying party.

If you want to create a card, click the identity selector's Add a Card button. This allows you to create one or more of your own cards.

As shown in Figure 3-2, self-issued cards contain claims that cover first and last name, email address, street address, multiple phone numbers, date of birth, gender, and web page.

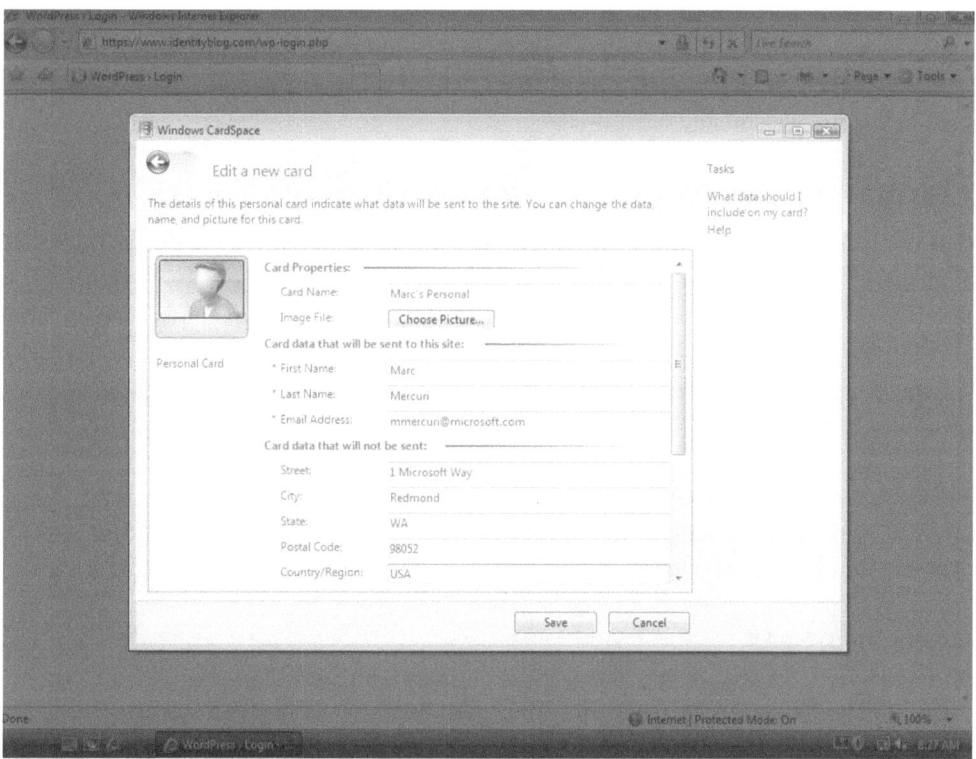

Figure 3-2. *Self-issuing an identity in CardSpace*

Information Cards on the Server

Microsoft also has plans for interacting with the metasystem on the server with an STS in the next version of Active Directory Federation Server. In addition, the company is also supporting extended validation SSL certificates.

Active Directory Federation Server 2.0

The Active Directory Federation Server (ADFS) will provide the ability to interact with the metasystem using Active Directory. The release date for this STS was not available at the time of this writing.

Extended Validation SSL Certificates

As stated earlier, the metasystem is based on two-way authentication. To add to the level of trust, Microsoft is recommending the use of extended validation (EV) SSL certificates.

EV SSL certificates inspire a stronger lever of trust. This is because these X.509 certificates have been issued only after a more significant investigation and confirmation about the claims being made by the owner. These certificates have both high fiduciary and legal guarantees.

In addition, these certificates contain a digitally signed bitmap of the owning company's logo. Used in conjunction with the identity selector, these certificates provide further visual assurance that the person requesting the claims is really who they claim to be.

These certificates provide additional levels of security and trust and provide visual cues in both the identity selector and the browser.

Information Card Support in the Development Tools

Microsoft is also providing support in the form of .NET namespaces and Windows Communication Foundation (WCF) support.

.NET Namespaces

With the installation of the .NET Framework 3.0 comes the addition of CardSpace-related assemblies.

System.IdentityModel.Selectors

System.IdentityModel.Selectors provides a series of exceptions that can be captured when triggering the identity provider via code.

System.IdentityModel

System.IdentityModel provides a set of classes that deal with claims, policies, and tokens. System.IdentityModel.Selectors—as found in System.IdentityModel—also includes classes for token providers and token authentication.

Windows Communication Foundation

Microsoft provides out-of-the-box support for CardSpace and information cards. Using one of the default bindings, wsFederationHttpBinding, it's straightforward to configure information card support in both services and clients. Listing 3-1 shows an example of this.

Listing 3-1. *Example WS-Federation Binding Configuration Where the Email Address Is Requested*

```
<wsFederationHttpBinding>
    <binding name='helloFederatedBinding' >
      <security mode='Message'>
        <message
          algorithmSuite='Basic128'
          issuedTokenType='urn:oasis:names:tc:SAML:1.0:assertion'
          issuedKeyType='SymmetricKey'>

          <claimTypeRequirements>
            <clear />
            <add claimType='http://schemas.xmlsoap.org/ws/2005/05/➥
identity/claims/emailaddress'
/>
          </claimTypeRequirements>
        </message>
      </security>
    </binding>
  </wsFederationHttpBinding>
```

For clients, System.IdentityModel.Selectors is referenced to handle CardSpace-related exceptions.

Browser Support

The CardSpace identity selector can be triggered by code present in web pages delivered to a browser. These pages can be served by any back-end server platform, regardless of whether it's running on Microsoft and ASP.NET or Linux and PHP.

The interpretation and handling takes place on the browser side. Support was enabled inside Microsoft Internet Explorer 7 by Microsoft and is being enabled in other browsers by third parties. One of the first such add-ins was written by Charlie Mortimer who created a Firefox plug-in available at his http://www.xmldap.org site. He also wrote the Java relying party sample found later in this book. Since the creation of that first plug-in, others have emerged, and now multiple plug-ins are available for the Mozilla Firefox and Safari browsers.

■**Note** I cover these third-party implementations in more detail later in the book.

The resulting token information is posted back to the server, where the token is decrypted and authentication, authorization, and personalization occur. Chapter 5 covers this in more detail.

Summary

After touring CardSpace in Chapter 2, in this chapter you learned about some of the rationale behind that user experience. I covered each of the Laws of Identity, with descriptions of why they're important and anecdotes that point to why earlier systems that violated the laws failed to find broader acceptance.

From there, you reviewed the pieces of the identity metasystem that's built on top of these laws. I went through each of the key areas of the metasystem, so you should have a decent understanding of what it is and why it's going to solve some of the most pressing identity challenges facing the online world today. You should also have a good understanding of which protocols are used within the metasystems.

The chapter completed with a quick review of how Microsoft will be providing support for the identity metasystem in its products. You saw that CardSpace provides functionality on the client to create, store, and select cards. In addition, you learned that WCF provides the ability to provide services that will trigger the CardSpace identity selector, as well as generate client applications that can interact with services that require certain claims be satisfied.

You also saw the support that was added in Internet Explorer 7 by Microsoft and learned of third-party support for other browsers such as Mozilla Firefox. The result is that any website can generate HTML that triggers the identity selector on the server and processes CardSpace-delivered tokens.

With all that covered, it's now time to start writing some code. You'll begin with using CardSpace with WCF in Chapter 4 and then move on to using it within the browser in Chapter 5. Both of these chapters are stand-alone topics, so depending on your interest level, feel free to read these two chapters out of order.

The Identity Metasystem Beyond CardSpace: A Look at Third-Party and Open Source Solutions

As you saw in Chapter 2, Microsoft provides an identity selector in CardSpace as well as a Security Token Server (STS) for issuing personal cards. These are provided as part of the .NET Framework, and Microsoft has also enabled its web browser, Internet Explorer, and its services stack, Windows Communication Foundation, with mechanisms to interact with the identity selector.

But as you've also read, CardSpace is built upon open standards. The concept of the identity metasystem is popular in numerous circles outside One Microsoft Way. Praise can be found, both online and in print, in many places you might not expect, including *Linux Journal*. In the March 2006 issue of *Wired Magazine*, Lawrence Lessig, the court-appointed "special master" in the United States vs. Microsoft case, went so far as to say this: "The solution is not only right, but it could be the most important contribution to Internet security since cryptography."

The identity metasystem is guided by the Laws of Identity. Given Law #5, "Pluralism of Operators and Technologies," and Law #7, "Consistent Experiences Across Contexts," it is clear that there will be no single technology implementation or platform limitations—be it on the client or the server—for the metasystem.

Although the focus of the book is on Microsoft's implementation, CardSpace, this chapter focuses on all things non-Microsoft—from browser support in Firefox and Safari to projects such as Higgins—and it concludes with a look at other approaches to user-centric identity solutions, namely, LID, OpenID, and i-names.

When reading this chapter, you will find that there are varying levels of depth on the contained topics. This is either because I cover them later in the book, because a given project is in the early stages of development, or because of a lack of readily available documentation.

Over the course of writing this book, I'm happy to report that this chapter changed the most. As time moves on, more and more is being done on interoperability between these approaches, which needless to say is a very good thing.

The following paragraphs provide high-level information about the major players and projects at the time of this writing.

> **Note** Special thanks to Jim Sermersheim from Novell for his review and contributions on the sections about OSIS, Higgins, Bandit, and the Pamela Project, as well as to Chuck Mortimore for his assistance with the identity selector for Firefox.

Identity Commons

From the wiki at `http://wiki.idcommons.net`, the purpose of the Identity Commons organization is to "support, facilitate, and promote the creation of an open identity layer for the Internet, one that maximizes control, convenience, and privacy for the individual while encouraging the development of healthy, interoperable communities."

The organization consists of a stewards council and a number of working groups. Each working group has a charter that includes milestones and deliverables. This organization is a great resource for anyone wanting to get a sense of what's happening in the Internet identity space.

The Open Source Identity System (OSIS)

At 2006's Harvard/Berkman Identity Mashup Conference, a number of individuals associated with various identity projects came together and put forward the Open Source identity selector (OSIS) agreement (OSIS was later renamed to the Open Source Identity System). The agreement was fairly significant, particularly as it relates to Law #7, because its members agreed to "establish architectural agreement on the key interfaces between the various open source digital identity software and service components under development."

Now, this agreement becomes significant only if the parties involved are key players in the industry. The individuals behind OSIS represent major corporations and major open source identity projects from across the world. Specifically, the OSIS steering committee boasts major vendors and projects including IBM, Novell, Red Hat, Sun, NetMesh, CA, Sxip, Oracle, Microsoft, Eclipse Higgins, Bandit, PamelaProject, and OpenXRI.

OSIS facilitates communication among identity system projects and vendors in order to reduce the duplication of work and promote interoperability among multiple parties in the open source community. Originally, OSIS was chartered to produce an open source identity selector that could be used where the CardSpace selector was absent. That work shifted primarily to the Eclipse Higgins project, and OSIS rechartered to oversee which open source projects would produce the specific components needed to implement the identity metasystem. In addition to that, and perhaps more important, it is currently focusing on ensuring interoperability between these different components.

This project (`http://osis.netmesh.org`) defines interoperability use cases (tests) and organizes events where participants can work side by side to ensure interoperability between their components.

Even though comprising multiple identity technologies, the first goal is interoperability with Microsoft's CardSpace. To aid in this, OSIS was instrumental in the latter stages of the Microsoft Open Specification Promise.

Eclipse Higgins

IBM, Novell, and Parity Communications announced the Eclipse Higgins project in late February 2006. Higgins was built to provide solutions for a user-centric identity that integrates identities, profiles, and relationships across multiple systems. It is a software framework that relies on service adapters to integrate with external systems.

Higgins is a citizen in good standing of the identity metasystem, currently designed to follow the seven Laws of Identity. It creates adapters that leverage existing protocols and interfaces to external systems. It doesn't compete with information cards, OpenID, or XRI; instead, Higgins can leverage the existing interfaces to support them via adapters.

One area that is different is the "link and sync" services that Higgins is targeting. With information cards, each card contains claims validated by an identity provider. In the real world, if you moved to a new address, you would contact your credit card companies and inform them of your change of address. If you had five credit cards, you would need to do this five times.

If you had information cards for five websites that contained your address information and you moved to a new address, you would also need to contact the issuers to inform them of the change. With link and sync, Higgins will attempt to provide the ability to make a single change and have that sync across all sources.

Note The name Higgins has its origins in the name of a long-tailed mouse in Tasmania. The architects thought in addition to mainstream environments, such as websites and enterprise applications, that the project would want to collect information from the "long tail" markets such as IM and social networks.

The target platforms for Higgins include Linux, Mac OS X, and Windows, as well as an Eclipse plug-in.

The Higgins project has working open source implementations of a browser extension, an identity selector, card providers, card stores, an STS, an identity attribute service, and a number of adapters used to expose identities from different stores.

Bandit

Prior to the Higgins project, a team at Novell created the open source Bandit project that wanted to "invent new identity DNA." The project was originally chartered to deliver components and solutions that provide consistent identity services for authentication, authorization, and auditing. Work began on a common identity framework, role engine, and audit framework.

Not long after delivering a common identity framework (APIs and code for dealing with identities from all kinds of different sources), it was discovered that the Higgins project had a number of goals that overlapped Bandit's—especially along the lines of common identity.

Rather than competing with the Higgins project, the Bandit team joined them and pooled their overlapping efforts. Now the Higgins project is focused on common identity framework architecture and components, and the Bandit project will continue to provider higher-level components and solutions around authentication, authorization, and auditing.

Pamela Project

The following describes the Pamela Project:

> *The Pamela Project is a grassroots organization dedicated to providing community support for both technical and non-technical web users and administrators who wish to use or deploy information card technologies. We hope to make it easier for people of all skill levels to understand and use this technology. Overall, the goal is to hasten adoption, lessen frustration, and improve the overall quality of information card relying party deployments on the Internet.*

—http://pamelaproject.com

The Pamela Project has been set up to do the following:

- Champion open source relying party code development and integration for information card technologies

- Foster evolutionary integration with existing web-based products and services

- Create and assist in architecting code that is user-friendly, secure, and ready for mass adoption (not just proof-of-concept)

- Support and encourage not just developers but also nontechnical end users and webmasters to deploy and use these technologies

User-Centric Identity Without Information Cards

In addition to the work being done with information cards, there are also some different approaches to user-centric identity. The following sections focus on several of these, including Shibboleth, LID, OpenID, and i-names.

Shibboleth

Shibboleth is an Internet2/Mace project that is targeted at higher education. It is an open source project that leverages the SAML 1.1 specification to provide single sign-on in both organizational and cross-organizational scenarios.

Per the Internet2 website, the project is "developing architectures, policy structures, practical technologies, and an open source implementation to support inter-institutional sharing of web resources subject to access controls. In addition, Shibboleth will develop a policy framework that will allow inter-operation within the higher education community.

"From a usage standpoint, an individual is authenticated by their home (campus) system. When attempting to access resources, this home system can then pass applicable information to the resource provider."

This may sound somewhat familiar. Although Shibboleth uses a number of familiar concepts, the terminology is different. Table 4-1 compares the terms between Shibboleth and CardSpace.

Table 4-1. *Comparison of CardSpace and Shibboleth Terminology*

CardSpace	Shibboleth
Resource provider	Relying party
Identity Provider	Home campus. (Not exclusively, but typically the home campus is the identity provider.)
Claim	Attribute

Federation in Shibboleth allows universities with disparate identity implementations to participate in cross-campus/cross-organizational scenarios. It allows the sharing of claims for authorization to resources. As you might imagine, there are scenarios where individuals who were members of one university were granted access to a resource. The affiliation with the university is the only claim of relevance, so personal information would not be shared.

I am originally from the Boston area, which has 28 universities in and around the city. It was fairly common for someone to take a course at another university. In a scenario where individuals from University A enrolled in a particular course, say Economics 101, at University B, Shibboleth could enable those students—regardless of their campus of origin—to access videos and market research associated with the course.

Shibboleth also enables scenarios where an individual claim can be used to determine authorization. This could facilitate scenarios where only named individuals would be given access to a resource, or it could enable individuals in a multicampus research project to leverage a specific claim.

Although there is no official road map on the interoperability between CardSpace and Shibboleth, given its widespread adoption in academia, it is definitely a compelling opportunity. A quick search for the terms *CardSpace* and *Shibboleth* online will return blog entries by individuals pursuing interoperability.

Liberty Alliance

The Liberty Alliance is an identity consortium that began in 2001, and it currently boasts more than 150 members. Companies such as AOL, Fidelity Investments, HP, Novell, Oracle, and Sun are on its management board. The focus on the consortium is the establishment of open standards, best practices, and guidelines for federated identity.

LID

Lightweight Identity (LID) is an approach whereby you use a URL for an identifier for an individual, persona, or entity. Table 4-2 lists some example LIDs.

Table 4-2. *Example LIDs*

LID	Description
http://www.marcmercuri.com/marcmercuri	Personal LID that represents me
http://www.marcmercuri.com/kathrynmercuri	Personal LID that represents my wife
http://www.contoso.com	Entity LID that represents Contoso Corporation
http://www.contoso.com/systemX	Entity LID that represents System X in the Contoso Corporation

vcards

Version 2.0 of LID introduced the concept of a *vcard*, which is an XML representation of claims. Through the use of XPath statements in a URL, you can reference specific claims.

For example, http://www.marcmercuri.com/marcmercuri?xpath=/VCARD/N/GIVEN would return my given name, while http://www.marcmercuri.com/marcmercuri?xpath=/VCARD/BDAY would return my birthday.

You can find the DTD for LID 2.0's vcard at http://lid.netmesh.org/dtds/VCARD.dtd.

OpenID

OpenID is another approach whereby you specify your identity not with cards but by providing either a URI or an extensible resource identifier (XRI). OpenID is focused on providing a way that proves that you own a URL and that the URL represents an identity. That URL can contain a document(s)—RSS, Atom, vcard, and so on—that can be used to provide more information about you.

OpenID has been in development since mid-2005 and has more than 15 million enabled accounts. LiveJournal, which is hosted blogging software, is one of the marquis "customers" for OpenID. It uses OpenID to identify individuals making comments to its blogs, as shown in Figure 4-1.

Note Currently, within OpenID there is no specification or requirements that define how the server asserts ownership of the identity.

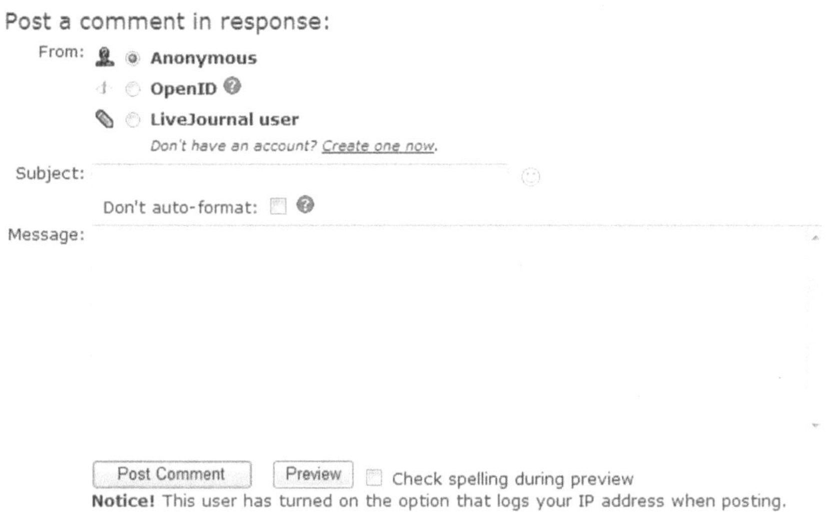

Post a comment in response:

From: ◉ **Anonymous**

⎯   ○ **OpenID** ❓

✎   ○ **LiveJournal user**

Don't have an account? Create one now.

Subject:

Don't auto-format: ☐ ❓

Message:

[Post Comment] [Preview] ☐ Check spelling during preview

Notice! This user has turned on the option that logs your IP address when posting.

Figure 4-1. *Leaving a comment with your OpenID on LiveJournal*

XRIs

XRIs are an OASIS digital identity standard used for sharing data and resources across domains. XRIs come in two varieties: i-names and i-numbers. Very much like user-friendly domain-names and machine/router-friendly IP addresses for web pages, XRI has user-friendly IDs in i-names and machine-friendly numeric addresses in i-numbers.

Just as domains are issued by registered brokers such as Network Solutions or GoDaddy, i-names and i-numbers are also issued by brokers, known as *i-brokers*. There are two formats for i-names, one for individuals and one for businesses and organizations. i-names for individuals are prefixed with an equals (=) sign, while those for businesses and organizations are prefixed with an at (@) sign. i-names are case-insensitive and can consist of any combination of letters and digits. Both the period (.) and hyphen (-) are also accepted. Although hyphens are accepted, it is *recommended* that i-name segments be separated using a period. Table 4-3 shows some example i-names.

Table 4-3. *Example i-names*

i-name	Description
=marc.mercuri	Example personal i-name
=marc.mercuri*spouse*Kathryn	Example personal community i-name
@duwamish.books	Example corporate i-name
@duwamish.books*employee* mercuri*marc	Example corporate community i-name

---

Note In addition to Latin characters, initial formats supported are Han (Simplified Chinese), Han (Japanese), and Hangul (Korean).

---

i-numbers, like i-names, maintain the = prefix for individuals and the @ prefix for businesses and organizations. To identify these as i-numbers and not as i-names, that prefix is followed by an exclamation mark (!). Also, there is support for community i-numbers. An exclamation point is used to separate the segments of the number.

There is also the addition of a network i-number. These are prefixed with two exclamation marks. Network i-numbers are reserved for accredited i-brokers. Table 4-4 shows some example i-names.

Table 4-4. *Example i-numbers*

i-number	Description
=!1000.a1b2.93d2.8c73	Example personal i-number
=!1000.a1b2.93d2.8c73!3ae2	Example personal community i-number
@!1000.9554.fabd.129c	Example corporate i-number
@!1000.9554.fabd.129c!2847.df4c	Example corporate community i-number
!!1000	Example network i-number
!!1000!de21.4536.2cb2.8074	Example network i-number

XRIs are resolved to an extensible resource description sequence (ERDS). ERDS is XML that, in addition to being used by OpenID, is also the basis for Yadis.

Yadis

Yadis is an initiative focused on a metadata discovery protocol, with its goal to make LID and OpenID interoperable.

When visiting a relying party, you would provide them with your identifier/URL. The relying party would then make an HTTP request that would either return a Yadis document or a pointer to a Yadis document.

The Yadis document contains information about what type of ID this is (such as OpenID) and what services are available.

OpenID and Information Card Integration

Chuck Mortimore, the individual who created the cross-platform identity selector plug-in for Mozilla, has prototyped his identity selector to provide support for OpenID.

This is done by allowing the user to specify the use of an OpenID in the identity selector (see Figure 4-2).

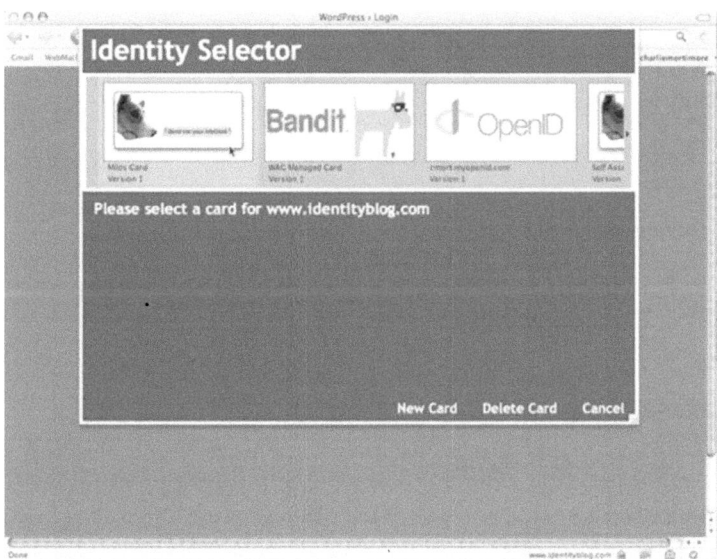

Figure 4-2. *Choosing to use an OpenID from within the identity selector*

This triggers the sign-in screen on the OpenID server. Here the user logs in to the server (see Figure 4-3).

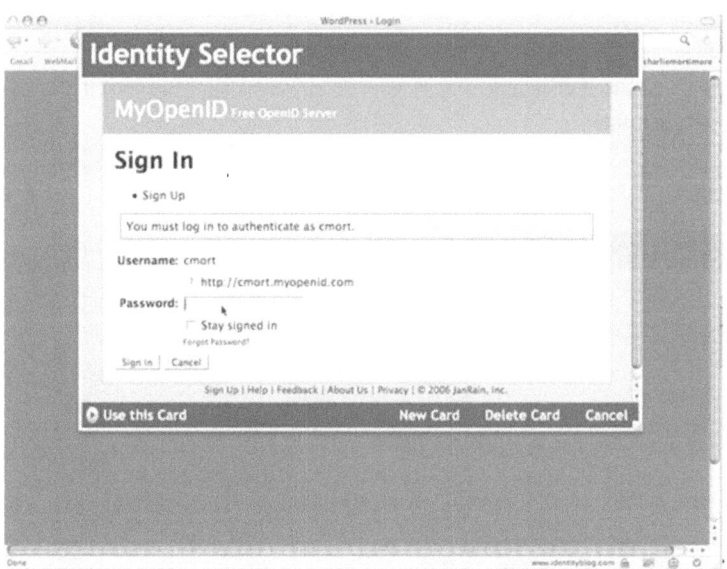

Figure 4-3. *Signing in to an OpenID server to authenticate the ID*

Upon successful login, the OpenID server will ask the user to select their persona and the claims that will be provided (see Figure 4-4).

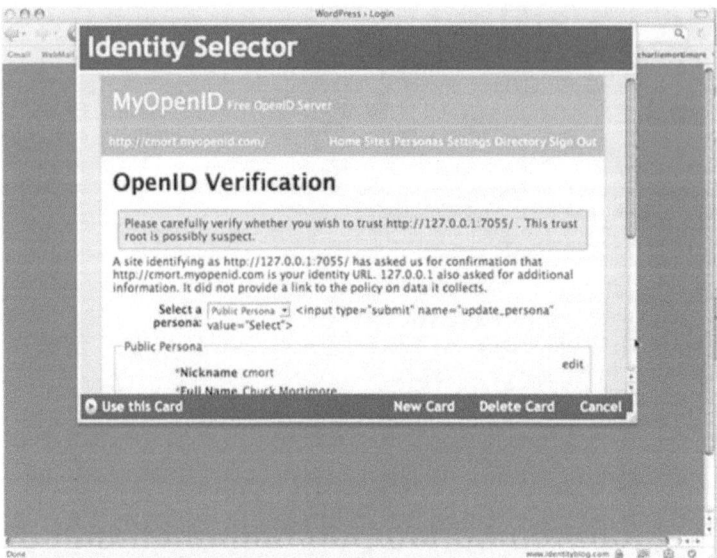

Figure 4-4. *Verifying that the relying party be trusted and verifying the persona from which to provide information*

The returned claims are then transformed into an information card, as displayed in Figure 4-5.

■ **Note** This selector offers some functionality not found in the v1.0 CardSpace identity selector. Rather than just approve or deny the request for claims, it offers the Allow Forever button, eliminating the need to display the selector when the user returns to a site.

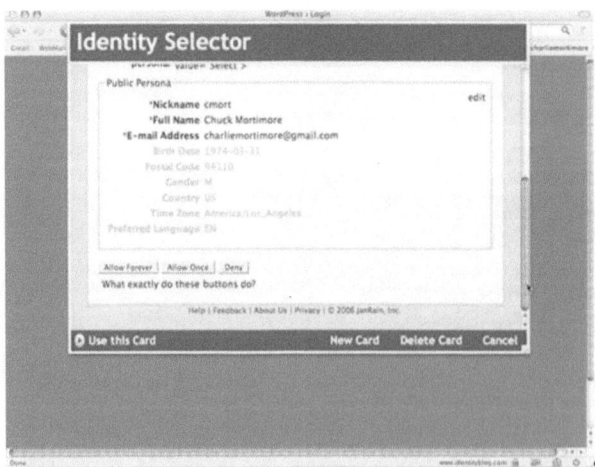

Figure 4-5. *The claims are transformed from an OpenID to an information card.*

VeriSign PIP

VeriSign currently has a service in beta called the Personal Identity Provider (PIP), as shown in Figure 4-6. PIP allows individuals to sign up for an identity. This service is built on open standards such as Yadis and OpenID.

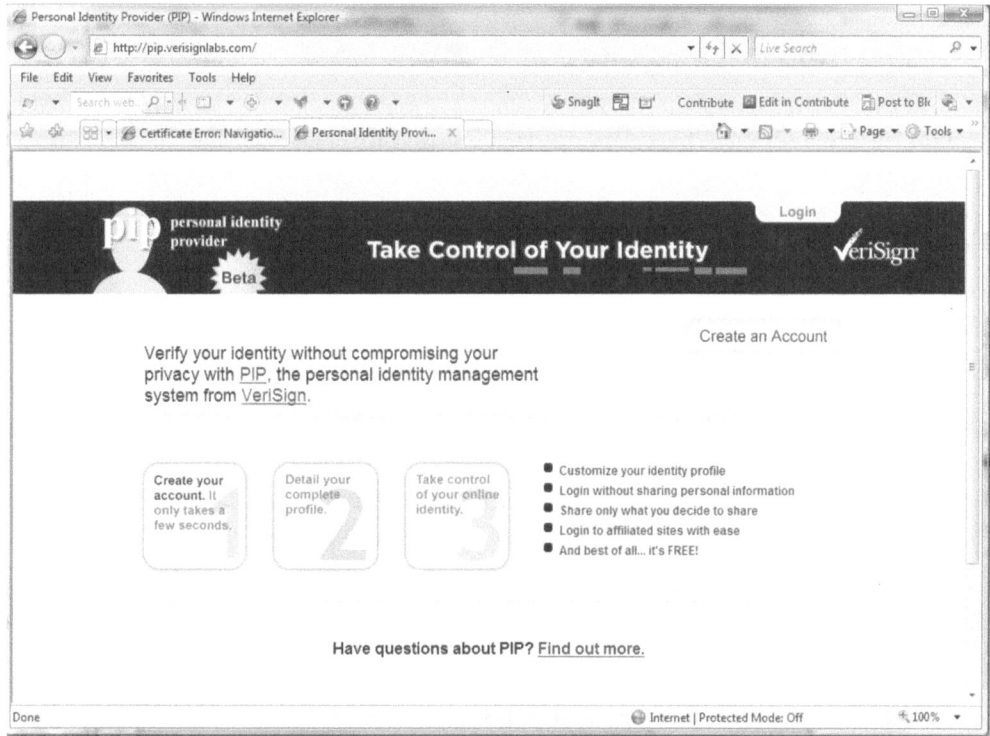

Figure 4-6. *Using VeriSign's PIP*

PingTrust

Ping Identity was the first company to produce a commercial STS. PingTrust is a stand-alone server written in Java that is supported on Windows Server 2003, Windows XP Professional SP2, Red Hat Enterprise Server 2.1, and Red Hat Enterprise Server 3.1.

PingTrust is based on WS-Trust and provides support for SAML, X.509, usernames and passwords, and Kerberos. SDKs are available for both Java and .NET development.

In addition, it provides an SDK to add support for custom tokens.

■**Note** Ping Identity has also released an open source token helper for use in the Apache web server.

Identity Selectors and Browser Support

At this point, you've already had hands-on experience with the CardSpace identity selector and the support for it built into Microsoft's web browser, Internet Explorer 7. In the following sections, you'll examine solutions where the CardSpace identity selector is leveraged outside Internet Explorer, as well as in other browsers.

Mozilla Firefox

If you or your customers use Mozilla Firefox, you have multiple solutions for information card support. Several individuals have developed add-ins that are freely available. There are two different types of add-ins.

Firefox Support on Microsoft OSs Using the CardSpace Identity Selector

Kevin Miller developed a plug-in for Mozilla running on the Windows platform. This plug-in interacts with the CardSpace identity selector and provides a comparable experience to what you see in Internet Explorer.

Cross-Platform Firefox Support

Firefox is an open source project with implementations on platforms other than Windows. Chuck Mortimore has developed support for information cards in Mozilla by creating both a token generator and an identity selector in Java. His xmldap.org identity selector can be used in Mozilla on platforms that support Java.

When a card is requested in this environment, the identity selector is displayed, as shown in Figure 4-7.

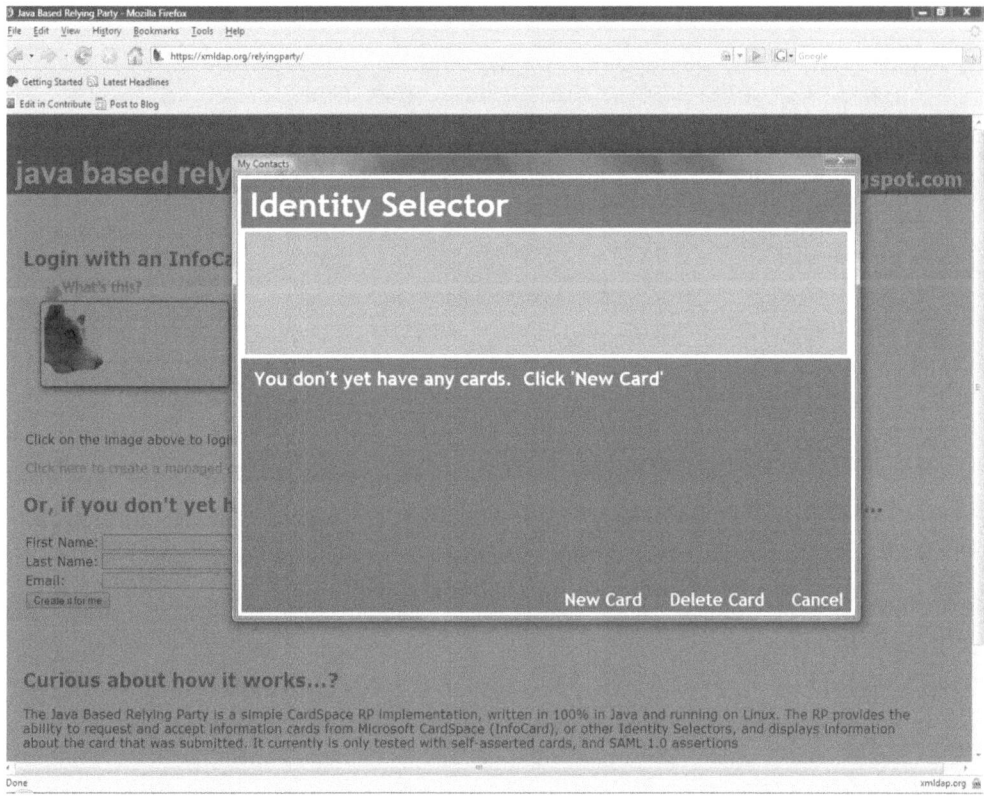

Figure 4-7. *The xmldap.org identity selector*

On first use, there are no information cards stored, so the user is prompted to create or import a new card. The xmldap.org identity selector has support for both personal/self-issued cards and managed cards, as shown in Figure 4-8.

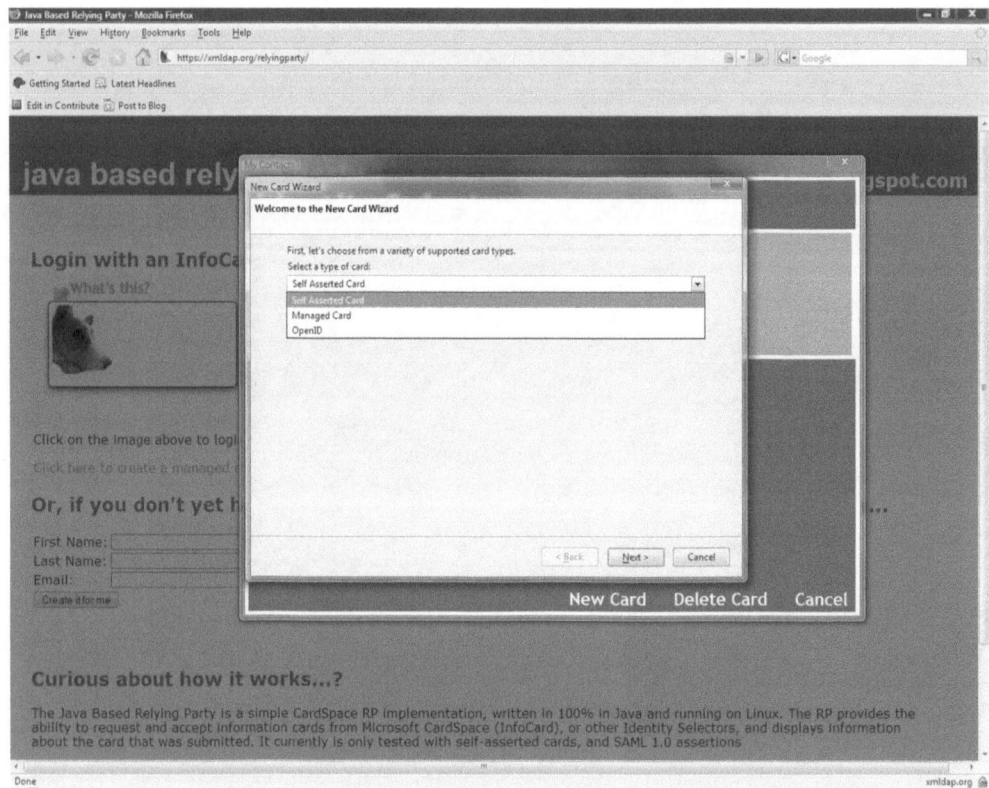

Figure 4-8. *xmldap.org's identity selector includes managed card support.*

Next, the user must specify the card location, as shown in Figure 4-9.

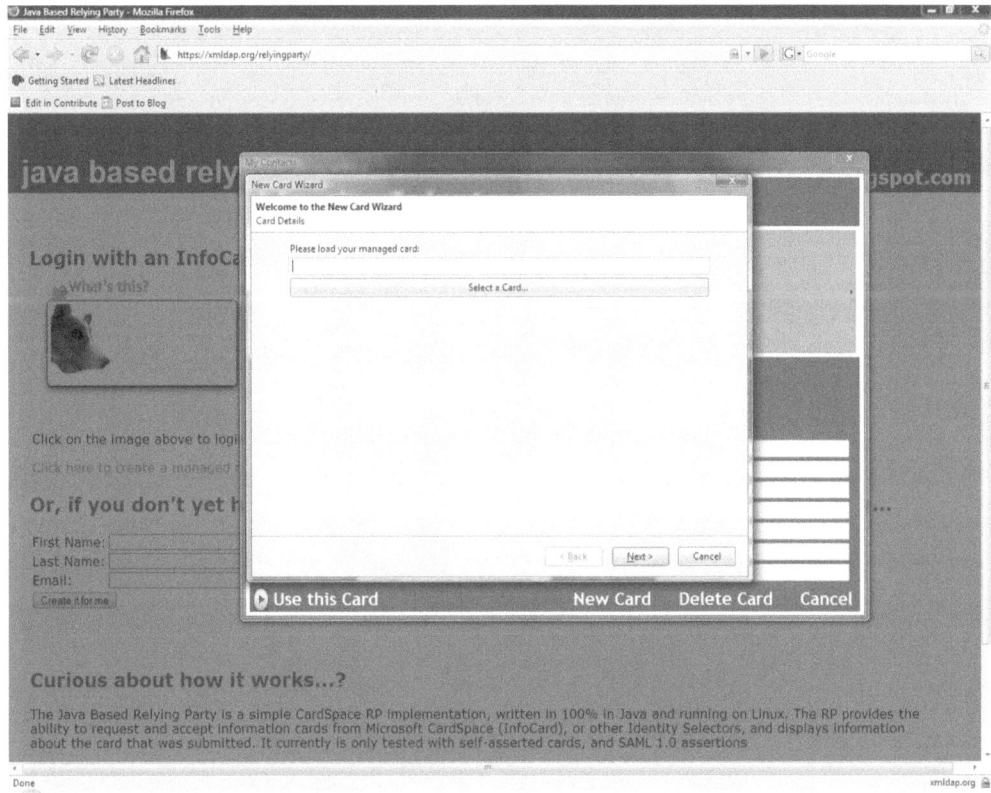

Figure 4-9. *Importing a managed card*

Once the card is imported, information about the card is displayed. In the upper left of the xmldap.org identity selector plug-in, the graphic for the card appears, as does the name. In the top center, the name of the identity provider appears. Below that, you can find the claims stored on the card, as shown in Figure 4-10.

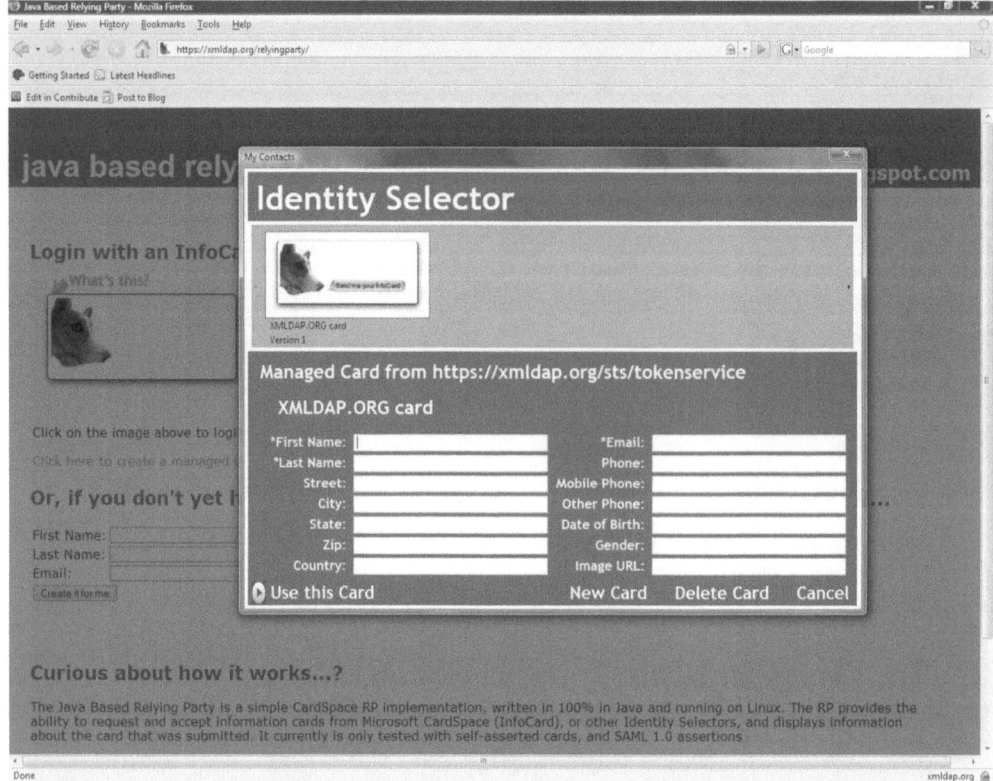

Figure 4-10. *The imported card*

This particular card requires the user to provide a username and password to authenticate the card on use, so a Card Authentication dialog box opens, as shown in Figure 4-11. This works just like it would in the Microsoft–provided identity selector.

If you're using Windows and Firefox and are not sure which selector to use, there's no need to panic. Because there is a great deal of cooperation in the identity space, Chuck Mortimore has introduced a hybrid, whereby you could select either his identity selector or the CardSpace identity selector at the time a card is requested.

■**Note** One benefit of the CardSpace identity selector is that, when shown, the background goes dark and the selector is displayed in a different "desktop." This makes the OS-based identity provider harder to spoof with a phishing attack. The use of a second desktop does not occur in the Java version. As you might imagine, given the number of potential OSs the Java version could be running on, this is definitely more of a challenge.

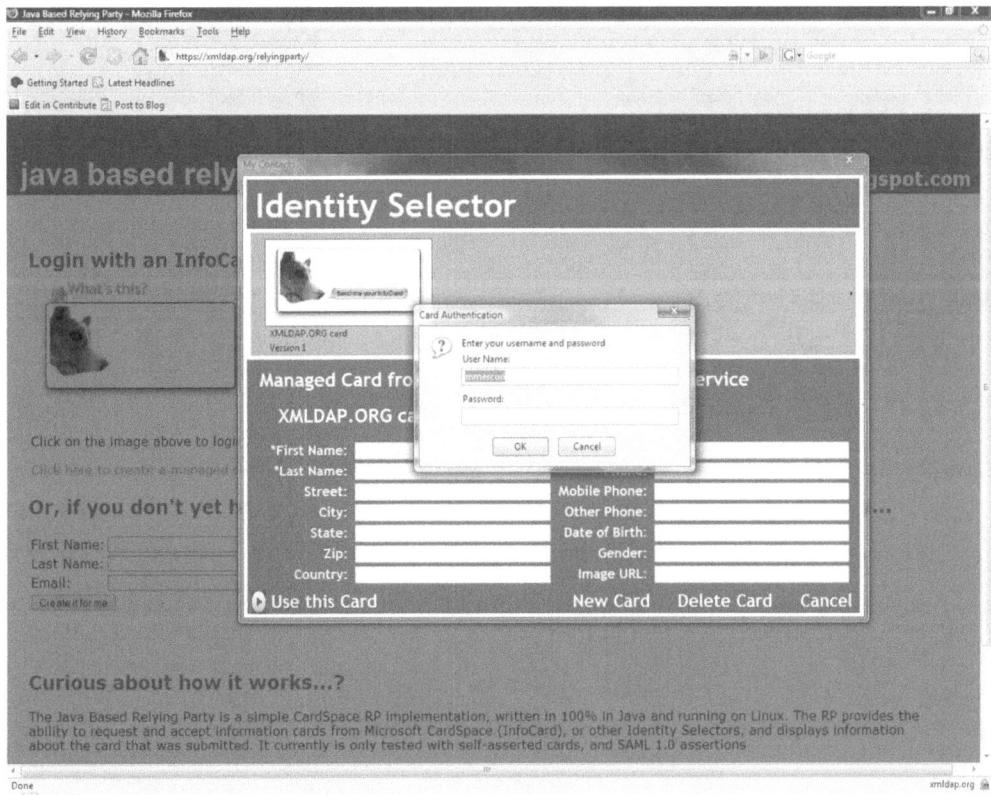

Figure 4-11. *Username and password-secured card*

Apple Safari

In addition to Internet Explorer and Firefox, someone has also built a plug-in to add information card support to Apple's Safari web browser. Ian Brown has developed an information card plug-in that retrieves information from the address book found in the Apple OS. Remember how I said there was actually a lot of "community" in the identity community? This plug-in is a great example, because the plug-in is a wrapper around Chuck Mortimore's Java-based work. This plug-in is provided in both PowerPC and Intel versions.

Here you'll note that the identity selector looks a bit different, displaying the address book icon in the upper left, as shown in Figure 4-12.

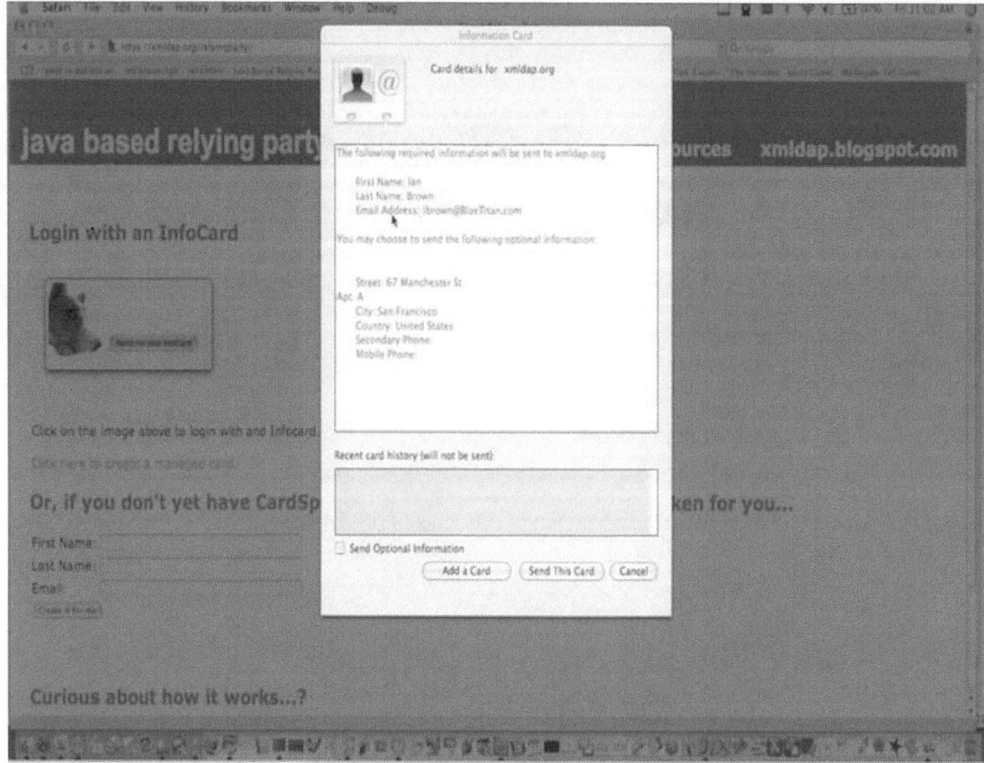

Figure 4-12. *Identity selector integrated with the Address Book*

Summary

As you saw in this chapter, many parties—more to the point, many of the right parties—believe in and are investing in user-centric identity and the identity metasystem.

In this chapter, you saw the projects and products that individuals outside of Microsoft are working on regarding identity selectors, token generators, and STSs. You also saw approaches beyond information cards such as LID, OpenID, and XRI. As we move forward, these systems are beginning to interoperate with each other.

■ ■ ■

CHAPTER 5

Introduction to Adding CardSpace to Your Web Applications

Earlier in the book, you created your own personal card and accessed third-party sites that use CardSpace and information cards. By the end of this chapter, you'll have working code that can serve as an example of how to accept CardSpace cards on your own site.

The chapter begins with a review of the challenges of today's de facto standard for authentication—username and password. Whether you're skeptical, curious, or a die-hard fan of CardSpace, before we get to the code, it's good to understand why the technology is important to implement on your site.

From there, you'll explore the two ways you can use CardSpace within your web pages, processing the tokens that are sent to your site and retrieving the claims that are contained within them.

Note The technologies used in this chapter are HTML, which is universal, and Microsoft's ASP.NET. Chapter 13 covers how to use information cards with Java.

Challenges Associated with Username and Passwords

There is no denying that website and web application usage has increased on a dramatic scale over the past decade. Equally, there is no denying that the de facto standard for logging in to these sites—username and password—is less than ideal and does not scale particularly well. This has led to the challenge of website users having to create and remember usernames and passwords and has led to an environment in which criminals could exploit those challenges.

Too Many Passwords

Imagine if you went to a shopping mall, and before you could make a purchase in any store in that mall, you were required to provide the store with a unique name that identified you and a password that conformed to certain rules. Then imagine this occurring with every merchant you encountered in the mall. Then add to this the grocery store, the ticket office at the baseball stadium, and the hot dog stand in that stadium.

That would be ridiculous, wouldn't it? But this is exactly the way things work on the Web today. Usernames and passwords don't scale well with humans. If you visit more than a few websites, this begins to get unmanageable. In some cases, if someone visits more than ten websites that require them to log in, they will put all the usernames and passwords in a spreadsheet. Most people, however, use the same username and password for every site or use a small set of username and passwords across these sites. End users are forced to have too many passwords and as a result have *password fatigue*.

The real world has few usernames and passwords. Instead, we use cards. The cards are issued by entities that the merchants trust—governments, banks, credit card companies, and so on. Whether through visual traits or phone or electronic verification, we can use these cards because the claims on them can be confirmed by the issuer. CardSpace begins to move us toward a similar model.

Phishing

Every so often I check my Junk Mail folder in my email client, Outlook. Each time I do, it is not uncommon to find emails from one or more online auction companies, banks, credit unions, and credit card companies. These emails have several aspects in common. The first is that each email informs me that there is an issue with my account and that the solution to that issue involves me going to a website and taking some action. The second is that although each email and the sites they link to look official, they are not.

These emails are not from who they say there are from; they are from someone or some group looking to steal my information. If I were to go to these legitimate-looking sites, they would prompt me for my username and password to log in. If I entered this information, they would capture it and either use it or trade it to someone who would use it for unscrupulous purposes. Perhaps they would clean out my bank account with a funds transfer or fraudulent online purchases. They might also use my information to access my auction account, from which they would launch "too good to be true" auctions that would swindle unwitting bidders out of their funds.

This is *phishing*, and it is a scourge on the Internet. It is bad, and it is getting worse. These emails used to arrive only occasionally, but now they arrive daily. In addition, these attacks are growing more organized. There are attacks now that will not just prompt you for your username and password once; they will prompt you multiple times until you repeat a username/password pair. Why? As mentioned in the previous section, many people have challenges remembering multiple passwords and use a limited number of username/passwords across all sites they encounter. This one type of attack could yield access to your bank account, your credit card, your auction site, or any other site you access.

That's just another reason why information cards—and their ability to replace usernames and passwords—is a very good thing for the future of the Web.

Configuring the Server

As mentioned previously in the book, websites that want to utilize information cards must publish those sites using Secure Sockets Layer (SSL). The steps to do this are different depending on whether you are using IIS 6 (Windows XP and Windows Server 2003) or IIS 7 (Windows Vista and Longhorn Server).

Based on the web server you have installed, configure SSL as directed in the following sections.

Configuring the IIS 6 Environment

To configure SSL with IIS 6, follow these steps:

1. If the directory C:\BeginningCardspace\Chapter5\Part1 does not exist, create it.

2. Open the Internet Information Services (IIS) Manager.

3. Right-click the default website, and select a new virtual directory.

4. This will display the Directory Creation Wizard. Click Next.

5. On the next screen of the wizard, enter **BeginningCardspace** as the alias, and click Next.

6. Enter **C:\BeginningCardspace** for the directory, and click Next.

7. Leave the default permissions, Read and Run Scripts, checked, and then click Next.

8. Click Finish.

Configuring the IIS 7 Environment

To configure SSL with IIS 7, follow these steps:

1. If the directory C:\BeginningCardspace\Chapter5\Part1 does not exist, create it.

2. Open the Internet Information Services (IIS) Manager (Control Panel ➤ Administrative Tools ➤ Internet Information Services).

3. In the Connections tree, expand Web Sites and Default Web Site.

4. Right-click Default Web Site, and select Add New Virtual Directory.

5. Name the directory **BeginningCardspace** as the alias, and specify **C:\BeginningCardspace** as the physical path.

6. Right-click the Chapter4 folder, and select Add Application.

7. Specify **Part1** as the alias, and specify **C:\BeginningCardspace\Chapter4\Part1** as the Physical Path setting.

8. Right-click the folder Part1, and select SSL Settings from the Features view.

9. Check the Require SSL and Require 128-bit SSL checkboxes, and click Ignore under Child Certificates, as shown in Figure 5-1.

10. Finally, click Apply.

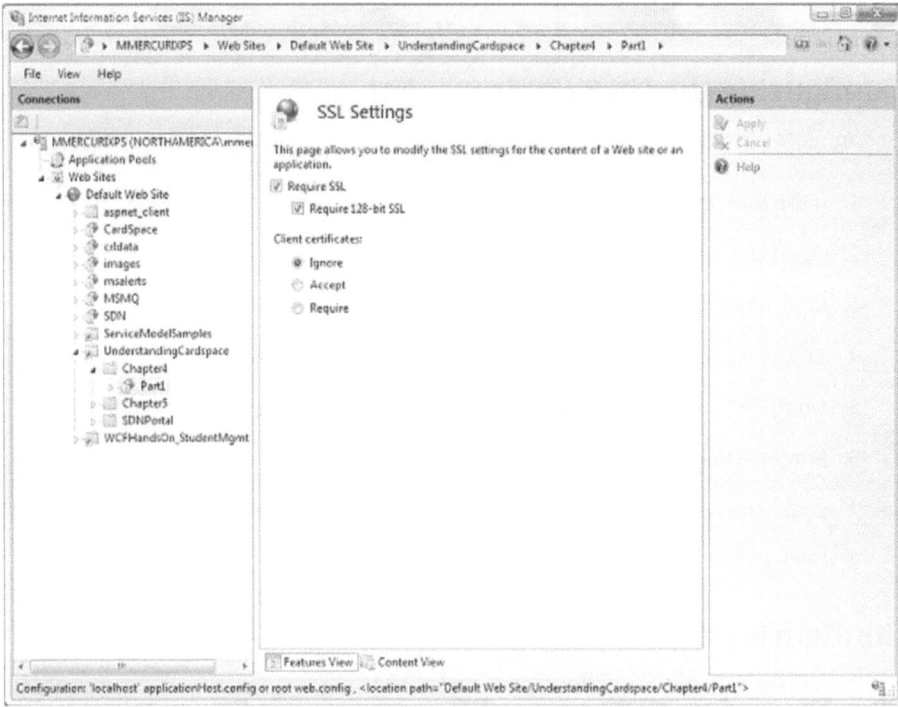

Figure 5-1. *Configuring SSL on IIS 7*

Triggering the Identity Selector via ActiveX

This section focuses on triggering the identity selector inside the browser. Follow these steps:

1. Begin by opening Visual Studio 2005.

2. From the menu, select File ➤ New ➤ Web Site.

3. Select Empty Web Site.

4. Confirm that Visual C# is specified in the Language drop-down list.

5. Name the website **C:\BeginningCardspace\Chapter5\Part1**, as shown in Figure 5-2.

6. Right-click the website, and select Add New Item.

7. Select HTML Page, and name it **Default.htm**.

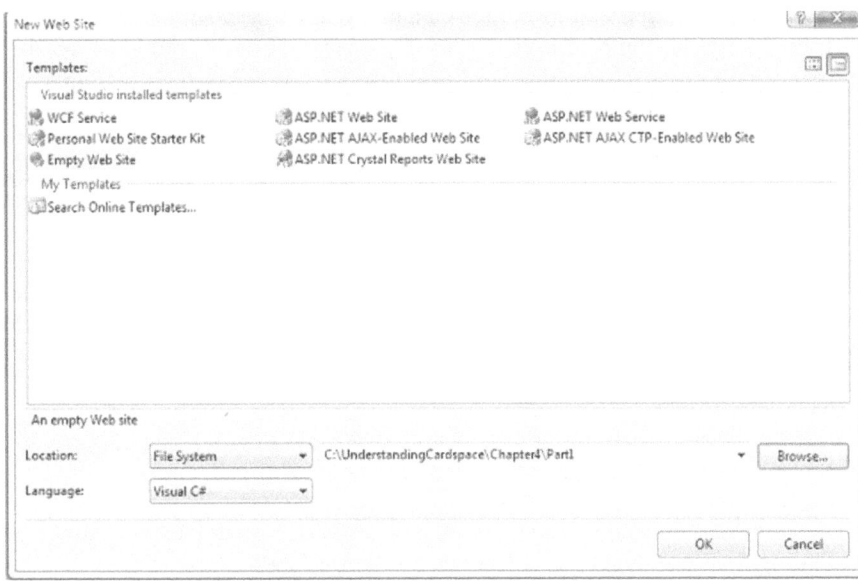

Figure 5-2. *New Web Site dialog box*

8. Modify Default.htm such that it contains the following HTML:

```
<!DOCTYPE html PUBLIC "-//W3C//DTD XHTML 1.0 Transitional//EN"
 "http://www.w3.org/TR/xhtml1/DTD/xhtml1-transitional.dtd">
<html xmlns="http://www.w3.org/1999/xhtml" >
<head>
    <title>ActiveX triggered identity selector</title>
</head>
<body>
    <form method=post action="Placeholder.aspx">
    <input  type="submit"  "Submit Information Card" />
        <object type="application/x-informationcard" name="xmlToken">
            <param name="tokenType"
 value="urn:oasis:names:tc:SAML:1.0:assertion" />
            <param name="issuer"
 value="http://schemas.xmlsoap.org/ws/2005/05/identity/issuer/self" />
            <param name="requiredClaims"
value="http://schemas.xmlsoap.org/ws/2005/05/identity/claims/givenname ➥
http://schemas.xmlsoap.org/ws/2005/05/identity/claims/surname ➥
http://schemas.xmlsoap.org/ws/2005/05/identity/claims/locality ➥
http://schemas.xmlsoap.org/ws/2005/05/identity/claims/country"
 />
        </object>

    </form>
</body>
</html>
```

This code is creating an information card object and does so utilizing three parameters: tokenType, issuer, and requiredClaims. The tokenType parameter identifies the type of token, in this case a token that conforms to the Security Assertion Markup Language (SAML) 1.0 specification. The issuer refers to the identity provider that issued the token; in this case, the issuer is self. This defines the requested issuer being the local STS used to create self-issued cards. The requiredClaims parameter provides a space-delimited list of the claims that are required. In this case, I've elected to require the given name, surname, locality, and country.

Also note that this object is located within a form that will post content to a file named Placeholder.aspx. For that post to occur, there is an input button on the page that will initiate the submission of the form.

9. Save Default.htm.

10. Right-click the website, and select Add New Item.

11. Select Web Form, and name it **Placeholder.aspx**.

12. Right-click Placeholder.aspx, and select View Designer.

13. In Designer view, click the Source tab.

14. Modify the page directive, adding the ValidateRequest attribute and setting it with a value of false, as shown here:

```
<%@ Page Language="C#" AutoEventWireup="true"
  CodeFile="Placeholder.aspx.cs" Inherits="Home"
   ValidateRequest="false"%>
```

■**Note** You do this because the token that will be posted contains XML tags, and ASP.NET would see this as a potential security issue.

---

15. Save Placeholder.aspx.

16. On that same page, add the text **Submitted** to the div element.

17. Open Internet Explorer, and navigate to https://www.fabrikam.com/BeginningCardspace/ Chapter5/Part1.

18. Click the Submit Information Card button.

This last step should trigger a post of the form. The object type of "application/ x-informationcard" will trigger the CardSpace identity selector. The token will then be sent to the Placeholder.aspx page created earlier. As with the previous example, the result will display Placeholder.aspx.

Triggering the Identity Selector via Binary

To trigger the identity selector via the binary, follow these steps:

1. Rename Default.htm to **Default1.htm**.

2. Right-click the website, and select Add New Item.

3. Select HTML Page, and name it **Default.htm**.

4. Modify Default.htm such that it contains the following HTML:

```html
<html xmlns="http://www.w3.org/1999/xhtml" xmlns:ic>
 <head><title>Binary Behavior</title>
 </head>
 <body>
 <form method="post" action="Placeholder.aspx">
  <ic:informationcard
   name='xmlToken'
   style='behavior: url(#default#informationCard)'
   issuer='http://schemas.xmlsoap.org/ws/2005/05/identity/issuer/self'
   tokenType='urn:oasis:names:tc:SAML:1.0:assertion'>
   <ic:add
 claimType='http://schemas.xmlsoap.org/ws/2005/05/identity/claims/givenname'
 optional='false' />
   <ic:add
 claimType='http://schemas.xmlsoap.org/ws/2005/05/identity/claims/surname'
 optional='false' />
   <ic:add
 claimType='http://schemas.xmlsoap.org/ws/2005/05/identity/claims/locality'
 optional='false' />
   <ic:add
 claimType='http://schemas.xmlsoap.org/ws/2005/05/identity/claims/country'
 optional='false' />
     </ic:informationcard>

   <input type="submit" name="CardspaceSignIn"
 value = "Login using CardSpace" id="InfocardSignin" />
   </form>
   </body>
   </html>
```

5. Open Internet Explorer, and navigate to https://www.fabrikam.com/BeginningCardspace/Chapter5/Part1.

6. Click the Submit Information Card button.

This last step should trigger a post of the form that will trigger the CardSpace identity selector. The token will then be sent to the Placeholder.aspx page created earlier.

The result of this test will be the display of that page. Because we haven't added code to process the token yet, the result is fairly boring, with only the word *Submitted* displayed.

Tip If the CardSpace identity selector is displayed but then you are shown a dialog box that says "Incoming policy failed validation," there's a good chance there's a spelling or capitalization issued in the `ic:informationCard` element.

Retrieving the Token

In the previous two examples, you've created pages that triggered the identity selector and posted the token to a secondary page. In this exercise, you'll expand on that solution to retrieve and display the token:

1. Right-click the website, and select Add New Item.

2. Select Web Form, and name the form **DisplayEncryptedToken.aspx**.

3. On the form, enter the text **This is your encrypted token:**.

4. Below the text, add a label to the form, and name it **lblEncryptedToken**.

5. In the designer, click the Source tab.

6. Modify the page directive to include `validateRequest="false"`.

7. Your page directive should look like this:

   ```
   <%@ Page Language="C#" AutoEventWireup="true"
   CodeFile="DisplayEncryptedToken.aspx.cs"
   Inherits="EncryptedToken" ValidateRequest="false" %>
   ```

8. From the menu bar in Visual Studio, select View ➤ Code.

9. In the form load event, enter the following code:

   ```
   protected void Page_Load(object sender, EventArgs e)
     {
         string xmlToken;
         xmlToken = Request.Params["xmlToken"];

         if (xmlToken == null || xmlToken == "")
         {
             xmlToken = "N/A. No token was provided.";
         }

         lblEncryptedToken.Text = xmlToken;

     }
   ```

10. Open `Default.htm`.

11. Replace the reference to `Placeholder.aspx` in the form action to `DisplayEncrypedtoken.aspx`.

12. Save `Default.htm`.

13. Open Internet Explorer, and navigate to `https://www.fabrikam.com/BeginningCardspace/Chapter5/Part1`, as shown in Figure 5-3.

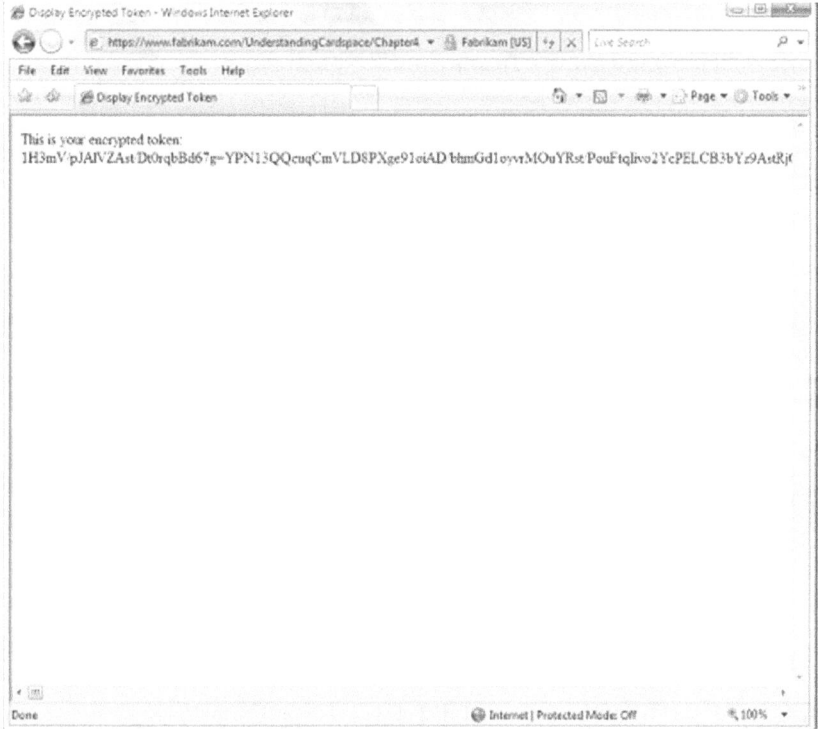

Figure 5-3. `DisplayEncryptedToken.aspx`

At this point, you've seen how to wire up an HTML page to trigger the identity selector and transmit the token to a page. You've also seen how to retrieve the encrypted token.

The next step is decrypting the token and retrieving the claims from the token.

Retrieving Claims from the Token

To retrieve the claims from the token, follow these steps:

1. Right-click the website, and select Add Reference.

2. Select System.ServiceModel, System.IdentityModel, and System.IdentityModel.Selectors, and click OK.

3. Right-click the website, and select Add Existing Item.

4. Select `TokenHelper.cs`.

■**Note** Microsoft provides this file. If you haven't already done so, please see the "Prerequisites" section at the beginning of the book. It provides information on where to get this and the certificates referenced in this chapter.

---

5. Open Default.html, and change the action attribute of the form element to DisplayUnencryptedClaims.aspx.

6. Right-click the website, and select Add New Item.

7. Select WebForm, and name it **DisplayUnencryptedClaims**.

8. Open DisplayUnencryptedClaims.cs.

9. From the Visual Studio menu bar, select View ➤ Designer.

10. Add the text **The claims found in the token are:**, and press Enter.

11. Beneath the text, add a TextBox control.

12. In the Properties window for the TextBox control, set the name to **tbClaims**, and set the text mode to **Multiline**.

13. From the Visual Studio menu bar, select View ➤ Code.

14. Add **Using System.IdentityModel.Samples** to the top of the file.

15. Add the following code to the form load event:

```
protected void Page_Load(object sender, EventArgs e)
    {
        string xmlToken;
        xmlToken = Request.Params["xmlToken"];

        if (xmlToken == null || xmlToken == "")
        {
            xmlToken = "N/A. No token was provided.";
        }
        else
        {
            TokenHelper tokenHelper = new TokenHelper(xmlToken);
```

```
        foreach(Claim claim in tokenHelper.IdentityClaims)
        {
            tbClaims.Text += "-------------------------------------\n";
            tbClaims.Text += "Claim Type:" + claim.ClaimType + "\n";
            tbClaims.Text += "Right:" + claim.Right + "\n";
            tbClaims.Text += "Resource:" +
claim.Resource.ToString() + "\n";

        }

    }
```

This code uses the TokenHelper class provided by Microsoft. This class receives the encrypted token and then decrypts it and uses the contents to populate a claimset. The claimset is then iterated through; the claim type, right, and resource are all interrogated; and their values are sent to the TextBox control.

Note Claimsets are covered in more detail in the previous chapter.

---

16. Open web.config.

17. Add the following elements to the configuration file:

```
<add key="CertificateSubject" value="www.fabrikam.com"/>
  <add key="StoreName" value="My"/>
  <add key="StoreLocation" value="LocalMachine"/>
  <add key="IdentityClaimType"
value=http://schemas.xmlsoap.org/ws/2005/05/identity/claims/➥
privatepersonalidentifier
/>
  <add key="MaximumClockSkew" value="60"/>
```

The relevance of these additions are covered in the next section.

18. Save all the files.

19. Open Internet Explorer, and navigate to https://www.fabrikam.com/BeginningCardspace/Chapter5/Part1. You should see the results as displayed in Figure 5-4.

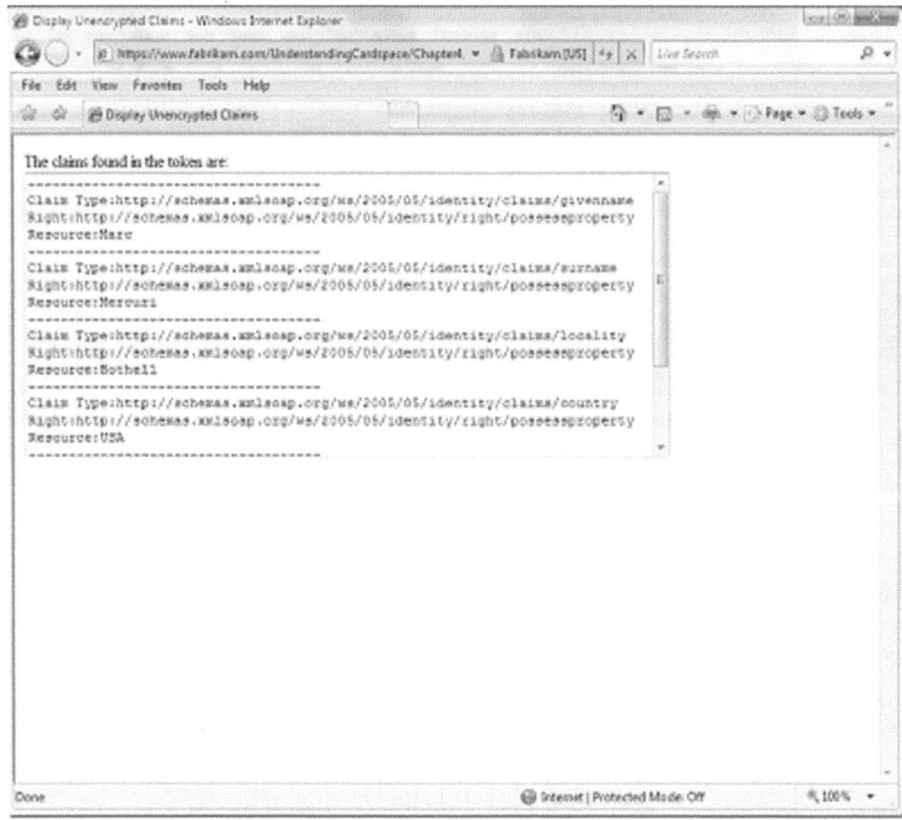

Figure 5-4. *Output from this exercise*

Taking a Closer Look at TokenHelper

In the previous exercise, you used TokenHelper.cs. Let's take a closer look at how it works:

```
TokenHelper tokenHelper = new TokenHelper(xmlToken);
```

This triggered the constructor for TokenHelper, which in turn called this other constructor, passing null for the certificateSubject value:

```
        public TokenHelper(String xmlToken, string certificatesubject)
        {

            StoreName storeName = StoreName.My;
            StoreLocation storeLocation = StoreLocation.LocalMachine;
            X509Certificate2 cert = null;

            string rpCertificateSubject =
System.Configuration.ConfigurationManager.AppSettings["CertificateSubject"];
            string rpStoreName =
```

```
ConfigurationManager.AppSettings["StoreName"];
            string rpStoreLocation =
ConfigurationManager.AppSettings["StoreLocation"];

            if (!string.IsNullOrEmpty(certificatesubject))
                rpCertificateSubject = certificatesubject;


            if (!string.IsNullOrEmpty(rpStoreName))
                storeName = (StoreName)Enum.Parse(typeof(StoreName),
 rpStoreName, true);

            if (!string.IsNullOrEmpty(rpStoreLocation))
                storeLocation =
(StoreLocation)Enum.Parse(typeof(StoreLocation),
rpStoreLocation, true);

            if (string.IsNullOrEmpty(rpCertificateSubject))
                throw new Exception("Relying Party Certificate➥
 Subject not specified");

            X509Store s = new X509Store(storeName, storeLocation);
            s.Open(OpenFlags.ReadOnly);

            foreach (X509Certificate2 xCert in s.Certificates)
            {
                if (xCert.Subject.StartsWith("CN=" +
rpCertificateSubject, StringComparison.CurrentCultureIgnoreCase))
                {
                    if (cert == null)
                        cert = xCert;
                    else
                        throw new Exception(string.Format("There are
more than one certificates matching CN={0}", rpCertificateSubject));
                }
            }

            if (cert == null)
                throw new Exception(string.Format("Relying Party➥
 Certificate ({0}) in {1}:{2} Not located",
 rpCertificateSubject, storeLocation.ToString(),
storeName.ToString()));

            ParseToken(xmlToken, cert);

        }
```

This code reads in the configuration information we specified in web.config. These entries in web.config provide definitions for the certificate subject, store name, and store location for the certificate for the relying party (this site).

Both the certificate and the token passed in from Default.htm are passed to the ParseToken method.

```
        private void ParseToken(string xmlToken, X509Certificate2 cert)
        {
            int skew = 300; // default to 5 minutes
            string tokenskew =
    System.Configuration.ConfigurationManager.AppSettings["MaximumClockSkew"];
            if (!string.IsNullOrEmpty(tokenskew))
                skew = Int32.Parse(tokenskew);

            XmlReader tokenReader =
    new XmlTextReader(new StringReader(xmlToken));
            EncryptedData enc = new EncryptedData();

            enc.TokenSerializer = WSSecurityTokenSerializer.DefaultInstance;

            enc.ReadFrom(tokenReader);

            List<SecurityToken> tokens = new List<SecurityToken>();
            SecurityToken encryptingToken = new X509SecurityToken(cert);
            tokens.Add(encryptingToken);

            SecurityTokenResolver tokenResolver =
    SecurityTokenResolver.CreateDefaultSecurityTokenResolver(tokens.AsReadOnly()
    , false);
            SymmetricSecurityKey encryptingCrypto;

            // an error here usually means that you have selected
    //the wrong key.
            encryptingCrypto =
    (SymmetricSecurityKey)tokenResolver.ResolveSecurityKey(enc.KeyIdentifier[0]);

            SymmetricAlgorithm algorithm =
    encryptingCrypto.GetSymmetricAlgorithm(enc.EncryptionMethod);

            byte[] decryptedData = enc.GetDecryptedBuffer(algorithm);

            SecurityTokenSerializer tokenSerializer =
    WSSecurityTokenSerializer.DefaultInstance;

            XmlReader reader = new XmlTextReader(new StreamReader(new
    MemoryStream(decryptedData), Encoding.UTF8));
```

```
            m_token =
 (SamlSecurityToken)tokenSerializer.ReadToken(reader, tokenResolver);



            SamlSecurityTokenAuthenticator authenticator = new
SamlSecurityTokenAuthenticator(new List<SecurityTokenAuthenticator>(
new SecurityTokenAuthenticator[]{

new RsaSecurityTokenAuthenticator(),

new X509SecurityTokenAuthenticator() }), new TimeSpan(0, 0, skew));



            if (authenticator.CanValidateToken(m_token))
            {
                ReadOnlyCollection<IAuthorizationPolicy> policies =
authenticator.ValidateToken(m_token);
                m_authorizationContext =
AuthorizationContext.CreateDefaultAuthorizationContext(policies);
                m_identityClaims = FindIdentityClaims(m_authorizationContext);
            }
            else
            {
                throw new Exception("Unable to validate the token.");
            }
        }
```

The ParseToken method decrypts the token using the certificate and, using classes available as part of System.IdentityModel.Selectors, takes the decrypted data and generates a SamlSecurityToken. That token is then evaluated against a SamlSecurityTokenAuthenticator, which validates the token. If the token is valid, the authorization claims and the authorization policies are extracted.

Finally, these claims are returned to the calling code, and the claimset is exposed via the identityClaims property.

Once you have the claims, you can use the information per your privacy policy. In addition to using it for authentication, you can use it for personalization and targeted recommendations.

Confirming That CardSpace Is Installed

Everything you've done thus far all works fine—if your client has CardSpace installed. Not everyone will have Internet Explorer 7 or a third-party browser with CardSpace support.

This section focuses on JavaScript, which can be used to help you determine whether Internet Explorer 7 or a supported browser is installed. Follow these steps:

1. Begin by opening Visual Studio 2005.

2. From the menu, select File ➤ New ➤ Web Site.

3. Select Empty Web Site.

4. Confirm that Visual C# is specified in the Language drop-down list.

5. Name the website **C:\BeginningCardspace\Chapter5\Part2**.

6. Right-click the website, and select Add New Item.

7. Select HTML Page, and name the file **Default.htm**.

8. Make changes to your Default.htm file such that it looks like the following code:

```
<!DOCTYPE html PUBLIC "-//W3C//DTD XHTML 1.0 Transitional//EN"
"http://www.w3.org/TR/xhtml1/DTD/xhtml1-transitional.dtd">
<html xmlns="http://www.w3.org/1999/xhtml" xmlns:ic>
<head>
    <title>Browser Support</title>

        <object type="application/x-informationcard" name="xmlToken"

id="informationCard">
            <param name="tokenType"

value="urn:oasis:names:tc:SAML:1.0:assertion" />
            <param name="issuer" ➥
value="http://schemas.xmlsoap.org/ws/2005/05/identity/issuer/self" />


            <param name="requiredClaims"
value="http://schemas.xmlsoap.org/ws/2005/05/identity/claims/givenname
http://schemas.xmlsoap.org/ws/2005/05/identity/claims/surname
http://schemas.xmlsoap.org/ws/2005/05/identity/claims/locality
http://schemas.xmlsoap.org/ws/2005/05/identity/claims/country
http://schemas.xmlsoap.org/ws/2005/05/identity/claims/➥
privatepersonalidentifier"
 />
        </object>
    <script type="text/javascript" language="javascript"
src="DetectSupport.js"></script>

</head>
<body>
  <div id="CardSpaceSupportTest">

  </div>
   <script type="text/javascript">

            if(IsCardSpaceSupported())
            {
                populateDiv("CardSpaceSupportTest",
"Cardspace is not supported in this browser");
```

```
            }
            else
            {
                 populateDiv("CardSpaceSupportTest",
   "Cardspace is supported in this browser");
            }



        </script>
   </body>
   </html>
```

9. Right-click the website, and select Add New File.

10. Select a JavaScript file, and name the file **DetectSupport.js**.

11. Populate **DetectSupport.js** with the following code:

```javascript
//Use this routine to populate divs via JavaScript

function populateDiv(id, text)
{
if (document.getElementById(id))
{
var element = document.getElementById(id);
element.innerHTML = text;
}

}

//This function examines the user agent and
//determines whether Internet Explorer is running
function RunningInternetExplorer()
{
    var runningIE = (navigator.userAgent.toUpperCase().indexOf("MSIE") >= 0);
    return (runningIE);
}

//This determines the version of IE
function GetIEVersion()
{
    if(RunningInternetExplorer())
    {
        if (new ➡
RegExp("MSIE ([0-9]{1,}[\.0-9]{0,})").exec(navigator.userAgent)➡
 != null)
            return parseFloat( RegExp.$1 );
    }
```

```
        else
        {
            return 0;
        }
    }

    function IsCardSpaceSupported()
    {
        var supported = false;

        try
        {
            var informationCard = document.getElementById(informationCard);

            if ( RunningInternetExplorer() )
            {
                //This is running a version of Internet Explorer

                if ( GetIEVersion() >= 7 )
                //This is running a version where
    //CardSpace/information cards could be supported
                {
                    if ( informationCard.isInstalled )
                    {
                        //Information card support is available
                         supported = true;
                    }
                }
            }
            else
            {

                if ( navigator.mimeTypes && navigator.mimeTypes.length )
                {
                    var ic = ➥
    navigator.mimeTypes['application/x-informationcard'];

                    if ( ic && ic.enabledPlugin ) //Installed and enabled
                        supported = true;
                }
            }
        }
```

```
      catch (e)
      {
          return false;
      }

      return supported;
   }x
```

The HTML you entered for `Default.htm` contains an object reference for an information card. This is nearly identical to those you've seen earlier in this chapter. The one exception is that this object also includes an `id` attribute that is set to `informationCard`.

In addition, you have a reference to a linked JavaScript file, `DetectSupport.js`. Also, note that there is a `div` with an `id` of `CardSpaceSupportText`, and it is followed by some JavaScript.

The script here calls a function in the JavaScript file `IsCardSpaceSupported`. This routine examines the user agent and determines whether this is Internet Explorer. If so, it determines which version of Internet Explorer it is, using version 7 as a baseline for CardSpace support. If this is not Internet Explorer, it will use the cross-platform functions to determine whether "application/x-informationcard" is a supported MIME type. If it is, it will determine whether it is enabled on the system.

That function returns a boolean response, and based on the result, the script inside `Default.htm` populates a `div` on the page with a certain value. In this case, the value is text that specifies whether CardSpace is supported in the browser. In a production application, you could use this to drive your user experience. For example, CardSpace-enabled browsers could default to a screen that allowed the presentation of an information card. Conversely, if a browser did not support information cards, HTML for a username and password entry could be placed into the `div`.

Summary

This chapter served as an introduction to using CardSpace in the browser. You learned how to trigger the identity selector, collect the claims that you're interested in, and decrypt and access the token and its contained claimset(s). In addition, you learned how to use JavaScript to determine whether CardSpace support is installed in the client browser so you can program your web application to render an appropriate user interface.

In the next chapter, we'll move beyond the basics and build a working sample where CardSpace is being used with ASP.NET membership to provide authentication for a website.

■ ■ ■

CHAPTER 6

CardSpace with ASP.NET 2.0 Forms Authentication and Membership

In Chapter 1, I introduced the concept of authentication. ASP.NET has several built-in options for authentication. The default is Windows authentication, which utilizes the same credentials as those used to log in to your Windows computer or network. In this chapter, you will use forms authentication. As the name implies, forms authentication requests authentication information from users via a form, as shown in Figure 6-1.

Forms authentication in ASP.NET provides controls, configuration settings, and back-end data store providers to enroll and authenticate users effortlessly. ASP.NET also includes functionality related to membership. Membership is implemented via providers, and those providers offer functionality to create, find, and update users programmatically. In addition, the underlying data store provides storage and stored procedures to support key tasks such as tracking failed password attempts, locking out accounts, and resetting passwords.

In this chapter, you'll learn how to extend that knowledge and incorporate CardSpace and information cards into the out-of-the-box functionality provided with forms authentication and membership in ASP.NET 2.0.

■**Note** Although ASP.NET can work with different providers, the focus of this chapter is SQL Server. You can apply the knowledge gained here to other scenarios such as Active Directory, Active Directory Lightweight Directory Services (formally called Active Directory Application Mode [ADAM]), third-party databases, and so on.

The chapter begins with a review of forms authentication and membership, moves on to a sample that implements standard forms authentication, and closes with enhancements for adding support for information cards.

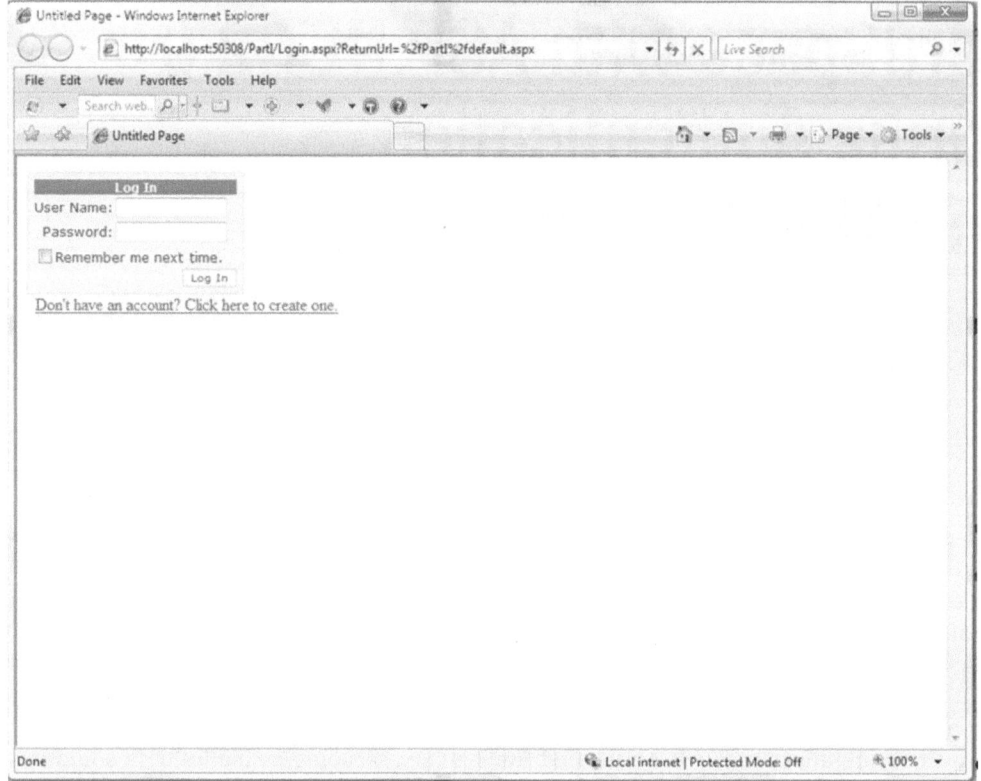

Figure 6-1. *Forms authentication in action*

Installing the Database

ASP.NET ships with an executable file, aspnet_regsql.exe, that will install the underlying tables used for forms authentication and membership. Follow these steps:

1. In a Visual Studio command prompt window, run aspnet_regsql.exe -S <local> -E -A all.

■**Note** You should replace <local> here with the name of your SQL Server, as in mmercuri1\sqlexpress.

This will result in the creation of the database (aspnetdb.mdf) that contains the tables and stored procedures for forms authentication and membership:

• The -S command-line parameter specifies the server. In this case, it is going against the local server; substitute your server name if it's different.

• The -E command-line parameter specifies that Windows authentication should be used to connect to the SQL Server database.

- The -A command line parameters specifies the features to add. 'all' specifies to include membership, profile, rolemanager, membership and SqlWebEventProvider.

The next step is to grant database access to the account running IIS.

2. Open Notepad.

3. Enter the following text in Notepad, and save the file as **GrantAccess.sql** in C:\BeginningCardspace\Chapter6:

```
Create a SQL Server login for the Network Service account

sp_grantlogin 'NT AUTHORITY\Network Service'


-- Grant the login access to the membership database

USE aspnetdb

GO

sp_grantdbaccess 'NT AUTHORITY\Network Service', 'Network Service'


-- Add user to database role

USE aspnetdb

GO

sp_addrolemember 'aspnet_Membership_FullAccess', 'Network Service'
```

4. Open the Visual Studio command prompt, and enter the following:

```
sqlcmd –S <server> -i C:\BeginningCardspace\Chapter6\GrantAccess.sql
```

5. Press Enter.

This will grant login rights to the ASP.NET membership database for the network service.

Note In this example, the default NT AUTHORITY\Network Service is used. If you are using a different account to run IIS, use it in place of NT AUTHORITY\Network Service.

Configuring Forms Authentication

Once a database is created, you can write applications that leverage SQL providers. When developing an ASP.NET application that utilizes forms authentication, you must define the configuration information. Here's a sample configuration section:

```
<authentication mode="Forms">
    <forms name="cookie"
 loginUrl="Login.aspx"
protection="All"
timeout="30"
requireSSL="false"
slidingExpiration="false"
cookieless="UseCookies"
defaultUrl="Default.aspx"
    />
</authentication>
```

When a new web configuration file is created, it is prepopulated with a default authentication mode of Windows. When using forms authentication, you will replace the value of Windows with Forms. Optionally, you can add a subelement of forms that can include any of 11 potential attributes. Each of these attributes is optional, because ASP.NET will use the default value for any attribute not specified.

Table 6-1 defines the full list of attributes.

Table 6-1. *Configuration Settings*

Name	Description	Default
Cookieless	Defines whether cookies are used and, if used, the method by which they should be implemented. The following are acceptable values for the attribute: UseCookies: Cookies will always be used. UseUri: Cookies will never be used. AutoDetect: Cookies will be used with devices that support cookies; otherwise, cookies will not be used. UseDeviceProfile: Cookies will be used if the browser supports cookies; otherwise, cookies will not be used. For devices that support cookies, no check is made to see whether cookies are enabled.	UseDeviceProfile
defaultUrl	Defines the default URL redirected to after authentication.	Default.aspx
Domain	Sets an optional domain on forms authentication cookies.	Empty string ("")
enableCrossAppRedirects	Specifies whether a user can be redirected to another web application.	False

Table 6-1. *Configuration Settings*

Name	Description	Default
loginUrl	Specifies the URL for the login page to which unauthenticated users will be redirected.	Login.aspx
Name	Specifies the HTTP cookie to use for authen-tication.	.ASPXAUTH
Path	Specifies the path for the cookies that are issued by the application.	/
Protection	Specifies the encryption type used to encrypt the cookie.	All
Timeout	Specifies an integer value for the time in minutes that a cookie is valid.	30 (30 minutes)
requireSSL	Specifies whether SSL is required.	False
slidingExpiration	If set to True, specifies that the cookie expiration be reset on each request. If set to False, cookie expiration is set to a fixed interval.	False

Note When slidingExpiration is set to True, the use of the timeout attribute value differs. In that scenario, the timeout window is reset with each page request (instead of set on the initial request).

The FormsAuthentication Class

ASP.NET provides a FormsAuthentication class that offers access to key functions tied to the authentication of the user. This includes authenticating the user, encrypting and decrypting the generated authentication ticket, and signing the user out of the system. Table 6-2 lists the methods of the FormsAuthentication class.

Table 6-2. *FormsAuthentication Methods (Excluding Those Inherited from Object)*

Name	Description
Authenticate	Using the supplied credentials, attempts to authenticate the provided credentials against those stored in the credential store
Decrypt	When provided with a valid encrypted authentication ticket, returns an instance of the FormsAuthenticationTicket class
Encrypt	Given a FormsAuthenticationTicket, produces an encrypted authentication ticket that can be used in an HTTP cookie

Table 6-2. *FormsAuthentication Methods (Excluding Those Inherited from Object) (Continued)*

Name	Description
GetAuthCookie	Creates an authentication cookie for a given username
GetRedirectUrl	Returns the URL to the page that was requested (prior to being redirected to the login page)
HashPasswordForStoringInConfigFile	As the name implies, produces a hash password suitable for storing in a configuration file
Initialize	Reads the web.config file, retrieving cookie values and encryption keys
RedirectFromLoginPage	Returns the user to the page that was requested (prior to being redirected to the login page)
RenewTicketIfOld	Updates the sliding expiration of a FormsAuthenticationTicket
SetAuthCookie	Creates an authentication ticket and adds it to the response's cookie collection
SignOut	Signs the user out, removing the authentication ticket

The Membership Class

When creating the database earlier, aspnet_regsql.exe added the membership-related structure and stored procedures to the database. In addition to the FormsAuthentication class, ASP.NET includes a class that provides the ability to easily interact with the underlying tables and stored procedures.

Table 6-3 lists the methods of the Membership class.

Table 6-3. *Membership Class Methods*

Name	Description
CreateUser	Creates a new user in the database
DeleteUser	Deletes a user from the database
FindUsersByEmail	Finds all users using the email address provided
FindUsersByName	Finds all users given the name provided
GeneratePassword	Generates a random password for the specified user
GetAllUsers	Gets a collection of all users in the database

Table 6-3. *Membership Class Methods*

Name	Description
GetNumberOfUsersOnline	Returns the number of users currently online and accessing an application
GetUser	Gets the membership information from the database for a given user
GetUserNameByEmail	Gets a username for a user, based on an email address
UpdateUser	Updates a user
ValidateUser	Verifies that the supplied username and password are valid

Configuring Standard Forms Authentication

To configure standard forms authentication, follow these steps:

1. In Visual Studio, create a new ASP.NET website, and place it at
   C:\BeginningCardspace\Chapter6\PartI, as shown in Figure 6-2.

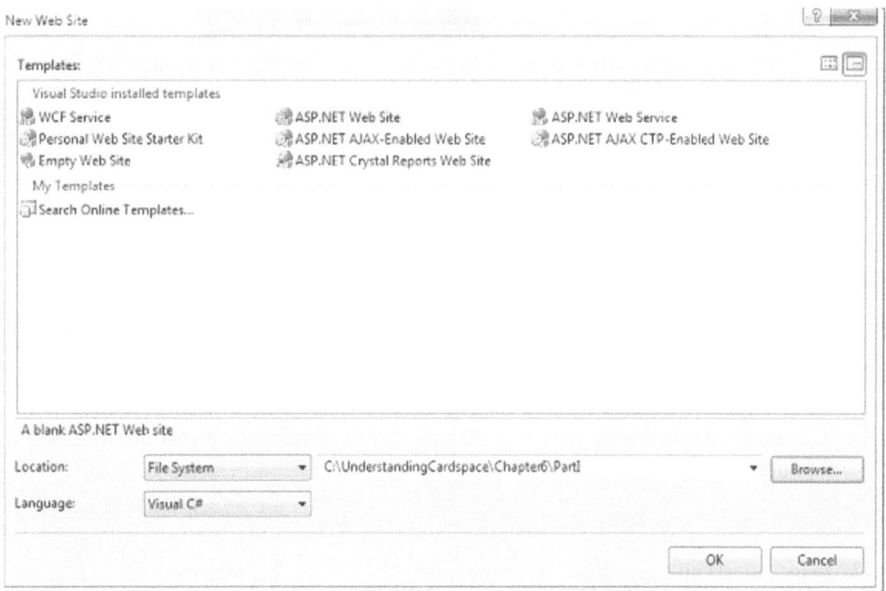

Figure 6-2. *Creating the new website*

2. Drag a LoginName control from the Toolbox onto the form.

3. Right-click the website name in Solution Explorer, and select Add New Item.

4. Select Web Form, and name it **Login.aspx**.

5. From the Toolbox, drag a Login control onto the form.

6. Click the smart tag on the control, and select AutoFormat.

7. Select the Professional format.

8. Drag a LinkButton control from the Toolbox, and position it under the control.

9. Modify the text property of the LinkButton to read **Don't have an account? Click here to create one.**

10. Drag a CreateUserWizard control onto the form, positioning it in the upper left of the form.

11. View the code for the form, and make the following additions:

```
public partial class Login : System.Web.UI.Page
{
    protected void Page_Load(object sender, EventArgs e)
    {
        LinkButton1.Click += new EventHandler(LinkButton1_Click);
        CreateUserWizard1.CreatedUser += new ➥
EventHandler(CreateUserWizard1_CreatedUser);
    }

    void CreateUserWizard1_CreatedUser(object sender, EventArgs e)
    {
        CreateUserWizard1.Visible = false;
    }

    void LinkButton1_Click(object sender, EventArgs e)
    {
        Login1.Visible = true;
        CreateUserWizard1.Visible = true;
    }
}
```

This code manipulates the page, specifically controlling the visibility of the CreateUserWizard control.

12. Right-click the website, and select Add New Item.

13. Select Web Configuration File, and select OK.

14. Open web.config.

15. The web.config file will contain an authentication section. Replace it with the following XML:

```
<authentication mode="Forms">
     <forms name="cookie"
loginUrl="Login.aspx"
protection="All"
timeout="30"
requireSSL="false"
slidingExpiration="false"
cookieless="UseCookies"
defaultUrl="Default.aspx"/>
</authentication>
<authorization>
     <deny users="?"/>
</authorization>
```

This code performs two key functions. The authorization section denies access to unauthenticated users. The authentication element establishes that this website will use forms authentication. I'll discuss the full list of attributes in a moment; for now just note that loginUrl points to Login.aspx. As you might imagine, for all unauthenticated users, the site will redirect all requests to Login.aspx.

16. Modify the connectionStrings element in the file by replacing it with the following XML:

```
  <connectionStrings>
<remove name="LocalSqlServer"/>
   <add name="LocalSqlServer" ➥
connectionString="Server=MMERCURIXPS\SQLEXPRESS;Integrated ➥
Security=True;Database=aspnetdb;Persist Security Info=True" />
  </connectionStrings>
```

Note The server listed in the previous XML is my personal SQL Server. Replace MMERCURIXPS\SQLExpress with the name of your local SQL Server or SQL Server Express.

Testing the Solution

At this point, your site is now configured and ready for testing, so start the debugger, and run the project.

The site will attempt to go to Default.aspx, but because you're not authenticated and this site is configured for forms authentication, it directs you to the loginUrl specified in the web.config file. You will be redirected to Login.aspx, which prompts you for your user credentials, as shown in Figure 6-3.

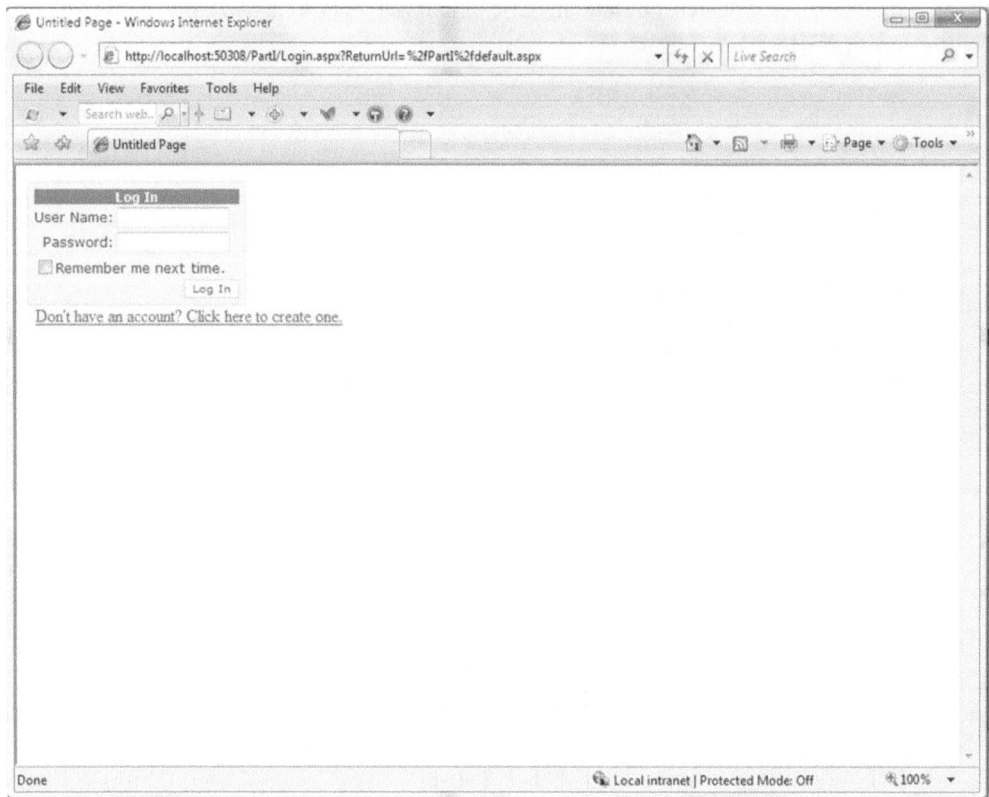

Figure 6-3. *The Login control*

Because you do not yet have an account for the site, click the hyperlink. This will display the CreateUserWizard control page, as shown in Figure 6-4. Enter the requested information, and click Create User.

■**Note** For the password, be sure to include at least one nonalphanumeric character.

If the login was created successfully, you'll see the login page. Enter the username and password for your newly created account, and click the login button. You should now be redirected to the Default.aspx page. You'll note that the text in the LoginName1 control displays the username you created and used to log in.

You've just configured the standard forms authentication functionality, created a user, and logged into the system. Now that you've covered the basics, it's time to add support for information cards.

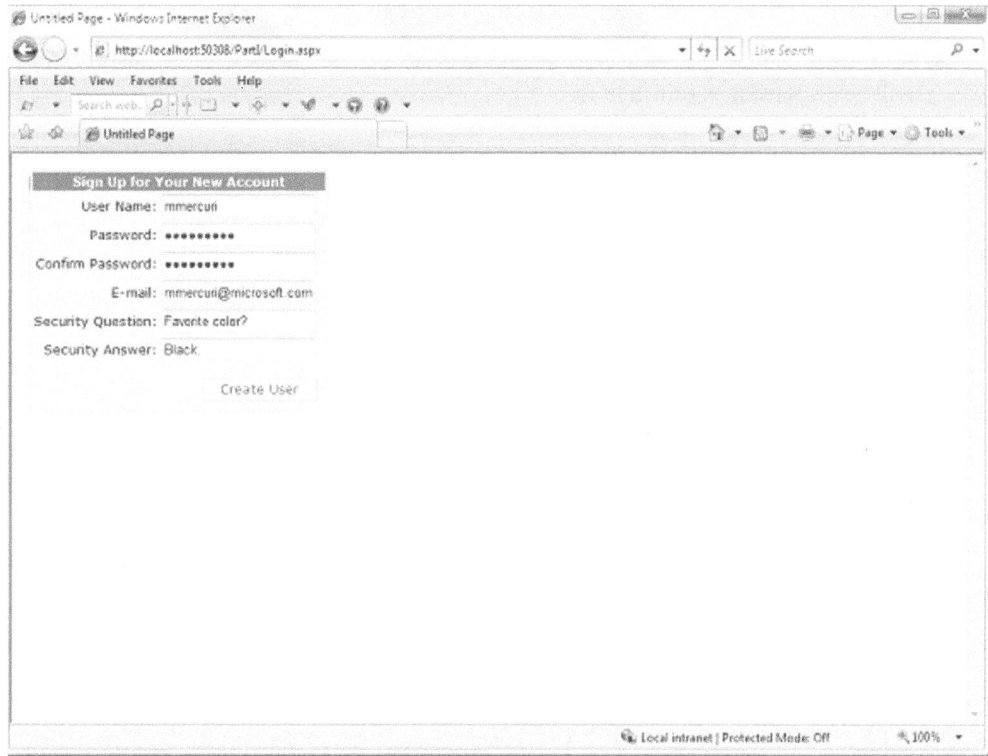

Figure 6-4. *Creating a user in the CreateUserWizard control*

Adding Support for Information Cards

The remainder of the chapter will illustrate how to extend the existing forms authentication and membership functionality to support information cards. The changes are focused in two areas—the underlying data structures and stored procedures and the login-related controls.

Updating the Table Structure

To update the table structure, follow these steps:

1. In Visual Studio, select View ➤ Server Explorer from the menu.

2. Right-click Data Connections, and select Add Connection. This will display an Add Connection dialog box.

3. In the box for the server name, select or enter the name of your server.

4. In the Select or Enter a Database Name box, select aspnetdb, and click OK.

5. This will add a new data connection in Server Explorer.

6. Click the plus sign to the left of the new database connection.

7. Click the plus sign to the left of the Stored Procedures folder.

8. Right-click aspnet_Users_CreateUser, and select Open. The code for the stored procedure will be displayed, as shown here:

```
ALTERPROCEDURE [dbo].[aspnet_Users_CreateUser]
    @ApplicationId    uniqueidentifier,
    @UserName         nvarchar(256),
    @IsUserAnonymous  bit,
    @LastActivityDate DATETIME,
    @UserId           uniqueidentifier OUTPUT
AS
BEGIN
    IF( @UserId IS NULL )
        SELECT @UserId = NEWID()
    ELSE
    BEGIN
        IF( EXISTS( SELECT UserId FROM dbo.aspnet_Users
                    WHERE @UserId = UserId ) )
            RETURN -1
    END

    INSERT dbo.aspnet_Users (ApplicationId, UserId, UserName, ➥
LoweredUserName, IsAnonymous, LastActivityDate)
    VALUES (@ApplicationId, @UserId, @UserName, LOWER(@UserName), ➥
@IsUserAnonymous, @LastActivityDate)

    RETURN 0
END
```

You can see how the default stored procedure creates users, and you can see what information is stored in the user table—the application ID, a username, a boolean that identifies whether the user is anonymous, a GUID that serves as a user ID, and a datetime field that stores the last date of activity for the user.

There currently is no storage for the private identifier stored in an information card. Because this is a table that is created by a script provided by the product team, it is open to change. To add support for information cards, you'll create a new table.

9. Within the data connection, click the plus sign to the left of the Tables folder.

10. Right-click the Tables folder, and select Add New Table.

11. Add the columns defined in Table 6-4.

Table 6-4. *The aspnet_UserInformationCards Table*

Column Name	Data Type	Allow Nulls
UserID	uniqueidentifier	No
PrivatePersonalIdentifier	char(20)	No
Active	bit	No
DateAdded	datetime	No
DateModified	datetime	No

12. Save the table, and name it **aspnet_UserInformationCards**.

    This table provides the ability to store multiple information cards for an account, as well as a flag to identify whether the card is active. This table will be used in addition to the tables provided for authentication and membership. It will facilitate the association of a card with a user, and it will deactivate cards associated with an account with the Active field.

    With the table created, let's create a new stored procedure to populate it.

13. In the data connection, right-click the Stored Procedures folder, and select Add New Stored Procedure.

14. Populate the query with the following SQL:

```
Create PROCEDURE [dbo].[aspnet_Users_AddUserInformationCard]
    @UserId          uniqueidentifier ,
     @PPID char(20)
AS
BEGIN
    BEGIN
        IF( EXISTS( SELECT UserId FROM dbo.aspnet_UserInformationCards
                    WHERE @UserId = UserId ) )
            RETURN -1
    END

    INSERT dbo.aspnet_UserInformationCards (UserID, ➥
PrivatePersonalIdentifier, Active, DateAdded,DateModified)
    VALUES (@UserID, @PPID, 1, GetDate(),GetDate())

    RETURN 0
END
```

15. Save the stored procedure. You've created a stored procedure to add a reference to an information card; you will now add one to remove it.

16. In the data connection, right-click the Stored Procedures folder, and select Add New Stored Procedure.

17. Populate the query with the following SQL:

```
Create PROCEDURE [dbo].[aspnet_Users_DeleteUserInformationCard]
    @UserId            uniqueidentifier ,
     @PPID char(20)
AS
BEGIN
    Delete from dbo.aspnet_UserInformationCards where UserID =➥
 @UserID and PrivatePersonalIdentifier = @PPID
       RETURN 0
END
```

18. Save the stored procedure. You may also want to just deactivate a card. The following are the steps to create a stored procedure for this task.

19. In the data connection, right-click the Stored Procedures folder, and select Add New Stored Procedure.

20. Populate the query with the following SQL:

```
CREATE PROCEDURE [dbo].[aspnet_Users_DeactivateUserInformationCard]
    @UserId            uniqueidentifier ,
     @PPID char(20)
AS
BEGIN
    UPDATE dbo.aspnet_UserInformationCards
    set Active=-1
    where UserID = @UserID and PrivatePersonalIdentifier = @PPID
    RETURN 0
END
```

21. Save the stored procedure. Next, you'll want to add stored procedures to enhance ASP.NET's out-of-the-box membership functionality. You'll begin by creating a stored procedure that will retrieve member records that use the PPID found in an information card.

22. In the data connection, right-click the Stored Procedures folder, and select Add New Stored Procedure.

23. Populate the query with the following SQL:

```
CREATE PROCEDURE [dbo].[aspnet_Membership_GetUserByInformationCard]
    @PPID               char(20),
    @Email              nvarchar(256),
     @CurrentTimeUtc     datetime,
    @UpdateLastActivity  bit = 0
AS
```

```
BEGIN
    IF ( @UpdateLastActivity = 1 )
    BEGIN
        DECLARE @UserID uniqueidentifier;
          SET @UserID = ( Select u.UserID from ➡
dbo.aspnet_Users u, dbo.aspnet_UserInformationCards i, ➡
dbo.aspnet_Membership m
                            where u.UserID = i.UserID
                          AND m.UserID = u.UserID
                                    AND
 i.PrivatePersonalIdentifier = @PPID
                                  AND   m.Email = @Email
                            )

         UPDATE    dbo.aspnet_Users
        SET       LastActivityDate = @CurrentTimeUtc
        FROM      dbo.aspnet_Users
        WHERE     @UserId = UserId

        IF ( @@ROWCOUNT = 0 ) -- User ID not found
            RETURN -1
    END

    SELECT  m.Email, m.PasswordQuestion, m.Comment, m.IsApproved,
            m.CreateDate, m.LastLoginDate, u.LastActivityDate,
            m.LastPasswordChangedDate, u.UserName, m.IsLockedOut,
            m.LastLockoutDate
    FROM    dbo.aspnet_Users u, dbo.aspnet_Membership m, ➡
dbo.aspnet_UserInformationCards i
    WHERE   u.UserID = i.UserID
                  AND m.UserID = u.UserID
          AND i.PrivatePersonalIdentifier ➡
 = @PPID AND  m.Email = @Email

    IF ( @@ROWCOUNT = 0 ) -- User ID not found
        RETURN -1

    RETURN 0
END
```

24. Save the stored procedure.

You may want to allow multiple users with the same information card (that is, I might use the same identifying card but have one account I use at work and a different one for personal use). If your site will allow this, you'll also want to add a FindUsersByInformationCard stored procedure. This will find all users who are registered with a particular PPID.

25. In the data connection, right-click the Stored Procedures folder, and select Add New Stored Procedure.

26. Populate the query with the following SQL:

```
CREATE PROCEDURE [dbo].[aspnet_Membership_FindUsersByInformationCard]
    @ApplicationName        nvarchar(256),
    @PPID                   nvarchar(256),
    @PageIndex              int,
    @PageSize               int
AS
BEGIN
    DECLARE @ApplicationId uniqueidentifier
    SELECT  @ApplicationId = NULL
    SELECT  @ApplicationId = ApplicationId FROM
dbo.aspnet_Applications WHERE LOWER(@ApplicationName) =
LoweredApplicationName
    IF (@ApplicationId IS NULL)
        RETURN 0

    -- Set the page bounds
    DECLARE @PageLowerBound int
    DECLARE @PageUpperBound int
    DECLARE @TotalRecords   int
    SET @PageLowerBound = @PageSize * @PageIndex
    SET @PageUpperBound = @PageSize - 1 + @PageLowerBound

    -- Create a temp table TO store the select results
    CREATE TABLE #PageIndexForUsers
    (
        IndexId int IDENTITY (0, 1) NOT NULL,
        UserId uniqueidentifier
    )

    -- Insert into our temp table
    INSERT INTO #PageIndexForUsers (UserId)
        SELECT u.UserId
        FROM    dbo.aspnet_Users u, dbo.aspnet_Membership m,
    dbo.aspnet_UserInformationCards i
        WHERE  u.ApplicationId = @ApplicationId AND m.UserId =
    u.UserId AND i.UserID = u.UserID
                and i.PrivatePersonalIdentifier = @PPID
        ORDER BY u.UserName
```

```
    SELECT  u.UserName, m.Email, m.PasswordQuestion, m.Comment, m.IsApproved,
            m.CreateDate,
            m.LastLoginDate,
            u.LastActivityDate,
            m.LastPasswordChangedDate,
            u.UserId, m.IsLockedOut,
            m.LastLockoutDate
    FROM    dbo.aspnet_Membership m, dbo.aspnet_Users u, #PageIndexForUsers p
    WHERE   u.UserId = p.UserId AND u.UserId = m.UserId AND
            p.IndexId >= @PageLowerBound AND p.IndexId <= @PageUpperBound
    ORDER BY u.UserName

    SELECT  @TotalRecords = COUNT(*)
    FROM    #PageIndexForUsers
    RETURN @TotalRecords
END
```

27. Save the stored procedure.

    You will also need a stored procedure that will return the user ID associated with an information card's PPID in the database. The user ID is the key used in the User- and Membership-related tables provided by ASP.NET. This will allow you to leverage the existing stored procedures and the Membership class.

    The following steps detail how to create a stored procedure that will return the user ID for a given user based on a PPID from an information card.

28. In the data connection, right-click the Stored Procedures folder, and select Add New Stored Procedure.

29. Populate the query with the following SQL:

```
ALTER PROCEDURE [dbo].[aspnet_Membership_GetUserIDByPPID]
    @PPID               char(20)

AS
BEGIN

    SELECT  u.UserID
    FROM    dbo.aspnet_UserInformationCards u
    WHERE   @PPID = u.PrivatePersonalIdentifier


    IF ( @@ROWCOUNT = 0 ) -- User ID not found
        RETURN -1

    RETURN 0
END
```

30. Execute the script to create the stored procedure.

Creating an Information Card–Aware Login Control

With the underlying data structure and stored procedures in place, you will now create enhanced versions of two of the controls shipped with ASP.NET—Login and CreateUserWizard—and a web application in which to test them. At the end of this exercise, you will have two user controls that will make it easy to add information card support to your applications. Follow these steps:

1. In Visual Studio, create a new ASP.NET website, and place it at C:\BeginningCardspace\ Chapter6\PartII.

2. Drag a LoginName control from the Toolbox onto the form named Default.aspx.

3. Right-click the website, and select Add New Item.

4. Select Web Configuration File, and select OK.

5. Open web.config.

6. The web.config file will contain an authentication element. Replace it with the following XML:

```
<authentication mode="Forms">
    <forms name="cookie"
     loginUrl="Login.aspx"
    protection="All"
    timeout="30"
    requireSSL="false"
    slidingExpiration="false"
    cookieless="UseCookies"
    defaultUrl="Default.aspx"/>
</authentication>
<authorization>
    <deny users="?"/>
</authorization>
```

7. The web.config file also contains the information for the database connection string. Change the connectionStrings element to the XML shown here:

```
<connectionStrings>
<remove name="LocalSqlServer"/>
    <add name="LocalSqlServer" ➥
connectionString="Server=MMERCURIXPS\SQLEXPRESS;Integrated ➥
Security=True;Database=aspnetdb;Persist Security Info=True" />
    </connectionStrings>
```

As in the earlier exercise, remember to replace MMERCURIXPS\SQLEXPRESS with the name of your server.

8. The enhancements will use the TokenHelper class used in earlier chapters. This class requires some configuration elements that are stored in the appSettings element:

```
<appSettings>
    <add key="CertificateSubject" value="www.fabrikam.com"/>
    <add key="StoreName" value="My"/>
    <add key="StoreLocation" value="LocalMachine"/>
    <add key="IdentityClaimType"➥
  value="http://schemas.xmlsoap.org/ws/2005/05/identity/claims/➥
privatepersonalidentifier"/>
    <add key="MaximumClockSkew" value="60"/>
  </appSettings>
```

9. Next, right-click the App_Code folder, and select Add Existing Item. Navigate to the TokenHelper.cs file, and add it to your project.

10. Right-click the website name in Solution Explorer, and select Add New Item.

11. Select Web Form, and name it **Login.aspx**.

12. Right-click the website name in Solution Explorer, and select Add New Item.

13. Select Web User Control, and name it **ICLogin.ascx**.

14. Drag a Login control onto ICLogin.ascx.

15. Right-click the website, and select Add Existing Item.

16. Add the image informationcard.gif.

17. Right-click the website, and select Add Existing Item.

18. Add the image informationcard_gray.gif. (These images will be used in the user interface for the control; you can find them with the code for this chapter.)

19. View the source of the ICLogin.ascx page, and replace it with the following:

```
<%@ Control Language="C#" AutoEventWireup="true" ➥
CodeFile="ICLogin.ascx.cs" Inherits="Login" %>
<!DOCTYPE html PUBLIC "-//W3C//DTD XHTML 1.0 Transitional//EN" ➥
"http://www.w3.org/TR/xhtml1/DTD/xhtml1-transitional.dtd">
<script type="text/javascript">
    function requestInformationCard()
     {
       icObject = '<object type="application/x-informationcard"➥
 name="xmlLoginToken">';
       icObject += '<param name="tokenType" ➥
value="urn:oasis:names:tc:SAML:1.0:assertion" />';
       icObject += '<param name="issuer" ➥
value="http://schemas.xmlsoap.org/ws/2005/05/identity/issuer/self" />';
       icObject += '<param name="requiredClaims" ➥
value=➥
"http://schemas.xmlsoap.org/ws/2005/05/identity/claims/givenname
http://schemas.xmlsoap.org/ws/2005/05/identity/claims/surname
```

```
http://schemas.xmlsoap.org/ws/2005/05/identity/claims/➥
privatepersonalidentifier ➥
http://schemas.xmlsoap.org/ws/2005/05/identity/claims/➥
emailaddress"➥
 />';
        icObject += '</object>'
        document.getElementById("InformationCardToLoginObjectContainer"➥
).innerHTML=icObject;
        document.getElementById("form1").submit();
    }
</script>
<div id="InformationCardToLoginObjectContainer">
  </div>

<asp:Panel ID="Panel1" runat="server" Height="368px" ➥
Style="position: relative; left: 0px; top: 0px;" Width="376px"➥
 BorderStyle="None">
    <asp:Panel ID="Panel2" runat="server" Height="160px"➥
 Style="left: 0px; position: relative;
        top: 0px; font-family: Verdana; text-align: center;" Width="384px">
        <table style="width: 384px; position: relative; ➥
height: 160px; left: 0px; top: 0px;">
            <tr>
                <td style="font-weight: bold; color: white;➥
 background-color: #5d7b9d;font-size:small';" colspan="3">
                    Sign In Using Your Information Card</td>
            </tr>
            <tr>
                <td style="width: 59px">
                </td>
                <td style="width: 50px">
                    <img id="Image1" src="informationcard.gif"➥
 style="position: relative; text-align: center;" ➥
onclick="requestInformationCard();" ➥
onmouseover="this.src='informationcard_gray.gif'" ➥
onmouseout="this.src='informationcard.gif'"  alt="Information ➥
Card"/></td>

                <td>
                </td>
            </tr>
            <tr>
                <td style="width: 59px">
                </td>
                <td style="width: 50px">
                </td>
                <td>
```

```
                    </td>
                </tr>
            </table>
            or<br />
        </asp:Panel>
        <asp:Panel ID="Panel3" runat="server" Height="96px" ➥
Style="left: 8px; position: relative;
        top: 32px; font-family: Verdana;" Width="384px">
            <table style="width: 384px; position: relative; ➥
left: -6px; top: -46px;">
            <tr>
                <td colspan="2" style="font-weight: bold; color:➥
 white; background-color: #5d7b9d;font-size:small'; ">
                    Sign in with your username and password</td>
            </tr>
            <tr>
                <td style="width: 128px">
                    <asp:Label ID="Label1" runat="server" ➥
Style="position: relative; font-family: Verdana;" Text="User➥
Name"></asp:Label></td>
                <td>
                    <asp:TextBox ID="tbUsername" runat="server"➥
 Style="position: relative"></asp:TextBox></td>
            </tr>
            <tr>
                <td style="width: 128px">
                    <asp:Label ID="Label2" runat="server" ➥
Style="position: relative" Text="Password" ➥
Font-Names="Verdana"></asp:Label></td>
                <td>
                    <asp:TextBox ID="tbPassword" runat="server"➥
 Style="position: relative"></asp:TextBox></td>
            </tr>
            <tr>
                <td style="width: 128px">
                </td>
                <td>
                    <asp:Button ID="btnSignIn" runat="server"➥
 Style="position: relative" Text="Sign In" /></td>
            </tr>
            <tr>
                <td colspan="2">
                    </td>
            </tr>
        </table>
        <asp:Label ID="lblError" runat="server" ➥
```

```
Font-Names="Verdana" ForeColor="DarkRed"
            Style="position: relative; left: 0px; ➡
top: -38px;"></asp:Label></asp:Panel>
</asp:Panel>
 
```

This code enhances the UI to include a section that displays the graphic for the information card. In the bold IMG tag shown in the previous code, you can see that there are attributes that change the actual image displayed based on whether the mouse pointer is positioned over it. In addition, if the image is clicked, it executes the JavaScript function named requestInformationCard.

This function is defined earlier in the code and is shown in bold. This code dynamically creates the object tag used to trigger the CardSpace identity selector and assigns that object XML to a div named InformationCardToLoginObjectContainer. Finally, it submits the form that triggers the display of the identity selector.

You may be asking why the object is created dynamically, particularly because it wasn't created dynamically in earlier chapters. The reason for this is that you want to trigger the identity selector only if the user clicks the image. If it was not assigned automatically, it would trigger every time—even if a user preferred to log in via username and password.

Also note that you did not provide the XML with an ID of xmlToken and instead provided an ID specific to this type of control. What was the reason for this? You may want to include the Register control (which will be created in the next section) on the same form, and you'll want to differentiate between the two.

With the markup modifications complete, it's time to modify the code for the control:

1. Open Login.ascx.cs.

2. Add using statements for Microsoft.IdentityModel.Samples, System.IdentityModel.Claims, and System.Data.SqlClient:

```
using System;
using System.Data;
using System.Configuration;
using System.Collections;
using System.Web;
using System.Web.Security;
using System.Web.UI;
using System.Web.UI.WebControls;
using System.Web.UI.WebControls.WebParts;
using System.Web.UI.HtmlControls;
using Microsoft.IdentityModel.Samples;
using System.IdentityModel.Claims;
using System.Data.SqlClient;
```

3. Add the member variables and properties as specified here:

```
public partial class Login : System.Web.UI.UserControl
{



#region MemberVariables

    private string _registerUrl;
    private string _ppid = "";
    private string _givenName = "";
    private string _surName = "";
    private string _email = "";
    private string _username = "";
    private ClaimSet _userClaims;
    #endregion

    #region Properties

    public string AssociatedInformationCardPPID
    {
        get { return _ppid; }
        set { _ppid = value; }
    }

    public string AssociatedInformationCardGivenName
    {
        get { return _givenName; }
        set { _givenName = value; }
    }

    public string AssociatedInformationCardSurName
    {
        get { return _surName; }
        set { _surName = value; }
    }

    public string AssociatedInformationCardEmail
    {
        get {return _email;}
        set {_email = value;}
    }

    #endregion
```

4. Modify the Page_Load event to add an event handler for the click event of btnSignIn. In addition, make changes to check for the existence of a token, and if it's present, call the operation SignInWithInformationCard.

```
protected void Page_Load(object sender, EventArgs e)
{
    btnSignIn.Click += new EventHandler(btnSignIn_Click);

    if (IsPostBack)
    {


        if (this.Visible == true)
        {
            //Check to see whether the user submitted an information card
            string xmlToken;
            xmlToken = Request.Params["xmlLoginToken"];

            if (xmlToken == null || xmlToken == "")
            {

            }
            else
            {

                //The user submitted an information card,
                //so process it.
                SignInWithInformationCard(xmlToken);

            }


        }
    }
}
```

5. Add the btnSignIn_Click event, and populate it with the code listed here. This code utilizes the built-in functionality in the FormsAuthentication class to authenticate users via a username and password.

```
void btnSignIn_Click(object sender, EventArgs e)
{
    bool isAuthenticated = ➡
AuthenticateUser(tbUsername.Text, tbPassword.Text);
    if (isAuthenticated)
    {
        FormsAuthentication.RedirectFromLoginPage(tbUsername.Text, true);
    }
```

```
        else
        {
            lblError.Text="The username and password ➥
pair provided was invalid.";
        }

    }
bool AuthenticateUser(string username, string password)
    {

        return FormsAuthentication.Authenticate(username, password);

    }
```

6. Next, create the operation SignInWithInformationCard, as shown here. This calls the AuthenticateInformationCardUser operation and, if authenticated, redirects to the originally requested URL.

```
void SignInWithInformationCard(string xmlToken)
    {

        RetrieveTokenClaims(xmlToken);
        bool isAuthenticated = ➥
AuthenticateInformationCardUser(xmlToken, _ppid, _email);
        if (isAuthenticated)
        {
            FormsAuthentication.RedirectFromLoginPage(_➥
givenName + " " + _surName, true);
        }
        else
        {
            lblError.Text = "The Information Card provided is not ➥
associated with an account.";
        }


    }
```

7. Next create the AuthenticateInformationCardUser operation. This will use ADO.NET to call the stored procedure created in the first part of this exercise:

```
    bool AuthenticateInformationCardUser(string xmlToken, ➥
string ppid, string email)
    {
        //Create a connection to the SQL Server;
        //modify the connection string for your environment.
        RetrieveTokenClaims(xmlToken);
        string connString =
            ConfigurationManager.ConnectionStrings["LocalSqlServer"].➥
```

```
ConnectionString;
        SqlConnection MyConnection = new SqlConnection(connString);
        MyConnection.Open();
        SqlCommand MyCommand = new ➥
SqlCommand("aspnet_Membership_GetUserBInformationCard", ➥
MyConnection);
        MyCommand.CommandType = CommandType.StoredProcedure;

        //Create and add a parameter to Parameters collection
        //for the stored procedure.
        MyCommand.Parameters.Add(new SqlParameter ("@Email", ➥
SqlDbType.NVarChar,256));
        //Assign the UserID value to the parameter.
        MyCommand.Parameters["@Email"].Value = _email;


        //Create and add a parameter to Parameters collection
        // for the stored procedure.
        MyCommand.Parameters.Add(new SqlParameter("@PPID", ➥
SqlDbType.Char, 20));
        //Assign the UserID value to the parameter.
        MyCommand.Parameters["@PPID"].Value = _ppid;


        //Create and add a parameter to Parameters collection
        //for the stored procedure.
        MyCommand.Parameters.Add(new SqlParameter(➥
"@CurrentTimeUtc", SqlDbType.DateTime));
        //Assign the UserID value to the parameter.
        MyCommand.Parameters["@CurrentTimeUtc"].Value = DateTime.Now;

    //Create and add a parameter to Parameters collection
    //for the stored procedure.
        MyCommand.Parameters.Add(new ➥
SqlParameter("@UpdateLastActivity", SqlDbType.Bit));
        //Assign the UserID value to the parameter.
        MyCommand.Parameters["@UpdateLastActivity"].Value = 1;


        SqlDataReader reader = MyCommand.ExecuteReader();
        Response.Write(reader.HasRows.ToString());

        return reader.HasRows;
        MyConnection.Close(); //Close the connection.

    }
```

8. Create the RetrieveTokenClaims operation, as shown here. This will parse the token provided from the information card and assign the contained values to the member variables of the control.

```
private void RetrieveTokenClaims(string xmlToken)
    {
        TokenHelper tokenHelper = new TokenHelper(xmlToken);

        _userClaims = tokenHelper.IdentityClaims;


        foreach (Claim claim in _userClaims)
        {

            switch (claim.ClaimType)
            {
                case ➥
"http://schemas.xmlsoap.org/ws/2005/05/identity/claims/givenname":
                    _givenName = claim.Resource.ToString();
                    break;
                case ➥
 "http://schemas.xmlsoap.org/ws/2005/05/identity/claims/surname":
                    _surName = claim.Resource.ToString();
                    break;
                case ➥
"http://schemas.xmlsoap.org/ws/2005/05/identity/claims/➥
privatepersonalidentifier":
                    _ppid = claim.Resource.ToString();
                    break;
                case ➥
"http://schemas.xmlsoap.org/ws/2005/05/identity/claims/emailaddress":
                    _email = claim.Resource.ToString();
                    break;
            }

        }


    }


}
```

Creating an Information Card–Aware Create User Wizard

To create an information card–aware Create User Wizard, follow these steps:

1. Right-click the website name in Solution Explorer, and select Add New Item.

2. Select Web User Control, and name it **ICRegister.ascx**.

3. Drag a CreateUserWizard control onto ICRegister.ascx.

4. The CreateUserWizard control is extensible and provides the ability to create new steps.

5. View the source of ICRegister.ascx, and make sure it maps to the following:

```
<%@ Control Language="C#" AutoEventWireup="true" ➥
CodeFile="ICRegister.ascx.cs" Inherits="ICRegister" %>

<asp:CreateUserWizard ID="CreateUserWizard1" runat="server" ➥
Style="position: relative" BackColor="#F7F6F3" ➥
BorderColor="#E6E2D8" BorderStyle="Solid" ➥
BorderWidth="1px" Font-Names="Verdana" Font-Size="0.8em" ➥
 AutoGeneratePassword="True" CreateUserButtonText="Next">
    <WizardSteps>
        <asp:CreateUserWizardStep runat="server">
            <ContentTemplate>
                <table border="0">
                    <tr>
                        <td align="center" colspan="2" ➥
style="font-weight: bold; color: white; background-color: #5d7b9d">
                            Sign Up for Your New Account</td>
                    </tr>
                  <tr>
                        <td align="right">
                        </td>
                        <td>
                        </td>
                    </tr>
                    <tr>
                        <td align="right">
                            <asp:Label ID="UserNameLabel" ➥
runat="server" AssociatedControlID="UserName">User ➥
Name:</asp:Label></td>
                        <td>
                            <asp:TextBox ID="UserName" ➥
runat="server"></asp:TextBox>
                            <asp:RequiredFieldValidator ➥
ID="UserNameRequired" runat="server" ControlToValidate="UserName"
                            ErrorMessage="User Name is required."➥
 ToolTip="User Name is required."➥
 ValidationGroup="CreateUserWizard1">*➥
</asp:RequiredFieldValidator>
                        </td>
                    </tr>
                    <tr>
                        <td align="right">
                            <asp:Label ID="PasswordLabel" ➥
```

```
runat="server"
AssociatedControlID="Password">Password:</asp:Label></td>
                          <td>
                                <asp:TextBox ID="Password" ➥
runat="server" TextMode="Password"></asp:TextBox>
                                <asp:RequiredFieldValidator ➥
ID="PasswordRequired" runat="server" ➥
ControlToValidate="Password"
                                      ErrorMessage=➥
"Password is required." ToolTip="Password is required." ➥
ValidationGroup="CreateUserWizard1">*</asp:RequiredFieldValidator>
                          </td>
                    </tr>
                    <tr>
                          <td align="right">
                                <asp:Label ID="ConfirmPasswordLabel" ➥
runat="server" AssociatedControlID="ConfirmPassword">Confirm ➥
Password:</asp:Label></td>
                          <td>
                                <asp:TextBox ID="ConfirmPassword" ➥
runat="server" TextMode="Password"></asp:TextBox>
                                <asp:RequiredFieldValidator ➥
ID="ConfirmPasswordRequired" runat="server" ➥
ControlToValidate="ConfirmPassword"
                                      ErrorMessage="Confirm Password is➥
 required." ToolTip="Confirm Password is required."
 ValidationGroup="CreateUserWizard1">*</asp:RequiredFieldValidator>
                          </td>
                    </tr>
                    <tr>
                          <td align="right">
                                <asp:Label ID="EmailLabel" ➥
runat="server" AssociatedControlID="Email">E-mail:</asp:Label></td>
                          <td>
                                <asp:TextBox ID="Email" runat="server">
</asp:TextBox>
                                <asp:RequiredFieldValidator➥
 ID="EmailRequired" runat="server" ControlToValidate="Email"➥
                                      ErrorMessage="E-mail is required."➥
 ToolTip="E-mail is required." ➥
ValidationGroup="CreateUserWizard1">*</asp:RequiredFieldValidator>
                          </td>
                    </tr>
                    <tr>
                          <td align="right">
                                <asp:Label ID="QuestionLabel" ➥
runat="server" AssociatedControlID="Question">Security ➥
```

```
Question:</asp:Label></td>
                            <td>
                                <asp:TextBox ID="Question" runat="server">
</asp:TextBox>
                                <asp:RequiredFieldValidator➡
 ID="QuestionRequired" runat="server" ControlToValidate="Question"➡
ErrorMessage="Security question is➡
 required." ToolTip="Security question is required."
ValidationGroup="CreateUserWizard1">*</asp:RequiredFieldValidator>
                            </td>
                        </tr>
                        <tr>
                            <td align="right">
                                <asp:Label ID="AnswerLabel" ➡
runat="server" AssociatedControlID="Answer">Security ➡
Answer:</asp:Label></td>
                            <td>
                                <asp:TextBox ID="Answer"
runat="server"></asp:TextBox>
                                <asp:RequiredFieldValidator➡
 ID="AnswerRequired" runat="server" ControlToValidate="Answer"➡
ErrorMessage="Security answer is required." ➡
ToolTip="Security answer is required."
 ValidationGroup="CreateUserWizard1">*</asp:RequiredFieldValidator>
                            </td>
                        </tr>
                        <tr>
                            <td align="center" colspan="2">
                                <asp:CompareValidator ➡
ID="PasswordCompare" runat="server" ➡
ControlToCompare="Password"
ControlToValidate="ConfirmPassword"➡
 Display="Dynamic" ➡
ErrorMessage="The Password and Confirmation Password must match."
                                ValidationGroup="CreateUserWizard1">
</asp:CompareValidator>
                            </td>
                        </tr>
                        <tr>
                            <td align="center" colspan="2" style="color: red">
                                <asp:Literal ID="ErrorMessage"➡
 runat="server" EnableViewState="False"></asp:Literal>
                            </td>
                        </tr>
                    </table>
                </ContentTemplate>
            </asp:CreateUserWizardStep>
```

```
        <asp:TemplatedWizardStep runat="server" ➡
Title="Associate Information Card" StepType="Step">
            <ContentTemplate>
<div id="InformationCardToRegisterObjectContainer">
  </div>

                  <script type="text/javascript">
     function requestInformationCard()
      {

        icObject = '<object type="application/x-informationcard"➡
 name="xmlRegisterToken">';
        icObject += '<param name="tokenType"➡
 value="urn:oasis:names:tc:SAML:1.0:assertion" />';
        icObject += '<param name="issuer" ➡
value=➡
"http://schemas.xmlsoap.org/ws/2005/05/identity/issuer/self"/>';
        icObject += '<param name="requiredClaims" ➡
value=➡
"http://schemas.xmlsoap.org/ws/2005/05/identity/claims/givenname➡
 http://schemas.xmlsoap.org/ws/2005/05/identity/claims/surname➡
http://schemas.xmlsoap.org/ws/2005/05/identity/claims/➡
privatepersonalidentifier" />';
        icObject += '</object>'


        document.getElementById(➡
"InformationCardToRegisterObjectContainer").innerHTML=icObject;
        document.getElementById("form1").submit();


     }
</script>
                  <table border="0" style="➡
font-size: 100%; font-family: Verdana">
                     <tr>
                        <td align="right" colspan="2" ➡
style="text-align: center;font-weight: bold; color: white; ➡
background-color: #5d7b9d">
                              Associate Information Card</td>
                     </tr>
                     <tr>
                        <td align="right" style="➡
text-align: center; width: 126px;">
Select Card<br />
                           (Optional)
                        </td>
                        <td style="width: 166px">
```

```
    <img id="Img1" src="informationcard.gif" ➥
 style="position: relative; text-align: center; left: 0px;" ➥
 onmouseover="this.src='informationcard_gray.gif'" ➥
onmouseout="this.src='informationcard.gif'" ➥
alt="Information Card" onclick="requestInformationCard();"/></td>
                        </tr>
                    </table>
                </ContentTemplate>
            </asp:TemplatedWizardStep>
            <asp:CompleteWizardStep runat="server">
                <ContentTemplate>
                    <table border="0" ➥
style="font-size: 100%; font-family: Verdana">
                        <tr>
                            <td align="center" colspan="2" ➥
style="font-weight: bold; color: white; background-color: #5d7b9d">
                                Complete</td>
                        </tr>
                        <tr>
                            <td>
                                Your account has been successfully created.</td>
                        </tr>
                        <tr>
                            <td align="right" colspan="2">
                                <asp:Button ID="ContinueButton"➥
 runat="server" BackColor="#FFFBFF" BorderColor="#CCCCCC"
                                BorderStyle="Solid" BorderWidth="1px" ➥
CausesValidation="False" CommandName="Continue"
 Font-Names="Verdana" ➥
 ForeColor="#284775" OnClick="ContinueButton_Click" Text="Continue" ➥
ValidationGroup="CreateUserWizard1" />
                            </td>
                        </tr>
                    </table>
                </ContentTemplate>
            </asp:CompleteWizardStep>
        </WizardSteps>
        <SideBarStyle BackColor="#5D7B9D" BorderWidth="0px" ➥
Font-Size="0.9em" VerticalAlign="Top" />
        <TitleTextStyle BackColor="#5D7B9D" Font-Bold="True" ForeColor="White" />
        <SideBarButtonStyle BorderWidth="0px" ➥
Font-Names="Verdana" ForeColor="White" />
        <NavigationButtonStyle BackColor="#FFFBFF" ➥
BorderColor="#CCCCCC" BorderStyle="Solid"
            BorderWidth="1px" Font-Names="Verdana" ForeColor="#284775" />
        <HeaderStyle BackColor="#5D7B9D" ➥
BorderStyle="Solid" Font-Bold="True" Font-Size="0.9em"
```

```
            ForeColor="White" HorizontalAlign="Center" />
        <CreateUserButtonStyle BackColor="#FFFBFF" ➥
    BorderColor="#CCCCCC" BorderStyle="Solid"
            BorderWidth="1px" Font-Names="Verdana" ForeColor="#284775" />
        <ContinueButtonStyle BackColor="#FFFBFF" ➥
    BorderColor="#CCCCCC" BorderStyle="Solid"
            BorderWidth="1px" Font-Names="Verdana" ForeColor="#284775" />
        <StepStyle BorderWidth="0px" />
    </asp:CreateUserWizard>
```

The bold lines in the previous code identify the custom wizard step. You'll see some similarities to what you did for the Login control. If a user clicks the information card graphic, a div is populated with an information card object, and the div then submits the form.

Note Because not all users will have an information card, the association of an information card is strictly optional, and users can skip this step and complete the wizard.

With the new wizard step added to the user interface, it's time to write the code to implement the functionality behind the scenes:

1. Open ICRegister.ascx.cs.

2. Add using statements for Microsoft.IdentityModel.Samples, System.IdentityModel. Claims, and System.Data.SqlClient:

```
using System;
using System.Data;
using System.Configuration;
using System.Collections;
using System.Web;
using System.Web.Security;
using System.Web.UI;
using System.Web.UI.WebControls;
using System.Web.UI.WebControls.WebParts;
using System.Web.UI.HtmlControls;
using Microsoft.IdentityModel.Samples;
using System.IdentityModel.Claims;
using System.Data.SqlClient;
```

3. Add member variables and properties to the control, as shown here:

```
public partial class ICRegister : System.Web.UI.UserControl
{

    #region MemberVariables
```

```
private string _ppid = "";
private string _givenName = "";
private string _surName = "";
private string _email = "";
private string _username = "";
private ClaimSet _userClaims;
#endregion

#region Properties
public string AssociatedInformationCardPPID
{
    get { return _ppid; }
    set { _ppid = value; }
}

public string AssociatedInformationCardGivenName
{
    get { return _givenName; }
    set { _givenName = value; }
}

public string AssociatedInformationCardSurName
{
    get { return _surName; }
    set { _surName = value; }
}

public string AssociatedInformationCardEmail
{
    get {return _email;}
    set {_email = value;}
}

#endregion
```

4. Modify the Page_Load operation to associate an information card with an account. The Page_Load operation in your file should resemble the following:

```
protected void Page_Load(object sender, EventArgs e)
{

    if (this.IsPostBack)
    {
        if (this.Visible == true)
        {
            //Check to see whether the user submitted an information card
            string xmlToken;
            xmlToken = Request.Params["xmlRegisterToken"];
```

```
              if (xmlToken == null || xmlToken == "")
              {
                  //No card provided
              }
              else
              {
                  //The user submitted an information card,
                  //so process it.
                  AssociateInformationCard(xmlToken);
                  FormsAuthentication.RedirectFromLoginPage(➥
this.CreateUserWizard1.UserName, false);
              }


          }
       }
    }
```

5. Add a new operation, AssociateInformationCard, to associate an information card with a member. The code for AssociateInformationCard is as follows:

```
void AssociateInformationCard(string xmlToken)
    {
        //Create a connection to the SQL Server;
        //modify the connection string for your environment.
        RetrieveTokenClaims(xmlToken);
        string connString =
            ConfigurationManager.ConnectionStrings["LocalSqlServer"].➥
ConnectionString;
        SqlConnection MyConnection = new SqlConnection(connString);
        MyConnection.Open();
        SqlCommand MyCommand = new ➥
SqlCommand("aspnet_Users_AddUserInformationCard", ➥
MyConnection);
        MyCommand.CommandType = CommandType.StoredProcedure;
        //Create and add a parameter to Parameters collection
        //for the stored procedure.
        MyCommand.Parameters.Add(new SqlParameter("@UserId", ➥
SqlDbType.UniqueIdentifier));
        //Assign the UserID value to the parameter.
        MyCommand.Parameters["@UserId"].Value =➥
 RetrieveUserIDByUserName(this.CreateUserWizard1.UserName, ➥
this.CreateUserWizard1.Password);
        //Create and add a parameter to Parameters collection
        //for the stored procedure.
        MyCommand.Parameters.Add(new SqlParameter("@PPID", ➥
SqlDbType.Char, 20));
```

```
        //Assign the UserID value to the parameter.
        MyCommand.Parameters["@PPID"].Value = _ppid;


        MyCommand.ExecuteScalar();
        MyConnection.Close(); //Close the connection.

    }
```

6. Add the operation RetrieveUserIDByUsername, which will retrieve a user ID for use in the control. Your code should map to the code shown here:

```
    private Guid RetrieveUserIDByUserName(string username, string password)
    {
        //Create a connection to the SQL Server;
        //modify the connection string for your environment.
        string connString =
            ConfigurationManager.ConnectionStrings["LocalSqlServer"].➥
ConnectionString;


            SqlConnection MyConnection = new SqlConnection(connString);
            MyConnection.Open();
        SqlCommand MyCommand = new ➥
SqlCommand("aspnet_Membership_GetUserIDByUserName", ➥
MyConnection);
            MyCommand.CommandType = CommandType.StoredProcedure;
            //Create and add a parameter to Parameters collection
            // for the stored procedure.
            MyCommand.Parameters.Add(new SqlParameter(➥
"@UserName", SqlDbType.NVarChar,256));
            //Create and add a parameter to Parameters collection
            //for the stored procedure.
            MyCommand.Parameters["@UserName"].Value = username;


            Guid userId = (Guid) MyCommand.ExecuteScalar();
                MyConnection.Close(); //Close the connection.
                return userId;
    }
```

7. Add the operation RetrieveTokenClaims, as shown here, which will parse the information card–related token and assign the claims to properties on the control:

```
    private void RetrieveTokenClaims(string xmlToken)
    {
        TokenHelper tokenHelper = new TokenHelper(xmlToken);

        _userClaims = tokenHelper.IdentityClaims;


        foreach (Claim claim in _userClaims)
        {

            switch (claim.ClaimType)
            {
                case ➥
"http://schemas.xmlsoap.org/ws/2005/05/identity/claims/givenname":
                    _givenName = claim.Resource.ToString();
                    break;
                case ➥
"http://schemas.xmlsoap.org/ws/2005/05/identity/claims/surname":
                    _surName = claim.Resource.ToString();
                    break;
                case ➥
"http://schemas.xmlsoap.org/ws/2005/05/identity/claims/➥
privatepersonalidentifier":
                    _ppid = claim.Resource.ToString();
                    break;
                case ➥
"http://schemas.xmlsoap.org/ws/2005/05/identity/claims/emailaddress":
                    _email = claim.Resource.ToString();
                    break;
            }

        }


    }
```

8. Add a line to the ContinueButton_Click event to redirect after creating the account and logging the user into the site:

```
    protected void ContinueButton_Click(object sender, EventArgs e)
    {
        FormsAuthentication.RedirectFromLoginPage(➥
this.CreateUserWizard1.UserName, false);
    }
}
```

Configuring the Website in IIS

Follow these steps to configure the website in IIS:

1. Open the IIS Manager application.

2. Right-click Default Web Site, and add a new web application.

3. Name the application **USChapter6**, and point it to C:\BeginningCardspace\ Chapter6\PartII.

Testing the ICRegister Control

Follow these steps to test the ICRegister control:

1. Drag the ICRegister control onto Login.aspx.

2. Open Internet Explorer, and navigate to https://www.fabrikam.com/USChapter6.

3. You will be redirected to Login.aspx, and the ICRegister control will be displayed.

4. Provide the information requested on the first page of the wizard, and then click Next.

5. This will display the Associate Information Card step in the wizard, as displayed in Figure 6-5.

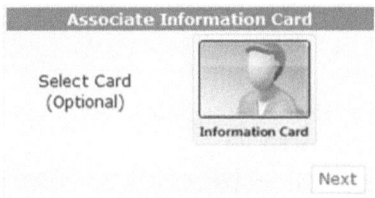

Figure 6-5. *Associating an information card with a new account*

6. Click the information card graphic, and associate a card.

7. You will be redirected to Default.aspx, and your username will be displayed.

Testing the ICLogin Control

Follow these steps to test the ICLogin control:

1. Delete ICRegister1 from Login.aspx

2. Drag the ICLogin control onto Login.aspx.

3. Open Internet Explorer, and navigate to https://www.fabrikam.com/USChapter6.

4. You will be redirected to Login.aspx, and the ICLogin control will be displayed, as shown in Figure 6-6.

Figure 6-6. *Logging in with a username and password or an information card*

5. Click the information card graphic.

6. Select an information card, and continue.

7. You will be redirected to Default.aspx, and your username will be displayed.

Summary

ASP.NET provides functionality for forms authentication and membership. In this chapter, I covered the basics of both, as well as the implementation of a simple site with forms authentication.

The remainder of the chapter stepped through specifics on how to extend the data structure, stored procedures, and controls, so now you can readily add support to both register and log in with information cards.

CHAPTER 7

■ ■ ■

Software + Services with CardSpace and the Windows Communication Foundation

In this chapter, the focus moves to the development of what is referred to as *software + services.* Although there is no question that CardSpace in the browser is important and will be the most widely used scenario in CardSpace 1.0, there is a strong direction toward building applications that combine a rich user experience and local resources and is augmented by services in the "cloud."

With the release of Windows Vista, Microsoft has released the .NET Framework 3.0. This release of the .NET Framework includes several technologies—Windows Presentation Foundation (WPF), Windows Workflow Foundation (WF), Windows Communication Foundation (WCF), and the subject of this book, Windows CardSpace. These four technologies provide a truly potent combination for developing powerful client applications. WPF provides the ability to deliver rich visualization; WCF provides the ability to easily, securely, and reliably interact with services; CardSpace provides the ability to authenticate to those services; and Workflow Foundation provides the ability to drive everything from the coordination of those services to the workflow of the UI.

This chapter focuses on two of these technologies, Windows CardSpace and Windows Communication Foundation. By the end of the chapter, you will have an application that utilizes information card–secured WCF services and a WCF client. Along the way, I'll cover a number of topics, including exception handling of identity selector–specific issues, understanding claims, and providing personalization based on those claims.

Windows Communication Foundation

One of the best ways of accessing services is with WCF. For those unfamiliar with WCF, this chapter will provide a high-level introduction to the technology and briefly present a sample application that explains the basics. This chapter does *not* purport to provide comprehensive coverage of WCF. The goal of this chapter to is to provide an understanding of how you can use WCF to enable services that use CardSpace for authenticating and empowering clients to call CardSpace-secured services.

■**Note** If you are unfamiliar with WCF, I recommend both the book I coauthored on the subject, *Windows Communication Foundation: Hands On* (Sams, 2006), and the resources on the .NET Framework 3.0 community site, http://www.netfx3.com/.

Introduction to WCF

Historically, if you were tasked with developing a distributed application, you'd have to determine which communication stack(s) to use in your solution. Over the years, a number of stacks have been available from various software vendors. Microsoft alone offers five options—ASMX web services, Web Services Enhancements (WSE), Enterprise Services, .NET Remoting, and MSMQ—each with its own distinct benefits (see Table 7-1).

Table 7-1. *Key Benefits of Each Microsoft Communication Stack*

Communication Stack	Benefit
ASMX web services	Interoperability between platforms
Web Services Enhancements (WSE)	Support for the WS-* protocols
Enterprise Services	Attribute-based programming
Remoting	Extensibility and location transparency
Microsoft Message Queue (MSMQ)	Message-oriented programming

Choosing a communication stack historically has been a significant commitment. Why? Consider this common scenario: the initial needs of your business require the ability to interoperate in a way that is agnostic to language, platform, and location. Based on this requirement, you decide to develop your solution using ASMX web services.

As you're aware, requirements often change over time. If new requirements dictate that there is now a requirement that the service be secured at the message level via WS-Security, you'd likely look to Web Services Enhancements (WSE) to provide this functionality. Adding support with WSE is not effortless. It requires learning this new stack, porting code from ASMX to WSE, testing the code, and redeploying. This can be done, but it requires time, money, and effort.

Although every stack contains benefits, each stack also contains a separate API. As was evident in the example, this presents a number of challenges in regard to agility. The overhead required to learn and maintain knowledge of each stack's APIs, rearchitect the application, make code changes, test those changes, and get them deployed is nontrivial.

The reality is that there's no reason why you should need to learn five separate APIs for communication. Microsoft recognized this and developed a unified API for distributed application development called Windows Communication Foundation.

Windows Communication Foundation provides a single API that encompasses the key benefits of these five stacks as well as robust extensibility that provides tremendous agility.

The ABCs of WCF

When thinking about services in the Windows Communication Foundation, it is helpful to think of it in terms of the ABCs—address, binding, and contract. The address identifies where the service can be accessed, that is, `http://www.fabrikam.com/MyService`. If the address identifies the where, then the binding identifies the how. In the binding, you'll find information on the transport, security, and encoding. Here you can define things such as if you're using HTTP or TCP/IP, message (WS-Security) or transport-level (HTTPS) security, and binary or text encoding. The contract specifies the what. There are actually multiple types of contracts. Contracts define the operations of the service, the data that is exchanged by those operations, and the fault messages that are returned when there's an error.

By looking at services in terms of ABCs, you can also more readily recognize and allocate ownership. Developers need to focus on the operations and the messages exchanged by those operations; thus, they own the contracts, and IT operations will typically own the address and the binding. The rationale is that although it's key for developers to focus on the operations and the messages that are exchanged, IT has the responsibility of ensuring that the services are exposed in conformance with corporate policies. With WCF, configuration can be handled external to the code, allowing IT to easily control the binding and the contracts.

If the scenario with the changing requirements were to occur in a WCF application, the change would not be in the contract, but in the binding and perhaps in the address. The change could be made by IT through configuration.

Service Hosting

With ASMX services, you had a single hosting option: Internet Information Services (IIS). This worked well for exposing web services that used HTTP for their transport. With Windows Communication Foundation, however, the focus is on services—not just web services. As a result, there is a desire to be able to host services with transports other than HTTP and host those services both in and out of IIS.

From a hosting perspective, WCF provides tremendous flexibility. WCF services can be hosted in any .NET application, which means anything from a console application to a Windows Forms application to an NT service to a web server can host WCF.

In addition, IIS 7 has evolved to support two additional types of traffic for WCF services—binary and named pipes.

This flexible hosting combined with the flexibility of transports empowers you to build service-oriented designs that extend from the data center to the desktop, utilizing a mix of hosting, transports, security, and reliability to make software + services easy to implement.

Building an Application with WCF

Prior to showing how to build a information card secured service, I'll show you how to build a simple WCF solution. In the process, you'll learn about data contracts, service contracts, WCF services, and WCF clients.

Creating the Data Contract

The *C* of the ABCs stands for *contract*. The data that is used in WCF services can be defined using data contracts. As you'll see in this section, creating data contracts isn't all that different from creating a class in .NET:

1. Begin by opening Visual Studio 2005.

2. From the menu, select File ➤ New ➤ Project.

3. Select Visual C# ➤ Class Library.

4. Name the library **DataContracts**.

5. Name the solution **Software+Services**.

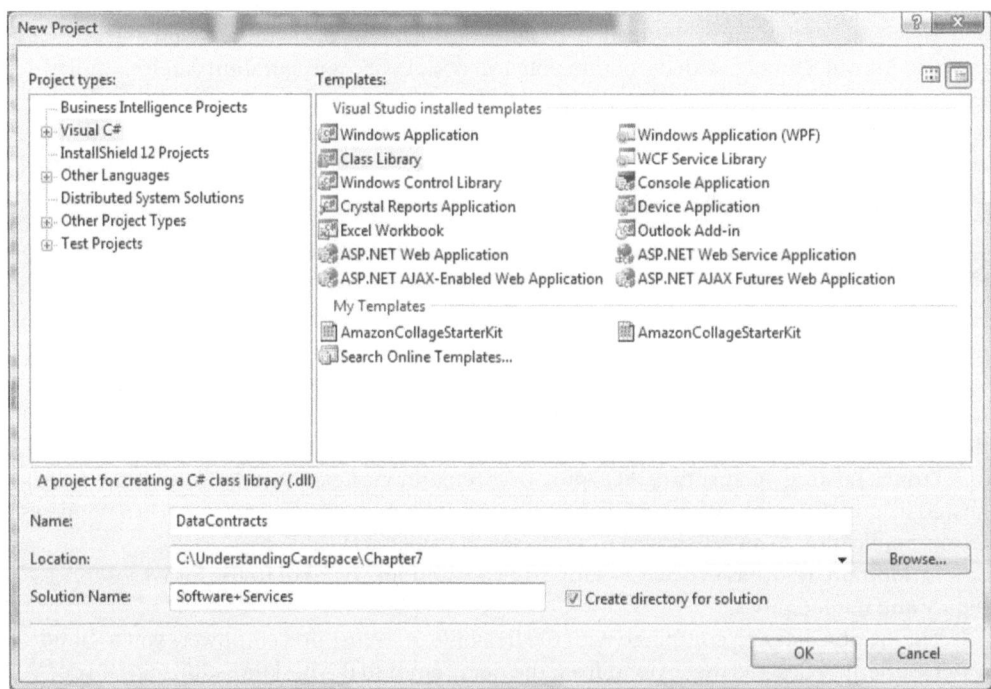

Figure 7-1. *New Web Site dialog box*

6. The new project will contain a file named Class1.cs. Rename this file to **Alert.cs**.

7. Right-click References in the project, and select Add Reference.

8. Select System.Runtime.Serialization, and click the OK button.

9. Open the file Alert.cs, and add **Using System.Runtime.Serialization** to the top of the file.

10. Populate the Alert.cs class such that it resembles the code shown here:

```
using System;
using System.Collections.Generic;
using System.Text;
using System.Runtime.Serialization;

namespace DataContracts
{
    [DataContract]
    public class Alert
    {
        private string _title;
        private string _alertText;
        private string _alertHTML;

        [DataMember]
        public string Title
        {
            get { return _title; }
            set { _title = value; }

        }

        [DataMember]
        public string AlertText
        {
            get { return _alertText; }
            set { _alertText = value; }

        }

        [DataMember]
        public string AlertHTML
        {
            get { return _alertHTML; }
            set { _alertHTML = value; }

        }

    }
}
```

As a result of adding a reference to System.Runtime.Serialization earlier in the exercise, the attributes [DataContract] and [DataMember] are available for use. As you can see in the code, the class is decorated with the [DataContract] attribute. This flags the class, as you might imagine, as a data contract. For each of the data members you'd like to expose, decorate them with the [DataMember] attribute.

> **Note** The [DataMember] attribute does not recognize the scope attached to the underlying member of the class. This means a class could have a member scoped as private that was also attributed with [DataMember], and it *would* be exposed in the data contract but not in regular use of the class.

Creating a Service Contract

Data contracts specify data structures, and service contracts define the structure of the service. In this section, you will create the contract for the service that will expose a single operation, GetAlerts:

1. Right-click the solution, and select Add New Project.

2. Select Visual C# ➤ Class Library.

3. Name the library **ServiceContracts**.

4. The new project will contain a file named Class1.cs. Rename this file to **IAlertService.cs**.

5. Right-click References in the project, and select Add Reference.

6. Select System.Runtime.Serialization and System.ServiceModel, and click the OK button.

7. Right-click References in the project, and select Add Reference.

8. Click the Projects tab, select the DataContracts project, and click OK.

9. Open the file IAlertService.cs.

10. Add using statements for System.Runtime.Serialization, System.ServiceModel, and DataContracts.

11. Modify the code to change class to **interface**.

12. Change the scope of the interface to public.

13. Populate the class such that it resembles the code shown here:

```
using System;
using System.Collections.Generic;
using System.Text;
using System.Runtime.Serialization;
using System.ServiceModel;
using DataContracts;
namespace ServiceContracts
{
    [ServiceContract]
    public interface IAlertService
    {
```

```
[OperationContract]
List<Alert> GetAlerts();

    }
}
```

Creating the Service Implementation

You've just defined the contract for the service, so it is now time to create the service implementation:

1. Right-click the solution, and select Add New Project.

2. Select Visual C# ➤ Class Library.

3. Name the library **Services**.

4. The new project will contain a file named Class1.cs. Rename this file to **AlertService.cs**.

5. Right-click References in the project, and select Add Reference.

6. Select System.Runtime.Serialization and System.ServiceModel, and click the OK button.

7. Right-click References in the project, and select Add Reference.

8. Click the Projects tab, select the DataContracts and Service Contracts projects, and click OK.

9. Open the file AlertService.cs.

10. Open the file Alert.cs, and add using statements for System.Runtime.Serialization, System.ServiceModel, ServiceContracts, and DataContracts to the top of the file.

11. Populate the class such that it resembles the code shown here:

```
using System;
using System.Collections.Generic;
using System.Text;
using ServiceContracts;
using DataContracts;

using System.ServiceModel;
namespace Services
{
    public class AlertService : IAlertService
    {
        #region IAlertService Members

        public List<Alert> GetAlerts()
        {
```

```
                List<Alert> la = new List<Alert>();

                Alert a = new Alert();
                a.Title = "Scheduled Downtime";
                a.AlertText = "Fabrikam's website will be offline" +CCC
    "tomorrow from 8am to 9am PST.";
                a.AlertHTML = "<HTML><HEAD/><BODY>";
                a.AlertHTML += a.AlertText;
                a.AlertHTML += "</BODY></HTML>";

                la.Add(a);


                return la;
            }


        }
            #endregion
            }
```

The class implements the interface IAlertService that contains your service contract. The implementation generates a new alert and will return it to the caller.

Creating a Service Host

Now that the service has been created, it needs to be hosted. If you've created web services on the .NET platform in the past, you've traditionally hosted them in IIS. Services that use HTTP as a transport can still be hosted in IIS 6, and IIS 7 extends this with additional support for TCP and named pipes transports.

In addition to IIS, WCF provides the ability for you to host your services in any .NET application. This includes console applications, Windows Forms applications, Windows Presentation Foundation applications, and NT services.

In this chapter, you will learn how to self-host the services in a console application. Here's how:

1. Right-click the solution, and select Add New Project.

2. Select Visual C# ➤ Console Application.

3. Name the library **WCFServiceHost**.

4. Right-click References in the project, and select Add Reference.

5. Select System.Runtime.Serialization and System.ServiceModel, and click the OK button.

6. Right-click References in the project, and select Add Reference.

7. Click the Projects tab, select the Services and Service Contract projects, and click OK.

8. Open `Program.cs`, and modify it to resemble the code shown here:

```
using System;
using System.Collections.Generic;
using System.Text;
using System.ServiceModel;
using System.Runtime.Serialization;


namespace WCFServiceHost
{
    class Program
    {
        static void Main(string[] args)
        {

            ServiceHost shAlerts = ➥
new ServiceHost(typeof(Services.AlertService),➥
new Uri("http://localhost:1972/Alerts"));
            shAlerts.Open();
            Console.WriteLine("Alert Service Is Now Online");
            Console.WriteLine("---------------------------------------");


            Console.WriteLine("To Stop Service, Press Enter.");
            Console.ReadLine();
            shAlerts.Close();
        }
    }
}
```

To create the service host, you create a new instance of the ServiceHost class found in System.ServiceModel. When creating the service, you specify the type of service to create an instance of and the base address for the service.

Note Although you can specify the base address in code, as in this exercise, you will typically store it externally, such as in the `app.config` file.

The service host is not complete yet, however; you need to configure the bindings:

9. Right-click the project, and select Add New Item.

10. Select Application Configuration File.

11. This will create app.config. Open the file, and add the configuration information shown here:

```xml
<?xml version="1.0" encoding="utf-8" ?>
<configuration>

<system.serviceModel>
  <services>
    <service behaviorConfiguration="AlertServiceBehavior"
name="Services.AlertService">
      <endpoint
                     address="Alerts"
                     binding="basicHttpBinding"
                     name="Alerts"
                     contract="ServiceContracts.IAlertService">
      </endpoint>
      <endpoint address="mex" binding="mexHttpBinding"
contract="IMetadataExchange" />
    </service>
  </services>

  <behaviors>
    <serviceBehaviors>
      <behavior name="AlertServiceBehavior">
        <serviceMetadata httpGetEnabled="true"/>
      </behavior>
    </serviceBehaviors>
  </behaviors>
</system.serviceModel>
</configuration>
```

You'll note that all configuration is held within the system.serviceModel element and the services within the services element. For the Alert service configuration, there are several items of note. The service element is populated with behaviorConfiguration and name attributes.

The name attribute maps to the class used for the service implementation, in this case, Services.AlertService. The behaviorConfiguration attribute specifies a behavior to attach to this service. This will be described more, later in this section.

Within the service, you'll find that there is an endpoints element that contains one or more endpoints for the service. The ABCs are specified for each endpoint, and a service can be exposed on multiple endpoints.

In this exercise, you'll use a single endpoint with a simple binding. You'll specify the address as Alerts. This specifies where the endpoint is accessible from. This is in relationship to the base address provided when creating the ServiceHost object, effectively <baseaddress>/Alerts. The binding is specified as basicHttpBinding. This will expose the service on an HTTP transport that supports Basic Profile 1.0 interoperability. The contract refers to the service contract for the endpoint, in this case, ServiceContracts.IAlertService.

There is a second endpoint that uses mexHttpBinding. This endpoint serves to provide information about the service via WS-MetadataExchange. This returns the discussion to behaviors. The Windows Communication Foundation provides a means to modify the behavior of services. A behavior is given a name, which can be applied in a service via behaviorConfiguration. In this instance, you want to modify the behavior of the service so it will provide metadata via an HTTP GET mechanism.

Note If you're running this code on Windows Vista, you'll need to configure a namespace reservation for the service. Reservation and registration are the operations by which the HTTP server API gives access to the URL namespace on a machine. On Windows Vista, you make a registration using the following syntax:

```
netsh http add urlacl url=http://+:80/MyUri user=DOMAIN\user
```

Another option is to turn off User Account Control. You can do this by navigating to Start ➤ Control Panel ➤ Security Center and turning off the User Account Control. This is less recommended because turning off the User Account Control (UAC) lessens the level of security of your Windows Vista system.

You're now ready to test the service. Compile and run the application.

Now open a web browser, and navigate to http://localhost:1972/Alerts. You should see the screen represented in Figure 7-2. You'll see that this page displays two pieces of information—how to create a proxy using the Service Metadata Utility (svcutil.exe) and how to call the resulting proxy in C# or Visual Basic.

1. From the Start menu, navigate to Visual Studio ➤ Visual Studio Tools.

2. Click the Visual Studio 2005 Command Prompt icon.

3. Navigate to the BeginningCardspace\Chapter7\Exercise1 directory.

4. Run svcutil.exe using the command line specified in the web browser:

   svcutil.exe http://localhost:1972/Alerts?wsdl.

This will generate two files, AlertService.cs and output.config, that will be used when creating the client.

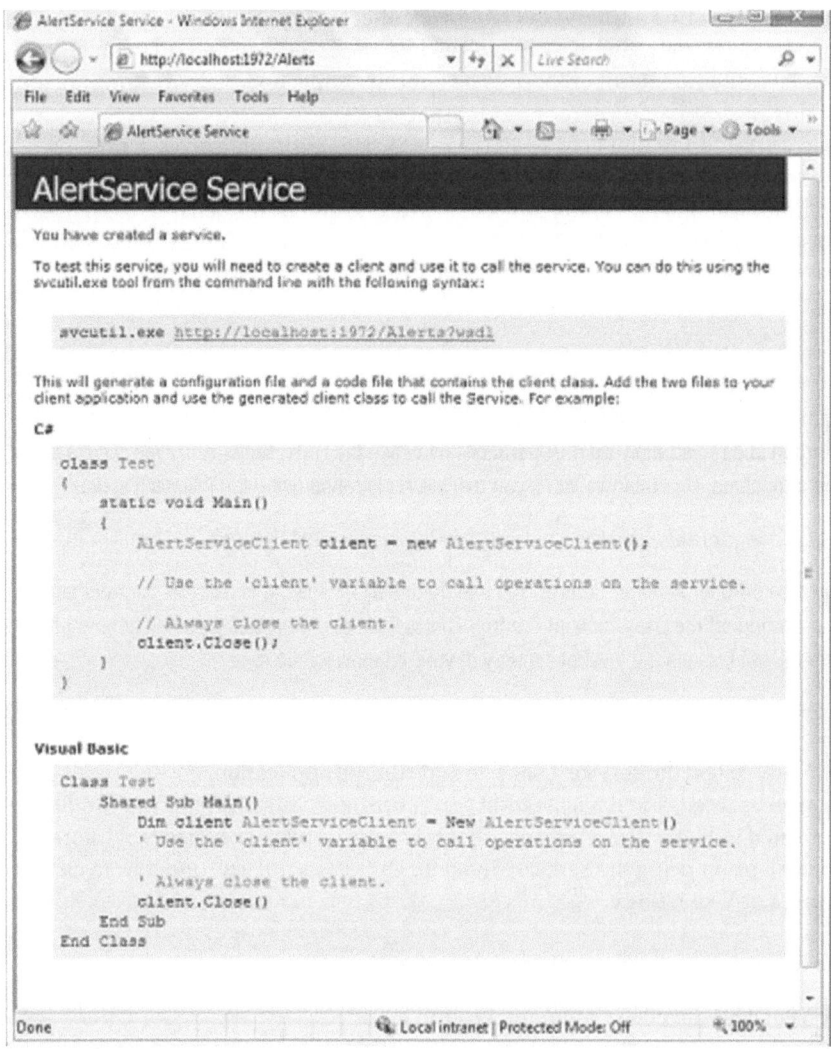

Figure 7-2. *Metadata for AlertService*

Creating a Client

To create the client, follow these steps:

1. Right-click the solution, and select Add New Project.

2. Select Visual C# ➤ Windows Application.

3. Name the library **WCFClient**.

4. Right-click References in the project, and select Add Reference.

5. Select System.Runtime.Serialization and System.ServiceModel, and click the OK button.

6. Right-click References in the project, and select Add Reference.

7. Click the Projects tab, select the Services and ServiceContracts projects, and click OK.

8. Rename Form1.cs to **AlertCenter.cs**.

9. Open AlertCenter.cs in design mode.

10. Add a ListBox control to the form, and name it **lbAlerts**.

11. Add a Label control to the form, name it **lblSystemAlerts**, and set the Text property to **System Alerts**.

12. Add a Label control to the form, and name it **lblTitle**.

13. Add a WebBrowser control to the form, and name it **webAlert**.

14. Arrange the controls so they resemble the layout in Figure 7-3.

Figure 7-3. *Control layout for the client*

15. Create a form load event for the form, and add the code shown here. This code runs when the application is started and will retrieve alerts from the alert service. Each of the alerts is added to the ListBox control, which is bound to the Title property of the Alert class.

```
AlertServiceClient alertService = new AlertServiceClient();
DataContracts.Alert[] systemAlerts = alertService.GetAlerts();
```

```
                foreach (DataContracts.Alert alert in systemAlerts)
                {
                    lbAlerts.Items.Add(alert);
                    lbAlerts.DisplayMember = "Title";
```

16. Next add the SelectedIndexChanged event for lbAlerts, and populate it with the code shown here. When a user clicks an item in the ListBox control, it will retrieve the alert and display the title in lblTitle and the alert itself in the WebBrowser control.

```
    private void lbAlerts_SelectedIndexChanged(object sender, EventArgs e)
        {
            if (lbAlerts.SelectedIndex > -1)
            {
                DataContracts.Alert alert = ➥
(DataContracts.Alert)lbAlerts.Items[lbAlerts.SelectedIndex];
                webAlert.DocumentText = alert.AlertHTML;
                lblTitle.Text = alert.Title;


            }
        }
```

17. Right-click the project, and select Add Existing Item.

18. Navigate to and select the directory where you ran svcutil.exe, and in the Files of Type drop-down list, select All Files.

19. Select AlertCenter.cs and output.config, and click OK.

    If you open the AlertCenter.cs file, you'll see that svcutil.exe read the metadata from AlertService and generated both a proxy *and* the data contract. This was done using standards, and svcutil.exe works just as well against services written in other stacks, on both Windows and non-Windows platforms.

20. Rename output.config to **app.config**.

21. Open app.config.

svcutil.exe also generated an application configuration file for use on the client. This—in combination with the proxy client class that was generated—will allow you to quickly build clients using WCF.

Although app.config will work without incident, you'll note that it has more information in it than what we specified in our service, particularly more attributes.

This is because on the service, we specified one of the six preconfigured bindings available with WCF, basicHttpBinding. The binding has a number of elements and attributes that are associated with it that are hidden behind the common name but are exposed as metadata to those querying the service.

This new binding is interchangeable with the preconfigured binding information specified on the service. To provide this, replace the body of the app.config file so that it mirrors the configuration shown here:

```
<?xml version="1.0" encoding="utf-8"?>
<configuration>
    <system.serviceModel>
        <client>
            <endpoint address=http://localhost:1972/Alerts/Alerts
 binding="basicHttpBinding"
                contract="IAlertService" name="Alerts">

            </endpoint>

        </client>
    </system.serviceModel>
</configuration>
```

Testing the Solution

To test the solution, follow these steps:

1. Right-click the solution, and select Properties.

2. Select Multiple Startup Projects.

3. Specify WCFServiceHost and WCFClient as startup applications (with WCFServiceHost starting first), as shown in Figure 7-4, then click OK.

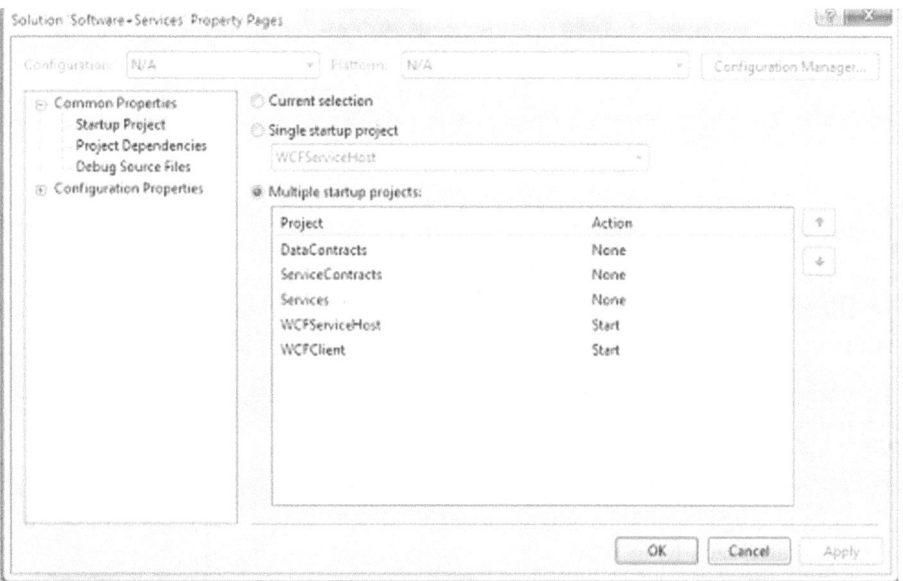

Figure 7-4. *Configuring the start-up projects*

4. Compile and run the application.

5. Click the item Scheduled Downtime. A successful test will result in the screen displayed in Figure 7-5.

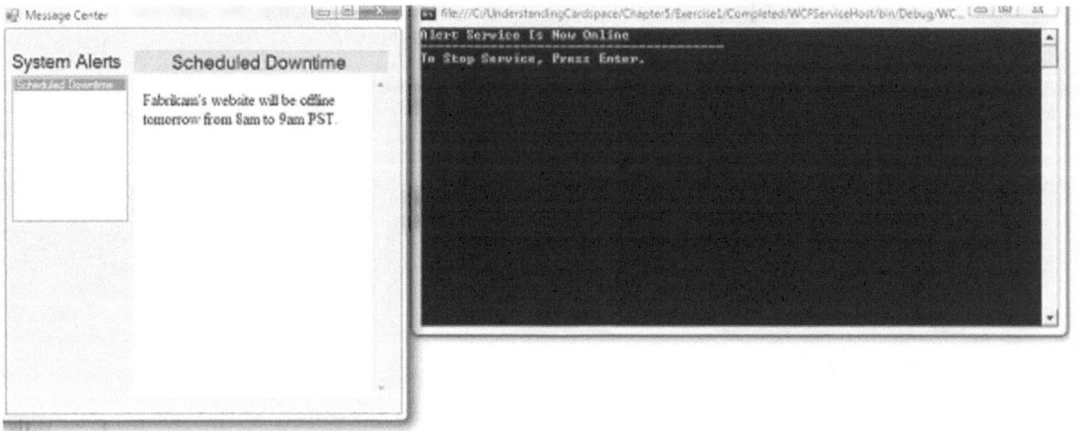

Figure 7-5. *The working solution*

Adding WS-Security to the Solution

Earlier in the chapter, there was a scenario where a project's requirements changed, requiring a shift to support message-level security with WS-Security. In the pre-WCF scenario, that change required moving from one communication stack (ASMX) to another (WSE).

Making this change in WCF is a straightforward task:

1. Open the app.config file in the WCFServiceHost project.

2. Modify the binding from basicHttpBinding to wsHttpBinding.

3. Open the app.config file in the WCFClient project.

4. Modify the endpoint binding from basicHttpBinding to wsHttpBinding.

The application now is configured to support message-level security via WS-Security. The configuration was quick, simple, and done externally to the application.

Using CardSpace with WCF

At this point, you've had a crash course in WCF—you've created contracts, services, and clients, and you've changed binding configurations. In the following sections, I'll expand on this and cover federated security in WCF.

In this part of the chapter, you'll enhance the application created in the first exercise to support information cards on both the service and the client. This will introduce a new service, MyAlertsService.

Creating a Service Contract

As in many scenarios, you will want to have both secured and nonsecured services. Begin by creating the service contract for the new secured service:

1. Right-click the ServiceContracts project, and select Add New Item.

2. Select Interface.

3. Name the interface **IMyAlertsService**.

4. Open the file IMyAlertsService.cs.

5. Add using statements at the top of the file for System.ServiceModel and DataContracts.

6. Populate the class so it resembles the code shown here:

```
using System;
using System.Collections.Generic;
using System.Text;
using System.ServiceModel;
using DataContracts;

namespace ServiceContracts
{
    [ServiceContract]
     public interface IMyAlertsService
     {

         [OperationContract]
         List<Alert> GetMyAlerts();

     }
}
```

Creating a Service Implementation

With the service contract created, it's time to create the service implementation:

1. Right-click References in the Services project, and select System.IdentityModel Right.

2. Click the Services project, and select Add New Item.

3. Select Class, and name the file **MyAlertService.CS**.

4. Open MyAlertService.cs.

5. Add using statements for ServiceContracts, DataContracts, System.IdentityModel.Claims, System.IdentityModel.Policy, and System.ServiceModel.

6. Modify the class to contain the following code:

```
using System;
using System.Collections.Generic;
using System.Text;
using ServiceContracts;
using DataContracts;
using System.IdentityModel.Claims;
using System.IdentityModel.Policy;
using System.ServiceModel;
namespace Services
{
    public class MyAlertService : IMyAlertsService
    {
        #region IMyAlertService Members


        public List<Alert> GetMyAlerts()
        {


            AuthorizationContext ctx = ➥
OperationContext.Current.ServiceSecurityContext.AuthorizationContext;


            foreach (ClaimSet claimSet in ctx.ClaimSets)
            {
                foreach (Claim claim in claimSet)
                {

                    Console.WriteLine("Claim Type:" + claim.ClaimType);
                    Console.WriteLine("Resource:" + ➥
claim.Resource.ToString());
                    Console.WriteLine("Right:" + claim.Right);

                }

            }


            List<Alert> la = new List<Alert>();

            Alert a = new Alert();
            a.Title = "Test";
            a.AlertText = "This is a test alert.";
            a.AlertHTML = "<HTML><HEAD/><BODY>";
            a.AlertHTML += a.AlertText;
```

```
            a.AlertHTML += "</BODY></HTML>";

            la.Add(a);

        return la;
    }
}
#endregion
}
```

This code presents a hybrid of what you saw in the initial exercise for the GetAlerts operation on AlertService and code specific to access claims information provided in the information card.

The code in the previous operation is executed on every call to the service and passes the authorization context to a local variable. AuthorizationContext is result of evaluating authorization policies. We'll establish the policy for this service later in the chapter.

Each authorization context contains properties as well as a collection of claimsets, as illustrated in Figure 7-6. *Claimsets*, as you might imagine, are a set of claims.

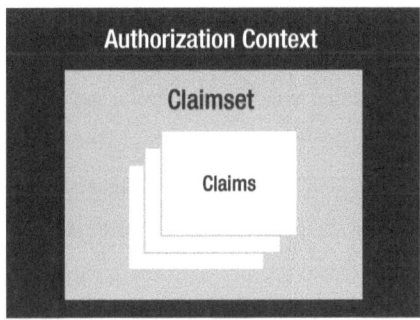

Figure 7-6. *An authorization context contains claim sets, which contain claims.*

As defined in the online documentation for WCF, a claim is the expression of a right with respect to a particular value. Each claim contains a claim type, a right, and a resource, as shown in Figure 7-7. A claim contains the URI that represents the claim.

One example of a claim would be a claim type of File with the right Read over the value for the resource of BeginningCardspace.doc; this would indicate that the entity that is presenting the claimset can read the document named BeginningCardspace.doc.

Claim

Claim Type
Right
Resource

Figure 7-7. *A claim contains a claim type, a right, and a resource.*

In the examples in this chapter, the focus is on those claims available on a self-issued information card, as detailed in Table 7-2. The right in this case will be PossessProperty. If a service were to request my given (first) name, the claim would be givenname, the right would be PossessProperty, and the resource value would be Marc. In this case, the entity presenting the card possesses a given name of Marc.

Table 7-2. *Claim Types in Self-Issued Cards*

Claim	Claim Type
Given Name	http://schemas.xmlsoap.org/ws/2005/05/identity/claims/givenname
Surname	http://schemas.xmlsoap.org/ws/2005/05/identity/claims/surname
Email Address	http://schemas.xmlsoap.org/ws/2005/05/identity/claims/emailaddress
Street Address	http://schemas.xmlsoap.org/ws/2005/05/identity/claims/streetaddress
Locality	http://schemas.xmlsoap.org/ws/2005/05/identity/claims/locality
State/Province	http://schemas.xmlsoap.org/ws/2005/05/identity/claims/stateorprovince
Postal Code	http://schemas.xmlsoap.org/ws/2005/05/identity/claims/postalcode
Country	http://schemas.xmlsoap.org/ws/2005/05/identity/claims/country
Home Phone	http://schemas.xmlsoap.org/ws/2005/05/identity/claims/homephone
Other Phone	http://schemas.xmlsoap.org/ws/2005/05/identity/claims/otherphone
Mobile Phone	http://schemas.xmlsoap.org/ws/2005/05/identity/claims/mobilephone
Date of Birth	http://schemas.xmlsoap.org/ws/2005/05/identity/claims/dateofbirth
Gender	http://schemas.xmlsoap.org/ws/2005/05/identity/claims/gender
PPID	http://schemas.xmlsoap.org/ws/2005/05/identity/claims/privatepersonalidentifier

Returning to the airline example from earlier in the book, when you attempt to check in for a flight, the clerk from the airline will accept only certain forms of identification. More specifically, in the United States a driver's license issued by a U.S. state or a passport issued by a recognized country is acceptable.

Having claims is not enough, because there needs to be a level of trust associated with the identity provider. Claimsets are associated with an issuer, and it is that issuer who assures the validity of the claims on the token. Just like the clerk at the airline desk, a relying party has discretion over which issuers it trusts.

Issuers are themselves identified by claims. It is possible to have multiple levels of claim sets that were issued by other claimsets. In some cases, a claimset could be self-issued and refer to itself, as shown in Figure 7-8.

The code in this exercise iterates through the claimsets and then through the claims in those claimsets. For each claim, it will write the claim type, the right, and the resource value to the console window.

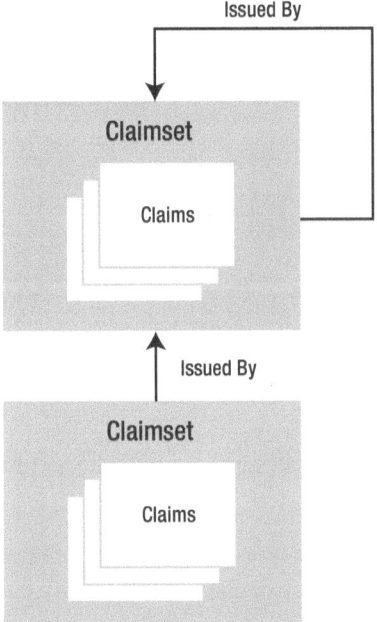

Figure 7-8. *Claimset are issued by issuers, which are claimsets themselves.*

Hosting the Service

The service hasn't been completely configured yet; there are additions that need to be made to the ServiceHost object and the app.config file:

1. Open Program.cs in the WCFServiceHost project.

2. Add lines to both create and open as well as close a new ServiceHost object. The ServiceHost object will be for a service of type Services.MyAlertServices with a base address of http://localhost:1972/Alerts/My. The code for Program.cs should match the code shown here:

```
class Program
  {
      static void Main(string[] args)
      {

          ServiceHost shAlerts = new ➥
ServiceHost(typeof(Services.AlertService), new ➥
 Uri("http://localhost:1972/Alerts"));
          shAlerts.Open();
          Console.WriteLine("Alert Service Is Now Online");
          Console.WriteLine("---------------------------------------");
```

```
            ServiceHost shMyAlerts = new ➥
ServiceHost(typeof(Services.MyAlertService), new ➥
Uri("http://localhost:1972/Alerts/My"));
            shMyAlerts.Open();


                Console.WriteLine("To Stop Service, Press Enter.");
                Console.ReadLine();
                shMyAlerts.Close();
            shAlerts.Close();
                }
            }
```

3. Open the app.config file.

4. Modify the bindings section, adding a behavior named MyAlertsServiceBehavior. The
   behaviors section of app.config should look like this:

```
<behaviors>
    <serviceBehaviors>
      <behavior name="AlertServiceBehavior">
        <serviceMetadata httpGetEnabled="true"/>
      </behavior>
  <behavior name="MyAlertsServiceBehavior" >
    <serviceMetadata httpGetEnabled="true"/>
    <serviceCredentials>
      <issuedTokenAuthentication allowUntrustedRsaIssuers="true"/>
      <serviceCertificate
                   findValue="www.fabrikam.com"
                   storeLocation="LocalMachine"
                   storeName="My"
                   x509FindType="FindBySubjectName"/>
    </serviceCredentials>

  </behavior>
    </serviceBehaviors>
  </behaviors>
```

In addition to the serviceMetadata element you saw in the first exercise in this chapter,
there is an additional element for serviceCredentials. Note the serviceCertificate
element. This element contains attributes that point to an X.509 certificate in the local
store. This is a reference to the private key to be used for signing and decrypting within
the service. Services are secured using certificates, preferably using Extended Validation
(EV) certificates. EV certificates contain embedded images that provide further assur-
ances of identity of the service to which it is attached.

5. Within the services element, add the following XML to the configuration file:

```
  <service behaviorConfiguration="MyAlertsServiceBehavior"
name="Services.MyAlertService">
      <endpoint address="MyAlerts" binding="wsFederationHttpBinding"
       bindingConfiguration="CardSpaceAlertsBinding" name="AlertsCardSpace"
       contract="ServiceContracts.IMyAlertsService">
        <identity>
           <certificateReference
                              storeName="My"
                              storeLocation="LocalMachine"
                              x509FindType="FindBySubjectName"
                              findValue="www.fabrikam.com"
               />
        </identity>
      </endpoint>
      <endpoint address="mex" binding="mexHttpBinding"
contract="IMetadataExchange" />
    </service>
```

This provides the configuration for the service. In this section, the behavior that was created in the previous step, MyAlertsServiceBehavior, is referenced via the behaviorConfiguration attribute on the service. In addition, we need to provide an identity reference for the endpoint that associates the certificate with it.

Note that the binding for this service is wsFederationHttpBinding, and there is a bindingConfiguration attribute that is defined. Although there are six predefined bindings for WCF, these bindings can be reconfigured through configuration.

6. Add a bindings section to the app.config file that includes the following code:

```
<bindings>

    <wsFederationHttpBinding>
      <binding name="CardSpaceAlertsBinding">
        <security mode="Message">
          <message algorithmSuite="Basic128"
                              issuedTokenType=➦
"urn:oasis:names:tc:SAML:1.0:assertion"


                              issuedKeyType="SymmetricKey"
            >
          <issuer
                      address=➦
http://schemas.xmlsoap.org/ws/2005/05/identity/issuer/self


             />
```

```
            <claimTypeRequirements>
               <add
claimType=➡
"http://schemas.xmlsoap.org/ws/2005/05/identity/claims/givenname"/>
               <add claimType=➡
"http://schemas.xmlsoap.org/ws/2005/05/identity/claims/surname"/>
               <add claimType=➡
"http://schemas.xmlsoap.org/ws/2005/05/identity/claims/locality"/>
               <add claimType=➡
"http://schemas.xmlsoap.org/ws/2005/05/identity/claims/country"/>
            </claimTypeRequirements>

          </message>
        </security>
      </binding>
    </wsFederationHttpBinding>
  </bindings>
```

Within the security element, we define the policy that will be applied for the service. It is established that it will be message-level security. The issuer that will be accepted is self-issued. This is identified in the issuer element via the address attribute.

This is also where the claims the server is requesting are specified. Here, you can see that the given name, the surname, the locality, and the country are requested.

Note All four of these claims are requested and required for access to the service. It is possible to request claims and specify that they are optional and not required. This is done by adding the attribute isOptional="true" to the add element.

Now that the service has been configured, it is time to configure the client:

1. Right-click the WCFServiceHost project, and select Debug ➤ Start New Instance. This will create an instance of the service.

2. Test that the service is online. Open a web browser, and go to http://localhost:1972/Alerts/my. You should see the screen shown in Figure 7-9.

3. From the Start menu, navigate to Visual Studio ➤ Visual Studio Tools.

4. Click the Visual Studio 2005 Command Prompt icon.

5. Navigate to the BeginningCardspace\Chapter7\Exercise2 directory.

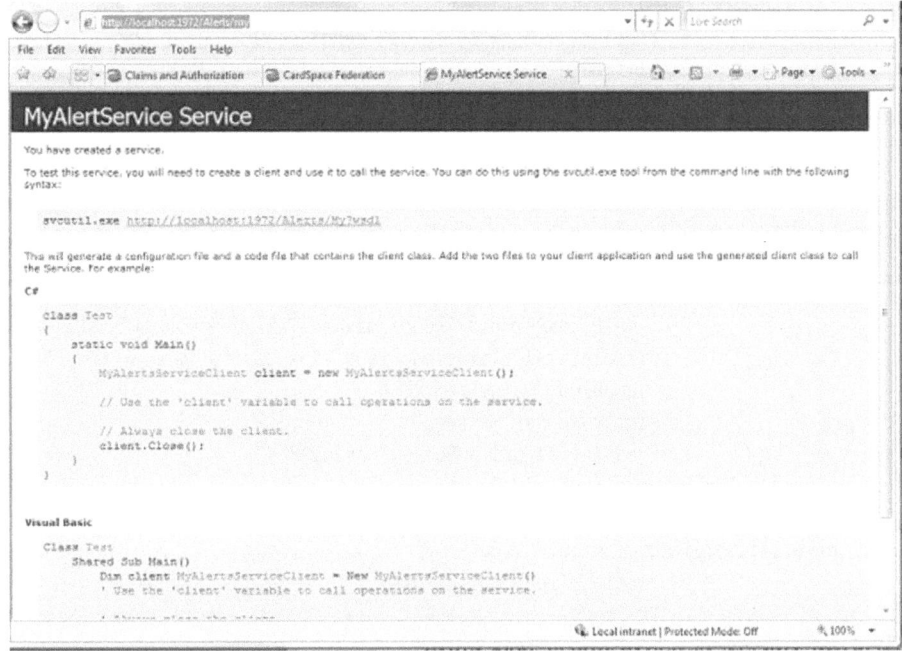

Figure 7-9. *Metadata for the MyAlertService*

6. Run `svcutil.exe` using the command line specified in the web browser:

   `svcutil.exe http://localhost:1972/Alerts/My?wsdl`.

   This will generate `MyAlertService.cs`, which contains a proxy client, and `output.config`, which contains the configuration information.

7. Add `MyAlertService.cs` to the WCFClient project.

8. Add `output.config` to the WCFClient project.

9. Copy the `service` element from `app.config`, and paste it into `output.config`.

10. Copy the `service` behavior `AlertServiceBehavior` from `app.config` to `output.config`.

11. Delete `app.config`.

12. Rename `output.config`to **app.config**.

13. Your merged `app.config` file should look like this:

```
<?xml version="1.0" encoding="utf-8"?>
<configuration>
    <system.serviceModel>
        <bindings>
            <wsFederationHttpBinding>
                <binding name="AlertsCardSpace" closeTimeout="00:01:00"
```

```
openTimeout="00:01:00"
                receiveTimeout="00:10:00" sendTimeout="00:01:00"
bypassProxyOnLocal="false"
                transactionFlow="false"
hostNameComparisonMode="StrongWildcard"
                maxBufferPoolSize="524288" maxReceivedMessageSize="65536"
                messageEncoding="Text" textEncoding="utf-8"
useDefaultWebProxy="true">
                <readerQuotas maxDepth="32"
maxStringContentLength="8192" maxArrayLength="16384"
                    maxBytesPerRead="4096" maxNameTableCharCount="16384" />
                <reliableSession ordered="true" inactivityTimeout="00:10:00"
                    enabled="false" />
                <security mode="Message">
                    <message algorithmSuite="Basic128"
issuedKeyType="SymmetricKey"
                        issuedTokenType="urn:oasis:names:tc:SAML:1.0:assertion"
negotiateServiceCredential="true">
                        <claimTypeRequirements>
                        <add
 claimType=➡
"http://schemas.xmlsoap.org/ws/2005/05/identity/claims/givenname"
                            isOptional="false" />
                        <add
claimType=➡
"http://schemas.xmlsoap.org/ws/2005/05/identity/claims/surname"
                            isOptional="false" />
                        <add
claimType=➡
"http://schemas.xmlsoap.org/ws/2005/05/identity/claims/locality"
                            isOptional="false" />
                        <add
claimType=➡
"http://schemas.xmlsoap.org/ws/2005/05/identity/claims/country"
                            isOptional="false" />
                        </claimTypeRequirements>
                        <issuer
 address=➡
"http://schemas.xmlsoap.org/ws/2005/05/identity/issuer/self" />
                    </message>
                </security>
            </binding>
        </wsFederationHttpBinding>

    </bindings>
    <client>
        <endpoint address="http://localhost:1972/Alerts/Alerts"
```

```
binding="wsHttpBinding"
              contract="IAlertService" name="Alerts">

          </endpoint>

          <endpoint address="http://localhost:1972/Alerts/My/MyAlerts"
            binding="wsFederationHttpBinding"
bindingConfiguration="AlertsCardSpace"
            contract="IMyAlertsService" name="AlertsCardSpace">
            <identity>
              <certificateencodedValue=➥
```

"AwAAAAEAAAAUAAAA1H3mV/pJAlVZAst/Dt0rqbBd67ggAAAAA➥
QAAAEgGAAAwggZEMIIFLKADAgECAgooKOI4AAAAAAvMAOGCSqGSIb3DQEBBQUA➥
MG4xEzARBgoJkiaJk/IsZAEZFgNjb2OxGTAXBgoJkiaJk/IsZAEZFgltaWNyb3N➥
vZnQxFDASBgoJkiaJk/IsZAEZFgRjb3JwMRUwEwYKCZImiZPyLGQBGRYFbnRkZX➥
YxDzANBgNVBAMTBkFkYXR1bTAeFwOwNjA1MTkyMzQyMzNaFwOxMTAzMTAxODI3N➥
TZaMGIxCzAJBgNVBAYTAlVTMRMwEQYDVQQIEwpXYXNoaW5ndG9uMRAwDgYDVQQH➥
EwdSZWRtb25kMREwDwYDVQQKEwhGYWJyaWthbTEZMBcGA1UEAxMQd3d3LmZhYnJ➥
pa2FtLmNvbTCCASIwDQYJKoZIhvcNAQEBBQADggEPADCCAQoCggEBAMACp5TXWi➥
J711p87W5r15bwnecarGdh4nnMTVj+WOhaUCIiRKev5OfBRyrjeJfEy4gv9B1ME➥
6pJJguIlfk7RMyx5Titica5J/aBWW21BxaDq05r9T+wZffsnxvqYcwWw6yG6/oG➥
3sDk+Trv2/mpE8SNJVgEcqlD7hvWIPa3opjk8AMD8gmoOk3Hw6gHt8xmnAEsb57➥
gOzLmHAo8+iLfs+uOi8efBnfgLrkO/rAaet74fSUS56bXmGyNvU5FF6rELEGOLk➥
WfH/LK82EmlToakCocEOmQmFCkNpQhQHyepwKndFOAmjVJ57M5jHOEewOEpkIuK➥
PJMRJwn/gtxW8MWhBMCAwEAAaOCAu4wggLqMA4GA1UdDwEB/wQEAwIE8DBEBgkq➥
hkiG9w0BCQ8ENzA1MA4GCCqGSIb3DQMCAgIAgDAOBggqhkiG9w0DBAICAIAwBwY➥
FKw4DAgcwCgYIKoZIhvcNAwcwHQYDVR0OBBYEFJfyWkB2bCNfu9uY6UHUlXjBLC➥
TEMBMGA1UdJQQMMAoGCCsGAQUFBwMBMB8GA1UdIwQYMBaAFOyhvEbGfwt7MxHOk➥
dVD6eGG/la6MDkGA1UdHwQyMDAwLqAsoCqGKGhOdHA6Ly93d3cuYWRhdHVtLmNv➥
bS9jcmxkYXRhL2FkYXR1bS5jmwwggEKBggrBgEFBQcBAQSB/TCB+jB6BggrBgE➥
FBQcwAoZuaHROcDovL3Rob24tdGVzdDEtMjAwMy5udGRldi5jb3JwLm1pY3Jvc2➥
9mdC5jb2OvQ2VydEVucm9sbC90aG9uLXR1c3QxLTIwMDMubnRkZXYuY29ycC5ta➥
WNyb3NvZnQuY29tX0FkYXR1bS5jcnQwfAYIKwYBBQUHMAKGcGZpbGU6Ly9cXHRo➥
b24tdGVzdDEtMjAwMy5udGRldi5jb3JwLm1pY3Jvc29mdC5jb21cQ2VydEVucm9➥
sbFx0aG9uLXR1c3QxLTIwMDMubnRkZXYuY29ycC5taWNyb3NvZnQuY29tX0FkYX➥
R1bS5jcnQwgdoGCCsGAQUFBwEMBIHNMIHKoWGgXzBdMFswWRYJaW1hZ2UvZ2lmM➥
CEwHzAHBgUrDgMCGgQUBO3hqsI4zqGA3bRTvpSU6LEiObwwKRYnaHROcDovL3d3➥
dy5hZGFOdWOuY29tL2ltYWdlcy9hZGFOdWOuZ2lmomomWgYzBhMF8wXRYJaW1hZ2U➥
vZ2lmMCEwHzAHBgUrDgMCGgQU8+uAcGo7FFJINSouwXzviKfnVGswLRYraHROcD➥
ovL3d3dy5mYWJyaWthbS5jb2OvaW1hZ2VzL2ZhYnJpa2FtLmdpZjAXBgNVHSAEE➥
DAOMAwGCisGAQQBgjc8ZAEwDQYJKoZIhvcNAQEFBQADggEBAEzYsXIBjTGbbuHI➥
Ubv+/7KFEWzSf3u23koOBlvzIHU6iXD64mdhrXr1G9qU39tE6fKxybfCp86U03N➥
Mb93SIHRtC2JvE/AJcNs4Oq9SF5VCGFGMBNAXKBBuJysrcQ2fgCvvscaNE8OmyA➥
tWOIBzHqqpRO6rfcdzRE/m1UyyHtnuqdAPUBXqiE7xR7BEw7hHDPzc4fTFMU9er➥
s3cjBZ9scwcBL6NIU47RL/vKqaIzlksII845egRr6LEHOaTyozk9IdOEL5W9JQe➥
Y2X2Ekb3+MtLNI5fAzUmsMkZO3JRuTxdZsOmmLYEqc9OfTkWeC53k+sAtW69NoM➥
jI91+Vo/O4RO=" />
```
```

```
                </identity>
              </endpoint>
            </client>
        </system.serviceModel>
    </configuration>
```

14. Next, add controls and code to call and use the results of the new service. In the WCFClient project, add a Label control named lblMyAlerts to the form, and set the Text property to **MyAlerts**.

15. Add a ListBox control to the form, and name it **lbMyAlerts**.

16. Add the following code to the existing form load event. This will create a new client for the new service:

```
        MyAlertsServiceClient myAlertService = new MyAlertsServiceClient();

        DataContracts.Alert[] myAlerts = myAlertService.GetMyAlerts();

        foreach (DataContracts.Alert alert in myAlerts)
        {
            lbMyAlerts.Items.Add(alert);
            lbMyAlerts.DisplayMember = "Title";
```

17. Add a SelectedIndexChanged event for the new ListBox control called lbMyAlerts, and add the code shown here:

```
        if (lbMyAlerts.SelectedIndex > -1)
        {
            DataContracts.Alert alert =
(DataContracts.Alert)lbMyAlerts.Items[lbMyAlerts.SelectedIndex];
            webAlert.DocumentText = alert.AlertHTML;
            lblTitle.Text = alert.Title;



        }
```

This code performs the same task as in the first exercise, but operating with data from the new ListBox control.

18. Assemble the controls on the form so they look like Figure 7-10.

19. Your project is now ready to be compiled and run. Run the project, and you will be prompted to select an information card. Select a card, and you will see that myAlertsService was successfully called and the claims were printed to the console, as shown in Figure 7-11.

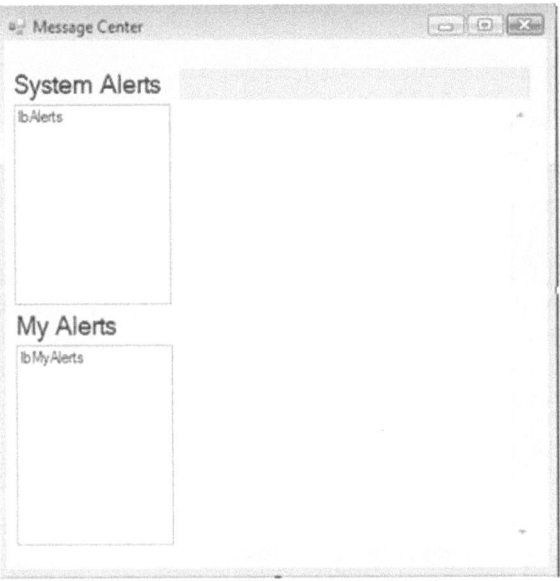

Figure 7-10. *The form layout*

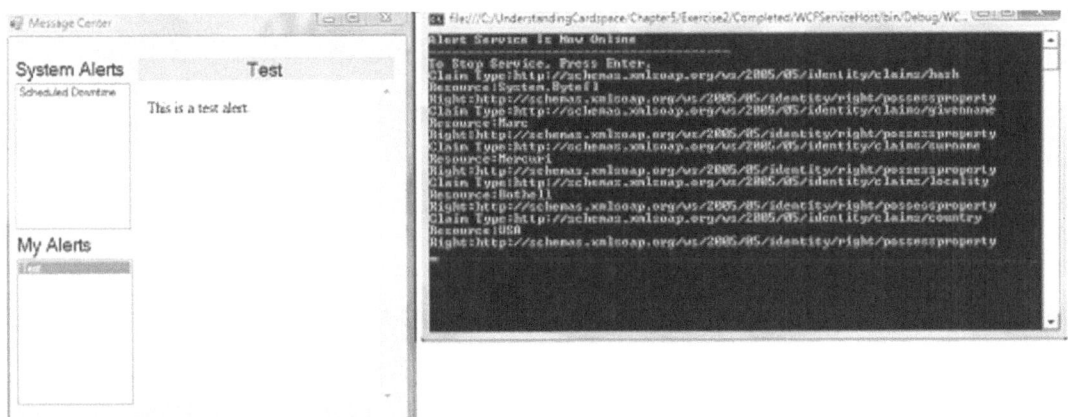

Figure 7-11. *Application showing information card holder–specific alerts*

Private Personal Identifier (PPID)

In the claims listed earlier in Table 7-1, the last claim listed was PPID. This stands for Private Personal Identifier. Every personal card is created with a *master key*. When the user is about to send a card to a site or service, the master key and data from the site's certificate are used to generate the PPID and the public/private key pair are used for signing. The PPID is unique for each site or service that you connect with.

The PPID is a standard claim and can be added to the claimRequirements element in the bindings section of the app.config file:

1. Add the following element in the claimRequirements in the service's app.config file:

```
<add
claimType=➡
"http://schemas.xmlsoap.org/ws/2005/05/identity/claims/privatepersonalidentifi-
er"/>
```

2. Add that same line to the client's app.config file.

Run the application, and you'll see the PPID added to the list of claims printed to the console. Recognize that if a new card is created or a different card is used, the PPID is different. I recommend you don't use the PPID as a primary key in a database, but instead either as a natural key or in a separate table linked by an internal key for the user. The latter facilitates the ability to associate multiple cards with a single account.

Adding Personalization

The previous section talked about how a PPID claim could be used to authenticate a user; this section introduces how claims can be used for personalization.

A simple example would be to incorporate the card holder's name in a response or return information based on information contained on the card.

Personalization is covered in more detail later in this book, but to see a simple example, replace the code in the GetMyAlerts operation in Services.MyAlertServices with the following:

```
public List<Alert> GetMyAlerts()
    {

        string locality ="";
        string country ="";
        string givenname ="";
        string surname ="";
        AuthorizationContext ctx =
OperationContext.Current.ServiceSecurityContext.AuthorizationContext;


        foreach (ClaimSet claimSet in ctx.ClaimSets)
        {
            foreach (Claim claim in claimSet)
            {

                if (claim.ClaimType == ClaimTypes.Locality)
                        {locality = claim.Resource.ToString();}
                if (claim.ClaimType == ClaimTypes.Country)
                        { country = claim.Resource.ToString(); }
                if (claim.ClaimType == ClaimTypes.GivenName)
                        { givenname = claim.Resource.ToString(); }
                if (claim.ClaimType == ClaimTypes.Surname)
                        { surname = claim.Resource.ToString(); }
            }
```

```
                }

                List<Alert> la = new List<Alert>();

                Alert a = new Alert();
                a.Title = "Special Offer";
                a.AlertText = givenname + " " + surname + ➥
", we wanted to let you know that Fabrikam has special offers for➥
 customers living in  " + locality + ➥
". These offers are open to all " + country + " citizens.";
                a.AlertHTML = "<HTML><HEAD/><BODY>";
                a.AlertHTML += a.AlertText;
                a.AlertHTML += "</BODY></HTML>";

                Alert b = new Alert();
                b.Title = "Statement Available";
                b.AlertText = givenname + " " + surname + ➥
", we wanted to let you know that your account statement for the➥
 period ending" + DateTime.Now.ToShortDateString() + ➥
" is now available.";
                b.AlertHTML = "<HTML><HEAD/><BODY>";
                b.AlertHTML += b.AlertText;
                b.AlertHTML += "</BODY></HTML>";


                la.Add(a);
                la.Add(b);

                return la;
            }
```

As the claimsets are iterated, the claims are evaluated against the ones of interest. The evaluation is done using the ClaimType enumeration, which contains all claim types found in a self-issued card, as well as some others.

The claims are copied to local values, and personalized alerts are created and delivered to the user. In a production environment, you would typically return different results and/or customized advertising based on the claims provided.

Adding Error Handling on the Client

Microsoft provides a class in System.IdentityModel.Selectors that offers exceptions tied to the identity selector in CardSpace.

For testing, the easiest exception to trigger is UserCancellationException. This exercise will add exception handling for all identity selector–specific exceptions and will display a message box if UserCancellationException is triggered. That exception is triggered if the identity selector is canceled and no card is submitted.

1. In the WCFClient project, right-click References, and select Add Reference.

2. Select System.IdentityModel.Selectors.

3. Open the form in the WCFClient project, and select View Code.

4. Add a using statement for System.IdentityModel.Selectors to the top of the file.

5. Modify the form load event to reflect the changes in bold shown here:

```
AlertServiceClient alertService = new AlertServiceClient();
DataContracts.Alert[] systemAlerts = alertService.GetAlerts();

foreach (DataContracts.Alert alert in systemAlerts)
{
    lbAlerts.Items.Add(alert);
    lbAlerts.DisplayMember = "Title";
}


try
{
    MyAlertsServiceClient myAlertService = ➥
new MyAlertsServiceClient();
    DataContracts.Alert[] myAlerts = myAlertService.GetMyAlerts();
    foreach (DataContracts.Alert alert in myAlerts)
    {
        lbMyAlerts.Items.Add(alert);
        lbMyAlerts.DisplayMember = "Title";
    }
}
catch (UserCancellationException uce)
{
    System.Windows.Forms.MessageBox.Show("User➥
Cancelled Out of the CardSpace UI.");

}
catch (UntrustedRecipientException ure)
{ }
catch (ServiceNotStartedException snse)
{ }
catch (CardSpaceException cse)
{ }
catch (Exception e)
{ }
```

Summary

This chapter focused on Windows CardSpace used with Windows Communication Foundation. At this point, you have an application that utilizes information card–secured WCF services and a WCF client. Along the way, you were introduced to a number of topics, including handling identity selector–specific exceptions, understanding claims, and implementing personalization based on those claims.

CHAPTER 8

■ ■ ■

Consuming Multiple Information Card–Secured Services in Smart Client Applications

The previous chapter introduced you both to Windows Communication Foundation (WCF) and to how to secure WCF services with information cards. This chapter continues the exploration of using WCF and information cards and shows how to create service-powered smart clients.

We'll begin by extending the MyAlerts sample from the previous chapter. In that application, a client polled an information card–secured service, retrieving user-specific alerts. Also, the service checked for alerts only once, on start-up. It's easy to imagine a scenario where the alert service is being called multiple times during a user session. What would happen if you checked for alerts periodically? When I first started developing with WCF and CardSpace, the result was not what I expected.

In this first exercise, you'll modify that application to see what happens:

1. Copy the completed code from Chapter 7 to C:\BeginningCardspace\Chapter8\PartI.

2. Open the project in Visual Studio.

3. Open the form AlertCenter.cs.

4. Add a new button to the form, and place it below the My Alerts listbox, lbMyAlerts.

5. Name the button **btnCheckAlerts**, and change the button text to **Check Alerts**.

6. Double-click the button to create a click event, and populate it with the following code:

```
private void btnCheckAlerts_Click(object sender, EventArgs e)
    {
        try
        {
```

```
                    MyAlertsServiceClient myAlertService = ➥
    new MyAlertsServiceClient();

                    DataContracts.Alert[] myAlerts =
myAlertService.GetMyAlerts();
                    lbMyAlerts.Items.Clear();
                    foreach (DataContracts.Alert alert in myAlerts)
                    {
                        lbMyAlerts.Items.Add(alert);
                        lbMyAlerts.DisplayMember = "Title";

                    }
                }
                catch (UserCancellationException uce)
                {
                    System.Windows.Forms.MessageBox.Show("User➥
    Cancelled Out of the CardSpace UI.");

                }
                catch (UntrustedRecipientException ure)
                { }
                catch (ServiceNotStartedException snse)
                { }
                catch (CardSpaceException cse)
                { }
                catch (Exception e1)
                { }
            }
```

If you now run the application, the form load event will be executed, a call to the MyAlerts service will be made, and you will be presented with the identity selector. You will select a card and authorize the identity provider (in this case, the personal security token server) to provide a token for the service. This is the expected behavior you saw in the previous chapter.

Now, if you click the Check Alerts button, the identity selector is displayed again. Click the Check Alerts button again—surprise, the identity selector is displayed again.

Why does this happen? WCF stores credentials on a per-channel basis. In this example, the client—and the underlying channel—is being created and destroyed each time the service is called. For every new instance of the client, there is no history of the user's authorization to provide claims to a service. This is a strict interpretation of Law #1, "User Control and Consent."

Now, you might be saying to yourself, "Marc, c'mon, that's easy enough to work around. Just create a single instance of the service client instead of creating/disposing of a channel with each call." Because the channel lifetime would be extended, this does work—and when I first began using WCF and information cards, I shifted my code to this approach. However, I soon learned, as you will now, that this usability challenge was only part of a larger one.

When developing applications of significance, you'll likely not be using a single service. You'll have multiple services with different contracts residing at different endpoints. When implementing such an application solely with the out-of-the-box features of WCF and Windows

CardSpace, you'll see that for every channel you create in WCF, the identity selector will be displayed.

If each of the services were provided by a different company—say one by Amazon and one by the federal government—this would make sense. These are very different organizations, and I may not want to use the same card with both of them. Furthermore, I may be more willing to share some information with the government than I would with Amazon (or vice versa). Following Law #1, "User Control and Consent," this behavior makes sense. In that case, you would want the identity selector displayed once for each service.

Many times, however, you'll be accessing multiple services from the same provider. In the MyAlerts application, there were two services—Alerts and MyAlerts—and only one of them was secured with an information card. But what would happen if they were both secured with information cards? Even though they're both provided by the same company and secured with the same certificate, because each service client would open its own channel, you would be prompted for an information card twice. It's not difficult to imagine the experience if you built a smart client that incorporated five services from the same company—the identity selector would be displayed five times. The display of the identity selector is very noticeable—the screen dims, and the identity selector appears in a separate desktop. Even if a client/channel was created and persisted for each of the services for the life of the application, having the identity selector display five times in succession is going to lead to unhappy users.

When building smart clients that utilize multiple information card–secured services, this would have introduced some *major* usability challenges. Speaking with the CardSpace product team, we talked about caching the token and reusing it. Early discussions with the product group indicated this might not be possible in version 1.

Fortunately, Vittorio Bertocci, a former teammate of mine who focuses on .NET Framework 3.0 projects in Fortune 500 companies, spent a fair bit of time looking at the issue and found a way to enable the caching of tokens via a WCF custom behavior.

One of the great aspects of Windows Communication Foundation is that it is so readily extensible. We'll leverage that extensibility to provide a satisfactory experience for the end user—helping avoid "User Control and Consent" resulting in user annoyance and frustration.

Enabling Token Caching

When working with an information card–secured service in a WCF client application, the client interacts with a `ClientCredentials` object. As you might imagine, this object handles credentials for the client. Credentials can take many forms—username and password, Windows client, x.509 certificates, and so on. `ClientCredentials` also includes support for information card tokens, and if you examine the metadata for `ClientCredentials`, you'll find an operation named `GetInfoCardSecurityToken`.

The default functionality of this method results in the identity selector being displayed. In the next exercise, you will create a new version of `ClientCredentials` and override the `GetInfoCardSecurityToken` method such that it caches tokens on their first appearance in a static dictionary object.

On each subsequent request, the new code will perform two tasks. First, it will check whether the token exists. Second, if the token does exist, it will examine whether it is still valid. If the token doesn't exist or is invalid, the identity selector will be displayed, and a new token will be retrieved. If the token is present and valid, it will not display the identity selector and instead use the cached token. This new implementation of `ClientCredentials` will be named

CachedInformationCardClientCredentials and will require some additional classes to be implemented.

As mentioned earlier, the tokens are cached in a dictionary object, and on each call of GetInfoCardSecurityToken, the dictionary will be queried to see whether there is a cached SecurityToken that conforms to values in the current request. To provide an easy way to perform this query, you will create a new class that contains key pieces of information. This class, CardspacePolicyInfo, stores three key pieces of information about a token—including the issuer of the token, the base URI of the relying party that requested it, and information from the certificate. This object will also implement a custom Equals evaluator that utilizes these three pieces of information.

You'll also need to create a new TokenManager that will support CachedInformationCardClientCredentials.

Once these classes are created, you'll want to enable them on your endpoints using custom behaviors. You'll create a class that makes it easy to add this functionality via the configuration file, and you'll learn the settings to add to the configuration file both to recognize your new credentials and to apply them to your endpoint.

Now that you've got an idea of how this will work, it's time to roll up your sleeves and begin interpreting this into code.

Setting Up the New Project

You'll begin by modifying the solution used earlier in this chapter:

1. Right-click the software + services solution in the Solution Explorer, and select Add New Project.

2. Select Class Library.

3. Name the project **CardpaceTokenCaching**, and have it created in C:\BeginningCardspace\Chapter8\PartI. Right-click References for this project in the Solution Explorer, and select Add Reference.

4. Add references to System.Configuration, System.ServiceModel, System.IdentityModel, System.IdentityModel.Selectors, System.Xml, and System.Runtime.Serialization.

5. Right-click the project, and select Properties.

6. Change the default namespace to **BeginningCardspace**.

Creating the PolicyInfo Class

To create the PolicyInfo class, follow these steps:

1. The new project will include a default class, Class1.cs. Rename this class to **CardspacePolicyInfo**.

2. Add using statements for System.IdentityModel.Selectors, System.ServiceModel, System.Xml, and System.IO to the top of the file:

```
using System;
using System.Collections.Generic;
using System.Text;
using System.IdentityModel.Selectors;
using System.ServiceModel;
using System.Xml;
using System.IO;
```

3. Change the namespace in the file to **BeginningCardspace**.

■ **Note** You're changing this namespace manually because it was created before you defined
BeginningCardspace as the default.

You'll now populate the body of the class. You'll begin by creating the member variables
to store the three pieces of information you'll use to find tokens—the identity provider,
the certificate, and the relying party. You'll also include a list of the claims for the token.

4. Enter the following code into the class:

```
public class CardspacePolicyInfo
{
    string _identityProvider;
    string _certificate;
    string _relyingParty;


    List<string> _requiredClaims;

    public string IdentityProvider
    {
       get { return _identityProvider; }
       set { _identityProvider = value; }

    }
    public string Certificate
    {
       get { return _certificate; }
       set { _certificate = value; }

    }
    public string RelyingParty
    {
       get { return _relyingParty; }
       set { _relyingParty = value; }
```

```
        }
        public List<string> RequiredClaims
        {
            get { return _requiredClaims; }
            set { _requiredClaims = value; }
        }
```

5. You'll now override the Equals method for the class. This method will compare the identity provider, relying party, claims, and certificate information of the current object to the one it's being asked to evaluate. The value of true will be returned if all these values match. If one of the requested claims is not present, it will return false. Enter the following code:

```
        public override bool Equals(object obj)
        {
            if (obj != null)
            {
                if (obj.GetType() == this.GetType())
                {
                    CardspacePolicyInfo policyToCompare = ➥
(CardspacePolicyInfo)obj;
                    bool includesAllClaims = true;

        foreach (string claim in policyToCompare.RequiredClaims)
                    {
                        if (!this.RequiredClaims.Contains(claim))
                        {
                            includesAllClaims = false;

                        }
                    }

                    return (policyToCompare.IdentityProvider ==➥
    this.IdentityProvider &&

                        policyToCompare.RelyingParty == ➥
this.RelyingParty &&

                        policyToCompare.Certificate == this.Certificate &&
                        includesAllClaims);


                }
                else
                {
                    return false;
                }

            }
```

```
        else
        {
            return false;
        }

    }
```

6. You'll next override the GetHashCode operation for the class. You'll leverage the relying party, identity provider, and certificate information. If the identity provider is not available (null), only the relying party and certificate will be provided.

```
    public override int GetHashCode()
    {
        return (_identityProvider == null ? ➥
_relyingParty.GetHashCode() ^ _certificate.GetHashCode() :➥
                _relyingParty.GetHashCode() ➥
^ _certificate.GetHashCode() ^ _identityProvider.GetHashCode());
    }
```

7. You will now create the constructor for the class. This will accept an array of CardSpacePolicyElement. This value is provided in the ClientCredentials class's GetInfoCardSecurityToken operation that you will work with shortly.

In the constructor, if the array is nonzero, you'll extract the information for the three values and populate the local member variables. To do this, you'll need to jump through some hoops, reading XML from the policy elements to a TextReader, passing that to a XmlTextReader, passing that to an XmlDictionaryReader, and then using that to populate an EndpointAddress object.

From there, the three variables will be assigned values. The identity provider variables will map to the issuer of the token, and the relying party will map to the host of the relying party.

Using the exact URI for the relying party would facilitate the scenario discussed in the beginning of the chapter. Specifically, you would be able to contact the same service multiple times and display the identity selector only once—even if multiple channels are used.

By instead using the host, the same functionality is enabled even when using multiple services from the same host.

The overridden Equals function will use these values to determine whether the host is the same but the requested claims differ.

8. Enter the following code:

```
public CardspacePolicyInfo(CardSpacePolicyElement[] policyElements)
{

    _requiredClaims = new List<string>();

    if (policyElements.Length > 0)
    {
        System.IO.TextReader tr = new ➡
System.IO.StringReader(policyElements[0].Target.OuterXml.ToString());
        XmlTextReader xmltr = new XmlTextReader(tr);
        XmlDictionaryReader xmldr = ➡
XmlDictionaryReader.CreateDictionaryReader(xmltr);
        EndpointAddress endpointAddress =➡
 EndpointAddress.ReadFrom(xmldr);
        _relyingParty = endpointAddress.Uri.Host;
        foreach (XmlElement xmlPolicyElement in ➡
policyElements[0].Parameters)
        {
            if (xmlPolicyElement.Name == "t:Claims")
            {
                XmlNode claimsNode = xmlPolicyElement;
                foreach (XmlNode claimNode in claimsNode.ChildNodes)
                {
_requiredClaims.Add(claimNode.Attributes["Uri"].Value);

                }
            }

        }
        X509CertificateEndpointIdentity endpointIdentity =➡
 (X509CertificateEndpointIdentity)endpointAddress.Identity;
        _certificate = endpointIdentity.Certificates[0].➡
GetCertHashString();

        if (policyElements[0].Issuer != null)
        {
            tr = new ➡
```

```
            System.IO.StringReader(policyElements[0].Issuer.OuterXml.ToString());
                    xmltr = new XmlTextReader(tr);
                  xmldr = XmlDictionaryReader.CreateDictionaryReader(xmltr);
                  endpointAddress = EndpointAddress.ReadFrom(xmldr);
                  _identityProvider = endpointAddress.Uri.ToString();
              }




          }



      }
```

This completes the `CardspacePolicyInfo` class; it's now time to create the new `ClientCredentials` class.

Creating a New ClientCredentials Class

To create a new `ClientCredentials` class, follow these steps:

1. Right-click the project, and select Add ➤ Class.

2. Name the class **CachedInformationCardClientCredentials**.

3. Add using statements to the class for System.Security.Permissions, System.ServiceModel, System.ServiceModel.Description, System.ServiceModel.Security.Tokens, System.IdentityModel.Tokens, and System.IdentityModel.Selectors:

```
using System;
using System.Collections.Generic;
using System.Text;

using System.Security.Permissions;
using System.ServiceModel;
using System.ServiceModel.Description;
using System.ServiceModel.Security.Tokens;
using System.IdentityModel.Tokens;
using System.IdentityModel.Selectors;
```

4. This class will have a static dictionary that will contain the cached tokens. This dictionary will use your newly created CardspacePolicyInfo class as the keys and store SecurityTokens as the values. Enter the following code:

```
namespace BeginningCardspace
{
    public class CachedInformationCardClientCredentials: ClientCredentials
    {
        //----------------------------------------
        //storage for the cached credentials
        //----------------------------------------
        static Dictionary<CardspacePolicyInfo, SecurityToken> ➥
_cachedInformationCardTokens;
        public Dictionary<CardspacePolicyInfo, SecurityToken> ➥
CachedInformationCardTokens
        {
            get
            {
                return _cachedInformationCardTokens;
            }
            set
            {
                _cachedInformationCardTokens = value;
            }
        }
}
```

Next you will override the GetInfoCardSecurityToken method. You'll begin by taking the CardSpacePolicyElement array passed into the method and creating a CardspacePolicyInfo object. You'll next add code to check for the existence of a token that reflects the policy for the current request. If one is found, you'll confirm that the cached token is still valid by evaluating the associated token's ValidFrom and ValidTo dates. Because the Web spans all time zones, you will also add code to convert these to the local time prior to evaluation. If the token exists and is valid, this code will return it. If it's not cached or is invalid, this code will call the base GetInfoCardSecurityToken, which will display the identity selector. In the latter case, the token returned from the base method will be placed into the cache.

5. Enter the following code:

```
        protected override SecurityToken ➥
GetInfoCardSecurityToken(bool requiresInfoCard,➥
 System.IdentityModel.Selectors.CardSpacePolicyElement[] chain,➥
 System.IdentityModel.Selectors.SecurityTokenSerializer ➥
tokenSerializer)
        {
            CardspacePolicyInfo policyInfo = new CardspacePolicyInfo(chain);
            TimeZone localTimeZone = TimeZone.CurrentTimeZone;
```

```
                if (      //Does the cache contain a token with the specified policy
info?
                     _cachedInformationCardTokens.ContainsKey(policyInfo) &&
                     //Is the token is still valid?
                     localTimeZone.ToLocalTime(➥
_cachedInformationCardTokens[policyInfo].ValidFrom) < ➥
DateTime.Now &&
                     localTimeZone.ToLocalTime(➥
_cachedInformationCardTokens[policyInfo].ValidTo) >➥
 DateTime.Now
                  )
                {

                    return CachedInformationCardTokens[policyInfo];

                }
                else
                {
                    lock (CachedInformationCardTokens)
                    {

                        SecurityToken newInformationCardToken =➥
  base.GetInfoCardSecurityToken(requiresInfoCard, chain,➥
 tokenSerializer);
CachedInformationCardTokens.Add(policyInfo,➥
 newInformationCardToken);
                        return newInformationCardToken;

                    }
                }


            }
```

6. Next, you'll create the three constructors for the class. Enter the following code:

```
        public CachedInformationCardClientCredentials()
            : base()
        {
            if (_cachedInformationCardTokens == null)
            {
                _cachedInformationCardTokens = ➥
 new Dictionary<CardspacePolicyInfo, SecurityToken>();
            }
        }
```

```
            CachedInformationCardClientCredentials(➥
CachedInformationCardClientCredentials ➥
existingCachedInformationCardClientCredentials,➥
 Dictionary<CardspacePolicyInfo, SecurityToken> ➥
cachedInformationCardTokens)
            : base(existingCachedInformationCardClientCredentials)
        {
            _cachedInformationCardTokens = cachedInformationCardTokens;
        }

            CachedInformationCardClientCredentials(➥
CachedInformationCardClientCredentials ➥
existingCachedInformationCardClientCredentials)
            : base(existingCachedInformationCardClientCredentials)
        {
        }
```

7. Next, add overrides for the CloneCore and CreateSecurityTokenManager operations to
   return CachedInformationCardClientCredentials and
   CardspaceCachedClientCredentialTokenManager objects:

```
            protected override  ClientCredentials CloneCore()
        {
            return new CachedInformationCardClientCredentials(this);
        }

        public override SecurityTokenManager CreateSecurityTokenManager()
        {
            return new ➥
CardspaceCachedClientCredentialTokenManager(➥
(CachedInformationCardClientCredentials)this.Clone());
        }



    }
}
```

Creating a New TokenManager

Next, you'll create a new ClientCredentialsSecurityTokenManager:

1. Right-click the project, and select Add ➤ Class.

2. Name the class **CardspaceCachedClientCredentialTokenManager**.

3. Add using statements to the class for System.ServiceModel and
    System.IdentityModel.Tokens:

```
using System;
using System.Collections.Generic;
using System.Text;
using System.ServiceModel;using System.IdentityModel.Tokens;
```

4. Next, you'll create the class. Here, you'll create a new
    ClientCredentialsSecurityTokenManager using
    CachedInformationCardClientCredentials:

```
namespace BeginningCardspace
{
    class CardspaceCachedClientCredentialTokenManager:CCC
  ClientCredentialsSecurityTokenManager
    {

            Dictionary<CardspacePolicyInfo, SecurityToken> ➥
_cachedInformationCardTokens;

            public ➥
CardspaceCachedClientCredentialTokenManager(➥
CachedInformationCardClientCredentials clientCredentials)
                : base(clientCredentials)
            {
                this._cachedInformationCardTokens = ➥
clientCredentials.CachedInformationCardTokens;
            }
        }


    }
```

At this point, you've created the ability to cache tokens, so what you must do next is create
a class that allows you to attach this functionality to your service(s).

Creating the Custom Behavior Configuration Handler

As mentioned earlier, WCF provides powerful extensibility mechanisms. One of those is
the ability to affect a service's behavior. In this section, you will create a custom behavior
configuration handler. This class will provide the ability to add support for
CachedInformationCardClientCredentials via the app.config file.

1. Right-click the project, and select Add ➤ Class.

2. Name the class **CachedInformationCardClientCredentialsConfigHandler**.

3. Add a using statement to the class for System.ServiceModel.Configuration.

4. Add the following code:

```
using System;
using System.Collections.Generic;
using System.Text;
using System.ServiceModel.Configuration;

namespace BeginningCardspace
{

    public class ➡
CachedInformationCardClientCredentialsConfigHandler : ➡
ClientCredentialsElement
        {

            public override Type BehaviorType
            {
                get { return typeof(CachedInformationCardClientCredentials); }
            }

            protected override object CreateBehavior()
            {
                CachedInformationCardClientCredentials➡
  cachedInformationCardClientCredentials = new ➡
CachedInformationCardClientCredentials();
base.ApplyConfiguration(cachedInformationCardClientCredentials);
                return cachedInformationCardClientCredentials;
            }
        }
    }
```

Modifying app.config on the Client

You're now ready to configure the service.

Adding the Custom Behavior Extension

Follow these steps for the custom behavior extension:

1. In the WCFClient project, open the app.config file.

2. Within the System.ServiceModel section, you'll add a BehaviorExtension that references the new CardspaceTokenCaching project created earlier in this section. Add the following code:

```
<extensions>
      <behaviorExtensions>
        <add name="CachedInformationCardClientCredentials"➡
type="BeginningCardspace.➡
CachedInformationCardClientCredentialsConfigHandler, ➡
CardspaceTokenCaching, Version=1.0.0.0, Culture=neutral, ➡
PublicKeyToken=null" />
      </behaviorExtensions>
    </extensions>
```

Adding the Actual Custom Behavior

Next, you'll add a new behavior to the configuration file. In WCF, the extensibility mode provides for four types of behaviors: service behaviors, endpoint behaviors, contract behaviors, and operation behaviors. In this case, you are applying a behavior to the endpoint.

You do this by adding a behaviors section to app.config. Here, you will include a named endpoint behavior named CachedInformationCardTokenBehavior. Within the behavior, you will include a reference for a default certificate.

So, add the following XML within the System.ServiceModel section of the app.config file:

```
<behaviors>
  <endpointBehaviors>
    <behavior name='CachedInformationCardTokenBehavior'>
      <CachedInformationCardClientCredentials>
        <serviceCertificate>
          <authentication
            trustedStoreLocation='LocalMachine'
            revocationMode='NoCheck'/>
          <defaultCertificate
            findValue='www.fabrikam.com'
            storeLocation='LocalMachine'
            storeName='My'
            x509FindType='FindBySubjectName' />
        </serviceCertificate>
      </CachedInformationCardClientCredentials>
    </behavior>
  </endpointBehaviors>
</behaviors>
```

Applying the Custom Behavior to the Endpoint

Finally, you will apply that named behavior to your endpoint. To the endpoint element for the MyAlerts service, add a behaviorConfiguration attribute, and assign it the name of the behavior you just created, CachedInformationCardTokenBehavior:

```
<endpoint  address="http://localhost:1972/Alerts/My/MyAlerts"
        binding="wsFederationHttpBinding"➡
  bindingConfiguration="AlertsCardSpace"
        behaviorConfiguration="'CachedInformationCardTokenBehavior'"
```

Testing the Solution with One Service

Before testing the solution, you'll want to make a minor addition to `MyAlertService` so that you can see that the alerts are actually updating:

1. In the Services project, open `MyAlertService.cs`.

2. Add the following bold line to include the current time within the alert:

```
Alert b = new Alert();
                b.Title = "Statement Available";
                b.AlertText = givenname + " " + surname + ➡
", we wanted to let you know that your account statement for➡
 the period ending" + DateTime.Now.ToShortDateString() + ➡
" is now available.";
                b.AlertText += "Last updated:" + DateTime.Now.ToString();
                b.AlertHTML = "<HTML><HEAD/><BODY>";
                b.AlertHTML += b.AlertText;
                b.AlertHTML += "</BODY></HTML>";
```

Run the application, and as the form load event is executed, the identity selector is displayed. After selecting a card, you will find two alerts in the My Alerts listbox. Click the Statement Available alert. It will display in the main window and include the time the alert was created on the server.

Now, click the Check Alerts button. This time, the cached token will be used, and the identity selector will not be displayed. Click Statement Available, and you'll get validation that the service has been called again, and the update date/time will be different.

Testing the Solution with Two Services: Part 1

Now that you've proved this works effectively with a single service, you'll try it with two:

1. Copy the solution to a new folder, `C:\BeginningCardspace\Chapter8\PartII`.

2. Copy the folder `WCFServiceHost`, and paste it into the root folder of the solution.

3. Rename the folder to **WCFServiceHost2**.

4. Open the `WCFServiceHost2` folder, and rename the `WCFServiceHost.csproj` project file to **WCFServiceHost2.csproj**.

5. Copy the folder `Services`, and paste it into the root folder of the solution.

6. Rename the folder to **Services2**.

7. Open the `Services2` folder, and rename the project from `Services.csproj` to **Services2.csproj**

8. Open the solution in Visual Studio.

9. Right-click the solution name, and select Add Existing Project.

10. Select the WCFServiceHost2 project, and click OK.

11. Right-click the solution name, and select Add Existing Project.

12. Select the Services2 project, and click OK.

13. In the WCFServiceHost2 project, open References in the Solution Explorer.

14. Right-click Services in the References, and select Remove.

15. Add a reference to the Services2 project.

16. Right-click the Services2 project, and select Properties.

17. Change the assembly name from Services to **Services2** in the project's properties.

18. Open the Program.cs file, modify the code to point to the service on a different port, and append the number 2, as shown here:

```
static void Main(string[] args)
    {

            ServiceHost shAlerts = new ➥
ServiceHost(typeof(Services.AlertService), new ➥
Uri("http://localhost:1974/Alerts2"));
            shAlerts.Open();
            Console.WriteLine("Alert Service Is Now Online");
            Console.WriteLine("-------------------------------------");

            ServiceHost shMyAlerts = new➥
 ServiceHost(typeof(Services.MyAlertService), new ➥
Uri("http://localhost:1974/Alerts/My2"));
            shMyAlerts.Open();


            Console.WriteLine("To Stop Service, Press Enter.");
            Console.ReadLine();
            shMyAlerts.Close();
            shAlerts.Close();
    }
```

Next, you'll add code to call the second service host.

19. In the WCFClient application, open the app.config file.

20. Copy the endpoint element for the MyAlerts service, and paste it below the original endpoint.

21. You'll next need to change the endpoint element to point toward the new service and also give it a unique name, **AlertsCardSpace2**.

22. Modify the address attribute of the endpoint to point to the new service, as shown in the following XML:

```
<endpoint  address="http://localhost:1974/Alerts/My2/MyAlerts"
                   binding="wsFederationHttpBinding"➥
    bindingConfiguration="AlertsCardSpace"
                   behaviorConfiguration="CachedTokenBehavior"
                   contract="IMyAlertsService" name="AlertsCardSpace2">
```

23. Open the AlertCenter form, and modify the form load event. Specifically, in the creation of the myAlertService client, reference the first service, AlertsCardSpace:

```
MyAlertsServiceClient myAlertService = new ➥
MyAlertsServiceClient("AlertsCardSpace");
```

24. Next, make the same change in the btnCheckAlerts_Click event code.

25. You'll now create a new button that will call the new service. Add a new button below the Check Alerts button.

26. Rename the button to **btnCheckAlerts2**, and change the text on the button to **Check Alerts 2**.

27. Double-click the button to automatically generate the button's click event.

28. Copy and paste the following code into the button's click event:

```
try
            {

                    MyAlertsServiceClient myAlertService = new ➥
        MyAlertsServiceClient("AlertsCardSpace2");

                    DataContracts.Alert[] myAlerts =
myAlertService.GetMyAlerts();
                    lbMyAlerts.Items.Clear();
                    webAlert.DocumentText = "";
                    foreach (DataContracts.Alert alert in myAlerts)
                    {
                        lbMyAlerts.Items.Add(alert);
                        lbMyAlerts.DisplayMember = "Title";

                    }
            }
            catch (UserCancellationException uce)
            {
                    System.Windows.Forms.MessageBox.Show(➥
        "User Cancelled Out of the CardSpace UI.");

            }
```

```
                    catch (UntrustedRecipientException ure)
                    { }
                    catch (ServiceNotStartedException snse)
                    { }
                    catch (CardSpaceException cse)
                    { }
                    catch (Exception e1)
                    { }
            }
```

29. Right-click the solution, and select Set Startup Projects.

30. Select WCFServiceHost2, and under the Action column, select Start.

31. Using the arrows on the right of the dialog box, move the project above the WCFClient project.

You're now ready to test the solution. Start debugging, and the form load event will make the initial call to the first service host. This will trigger the identity selector and cache the token.

Click the Check Alerts button, and this same service will be called. Because the CardSpacePolicyInfo class matches the cached token, the cached token will be used.

Click the Check Alerts 2 button, and the second service/service host will be called. Again, because the policy for the requested service matches the CardSpacePolicyInfo values, no identity selector is displayed, and the cached token is used.

Testing the Solution with Two Services: Part 2

Even with organizations that share multiple services, some of those services may have different claims requests as part of their policies.

If the code had just matched on the issuer, relying party, and certificate, a token could appear to be a match but not include all of the claims. By including the RequiredClaims property in your CardspacePolicyInfo class, you'll ensure you send only those tokens that contain all the claims required.

To test this, you will modify the implementation of MyAlertsService used in ServiceHost2 and change the requested claims for that service to an email address and private personal identifier.

1. Begin by opening the MyAlertService.cs file in the Services2 project. Modify the GetMyAlerts operation to resemble the following code. You'll see that this implementation uses only the email address:

```
            public List<Alert> GetMyAlerts()
            {

                bool foundEmail = false;
                string email ="";
```

```
                    AuthorizationContext ctx = ➡
        OperationContext.Current.ServiceSecurityContext.AuthorizationContext;


                foreach (ClaimSet claimSet in ctx.ClaimSets)
                  {


                    foreach (Claim claim in claimSet)
                      {


                            if (claim.ClaimType == ClaimTypes.Email)
                            {
                                email = claim.Resource.ToString();


                            }


                      }

                  }

                    List<Alert> la = new List<Alert>();

                    Alert a = new Alert();
                    a.Title = "Confirm Email";
                    a.AlertText = "We have been unable to➡
        reach you at the email address you provided,<b>";
                    a.AlertText += email + ➡
        ".  Please contact us and provide a valid email address.";
                    a.AlertHTML = "<HTML><HEAD/><BODY>";
                    a.AlertHTML += a.AlertText;
                    a.AlertHTML += "</BODY></HTML>";



                    la.Add(a);

                    return la;



            }
```

2. In the ServiceHost2 project, open app.config.

3. Change `ClaimRequirements` for `CardSpaceAlertBinding` to the following:

```
<claimTypeRequirements>
    <add claimType=➡
"http://schemas.xmlsoap.org/ws/2005/05/identity/claims/email"/>➡
    <add claimType=➡
"http://schemas.xmlsoap.org/ws/2005/05/identity/claims/➡
privatepersonalidentifier"/>
</claimTypeRequirements>
```

4. In the WCFClient project, open `app.config`.

5. Change `ClaimRequirements` for the `AlertsCardpace2` binding to the following:

```
<claimTypeRequirements>
            <add claimType=➡
"http://schemas.xmlsoap.org/ws/2005/05/identity/claims/emailaddress"
            isOptional="false" />
            <add claimType=➡
"http://schemas.xmlsoap.org/ws/2005/05/identity/claims/➡
privatepersonalidentifier"/>
            </claimTypeRequirements>
            <issuer address=➡
"http://schemas.xmlsoap.org/ws/2005/05/identity/issuer/self" />
```

You are now ready to test the solution with two separate services on the same service host that utilize different claims.

Start debugging the project, and the identity selector will be displayed as it prepares to contact the first service. Once the application is running, click the Check Alerts button. The service will be called a second time, and the cached token will be used.

Next click the Check Alerts 2 button. This will trigger a call to the second service. Because this service is on the same host but requires different claims, the identity selector will be displayed. At this point, tokens for both services have been cached; you can now click either of these buttons, and the cached buttons will be used.

Summary

In this chapter, you saw the native functionality of CardSpace with WCF when dealing with tokens. Whether calling the same information card–secured service multiple times or calling multiple information card–secured services, the out-of-the-box functionality is to display the identity selector each time.

You saw how to modify this functionality by using WCF custom behaviors and by adding a behavior that caches tokens. Through the use of these custom behaviors, you can cache tokens across calls and across services from the same host.

CHAPTER 9

■ ■ ■

Using CardSpace with RSS and OPML

In the past five years, self-publishing on the web—including blog postings, podcasts, and videos—has exploded. Whether it's hosting a personal blog or posting video to a site such as YouTube, the creation and sharing of content is changing the content communication landscape. This was so prevalent in 2006 that *Time* magazine named You—as in you, the self-publisher—as Man of the Year.

Really Simple Syndication (RSS) and Outline Processor Markup Language (OPML) are two XML-based formats that help facilitate the sharing of content, and they have been large contributors to the content sharing and distribution explosion that has occurred. Another format, Atom, has also received a fair amount of attention, most notably from Google. Atom, like RSS and OPML, consists of structured XML documents that are consumed by either services, websites, or client applications referred to as *aggregators*.

Today, most of these feeds are free. They are static or dynamically created XML documents available on the public Web or on an intranet to be readily consumed. I'd argue that for content syndication to go to the next level, there needs to be a monetization model for content. There should be a way—just as we have in traditional media—to allow content publishers to sell their content in various forms.

Today, RSS is made profitable via advertising. Although this is one model, interesting opportunities exist to better monetize content.

Think of how syndication works in television. The television show *Law & Order* is produced by a production company, and the first-run rights for the shows are currently with the NBC network in the United States. Here, the content is presented on a marquis network/site, and advertising commands a premium price. That same show may later be rebroadcast on sister networks within NBC's parent company, NBC Universal. Those channels will have their own branding and have different advertising rates. Eventually, the show is available for purchase for use in other channels/markets. For example, the television show *Friends* is on five days a week on multiple networks as part of some syndication deal. Payments from these syndication deals are made to the production company, writers, and actors. In fact, Jerry Seinfeld, star and cocreator of the hit U.S. television program bearing his last name, is estimated to have made $225 million for that show's syndication rights.

Traditional syndication should be augmented with the current on-demand option that you can find in cable systems and online services such as Zune and iTunes.

The good news is that information cards and Windows CardSpace can help facilitate this scenario. From a subscription perspective, managed cards could be issued that could identify the subscription type and expiration date.

When you begin looking at the possibilities, you'll see you can monetize your content in multiple ways. One example is that you could have standard subscriptions based on duration (that is, three months or six months). You could also create interesting scenarios where subscriptions could be sold in silver, gold, and platinum. In this scenario, platinum cards could access new content on Monday, gold on Tuesday, and silver on Wednesday.

This chapter steps you through creating a RSS service and an RSS client, with the service leveraging information stored in information cards. The resulting solution will be a working example that can be implemented in real-world situations to offer subscription-based content.

Introducing the Formats

Today, there are several predominant formats for content syndication—RSS, OPML, and Atom. The following sections review examples of each format.

RSS

Listing 9-1 is an example of an RSS feed provided by Microsoft. This feed consists of the top-ten downloads on Microsoft's site at http://msdn.microsoft.com.

The first thing to note about the file is that just as in other mediums, such as television, content is provided in the context of a *channel*. Channels have titles, descriptions, and a URL that links to the website associated with the channel. Channels can also be tagged with categories, such as CardSpace, Web Services, Technology, and so on. The RSS specification identifies 20 potential subelements that can be contained within a channel; Table 9-1 lists them.

Listing 9-1. *An RSS Feed from Microsoft's Developer Network*

```
<?xml version="1.0" encoding="utf-8"?>
<rss version="2.0" xmlns:dc="http://purl.org/dc/elements/1.1/"
xmlns:xhtml="http://www.w3.org/1999/xhtml">
  <channel>
    <copyright>Copyright Microsoft Corporation 2004</copyright>
    <description>Microsoft downloads center</description>
    <link>http://www.microsoft.com/downloads</link>
    <title>Top 10 Downloads</title>
    <item>
      <title>.NET Framework Version 2.0 Redistributable Package (x86)</title>
      <link>http://www.microsoft.com/downloads/details.aspx?➥
FamilyID=0856EACB-4362-4B0D-8EDD-AAB15C5E04F5&amp;displaylang=en➥
    </link>
    </item>
    <item>
      <title>.NET Framework Version 1.1 Redistributable Package</title>
      <link>http://www.microsoft.com/downloads/details.aspx?➥
```

```
FamilyID=262D25E3-F589-4842-8157-034D1E7CF3A3&amp;displaylang=en    </link>
    </item>
    <item>
      <title>Microsoft .NET Framework 3.0 Redistributable Package</title>
      <link>http://www.microsoft.com/downloads/details.aspx?➥
FamilyID=10CC340B-F857-4A14-83F5-25634C3BF043&amp;displaylang=en    </link>
    </item>
    <item>
      <title>.NET Framework 1.1 Service Pack 1</title>
      <link>http://www.microsoft.com/downloads/details.aspx?➥
FamilyID=A8F5654F-088E-40B2-BBDB-A83353618B38&amp;displaylang=en    </link>
    </item>
    <item>
      <title>DirectX SDK - (October 2006)</title>
      <link>http://www.microsoft.com/downloads/details.aspx?➥
FamilyID=D625324C-59B4-4951-849E-640B508DC442&amp;displaylang=en    </link>
    </item>
    <item>
      <title>XML Notepad 2007</title>
      <link>http://www.microsoft.com/downloads/details.aspx?➥
FamilyID=72D6AA49-787D-4118-BA5F-4F30FE913628&amp;displaylang=en    </link>
    </item>
    <item>
      <title>Platform Software Development Kit ➥
Redistributable: Microsoft Layer for Unicode on ➥
Windows 95, 98, and Me Systems, 1.1.3790.0</title>
      <link>http://www.microsoft.com/downloads/details.aspx?➥
FamilyID=73BA7BD7-ED06-4F0D-80A4-2A7EEAEE17E2&amp;➥
displaylang=en    </link>
    </item>
    <item>
      <title>Windows Media Encoder 9 Series</title>
      <link>http://www.microsoft.com/downloads/details.aspx?➥
FamilyID=5691BA02-E496-465A-BBA9-B2F1182CDF24&amp;➥
displaylang=en    </link>
    </item>
    <item>
      <title>DirectX April 2006 Redistributable for Software Developers</title>
      <link>http://www.microsoft.com/downloads/details.aspx?➥
FamilyID=FB73D860-5AF1-45E5-BAC0-9BC7A5254203&amp;➥
displaylang=en    </link>
    </item>
    <item>
      <title>Microsoft XNA Game Studio Express 1.0</title>
      <link>http://www.microsoft.com/downloads/details.aspx?➥
```

```
FamilyID=A73A7E71-FF41-432D-A0EB-043E904A1905&amp; ➡
displaylang=en    </link>
    </item>
  </channel>
</rss>
```

Table 9-1. *The Subelements of an RSS Channel*

Subelement	Description
title	This is the name of the channel. This element is required.
link	This is the URL of the website for this channel. This element is required.
description	This is the description of the channel. This element is required.
category	A channel can be associated with categories that describe it. Categories are sometimes referred to as *tags*.
cloud	This allows consuming applications to register with a cloud for notifications. The intent here is a simple publish/subscribe system, where the consuming application is proactively notified of changes versus having to poll repeatedly.
copyright	This is the copyright notice for the channel.
docs	This is a URL that points to the documentation for the RSS format. Typically, this will point to http://www.rssboard.org/rss-specification.
generator	This is the text that identifies the program that generated the feed.
image	This is the URL for an image that represents the channel. The image should be in GIF, JPEG, or PNG format.
item	Channels can contain one or more items. Items are discussed in more detail later in this section.
language	This is the language in which the channel is written.
lastBuildDate	This is the date the channel was last changed.
managingEditor	This is the email address for the person responsible for the editorial content.
pubDate	This is the date that the channel was published.
rating	This is the Platform for Internet Content Selection (PICS) rating for this channel.
skipDays	This identifies the days that a feed is not updated. For example, if the channel contained content that was not published on weekends, the content for this element would be as follows: `<day>Saturday</day><day>Sunday</day>`
skipHours	This identifies the hours that a feed is not updated. For example, if the channel contained content that was published only after 6 a.m., the field would contain the following: `<hour>0</hour><hour>1</hour><hour>2</hour>` `<hour>3</hour><hour>4</hour><hour>5</hour>`
textInput	According to the RSS advisory board, the textInput element's purpose is a mystery. In fact, I've never seen this field used. If it is used, it must contain four subelements: title, description, name, and link.

Table 9-1. *The Subelements of an RSS Channel*

Subelement	Description
ttl	This is the time to live, which indicates the duration—in minutes—that the channel can be cached.
webmaster	This is the email address for the individual responsible for handling technical issues with the channel.

Within the channel, you'll find *items*, which are connected to one or more pieces of content.

Like channels, items have titles, descriptions, and a link URL for that item. The description and link fields are interesting, because different types of software handle them differently. In blog software, which is the most common RSS exporter, certain software packages will contain the HTML for the complete item; other packages will contain only an abstract in the description field, and the link element will contain a URL pointer to where the full item can be found. Table 9-2 provides a complete list of the subelements of an RSS item.

Table 9-2. *The Subelements of an RSS Item*

Subelement	Description
title	This is the name of the item. This element is required.
link	This is the URL for the item.
description	This is the description of the channel. This element is required.
category	A channel can be associated with categories that describe it. Categories are sometimes referred to as *tags*.
comments	This is the URL for a page where comments on this item can be made.
enclosure	This is a reference to media that is attached to the item. This is often used to reference things such as podcasts, video files, and so on.
guid	This is a global unique identifier (GUID) for this item.
pubDate	This is the date that this item was published.
source	This is the RSS channel from which this item came.

In my experience, the rationale for exposing only the abstracts is usually an issue of monetization. The content creator generates revenue via advertisements. By placing all the content in the XML, they are not receiving ad revenue. By forcing the reader to go to the content creator's site for the full item, the creator can then get the revenue.

Ideally, by using information cards, this issue could be bypassed, and the content could be displayed in the consumer's reader of choice.

RSS items also can contain enclosures. Enclosures are used to associate media with an item, such as an MP3 audio file for podcasts or a WMV videos for video blogs.

Listing 9-1 shows an example of an RSS file. This instance is from the Microsoft Developer Network (MSDN) and contains the channel called Top 10 Downloads. That channel contains items that point to the topmost downloaded items in December 2006.

OPML

OPML.org defines OPML as "an XML-based format that allows exchange of outline-structured information between applications running on different operating systems and environments." OPML effectively provides you with a mechanism by which to provide a hierarchical structure and have URLs associated with the items in the outlines. OPML has become popular for sharing lists of RSS channels in a structured way.

Like an HTML page, an OPML document is broken into two high-level sections: the <head> and the <body>. The specification has defined several elements for the head that contain metadata about the list, such as the title, date created, and owner name. The specification also identifies other elements that are tied to the user interface, such as the window position.

Within the body, you can define outline elements that reflect the items in your list. Outlines can be organized in a straight list or with hierarchies that go multiple levels deep.

One thing to note is that OPML does not use subelements to define an outline but instead each outline uses attributes. Table 9-3 lists the potential attributes.

Table 9-3. *Attributes of an Outline Element in OPML*

Attribute	Definition
text	The text to be used when displaying this outline item
count	The number of items contained within this outline item
xmlUrl	The URL that points to the location of this item
createdDate	The date that this outline item was created
type	The type of file, which provides information about how to interpret the OPML
version	The version of this OPML definition
description	A description of this outline item
imageUrl	The URL that points to an image for this item

The following XML represents an OPML *blog roll,* which is a simple list of RSS feeds. In this case, the OPML file contains a listing of two different feeds. One is for my blog, called Living in a World of Connected Systems, and the other is for Kim Cameron's Identity Blog. The name of the blog is associated with the outline via the text attribute. The link to the RSS feed for the blog is defined within the xmlUrl attribute.

```xml
<?xml version="1.0" encoding="ISO-8859-1"?>
<opml version="1.1">
    <head>
        <title>Blog Roll</title>
        <dateCreated>Sun, 10 Dec 2006 11:00:00 GMT</dateCreated>
        <dateModified>Sun, 10 Dec 2006 11:00:00 GMT</dateModified>
        <ownerName>Marc Mercuri</ownerName>
        <ownerEmail>mmercuri@microsoft.com</ownerEmail>
        <expansionState></expansionState>
        <vertScrollState>1</vertScrollState>
        <windowTop>0</windowTop>
        <windowLeft>0</windowLeft>
        <windowBottom>0</windowBottom>
        <windowRight>0</windowRight>
        </head>
    <body>
        <outline text="Living in a World of Connected Systems" count="50"
xmlUrl="http://www.marcmercuri.com/SyndicationService.asmx/GetRss"/>
        <outline text="Identity Blog" count="50"
xmlUrl="http://www.identityblog.com/?feed=rss2"/>
            </body>
    </opml>
```

Atom

Back in the days when videocassette recorders were entering the scene, there was a famous battle between two formats, namely, VHS and Betamax. Even though Betamax provided higher quality, VHS won out in the end.

The lesson learned? Being the best doesn't mean you win the hearts and minds of the masses. My stance on RSS and OPML is that there are problems with the specification (or what is referred to as a specification) and that there are some areas that were clearly not well thought out (such as specifying formats for date times, and so on).

Atom, in my opinion, is arguably a better-thought-out implementation for publishing data in a structured way. Unfortunately, it's Betamax. Nearly everyone uses RSS, with Google being the best-known exception to the rule.

Whether distributing films on cassette in the 1980s or distributing them via video blogs in the 21st century, as a content distributor you'll most likely use the format more people know how to read, so at the time of this writing RSS is the way to go.

The following XML is an example of an Atom file. You'll note that although some terms have been changed—for example, an RSS *item* is an Atom *entry*—the type of content being collected is very much the same in both formats.

```
<?xml version="1.0" encoding="utf-8"?>
<feed xmlns="http://www.w3.org/2005/Atom">
<title>Example Feed</title>
<subtitle>A subtitle.</subtitle>
<link href="http://example.org/"/>
<updated>2003-12-13T18:30:02Z</updated>
<author>
    <name>John Doe</name>
    <email>johndoe@example.com</email>
</author>
<id>urn:uuid:60a76c80-d399-11d9-b91C-0003939e0af6</id>
<entry>
    <title>Atom-Powered Robots Run Amok</title>
    <link href="http://example.org/2003/12/13/atom03"/>
    <id>urn:uuid:1225c695-cfb8-4ebb-aaaa-80da344efa6a</id>
    <updated>2003-12-13T18:30:02Z</updated>
    <summary>Some text.</summary>
</entry>
</feed>
```

Now that you have a baseline understanding of what RSS, OPML, and Atom are, it's time to build an RSS service and an RSS client.

Building the RSS Service

You'll begin by creating the RSS service.

Getting the Data Contracts

For this exercise, you'll need two basic .NET assemblies for consuming RSS and OPML. You can download them with the source of this book from Apress or via my blog at http://www.marcmercuri.com/downloads/cardspacechapter9.zip.

Download and extract the files to C:\BeginningCardspace\Chapter9\Part1.

Creating the Service Contracts

With the data contracts defined, you can now define the service contracts. Place these service contracts in a new project titled ServiceContracts:

1. Right-click the solution, and select Add New Project.

2. Select Class Library, and name the library **ServiceContracts**.

3. Right-click the project, and select Add Reference.

4. On the Browse tab, navigate to RSS.DLL, and click OK.

5. Right-click the project, and select Add Reference.

6. On the Browse tab, navigate to OPML.DLL, and click OK.

7. Right-click the project, and select Add Reference.

8. On the .NET tab, select System.ServiceModel, and click OK.

IOPMLService

First, you will create the service contract for a service that will serve up OPML:

1. Rename Class1.cs to **IOPMLService**.

2. This service will expose a single-operation GetOPML that returns an OPML object. Populate the class with the following code:

```
using System;
using System.Collections.Generic;
using System.Text;
using System.ServiceModel;
using Rss;

namespace ServiceContracts
{
    [ServiceContract]
    public interface IOPMLService
    {
        [OperationContract]
        Rss.OPML GetOPML();
    }
}
```

IRSSService

Next, you will create a service contract for a service that will serve up RSS to the requester:

1. Right-click the ServiceContracts project, and select Add New Item.

2. Specify Class, and name the class **IRSSService**.

3. Modify the contents of the file such that it resembles the following code:

```
using System;
using System.Collections.Generic;
using System.Text;
using Rss;
using System.ServiceModel;

namespace ServiceContracts
{
    [ServiceContract]
    public interface IRSSService
```

```
    {
        [OperationContract]
        Rss.RssFeed GetFeed();
    }
}
```

Creating the Services

Now that you have the service contracts defined, you can implement the services themselves:

1. Right-click the solution, and select Add New Project.

2. Select Class Library, and name the library **Services**.

3. Right-click the project, and select Add Reference.

4. On the Browse tab, navigate to RSS.DLL, and click OK.

5. Right-click the project, and select Add Reference.

6. On the Browse tab, navigate to OPML.DLL, and click OK.

7. Right-click the project, and select Add Reference.

8. On the .NET tab, select System.ServiceModel, System.IdentityModel, and System. IdentityModel.Selectors, and click OK.

OPMLService

First up is the OPML service. Three things need to happen—you implement the interface defined in the service contract, you investigate the incoming claims from the card used to access the site, and an OPML file is read in from a file and returned to the user.

In this test service, the OPML is being read from an XML file. In a more complex system, this feed could utilize the incoming claims from the information card and dynamically generate a list of services for the consumer.

1. Rename `Class1.cs` to **OPMLService**.

2. Open the file, and enter the following code:

```
using System;
using System.Collections.Generic;
using System.Text;
using ServiceContracts;
using System.ServiceModel;
using Rss;
using System.IdentityModel.Claims;
using System.IdentityModel.Policy;
namespace Services
{
```

```csharp
    public class OPMLService : IOPMLService
    {
        #region IOPMLService Members

        public OPML GetOPML()
        {
            string locality = "";
            string country = "";
            string givenname = "";
            string surname = "";
            AuthorizationContext ctx =
OperationContext.Current.ServiceSecurityContext.AuthorizationContext;


            foreach (ClaimSet claimSet in ctx.ClaimSets)
            {
                foreach (Claim claim in claimSet)
                {

                    if (claim.ClaimType == ClaimTypes.Locality)
                    { locality = claim.Resource.ToString(); }
                    if (claim.ClaimType == ClaimTypes.Country)
                    { country = claim.Resource.ToString(); }
                    if (claim.ClaimType == ClaimTypes.GivenName)
                    { givenname = claim.Resource.ToString(); }
                    if (claim.ClaimType == ClaimTypes.Surname)
                    { surname = claim.Resource.ToString(); }

                }

            }

            Rss.OPML opml = new OPML(➥
    @"C:\BeginningCardspace\Chapter9\PartI\test.opml");
            return opml;
        }

        #endregion
    }
}
```

RSSService

Next up is the RSS service. For the sake of testing, this service is consuming my publicly exposed blog, Living in a World of Connected Systems, and delivering it through its own information card–secured interface.

In a production system, you would use the claims information passed in with the call and provide access to a nonpublic RSS feed. That feed could be static or could be created dynamically from a database utilizing the joining of data from an information card's claims with data stored in the services database. An example might be the following—if I access a LocalNews feed and my state information is requested from my information card, the service could provide me with an aggregation of news stories pertaining to Washington state.

To create the service, perform the following steps:

1. Right-click the Services project, and select Add New Item.

2. Specify Class, and name the class **RSSService**.

3. Modify the contents of the file so it resembles the following code:

```
using System;
using System.Collections.Generic;
using System.Text;
using ServiceContracts;
using Rss;
using System.ServiceModel;
using System.IdentityModel.Claims;
using System.IdentityModel.Policy;
namespace Services
{

    public class RSSService : IRSSService
    {

        #region IRSSService Members

        public Rss.RssFeed GetFeed()
        {
            string locality = "";
            string country = "";
            string givenname = "";
            string surname = "";
            AuthorizationContext ctx =➡
    OperationContext.Current.➡
ServiceSecurityContext.AuthorizationContext;


            foreach (ClaimSet claimSet in ctx.ClaimSets)
            {
                foreach (Claim claim in claimSet)
                {
```

```
                    if (claim.ClaimType == ClaimTypes.Locality)
                    { locality = claim.Resource.ToString(); }
                    if (claim.ClaimType == ClaimTypes.Country)
                    { country = claim.Resource.ToString(); }
                    if (claim.ClaimType == ClaimTypes.GivenName)
                    { givenname = claim.Resource.ToString(); }
                    if (claim.ClaimType == ClaimTypes.Surname)
                    { surname = claim.Resource.ToString(); }

                }

            }



            string feedUri = ➡
    "http://www.marcmercuri.com/SyndicationService.asmx/GetRss";
            Rss.RssFeed feed = new RssFeed(new Uri(feedUri));

            return feed;
        }

        #endregion
    }
}
```

Note As with OPMLService, you can see that you interrogate the incoming claims on the information card.

Creating the Service Host

For the services to be accessible by the client, they'll need to be hosted. For this example, you'll self-host the services inside a console application. In the service host projects, a service host is created for both the OPML and RSS services. The services are hosted at the addresses `http://localhost:1972/BeginningCardspace/OPML` and `http://localhost:1972/BeginningCardspace/`, respectively.

Note The console application is the easiest to build and debug. It does not, however, have all the built-in scalability benefits of more robust hosts. For production use, you would want to investigate hosting these types of services in IIS or a Windows service.

---

1. Right-click the solution, and select Add New Project.

2. Select Console Application, and name the project **ServiceHost**.

3. Right-click the project, and select Add Reference.

4. On the Browse tab, navigate to RSS.DLL, and click OK.

5. Right-click the project, and select Add Reference.

6. On the Browse tab, navigate to OPML.DLL, and click OK.

7. Right-click the project, and select Add Reference.

8. On the .NET tab, select System.ServiceModel, and click OK.

9. Open `Program.cs`, and modify the file such that it contains the following code:

```
using System;
using System.Collections.Generic;
using System.Text;
using System.ServiceModel;
using Services;
using ServiceContracts;
using Rss;

namespace CardSpaceRSS
{
    class Program
    {
        static void Main(string[] args)
        {

            ServiceHost shOPML = new ➡
ServiceHost(typeof(Services.OPMLService),➡
 new Uri("http://localhost:1972/BeginningCardspace/OPML"));
            shOPML.Open();
            Console.WriteLine("OPML Service Is Now Online");
            Console.WriteLine("--------------------------------------");


            ServiceHost shRSS = new ServiceHost(typeof(Services.RSSService),➡
 new Uri("http://localhost:1972/BeginningCardspace"));
            shRSS.Open();
            Console.WriteLine("RSS Service Is Now Online");
            Console.WriteLine("--------------------------------------");
```

```
        Console.WriteLine("To Stop Service, Press Enter.");
        Console.ReadLine();
        shRSS.Close();
        shOPML.Close();

    }


    }
}
```

Populating the Configuration File

For the services to be hosted, you must also configure them in the application's configuration file. If the configuration information looks familiar, it mirrors the configuration entered earlier in the book when exploring how to use WCF with information cards and CardSpace. For more details, refer to Chapter 7.

1. Right-click the project, and select New Item.

2. Select Application Configuration File, and accept the default name (app.config).

3. Click OK.

4. Open app.config, and enter the following XML:

```
<?xml version="1.0" encoding="utf-8" ?>
<configuration>

  <system.serviceModel>
    <services>

      <service behaviorConfiguration=➥
"RSSServiceBehavior" name="Services.RSSService">
        <endpoint address="GetRSS" binding="wsFederationHttpBinding"
         bindingConfiguration="CardSpaceRSSBinding" name="RSSCardSpace"
         contract="ServiceContracts.IRSSService">

          <identity>
            <certificateReference
                        storeName="My"
                        storeLocation="LocalMachine"
                        x509FindType="FindBySubjectName"
                        findValue="www.fabrikam.com"
            />
          </identity>
        </endpoint>
        <endpoint address="mex" binding="mexHttpBinding" ➥
```

```
        contract="IMetadataExchange" />
          </service>
          <service behaviorConfiguration="RSSServiceBehavior" ➡
  name="Services.OPMLService">
            <endpoint address="GetOPML" binding="wsFederationHttpBinding"
              bindingConfiguration="CardSpaceRSSBinding" name="RSSCardSpace"
              contract="ServiceContracts.IOPMLService">

              <identity>
                <certificateReference
                              storeName="My"
                              storeLocation="LocalMachine"
                              x509FindType="FindBySubjectName"
                              findValue="www.fabrikam.com"
                 />
              </identity>
            </endpoint>
            <endpoint address="mex" binding="mexHttpBinding"➡
    contract="IMetadataExchange" />
          </service>
        </services>
        <bindings>

          <wsFederationHttpBinding>
            <binding name="CardSpaceRSSBinding" closeTimeout="10:00"➡
  sendTimeout="10:00" receiveTimeout="10:00">

              <security mode="Message">
                <message algorithmSuite="Basic128"
                               issuedTokenType=➡
  "urn:oasis:names:tc:SAML:1.0:assertion"
                                        ➡
  issuedKeyType="SymmetricKey"
                 >
                  <issuer
                                address="http://schemas.xmlsoap.org/ws/2005/05/➡
  identity/issuer/self"
                 />

                  <claimTypeRequirements>
                    <add claimType="http://schemas.xmlsoap.org/ws/2005/05/➡
  identity/claims/givenname"/>
                      <add claimType="http://schemas.xmlsoap.org/ws/2005/05/➡
  identity/claims/surname"/>
                      <add claimType="http://schemas.xmlsoap.org/ws/2005/05/➡
```

```
identity/claims/locality"/>
                <add claimType="http://schemas.xmlsoap.org/ws/2005/05/➥
identity/claims/country"/>
                <add
claimType="http://schemas.xmlsoap.org/ws/2005/05/➥
identity/claims/privatepersonalidentifier"/>
            </claimTypeRequirements>

          </message>
        </security>
      </binding>
    </wsFederationHttpBinding>
  </bindings>
  <behaviors>
    <serviceBehaviors>

      <behavior name="RSSServiceBehavior" >
        <serviceMetadata httpGetEnabled="true"  />
        <serviceDebug httpHelpPageEnabled="true"➥
 includeExceptionDetailInFaults="true"/>

        <serviceCredentials>
          <issuedTokenAuthentication allowUntrustedRsaIssuers="true"/>
          <serviceCertificate
                          findValue="www.fabrikam.com"
                          storeLocation="LocalMachine"
                          storeName="My"
                          x509FindType="FindBySubjectName"/>
        </serviceCredentials>

      </behavior>

    </serviceBehaviors>

  </behaviors>
 </system.serviceModel>
</configuration>
```

▌Note This configuration file specifies that the service will return metadata via HTTP, and it will also include exception detail in faults. For product use, you'll want to definitely turn off the latter (and potentially both of these settings).

Building the RSS Reader

The services should now be ready to be served, so it's time to create a client that can consume them:

1. Right-click the solution, and select Add New Project.

2. Select Console Application, and name the project **RssClient**.

3. Right-click the project, and select Add Reference.

4. On the Browse tab, navigate to RSS.DLL, and click OK.

5. Right-click the project, and select Add Reference.

6. On the Browse tab, navigate to OPML.DLL, and click OK.

7. Right-click the project, and select Add Reference.

8. On the .NET tab, select System.ServiceModel and System.Runtime.Serialization, and click OK.

Creating Proxies for Your Services

Now create proxies for your services:

1. Start the ServiceHost project.

2. Select Files ➤ Visual Studio 2005 ➤ Visual Studio 2005 Command Prompt.

3. Navigate to C:\BeginningCardspace\ChapterI\RssClient.

4. Type **svcutil.exe http://localhost:1972/BeginningCardspace/OPML**. This will create an output.config file and an OPMLService.cs file.

5. Rename output.config to **app.config**.

6. Type **svcutil.exe http://localhost:1972/BeginningCardspace/**. This will create an output.config file and an RSService.cs file.

7. Within Visual Studio, right-click the RSSClient project, and select Add Existing Item.

8. Select OPMLService.cs, RSSService.cs, and app.config.

Modifying the Configuration

You need to modify the configuration file in three key places—you'll need to make a reference to the RSSService service, you'll need to modify the maximum message size, and you'll need to increase the reader maximum string size.

Adding RSSService

Because the bindings and behaviors for this service are the same as the OPML service, it's straightforward to add support for the RSS service to the configuration file:

1. Open app.config, and select the sole endpoint element listed.

2. Copy and paste the endpoint element within the client element.

3. Change the address on the endpoint to point to http://localhost:1972/ BeginningCardspace/GetRSS.

4. Change the contract on the endpoint to IRSSService. Your endpoint entry should match the one shown here:

```
        <endpoint ➥
address="http://localhost:1972/BeginningCardspace/GetRSS"
            binding="wsFederationHttpBinding" ➥
bindingConfiguration="RSSCardSpace"
            contract="IRSSService" name="RSSCardSpace" >

        <identity>
            <certificate encodedValue=➥
" AwAAAAEAAAAUAAAA1H3mV/pJAlVZAst/DtOrqbBd67ggAAAAAQAA➥
AEgGAAAwggZEMIIFLKADAgECAgooKOI4AAAAAAAvMAOGCSqGSIb3DQ➥
EBBQUAMG4xEzARBgoJkiaJk/IsZAEZFgNjb20xGTAXBgoJkiaJk/IsZAEZFg➥
ltaWNyb3NvZnQxFDASBgoJkiaJk/IsZAEZFgRjb3JwMRUwEwYKCZImiZPyLGQB➥
GRYFbnRkZXYxDzANBgNVBAMTBkFkYXR1bTAeFwOwNjA1MTkyMzQyMzNaFw➥
OxMTAzMTAxODI3NTZaMGIxCzAJBgNVBAYTAlVTMRMwEQYDVQQIEwpXYXN➥
oaW5ndG9uMRAwDgYDVQQHEwdSZWRtb25kMREwDwYDVQQKEwhGYWJya➥
WthbTEZMBcGA1UEAxMQd3d3LmZhYnJpa2FtLmNvbTCCASIwDQYJKoZIhvcN➥
AQEBBQADggEPADCCAQoCggEBAMACp5TXWiJ711p87W5r15bwnecarGdh4nn➥
MTVj+WOhaUCIiRKev5OfBRyrjeJfEy4gv9B1ME6pJJguIlfk7RMyx5Titica5J/aBWW➥
21BxaDqO5r9T+wZffsnxvqYcwWw6yG6/oG3sDk+Trv2/mpE8SNJVgEcqlD7hvWIP➥
a3opjk8AMD8gmoOk3Hw6gHt8xmnAEsb57gOzLmHAo8+iLfs+uOi8efBnfgLrkO/rAae➥
t74fSUS56bXmGyNvU5FF6rELEGOLkWfH/LK82EmlToakCocEOmQmFCkNpQhQH➥
yepwKndFOAmjVJ57M5jHOEewOEpkIuKPJMRJwn/gtxW8MWhBMCAwEAAaOCAu4➥
wggLqMA4GA1UdDwEB/wQEAwIE8DBEBgkqhkiG9w0BCQ8ENzA1MA4GCCqGSIb➥
3DQMCAgIAgDAOBggqhkiG9wODBAICAIAwBwYFKw4DAgcwCgYIKoZIhvcNAwcwH➥
QYDVROOBBYEFJfyWkB2bCNfu9uY6UHUlXjBLCTEMBMGA1UdJQQMMAoGCCsGA➥
QUFBwMBMB8GA1UdIwQYMBaAFOyhvEbGfwt7MxHOkdVD6eGG/la6MDkGA1UdHw➥
QyMDAwLqAsoCqGKGhOdHA6Ly93d3cuYWRhdHVtLmNvbS9jcmxkYXRhL2FkYXR1b➥
S5jcmwwggEKBggrBgEFBQcBAQSB/TCB+jB6BggrBgEFBQcwAoZuaHR0cDovL3Rob2➥
4tdGVzdDEtMjAwMy5udGR1di5jb3JwLm1pY3Jvc29mdC5jb20vQ2VydEVucm9sbC90a0aC➥
9uLXRlc3QxLTIwMDMubnRkZXYuY29ycC5taWNyb3NvZnQuY29tX0FkYXR1bS5jcnQwf➥
AYIKwYBBQUHMAKGcGZpbGU6Ly9cXRob24tdGVzdDEtMjAwMy5udGRldi5jb3JwLm➥
1pY3Jvc29mdC5jb21cQ2VydEVucm9sbFx0aG9uLXRlc3QxLTIwMDMubnRkZXYuY29yc➥
C5taWNyb3NvZnQuY29tX0FkYXR1bS5jcnQwgdoGCCsGAQUFBwEMBIHNMIHKoWGg➥
XzBdMFswWRYJaW1hZ2UvZ2lmMCEwHzAHBgUrDgMCGgQUBO3hqsI4zqGA3bRTvpS➥
U6LEiObwwKRYnaHR0cDovL3d3dy5hZGF0dW0uY29tL2ltYWdlcy9hZGF0dW0uZ2lmmom➥
WgYzBhMF8wXRYJaW1hZ2UvZ2lmMCEwHzAHBgUrDgMCGgQU8+uAcGo7FFJINSou➥
wXzviKfnVGswLRYraHR0cDovL3d3dy5mYWJyaWthbS5jb20vaW1hZ2VzL2ZhYnJpa2Ft➥
LmdpZjAXBgNVHSAEEDAOMAwGCisGAQQBgjc8ZAEwDQYJKoZIhvcNAQEFBQADgg➥
EBAEzYsXIBjTGbbuHIUbv+/7KFEWzSf3u23koOBlvzIHU6iXD64mdhrXr1G9qU39tE6fKx➥
```

```
ybfCp86Uo3NMb93SIHRtC2JvE/AJcNs4Oq9SF5VCGFGMBNAXKBBuJysrcQ2fgCvvsca➥
NE8OmyAtWOIBzHqqpRO6rfcdzRE/m1UyyHtnuqdAPUBXqiE7xR7BEw7hHDPzc4fTFMU➥
9ers3cjBZ9scwcBL6NIU47RL/vKqaIzlksII845egRr6LEHOaTyozk9IdOEL5W9JQeY2X2Ek➥
b3+MtLNI5fAzUmsMkZO3JRuTxdZsOmmLYEqc9OfTkWeC53k+sAtW69NoMjI91+➥
Vo/O4RO=" />
```

```
                    </identity>
                </endpoint>
```

Setting maxReceivedMessageSize

With the default settings for the maximum received message size, this application would fail consistently. This was resolved via the binding for the service. The binding has an attribute, `maxReceivedMessageSize`, which is of type int. Increase the size of the attribute to one you're comfortable with. In this sample, you'll leverage the maximum size for an integer, 2147483647.

Modify your `app.config` file on the client so it resembles the following:

```
    <binding name="RSSCardSpace" closeTimeout="00:10:00" openTimeout="00:10:00"
                         receiveTimeout="00:10:00" sendTimeout="00:10:00" ➥
    bypassProxyOnLocal="false"
                         transactionFlow="false"
hostNameComparisonMode="StrongWildcard"
                         maxBufferPoolSize="524288" ➥
maxReceivedMessageSize="2147483647"
                         messageEncoding="Text" textEncoding="utf-8" ➥
    useDefaultWebProxy="true">
```

Setting ReaderQuotas

Once a message is received, it will need to be read. In addition to increasing the maximum received message size, you'll also want to change the setting for the `maxStringContentLength` attribute. Evaluate the number that makes sense for your particular scenario; in this case, I again chose the maximum size for an integer, 2147483647.

```
                         <readerQuotas maxDepth="32" ➥
    maxStringContentLength="2147483647" maxArrayLength="16384"
                             maxBytesPerRead="4096" maxNameTableCharCount="16384"
    />
```

Your modified configuration file should resemble the following:

```
    <?xml version="1.0" encoding="utf-8"?>
    <configuration>

        <system.serviceModel>
            <bindings>
                <wsFederationHttpBinding>
                    <binding name="RSSCardSpace" closeTimeout="00:10:00"
                        openTimeout="00:10:00" receiveTimeout="00:10:00"
                        sendTimeout="00:10:00" bypassProxyOnLocal="false"
```

```
                                    transactionFlow="false"➥
hostNameComparisonMode="StrongWildcard"
                                    maxBufferPoolSize="524288"➥
maxReceivedMessageSize="2147483647"
                                    messageEncoding="Text" textEncoding="utf-8"
                                    useDefaultWebProxy="true">
                                    <readerQuotas maxDepth="32"
                                        maxStringContentLength="2147483647"
                                        maxArrayLength="16384"
                                        maxBytesPerRead="4096"
                                        maxNameTableCharCount="16384" />
                                    <reliableSession ordered="true" inactivityTimeout="00:10:00"
                                        enabled="false" />
                                    <security mode="Message">
                                        <message algorithmSuite="Basic128"
                                            issuedKeyType="SymmetricKey"

issuedTokenType="urn:oasis:names:tc:SAML:1.0:assertion"
                                            negotiateServiceCredential="true">
                                            <claimTypeRequirements>
                                                <add
                                                    claimType=➥
      "http://schemas.xmlsoap.org/ws/2005/05/identity/claims/givenname"
                                                    isOptional="false" />
                                                <add claimType=
      "http://schemas.xmlsoap.org/ws/2005/05/identity/claims/surname"
                                                    isOptional="false" />
                                                <add claimType=➥
      "http://schemas.xmlsoap.org/ws/2005/05/identity/claims/locality"
                                                    isOptional="false" />
                                                <add claimType=➥
      "http://schemas.xmlsoap.org/ws/2005/05/identity/claims/country"
                                                    isOptional="false" />
                                                <add claimType=➥
      "http://schemas.xmlsoap.org/ws/2005/05/identity/claims/privatepersonalidentifier"
                                                    isOptional="false" />
                                            </claimTypeRequirements>
                                            <issuer address=➥
      "http://schemas.xmlsoap.org/ws/2005/05/identity/issuer/self" />
                                        </message>
                                    </security>
                                </binding>
                            </wsFederationHttpBinding>
                        </bindings>
                        <client>
                            <endpoint address=➥
```

```
"http://localhost:1972/BeginningCardspace/GetRSS"
            binding="wsFederationHttpBinding"
            bindingConfiguration="RSSCardSpace"
            contract="IRSSService" name="RSSCardSpace" >

        <identity>
            <certificate encodedValue=
```
"AwAAAAEAAAAUAAAA1H3mV/pJAlVZASt/Dt0rqbBd67ggAAAAAQAAAEgC➡
AAAwggZEMIIFLKADAgECAgooKOI4AAAAAAvMAOGCSqGSIb3DQEBBQU➡
AMG4xEzARBgoJkiaJk/IsZAEZFgNjb20xGTAXBgoJkiaJk/IsZAEZFgltaWNyb3➡
NvZnQxFDASBgoJkiaJk/IsZAEZFgRjb3JwMRUwEwYKCZImiZPyLGQBGRYF➡
bnRkZXYxDzANBgNVBAMTBkFkYXR1bTAeFwOwNjA1MTkyMzQyMzNaFwOx➡
MTAzMTAxODI3NTZaMGIxCzAJBgNVBAYTAlVTMRMwEQYDVQQIEwpXYXN➡
oaW5ndG9uMRAwDgYDVQQHEwdSZWRtb25kMREwDwYDVQQKEwhGYWJy➡
aWthbTEZMBcGA1UEAxMQd3d3LmZhYnJpa2FtLmNvbTCCASIwDQYJKoZIhv➡
cNAQEBBQADggEPADCCAQoCggEBAMACp5TXWiJ71lp87W5r15bwnecarGdh➡
4nnMTVj+WOhaUCIiRKev5OfBRyrjeJfEy4gv9B1ME6pJJguIlfk7RMyx5Titica5J/aB➡
WW21BxaDqO5r9T+wZffsnxvqYcwWw6yG6/oG3sDk+Trv2/mpE8SNJVgEcqlD7hv➡
WIPa3opjk8AMD8gmoOk3Hw6gHt8xmnAEsb57gOzLmHAo8+iLfs+uOi8efBnfgLrkO➡
/rAaet74fSUS56bXmGyNvU5FF6rELEGOLkWfH/LK82EmlToakCocEOmQmFCkN➡
pQhQHyepwKndFOAmjVJ57M5jHOEewOEpkIuKPJMRJwn/gtxW8MWhBMCAwEA➡
AaOCAu4wggLqMA4GA1UdDwEB/wQEAwIE8DBEBgkqhkiG9w0BCQ8ENzA1MA➡
4GCCqGSIb3DQMCAgIAgDAOBggqhkiG9wODBAICAIAwBwYFKw4DAgcwCgYIK➡
oZIhvcNAwcwHQYDVR0OBBYEFJfyWkB2bCNfu9uY6UHUlXjBLCTEMBMGA1Ud➡
JQQMMAoGCCsGAQUFBwMBMB8GA1UdIwQYMBaAFOyhvEbGfwt7MxHOkdVD➡
6eGG/la6MDkGA1UdHwQyMDAwLqAsoCqGKGhodHA6Ly93d3cuYWRhdHVtLmN➡
vbS9jcmxkYXRhL2FkYXR1bS5jcmwwggEKBggrBgEFBQcBAQSB/TCB+jB6BggrBg➡
EFBQcwAoZuaHROcDovL3Rob24tdGVzdDEtMjAwMy5udGRldi5jb3JwLm1pY3Jvc29➡
mdC5jb20vQ2VydEVucm9sbC90aG9uLXRlc3QxLTIwMDMubnRkZXYuY29ycC5taW➡
Nyb3NvZnQuY29tXOFkYXR1bS5jcnQwfAYIKwYBBQUHMAKGcGZpbGU6Ly9cXHR➡
ob24tdGVzdDEtMjAwMy5udGRldi5jb3JwLm1pY3Jvc29mdC5jb21cQ2VydEVucm9sb➡
Fx0aG9uLXRlc3QxLTIwMDMubnRkZXYuY29ycC5taWNyb3NvZnQuY29tXOFkYXR1b➡
S5jcnQwgdoGCCsGAQUFBwEMBIHNMIHKoWggXzBdMFswWRYJaW1hZ2UvZ2lm➡
MCEwHzAHBgUrDgMCGgQUBO3hqsI4zqGA3bRTvpSU6LEiObwwKRYnaHROcDovL➡
3d3dy5hZGF0dWOuY29tL2ltYWdlcy9hZGF0dWOuZ2lmomWgYzBhMF8wXRYJaW1➡
hZ2UvZ2lmMCEwHzAHBgUrDgMCGgQU8+uAcGo7FFJINSouwXzviKfnVGswLRYr➡
aHROcDovL3d3dy5mYWJyaWthbS5jb20vaW1hZ2VzL2ZhYnJpa2FtLmdpZjAXBgN➡
VHSAEEDAOMAwGCisGAQQBgjc8ZAEwDQYJKoZIhvcNAQEFBQADggEBAEzYs➡
XIBjTGbbuHIUbv+/7KFEWzSf3u23koOBlvzIHU6iXD64mdhrXr1G9qU39tE6fKxybfC➡
p86U03NMb93SIHRtC2JvE/AJcNs4Oq9SF5VCGFGMBNAXKBBuJysrcQ2fgCvvsc➡
aNE8OmyAtWOIBzHqqpRO6rfcdzRE/m1UyyHtnuqdAPUBXqiE7xR7BEw7hHDPzc4➡
fTFMU9ers3cjBZ9scwcBL6NIU47RL/vKqaIzlksII845egRr6LEHOaTyozk9IdOEL5W9J➡
QeY2X2Ekb3+MtLNI5fAzUmsMkZO3JRuTxdZsOmmLYEqc9OfTkWeC53k+sAtW69N➡
oMjI91+Vo/O4RO=" />
```
        </identity>
    </endpoint>
```

```
            <endpoint address="http://localhost:1972/BeginningCardspace/OPML/➡
GetOPML"
                        binding="wsFederationHttpBinding" ➡
bindingConfiguration="RSSCardSpace"
                        contract="IOPMLService" name="RSSCardSpace" >

            <identity>
                        <certificate encodedValue=
```

```
"AwAAAAEAAAAUAAAA1H3mV/pJAlVZAst/DtOrqbBd67ggAAAAAQAAAEgG➡
AAAAwggZEMIIFLKADAgECAgooKOI4AAAAAAvMAOGCSqGSIb3DQEBBQU➡
AMG4xEzARBgoJkiaJk/IsZAEZFgNjb2oxGTAXBgoJkiaJk/IsZAEZFgltaWNyb3➡
NvZnQxFDASBgoJkiaJk/IsZAEZFgRjb3JwMRUwEwYKCZImiZPyLGQBGRYF➡
bnRkZXYxDzANBgNVBAMTBkFkYXR1bTAeFwOwNjA1MTkyMzQyMzNaFwOx➡
MTAzMTAxODI3NTZaMGIxCzAJBgNVBAYTAlVTMRMwEQYDVQQIEwpXYXN➡
oaW5ndG9uMRAwDgYDVQQHEwdSZWRtb25kMREwDwYDVQQKEwhGYWJy➡
aWthbTEZMBcGA1UEAxMQd3d3LmZhYnJpa2FtLmNvbTCCASIwDQYJKoZIhv➡
cNAQEBBQADggEPADCCAQoCggEBAMACp5TXWiJ71lp87W5r15bwnecarGdh➡
4nnMTVj+WOhaUCIiRKev5OfBRyrjeJfEy4gv9B1ME6pJJguIlfk7RMyx5Titica5J/aB➡
WW21BxaDqO5r9T+wZffsnxvqYcwWw6yG6/oG3sDk+Trv2/mpE8SNJVgEcqlD7hv➡
WIPa3opjk8AMD8gmoOk3Hw6gHt8xmnAEsb57gOzLmHAo8+iLfs+uOi8efBnfgLrkO➡
/rAaet74fSUS56bXmGyNvU5FF6rELEGOLkWfH/LK82EmlToakCocEOmQmFCkN➡
pQhQHyepwKndFOAmjVJ57M5jHOEewOEpkIuKPJMRJwn/gtxW8MWhBMCAwEA➡
AaOCAu4wggLqMA4GA1UdDwEB/wQEAwIE8DBEBgkqhkiG9woBCQ8ENzA1MA➡
4GCCqGSIb3DQMCAgIAgDAOBggqhkiG9woDBAICAIAwBwYFKw4DAgcwCgYIK➡
oZIhvcNAwcwHQYDVROOBBYEFJfyWkB2bCNfu9uY6UHUlXjBLCTEMBMGA1Ud➡
JQQMMAoGCCsGAQUFBwMBMB8GA1UdIwQYMBaAFOyhvEbGfwt7MxHOkdVD➡
6eGG/la6MDkGA1UdHwQyMDAwLqAsoCqGKGhOdHA6Ly93d3cuYWRhdHVtLmN➡
vbS9jcmxkYXRhL2FkYXR1bS5jcmwwggEKBggrBgEFBQcBAQSB/TCB+jB6BggrBg➡
EFBQcwAoZuaHROcDovL3Rob24tdGVzdDEtMjAwMy5udGRldi5jb3JwLm1pY3Jvc29➡
mdC5jb20vQ2VydEVucm9sbC90oAG9uLXRlc3QxLTIwMDunRkZXYuY29ycC5taW➡
Nyb3NvZnQuY29tX0FkYXR1bS5jcnQwfAYIKwYBBQUHMAKGcGZpbGU6Ly9cXHR➡
ob24tdGVzdDEtMjAwMy5udGRldi5jb3JwLm1pY3Jvc29mdC5jb21cQ2VydEVucm9sb➡
FxOaG9uLXRlc3QxLTIwMDMunRkZXYuY29ycC5taWNyb3NvZnQuY29tX0FkYXR1b➡
S5jcnQwgdoGCCsGAQUFBwEMBIHNMIHKoWGgXzBdMFswWRYJaW1hZ2UvZ2lm➡
MCEwHzAHBgUrDgMCGgQUBO3hqsI4zqGA3bRTvpSU6LEiObwwKRYnaHROcDovL➡
3d3dy5hZGF0dWOuY29tL2ltYWdlcy9hZGF0dWOuZ2lmMGwGA1UdIIBkXRYJaW1➡
hZ2UvZ2lmMCEwHzAHBgUrDgMCGgQU8+uACGo7FFJINSouwXzviKfnVGswLRYr➡
aHROcDovL3d3dy5mYWJyaWthbS5jb20vaW1hZ2VzL2ZhYnJpa2FtLmdpZjAXBgN➡
VHSAEEDAOMAwGCisGAQQBgjc8ZAEwDQYJKoZIhvcNAQEFBQADggEBAEzYs➡
XIBjTGbbuHIUbv+/7KFEWzSf3u23koOBlvzIHU6iXD64mdhrXr1G9qU39tE6fKxybfC➡
p86UO3NMb93SIHRtC2JvE/AJcNs4Oq9SF5VCGFGMBNAXKBBuJysrcQ2fgCvvsc➡
aNE8OmyAtWOIBzHqqpRO6rfcdzRE/m1UyyHtnuqdAPUBXqiE7xR7BEw7hHDPzc4➡
fTFMU9ers3cjBZ9scwcBL6NIU47RL/vKqaIzlksII845egRr6LEHOaTyozk9IdOEL5W9J➡
QeY2X2Ekb3+MtLNI5fAzUmsMkZO3JRuTxdZsOmmLYEqc9OfTkWeC53k+sAtW69N➡
oMjI91+Vo/O4RO=" />
```

```
                    </identity>
                  </endpoint>
                </client>
            </system.serviceModel>
        </configuration>
```

Creating the User Interface

This application is an RSS client. It will retrieve an OPML feed from your service and display the results in a tailored DataGridView control. After selecting an item in the list, it will contact your GetFeed service. From the feed, it will assign the channel title and channel summary to Label controls and then populate a secondary DataGridView control with information about the items contained within that feed.

After clicking an item in the secondary DataGridView control, the title of the item will be assigned to a Label control, and the HTML found in the description element will be assigned to a WebBrowser control.

1. Open Form1.

2. Drag a Button control onto the designer surface.

3. Name the button **btnGetOPML**, and set the button's Text property to **Get OPML**.

4. Drag a new Button control onto the designer surface.

5. Name the button **btnGetFeed**, and set the button's Text property to **Get Feed**.

6. Drag a Label control onto the designer surface, and name it **lblChannelTitle**.

7. Drag a Label control onto the designer surface, and name it **lblChannelSummary**.

8. Drag a Label control onto the designer surface, and name it **lblItemTitle**.

9. Drag a DataGridView control onto the designer surface, and name it **dgvOPML**.

10. Drag a DataGridView control onto the designer surface, and name it **datagridItems**.

11. Drag a WebBrowser control onto the form, and accept the default name of **webBrowser1**.

12. Assemble and size your controls on the form so they resemble Figure 9-1.

13. Add a CellContentClick event for dgvOPML.

14. Add a CellContentClick event for datagridItems.

15. Add a click event for btnGetOPML.

16. Add a click event for btnGetFeed.

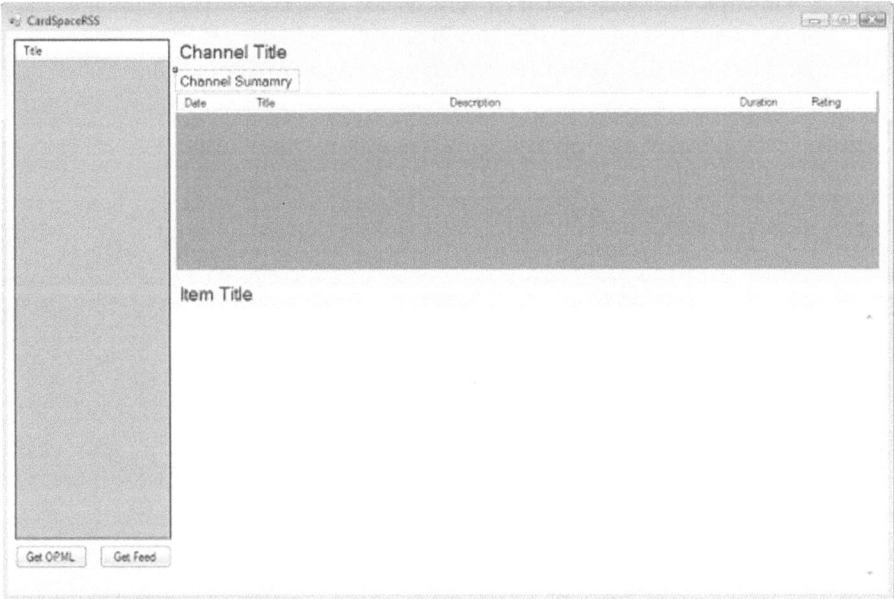

Figure 9-1. *Form 1 layout*

17. Populate the click event for GetFeed with the following code, which will call RSSService and populate a feed object with the result:

```
private void btnGetFeed_Click(object sender, EventArgs e)
{
RSSServiceClient client = new RSSServiceClient();
Rss.RssFeed feed = client.GetFeed();
DisplayChannel(feed.Channels[0]);
}
```

Note This code is helpful for testing that the service is working properly.

---

18. Populate the click event for GetOPML with the following code. This code will call RSSService and populate an OPML object with the result. This code then calls the DisplayOutlinesInControl operation, which displays a formatted version of the OPML in a DataGridView control.

```
private void btnGetOPML_Click(object sender, EventArgs e)
{
OPMLServiceClient client = new OPMLServiceClient();
Rss.OPML opml = client.GetOPML();
DisplayOutlinesInControl(opml);
}
```

19. Add the operation `DisplayOutlinesInControl` to `Form1.cs`. This routine will populate the DataGridView control with the items contained within the `OPML`. The outline itself is associated with the tag for a row within the grid and can be examined when responding to a cell click event.

```
private void DisplayOutlinesInControl(OPML opml)
{
    dgvOPML.Rows.Clear();
    int gridRowNbr = 0;
    int ParentIndex = 0;
    Color evenRowColorValue = Color.AliceBlue;
    Color oddRowColorValue = Color.LightSteelBlue;
    foreach (OPMLOutline outline in opml.Body.Outlines)
    {

        DataGridViewRow row = new DataGridViewRow();
        DataGridViewCheckBoxCell check = ➥
new DataGridViewCheckBoxCell();
        DataGridViewTextBoxCell count = new DataGridViewTextBoxCell();
        DataGridViewTextBoxCell text = new DataGridViewTextBoxCell();
        DataGridViewTextBoxCell categories = ➥
new DataGridViewTextBoxCell();
        DataGridViewTextBoxCell description = ➥
new DataGridViewTextBoxCell();
        DataGridViewTextBoxCell xmlUrl = ➥
new DataGridViewTextBoxCell();
        DataGridViewTextBoxCell type = new DataGridViewTextBoxCell();
        DataGridViewTextBoxCell version = ➥
new DataGridViewTextBoxCell();


        row.DefaultCellStyle.Font = this.Font;
        if (gridRowNbr % 2 == 0)
        {
            row.DefaultCellStyle.BackColor = oddRowColorValue;
        }
        else
        {
            row.DefaultCellStyle.BackColor = evenRowColorValue;
        }

        //Set the tag value for the row to the outline element
        row.Tag = outline;

        text.Value = outline.Text;
```

```
                    //Set the tool tile to the description
                    text.ToolTipText = outline.Description;
                    categories.Value = outline.Categories;
                    description.Value = outline.Description;
                    xmlUrl.Value = outline.XmlUrl;
                    type.Value = outline.Type;
                    version.Value = outline.Version;

                    row.Cells.Add(check);
                    row.Cells.Add(text);
                    row.Cells.Add(categories);
                    row.Cells.Add(description);
                    row.Cells.Add(xmlUrl);
                    row.Cells.Add(type);
                    row.Cells.Add(version);

                    dgvOPML.Rows.Add(row);

                    gridRowNbr++;
                }


            }
```

20. Populate the `CellContentClick` event for dgvOPML. This column that was clicked can be interrogated for the URL of the feed. In this case, for testing you're using the feed that's provided by the `GetFeed` operation on the service. The code to interrogate the URL information is as follows but is commented out:

```
        private void dgvOPML_CellContentClick(➥
object sender, DataGridViewCellEventArgs e)
        {
            switch (e.ColumnIndex)
            {
                case 0: //Check
                    break;
                case 1: //Text
                    //The following line would return the URL for the feed
                    //dgvOPML.Rows[e.RowIndex].Cells[4].Value.ToString();

                    //In the first part of this chapter, we use a fixed feed
                    RSSServiceClient client = new RSSServiceClient();
                    Rss.RssFeed feed = client.GetFeed();
                    DisplayChannel(feed.Channels[0]);
                    //Display the feed in the secondary data grid
```

```
                break;
        case 2: //Categories
                break;
        case 3: //Description
                break;
        case 4: //xmlUrl
                break;
        case 5: // type
                break;
        case 6: //version
                break;
        default:
                break;
    }
}
```

21. Next, add the DisplayChannel operation. This will iterate through an RSS channel and assign the items from that channel to a DataGridView control. In addition, it will assign the title of the channel and the summary of the channel to Label controls.

```
protected void DisplayChannel(Rss.RssChannel channel)
{
    datagridItems.Rows.Clear();

    lblChannelSummary.Text = channel.Summary;
    lblChannelTitle.Text = channel.Title;

    int ParentIndex;
    ParentIndex = 0;
    int ParentRow = ParentIndex + 1;



    string ChannelTitle;
    ChannelTitle = channel.Title;



    int gridRowNbr = ParentIndex + 1;
    ParentIndex = -1;
    foreach (RssItem item in channel.Items)
    {

        ///----------------------------------------
        ///
        DataGridViewRow row = new DataGridViewRow();
        DataGridViewTextBoxCell date = ➥
```

```
new DataGridViewTextBoxCell();
                DataGridViewTextBoxCell title = ➥
new DataGridViewTextBoxCell();
                DataGridViewTextBoxCell description = ➥
new DataGridViewTextBoxCell();
                DataGridViewTextBoxCell duration = ➥
new DataGridViewTextBoxCell();
                DataGridViewTextBoxCell rating = ➥
new DataGridViewTextBoxCell();

                datagridItems.Columns[0].Width = 75;
                datagridItems.Columns[1].Width = ➥
 (int)((double)(datagridItems.Width - 225) * (double).6);
                datagridItems.Columns[2].Width = ➥
 (int)((double)(datagridItems.Width - 225) * (double).39);
                datagridItems.Columns[3].Width = 75;
                datagridItems.Columns[4].Width = 75;


                if (gridRowNbr % 2 == 0)
                {
                    row.DefaultCellStyle.BackColor = Color.LightSteelBlue;
                }
                else
                {
                    row.DefaultCellStyle.BackColor = Color.AliceBlue;
                }


                date.Value = item.PubDate;
                date.Tag = item;
                title.Value = item.Title;

                if (item.Duration == null || item.Duration == "")
                { duration.Value = "None"; }
                else
                { duration.Value = item.Duration; }

                if (item.Subtitle == null || item.Subtitle == "")
                { description.Value = "None"; }
                else
                { description.Value = item.Subtitle; }
```

```
            if (item.Rating == null || item.Rating == "")
            { rating.Value = "None"; }
            else
            { rating.Value = item.Rating; }

            row.Cells.Add(date);
            row.Cells.Add(title);
            row.Cells.Add(description);
            row.Cells.Add(duration);
            row.Cells.Add(rating);

            datagridItems.Rows.Add(row);

            gridRowNbr++;
        }
        if (datagridItems.Rows.Count > 0)
        {
            datagridItems.Rows[0].Selected = false;
            datagridItems.Rows[0].Selected = true;
        }
    }
```

22. When an item is clicked, you'll want to display it in the WebBrowser control. By adding the DisplayItem operation, when an item in the datagridItems control is clicked, it will display the description of the item in the WebBrowser control and the title of the item in a Label control. Enter the following code:

```
private void DisplayItem(RssItem item)
{
    webBrowser1.DocumentText = item.Description;
    lblItemTitle.Text = item.Title;

}
```

23. Finally, populate the dataGridItems' CellContentClick event so it calls the DisplayItem operation:

```
    private void datagridItems_CellContentClick(➡
object sender, DataGridViewCellEventArgs e)
    {
        if (e.RowIndex > -1)
        {
            object o = datagridItems.Rows[e.RowIndex].Cells[0].Tag;
            if (o != null)
            {
                Type objectType = o.GetType();
```

```
                switch (objectType.Name)
                {
                    case "RssEnclosure":

                        break;
                    case "RssItem":
                        RssItem item = (RssItem)o;
                        DisplayItem(item);


                        break;
                    case "RssChannel":

                        break;
                    default:
                        break;
                }
            }
        }




    }
   }
}
```

Testing the Solution

With everything complete, you are now ready to test:

1. Right-click the solution, and specify ServiceHost and RSSClient as the start-up projects, with ServiceHost located higher in the list.

2. Run the solution.

3. The console service should display a note that the RSS service and the OPML service are online.

4. Form1 from the RSS client should be displayed. Click the GetOPML button.

5. You will be challenged for a CardSpace card, so provide one to the service, and an OPML list will be displayed.

6. Click one of the items in the OPML list, and it will trigger the GetFeed operation of RSSService. This will display all the items from the feed in the datagridItems control.

7. Click one of the items in the datagridItems list, and it will display the item in the WebBrowser control.

The resulting screen should look similar to Figure 9-2.

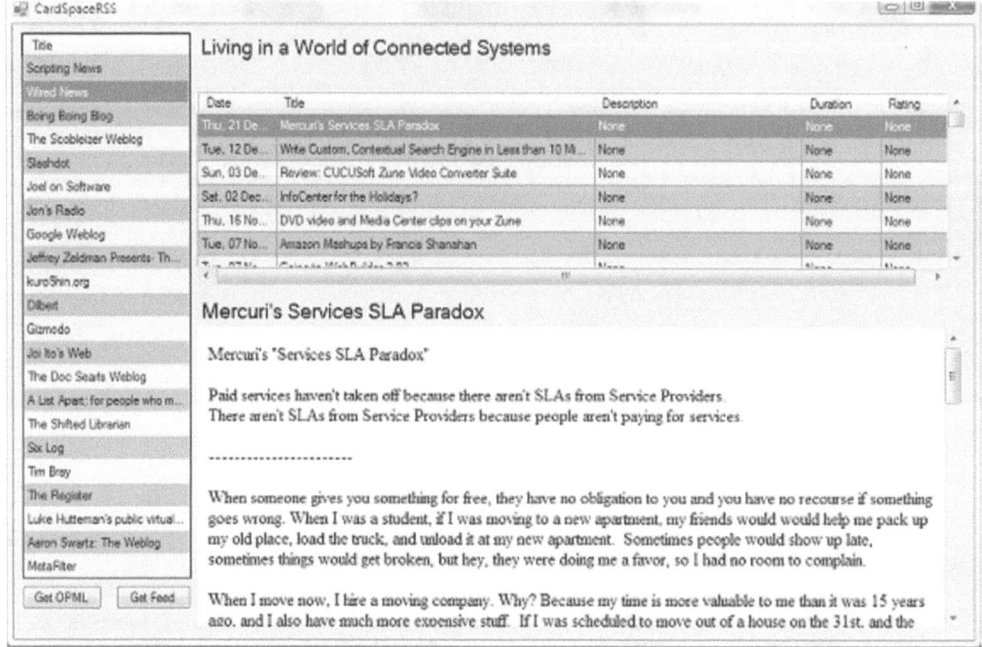

Figure 9-2. *The RSS client in action*

Summary

In this chapter, you learned about RSS, OPML, and Atom. You took that knowledge and built RSS and OPML services and clients to consume them. Along the away, you made these services CardSpace enabled.

You then brought everything together with a functional RSS client that retrieves and reads secured feeds from the RSS service.

Finally, you created a functional prototype that could easily be adapted to handle RSS feeds that are tied to subscription, that are personalized based on card information, or that are used to collect demographic information to be shared with advertisers.

CHAPTER 10

■■■

Security Token Services

Thus far in the book, I've focused primarily on two participants—the owner of an information card and the relying parties (RPs) that would accept that card. Starting with this chapter, the book will begin to focus on the third perspective—that of the identity provider.

It is the identity provider that issues the information cards in the first place and also provides the tokens that ultimately are delivered to the relying party. In this chapter, I first focus on token issuance, specifically the role of the identity provider (IP) and the Security Token Server (STS). Then I'll cover the Microsoft Simple-STS sample, and finally I'll show some code to enhance that sample by enabling additional functionality.

To Issue or Not to Issue

Today, if you look in your wallet, you will likely find just a handful of cards—a driver's license, a couple of credit cards, an auto club card, and an insurance card. Whether shopping at the mall, picking up a prescription, or renting a car, you can provide these cards to authenticate your identity and gain access to goods and services. Your universe of cards is relatively small.

Likewise, in the digital world, the reality is that the majority of relying parties will accept tokens that were issued by someone else. And for those who want to become identity providers, a good portion of them will use a commercial STS product. This is analogous to people using third-party web servers such as IIS and Apache instead of writing their own.

Note Chapter 12 provides more coverage of the pros and cons of issuing your own cards.

Creating a robust STS from scratch would take far more than a single chapter; in fact, it could be the subject of a separate book altogether. This chapter covers the concepts, and by the chapter's end, you'll have an understanding of how a STS fits into the metasystem and have a basic implementation upon which you can build. For those looking for lower-level details, Microsoft and Ping Identity have produced the document "A Guide to Interoperability with the Information Card Profile v1.0." This 73-page document provides that lower level of detail you may want. You can find the document at http://www.identityblog.com/wp-content/resources/profile/Infocard-Profile-v1-Guide.pdf.

Some individuals have found this document to be a bit daunting as an introduction to the subject. This and the next few chapters will provide an excellent primer for the low-level details of that document.

Exploring the Role of the STS

We'll begin by looking at the role of the STS. Figure 10-1 shows a sequence diagram that maps to a common scenario. That scenario consists of a user navigating to the login page of a website, logging into that site with an information card, and then being redirected to the home page of the site as an authenticated user.

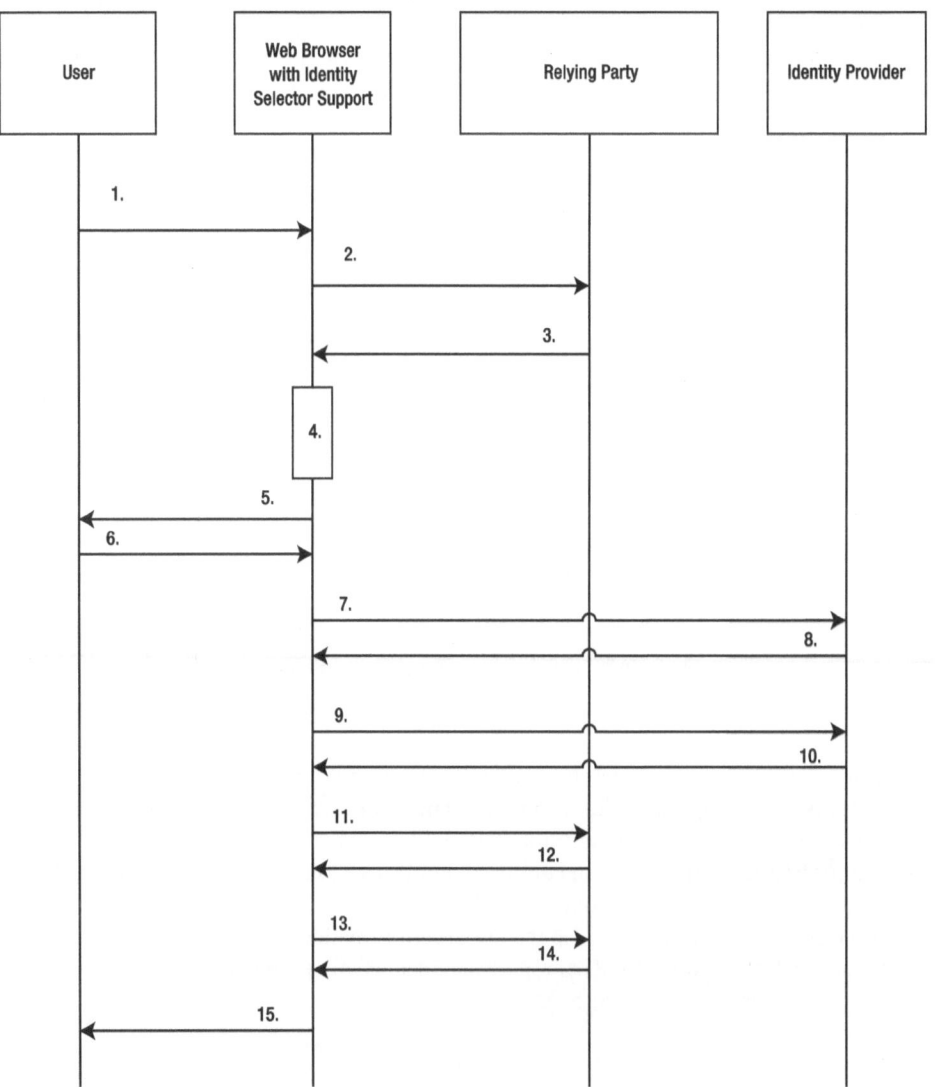

Figure 10-1. *Sequence for logging in to a website with an information card*

The steps in the sequence are as follows:

1. The user goes to the login page for a website.

2. An HTTP GET is sent to the relying party for the login page.

3. An HTML login page with the OBJECT tag is returned to the browser.

4. The user clicks a Log In with Information Card button, which triggers the identity selector to evaluate the policy of the relying party, as specified in the OBJECT tag. The selector then finds the subset of information cards that fit the policy.

5. The identity selector displays the subset of cards.

6. The user selects an information card to use.

7. The identity selector makes a request to the card issuer (identity provider) to retrieve the security policy.

8. The security policy is returned.

9. The user authenticates themself to the identity provider, and a request is sent to the identity provider for a security token, identifying the required claims. This is done using WS-Trust.

Note The credential to be used for authenticating the user to the identity provider is identified in the information card.

---

10. The security token is returned.

11. There is an HTTPS POST of the login page (with the security token) to the relying party.

12. An HTTP redirect to the home page with a cookie is returned.

13. An HTTP GET is sent to the relying party for the home page URL.

14. The HTML page is returned to the browser.

15. The user is now authenticated and able to access the website.

Note You'll note in this scenario that the user already has an information card. Although the STS will issue security tokens, it does not necessarily issue information cards. As you'll see in Chapters 11 and 12, you can create separate applications and services to automate the creation of cards that live outside the STS.

This sequence highlights two tasks that the STS does for the identity provider. An STS publishes the metadata for the service's security policy and also provides functionality for token issuance. You'll now look at the Simple-STS sample provided by Microsoft to see how that sample implements this functionality.

■**Note** For a lower-level look at the interactions, please see "A Guide to Interoperating with the Information Card Profile v1.0." Written by Microsoft and Ping Identity, this paper also covers scenarios outside the scope of this chapter, such as using delegate STS. You can find this document at `http://www.identityblog.com/ wp-content/resources/profile/Infocard-Profile-v1-Guide.pdf`.

Taking a Closer Look at Microsoft's Simple-STS Sample

You'll now examine the Simple-STS sample to get a better understanding of how an STS works. Later in the chapter, you'll learn how to extend this sample.

Getting the Bits

If you want to review the code for the sample, you'll need to download it. You can find the Simple-STS sample at `http://www.netfx3.com`. The sample is located in the Samples section in the Windows CardSpace part of the site. The URL to download this is `http://cardspace.netfx3.com/ files/folders/samples_rc_1/entry6082.aspx`.

Once you've downloaded the sample, you will want to unzip it and install it. You can find the installation documentation in the Documents subfolder of the sample's directory structure.

You will also want to download the managed card I created for the exercises in this chapter, which you can find on the Apress web page for this book or on my blog at `http:// www.marcmercuri.com`.

Exploring the Simple-STS Code

This section provides a quick walk-through of the Simple-STS sample. If you open the SampleSecurityTokenService project, this section covers what is happening as you trace through the code.

■**Note** This code is designed to work against the Simple-STS sample available at the time of this writing. If the Simple-STS sample is updated in the future, please check my blog at `http://www.marcmercuri.com` for any changes.

Each STS exposes an endpoint that provides a security policy and an endpoint that handles the actual token requests. As you can see in `Program.cs`, when starting the STS, the base URL addresses for the service and for the security policy are read from the `app.config` file:

```
<appSettings>
  <!-- The Identity Provider -->
  <add key="issuer" value="www.fabrikam.com" />
  <!-- The Thumbprint of the certificate to sign the RSTR-->
  <add key="certificateThumbprint" ➨
value="D47DE657FA4902555902CB7F0EDD2BA9B05DEBB8" />
  <!-- The Base address of the WS-Trust endpoint -->
  <add key="baseAddress" value="http://www.fabrikam.com:7000/sample/trust" />
  <!-- The Base address of the MEX endpoint -->
  <add key="baseMexAddress" value="https://www.fabrikam.com:7001/sample/trust" />
</appSettings>
```

Using those base addresses, three service hosts are created. These hosts represent three authentication types: smart card, self-issued SAML, and username and password. These hosts have endpoints for the service, as well as a Metadata Exchange (MEX) endpoint for the security policy. As you see in the code, the endpoint for each of these services is appended onto the base that was retrieved from the app.config file.

The three service types are represented by the classes CertificateAuthSTS, SelfIssuedSamlAuthSTS, and UserNameAuthSTS. All these classes derive from WsTrustResponder, which handles token requests.

The WsTrustResponder class contains four methods for handling token requests—Cancel, Issue, Renew, and Validate. Of those methods, only Issue is populated in the sample.

If you examine the Issue method, you will see it currently does the following:

1. Parses the incoming message into a RequestSecurityToken object

2. Processes the request and returns a RequestSecurityTokenResponse object

3. Takes the RequestSecurityTokenResponse object and places it in a new Message

4. Determines whether the original message specified an identifier and, if so, sets RelatesTo in the headers to that value, allowing for the caller to handle correlation

The resulting message is then returned to the client, which can pass on the contained token to the relying party.

Looking More Closely at the Simple-STS Sample

In the previous section, you took a quick lap through the code and established the high-level view of what happens when a client requests a token from the STS. You'll now look more closely at several aspects of this process.

Security Token Service Detail Stored in an Information Card

You'll begin by looking at the STS-related detail that's stored in the information card.

> ■ **Note** Chapter 11 will go into detail about the contents of an information card, but in the context of learning about the STS, I'll highlight a number of elements from the information card XML here.

Each card contains an identifier and version; you can see examples in the following XML:

```
<CardId>http://www.fabrikam.com/CardId/1234567890</CardId>
<CardVersion>1</CardVersion>
```

CardId provides an identifier for a card that can be utilized by the STS. For example, the STS could leverage this ID as a key by which to query a back-end data store for the claims associated with the card. CardVersion identifies the version of the card.

The information card also provides information that identifies where and how to contact the identity provider. If you examine the element TokenServiceList in the following XML, you'll see that it contains a list of all the security token services that can be contacted to get a token for this card. You'll see that each service is identified by a TokenService element and that the endpoints for both the service and the metadata (MEX) are identified.

```
<TokenServiceList>
<TokenService>
<wsa:EndpointReference>
<wsa:Address>http://www.fabrikam.com/sts</wsa:Address>
<wsa:Metadata>
<wsx:Metadata>
<wsx:MetadataSection
Dialect="http://schemas.xmlsoap.org/ws/2004/09/mex">
<wsx:MetadataReference>
<wsa:Address>https://www.fabrikam.com/sts/mex</wsa:Address>
</wsx:MetadataReference>
</wsx:MetadataSection>
</wsx:Metadata>
</wsa:Metadata>
</wsa:EndpointReference>
<UserCredential>
<UsernamePasswordCredential>
<Username>mmercuri</Username>
</UsernamePasswordCredential>
</UserCredential>
</TokenService>
</TokenServiceList>
```

In addition, each token service contains a UserCredential element. It is here that the client—that is, the identity selector—learns what type of authentication is required for the endpoint and provides a user interface to acquire it. In the following XML, you can see that the UsernamePasswordCredential element is specified. In this case, the UI would prompt for a username and password and would default the username to the value mmercuri.

Although not shown here, the user credential can also display a *hint*. This is text that is shown within the user interface. For UsernamePasswordCredential, this typically is a hint for the password.

Note Although UsernamePasswordCredential is specified here, you have four potential choices for UserCredential. You can specify UsernamePasswordCredential, KerberosV5Credential, X509V3Credential, and SelfIssuedCredential.

The card also specifies the types of tokens that the STS can issue. In the following XML, you can see that the STS will support SAML 1.0 tokens:

```
<SupportedTokenTypeList>
<wst:TokenType>urn:oasis:names:tc:SAML:1.0:assertion</wst:TokenType>
</SupportedTokenTypeList>
```

In the SupportedClaimTypeList, the information card also specifies which claims are available for this card:

```
<SupportedClaimTypeList>
<SupportedClaimType Uri="".../ws/2005/05/identity/claims/givenname"">
<DisplayTag>Given Name</DisplayTag>
</SupportedClaimType>
<SupportedClaimType Uri="".../ws/2005/05/identity/claims/surname"">
<DisplayTag>Last Name</DisplayTag>
</SupportedClaimType>
</SupportedClaimTypeList>
```

Requestor Authentication

If I were to request a token from an STS, how would it know that the requestor was Marc Mercuri? The reality is that without an authentication mechanism, it wouldn't.

If I find a credit card on the ground, what would stop me from using it at a local retail store? Most stores require that I provide a form of identification to authenticate my identity.

The Simple-STS sample contains services for three authentication mechanisms—smart card, self-issued SAML, and username and password. Each service facilitates a different way by which someone would authenticate themselves.

Note Although usernames and passwords and smart cards may be familiar concepts, self-issued SAML may not be. When users request information cards from an identity provider, that identity provider may allow users to identify themselves using existing self-issued information cards. For self-issued SAML, a user must possess that self-issued card—in addition to the card issued by the identity provider—to successfully authenticate.

Within the Issue method of WsTrustResponder, you'll see that there is a variable of type AuthorizationContext that's created:

```
AuthorizationContext ctx = ➥
OperationContext.Current.ServiceSecurityContext.AuthorizationContext;
```

You can use AuthorizationContext to retrieve additional details about the caller to perform further authentication from within the STS. Although I didn't show how to do this in this sample, I'll cover it later in this chapter.

RequestSecurityToken

The identity selector sends a message to the identity provider that requests a token containing claims. The following XML is an example of one of these RequestSecurityToken messages. This sample request is based on a card that contains a single claim, givenname.

```
<?xml version="1.0" encoding="utf-8"?>
<s:Envelope xmlns:s=http://www.w3.org/2003/05/soap-envelope➥
 xmlns:a="http://www.w3.org/2005/08/addressing" xmlns:u=➥
"http://docs.oasis-open.org/wss/2004/01/➥
oasis-200401-wss-wssecurity-utility-1.0.xsd">
  <s:Header>
    <a:Action s:mustUnderstand="1" u:Id="_2">➥
http://schemas.xmlsoap.org/ws/2005/02/trust/RST/➥
Issue</a:Action>
    <a:MessageID u:Id="_3">➥
urn:uuid:daa6b278-a668-457a-85a4-a08771d47cd7</a:MessageID>
    <a:ReplyTo u:Id="_4">
      <a:Address>http://www.w3.org/2005/08/addressing/anonymous</a:Address>
    </a:ReplyTo>
    <a:To s:mustUnderstand="1" u:Id="_5">➥
http://www.fabrikam.com:7000/sample/trust/selfissuedsaml/sts</a:To>
    <o:Security s:mustUnderstand="1" xmlns:o=➥
"http://docs.oasis-open.org/wss/2004/01/oasis-200401-wss-wssecurity-secext-1.0.xsd">
      <u:Timestamp u:Id=➥
"uuid-a4af06e2-0684-4274-aedd-7f1dee160477-32">
        <u:Created>2007-06-03T20:04:33.442Z</u:Created>
        <u:Expires>2007-06-03T20:09:33.442Z</u:Expires>
      </u:Timestamp>
      <c:SecurityContextToken u:Id=➥
"uuid-1f728028-ceb6-40c7-8653-95149066884e-4" ➥
xmlns:c="http://schemas.xmlsoap.org/ws/2005/02/sc">
        <c:Identifier>urn:uuid:954e9e8a-a77a-4007-ba2c-a1d41cbfdd5d</c:Identifier>
      </c:SecurityContextToken>
      <c:DerivedKeyToken u:Id=➥
"uuid-a4af06e2-0684-4274-aedd-7f1dee160477-30" ➥
xmlns:c="http://schemas.xmlsoap.org/ws/2005/02/sc">
        <o:SecurityTokenReference>
          <o:Reference ValueType=➥
```

```
"http://schemas.xmlsoap.org/ws/2005/02/sc/sct" URI=➡
"#uuid-1f728028-ceb6-40c7-8653-95149066884e-4" />
        </o:SecurityTokenReference>
        <c:Offset>0</c:Offset>
        <c:Length>24</c:Length>
        <c:Nonce>woZ5bO+FpVt/w1GORyQ9Qg==</c:Nonce>
      </c:DerivedKeyToken>
      <c:DerivedKeyToken u:Id=➡
"uuid-a4af06e2-0684-4274-aedd-7f1dee160477-31"➡
 xmlns:c="http://schemas.xmlsoap.org/ws/2005/02/sc">
        <o:SecurityTokenReference>
          <o:Reference ValueType=➡
"http://schemas.xmlsoap.org/ws/2005/02/sc/sct" ➡
URI="#uuid-1f728028-ceb6-40c7-8653-95149066884e-4" />
        </o:SecurityTokenReference>
        <c:Offset>0</c:Offset>
        <c:Length>24</c:Length>
        <c:Nonce>esvI+dFFOGWi+7SYaVz8+w==</c:Nonce>
      </c:DerivedKeyToken>
      <e:ReferenceList xmlns:e="http://www.w3.org/2001/04/xmlenc#">
        <e:DataReference URI="#_1" />
        <e:DataReference URI="#_6" />
      </e:ReferenceList>
      <e:EncryptedData Id="_6" Type=➡
"http://www.w3.org/2001/04/xmlenc#Element" ➡
xmlns:e="http://www.w3.org/2001/04/xmlenc#">
        <e:EncryptionMethod Algorithm=➡
"http://www.w3.org/2001/04/xmlenc#aes192-cbc" />
        <KeyInfo xmlns="http://www.w3.org/2000/09/xmldsig#">
          <o:SecurityTokenReference>
            <o:Reference ValueType=➡
"http://schemas.xmlsoap.org/ws/2005/02/sc/dk" ➡
URI="#uuid-a4af06e2-0684-4274-aedd-7f1dee160477-31" />
          </o:SecurityTokenReference>
        </KeyInfo>
        <e:CipherData>
          <e:CipherValue>➡
```
6vAGHhEmAqvXdOcN7piTtIgl5w63D3vg26lbgcB+L8g2o3tH6mSLwuripDGsWGSDZ➡
XZqCdO8Dch+Ep14x1BuGAA1OkTNtiGIFmRy3sGUXVtCqFJSLLIhLYiC8uNmrWZ6jZB➡
BnEAreMg8IRpKk6l7Me+219leHm6jSMmHLOPNA5YqmdlLkg/xbckGdUkQLePcbSvT➡
sU2rFOxvkdo4Pb8lYmu7D5sGczxVo8jZfweSypLGYBO6wPP9w1iinl9mSHrAwhOofKiqr➡
ETzBG7+Gb5r2E5z+Bv/cJLwgodGSQ9/yCKOiEiIf7Sk5LBS9cYGuw27jOberFHwMm26l➡
nubBtSV/B2snr4DOl+cvs3rk6HyzPljpsNrurX9gNoLX3nUMypGFEvE5zKWeUwUMCjv➡
gj4cmAwIcrLS7qEYQKplOz7jQ9aYQrnumz5J5yJMdxpRyZRHlLo6Td6asjx7psb15sU28➡
Njl4/Gkdllv9Xy3tpfWbERkxzow2GOkocMOUK3Xr53KoYYF5zwwFiPmdYbsA606LJyOr➡
61vKMO2GUvUzTTmy3t9gB/yU1pYJAo+OElHyvxsTzmtmdZW3ehK6XIpbSqbpn4m+➡
sIAPKv6tiCLJ3YIr2TL4leQcKnohx4IOnxefnPFW5UdLDdF8pUX9TdObQLyzr+HHCxyEN➡
```
```

```
+hAU5rT+U/OCblnKiREg1VHVuo4tmiJOYsGUDAXloiUnbPO3Z59K1VHj4IFRQxY9ZL➥
jqkd4y+5lRyj24xyy5p1wKafoB8rTLrCa5Y9LVryPiCTd+8X1vLjv65Ow6fADwAZ4mVRlg➥
Qx95iAE2H2JGxKugeKF2xf+3TVUDBfWa1/aVD7mMs+2C23KZtdQKahadANzNZPLA➥
aD6VueA3r/8sieMsn1QRhRcYAMJsS88JKAAIJu2p9KbCPBlmMKLaxYFPJiNbdEgdOFCf➥
l7p8+AKeiXmFJky9X+VxsL6Ost4vs9dOzUu6Hwmow6wfI71uFJU+N1f5GyAm4yil73Rv➥
Yr14RWiW1OqqSQBRN8JJStQPmPMY4rr/Gc541gyMa3b/U4sPdiB713M1csu4oGQUg➥
A6fSF4N2ST7yh7fw6pF8RwMgyOAJ6SeCwfWHwB6JkNs9qw8Z9zy5HeR6cffQ3+Qzns➥
bF7x30QVj5E5qa5WvNaDU7RuOTG28jxppBQv7fLKX+i/cpt+aJdtpcru6iCnSSMScXp9S➥
ESt1j/qxuA8NO7qC//CibkhuGbsAaz6CJu3AxT71GDOPMwaMQ9NSOmkt8WhOazYTsb➥
vizCHaoZ4YYxW/MWpOyMfATD4JlLEpAX3djy1MvaVzNp5GN1e8bO2OOTztZE4OxjYz➥
fcCtDp7RmNQvL7eoZDfagV7iOXAt8mbWzf5nO5DO/iHj+MgJsjpm3p1MI81ZhPLkJlUi➥
vUS8Sb+x3bz/riTlqSUwl8uZxfedmvQd+SHPLihRDiR7FYrqwIxpk1F3r5yaG4dpIgWFzZ➥
OutqJDKFcM93sOxnlVJK+ox/hVeJ3AzK3LQP+43hJMKttg9tKr8e9hKpZxIO+dqZUZB2➥
k+wtmJ6CfxlXM2rwk7X4TpTXmI7TUxZ7fkw18Kj+N4yPNooEs7LGtcWGhp8GoQcnFa5➥
M93vOUx3rHE2SoAihZNdFgjypei03XoR4uYEi1BySJOPDNy2W/cg5Coc3gmwTKq8JLk➥
efkypey7sdfO5FIgaUtNvsGg3KTXaXAyxSvZVISKAmuj42H+/g6kJlgFU3kBl35iZqt6Doo➥
YnAWXEXF8DG99GDOitA2QknhG11c8ho8y1ZzJg3d0xcoIxF+c31+is2wHwNu3SZoFQ➥
QIW8KGo88kJxZp9CMZa3dcZYmObBllItVX+zf4aGGInVWQlLfhrCn11sqqWFlLA7CkGV➥
ze9ZTI8tJIcSvTDe+SFj6mTEVGeGC5vAzU5YGrCR/FGTNe8D1N+JiHX7NOwHXdje3OC➥
XaaA6JlbiVOCEUXNidq9Nju5Ss+BavECX99gZWIwDSw2t+f63Q2mskZIl2pFQpS+WRX➥
wC9NQofbgnSerk49MAgpxMjnB2yenV83/Lib6aprtvNTOTDrZMhQe2eQ6Ec2+DrOOyI➥
7+Hg797gDzpjpx8rTXwjLuQgqpvOCg2waL8j8nQhhKMjicftxVncfY/XOSUG7bedsiQNV➥
K98QEgaOkKO60b46/qp6+lM/JevZ741MMlpyNJ2+HOF9kag7OZ5avG3QKfAm+27xc➥
e6l1OWbr+vOfe926Yvs/GpQteVX1J8ue74WOipu/MArpkAIr2Wmk/lhlku8Hey3LGt1ff7➥
29Qz+8B7OH4mWvQKDo5+zwWKHOwcnEkVnPdGPZBT+HOLpaJ7QP69ZVDZTVoBn➥
mk1fOKGzGefM1SoyuIBgiweKnbj62TOIxEAKvVWCtwGAMGbWSBT3QUlKM3jTgwsjM➥
/QEtZ8hgA12uKz41lymNPeoinJq1+OjiqSwJGqdSMFNs81UyIbBZy1wrQjFUn/EyF3VlN➥
DRrg6VrNJ5P1PUGoVjE4cyVcMtCtVg9gZbhiem26RCEwJWmyQQSa6Qo8DILMIU6hn/➥
xpReeMV6FO/UdgbUA5kOyh/N2ctaCxvmVYYoC657wDQX2Yn+kNELqYRPwdrodSHbn➥
81LhfLq2ortoQmM7x2IybMhbByLRHNymeuji6LU2KQiDr5mukeY9H1w+9ZkSqvsrEAr5➥
mG1iyHw79bvfOEE/U7BR4PrQqNZBmtHhTLOxjdKRIalut+5qHvtiCPn1TUzFf2XDnJx7TP➥
m+O/qmdfbytuqzL2cAo3mMLn5RTvyfYNs6DpSNLWMcandJ+JNUR+W4rOmkva4fJk➥
```
```
</e:CipherValue>
        </e:CipherData>
      </e:EncryptedData>
    </o:Security>
  </s:Header>
  <s:Body u:Id="_0">
    <wst:RequestSecurityToken Context=➥
"ProcessRequestSecurityToken" ➥
xmlns:wst="http://schemas.xmlsoap.org/ws/2005/02/trust">
      <wst:RequestType>http://schemas.xmlsoap.org/ws/2005/02/trust/Issue➥
</wst:RequestType>
      <wsid:InformationCardReference ➥
xmlns:wsid="http://schemas.xmlsoap.org/ws/2005/05/identity">
        <wsid:CardId>http://www.fabrikam.com/readercard/1234567890</wsid:CardId>
        <wsid:CardVersion>1</wsid:CardVersion>
```

```
      </wsid:InformationCardReference>
      <wst:Claims>
        <wsid:ClaimType Uri=➥
"http://schemas.xmlsoap.org/ws/2005/05/identity/claims/➥
givenname" ➥
xmlns:wsid="http://schemas.xmlsoap.org/ws/2005/05/identity" />
      </wst:Claims>
      <wst:KeyType>➥
http://schemas.xmlsoap.org/ws/2005/05/identity/NoProofKey</wst:KeyType>
      <ClientPseudonym xmlns=➥
"http://schemas.xmlsoap.org/ws/2005/05/identity">
        <PPID>VrOz8rmyCM+BA+EQVdOcOc/CLqrJ5+2OSO6ePhXt8Yo=</PPID>
      </ClientPseudonym>
      <wst:TokenType>urn:oasis:names:tc:SAML:1.0:assertion</wst:TokenType>
      <wsid:RequestDisplayToken xml:lang="en"➥
 xmlns:wsid="http://schemas.xmlsoap.org/ws/2005/05/identity" />
    </wst:RequestSecurityToken>
  </s:Body>
</s:Envelope>
```

The following are key elements of RequestSecurityToken.

RequestType

Within the RequestType element of RequestSecurityToken, you will see the type of request, in this case, Issue. As you'll recall, Issue is one of the four operations supported by the WsTrustResponder class.

```
      <wst:RequestType>http://schemas.xmlsoap.org/ws/2005/02/trust/Issue➥
</wst:RequestType>
```

InformationCardReference

Within RequestSecurityToken, you will find the InformationCardReference element. There you will find the identifier for the card that is making the request, as well as the card version that was in the information card that originated the request. As mentioned earlier, the STS can use this information when retrieving data for the card from a back-end store.

```
      <wsid:InformationCardReference ➥
xmlns:wsid="http://schemas.xmlsoap.org/ws/2005/05/identity">
        <wsid:CardId>http://www.fabrikam.com/readercard/1234567890</wsid:CardId>
        <wsid:CardVersion>1</wsid:CardVersion>
      </wsid:InformationCardReference>
```

Claims

The RequestSecurityToken XML also includes an element named Claims. As you might expect, it is here that the claims being requested from the STS are specified. In the following example, the request is for a single claim, givenname.

```
<wst:Claims>
    <wsid:ClaimType Uri=➠
"http://schemas.xmlsoap.org/ws/2005/05/identity/claims/➠
givenname" ➠
xmlns:wsid="http://schemas.xmlsoap.org/ws/2005/05/identity" />
</wst:Claims>
```

KeyType

The KeyType element identifies the type of proof key that the security token should contain. The requestor can specify that the proof key be asymmetric or symmetric or can opt for no proof key.

In the following XML, the request specifies NoProofKey:

```
<wst:KeyType>➠
http://schemas.xmlsoap.org/ws/2005/05/identity/NoProofKey</wst:KeyType>
```

■**Note** A relying party can specify the desired proof key in its policy. If it does not, an identity selector should default to requesting an asymmetric key token from the STS.

ClientPseudonym

The requestor may request that a specific PPID be used in the token generated by the identity provider. The desired PPID is then placed within the PPID element contained in the ClientPseudonym element, as shown in the following XML:

```
<ClientPseudonym xmlns=➠
"http://schemas.xmlsoap.org/ws/2005/05/identity">
    <PPID>VrOz8rmyCM+BA+EQVdOcOc/CLqrJ5+20SO6ePhXt8Yo=</PPID>
</ClientPseudonym>
```

The STS may use this value—but is not required to use it.

RequestDisplayToken

Identity selectors should be token agnostic, with the ability to simply serve as a router for delivering tokens from an identity provider to a relying party. From a user control and consent standpoint, it is desirable to display information about what will be transmitted to the relying party.

A RequestSecurityToken message can contain the RequestDisplayToken element. If provided, this specifies that a "display token" is requested and identifies the language for the display. The RequestDisplayToken element is optional for the requestor, and it is optional for the STS to respond with a display token.

In the following XML, you can see that a display token was requested and that the display language was English:

```
    <wsid:RequestDisplayToken xml:lang="en" ➡
xmlns:wsid="http://schemas.xmlsoap.org/ws/2005/05/identity" />
```

Note If you want to print the XML of an incoming `SecurityTokenRequest`, it's pretty straightforward to do so. In the `Issue` method, add the following code:

```
            //The following will write out the incoming request to a file
            System.Xml.XmlDictionaryWriter writer =➡
System.Xml.XmlDictionaryWriter.CreateDictionaryWriter(➡
System.Xml.XmlWriter.Create("C:\\SecurityTokenRequest" + ➡
Guid.NewGuid().ToString() + ".xml"));
            request.WriteMessage(writer);
            writer.Flush();
             writer.Close();
```

RequestSecurityTokenResponse

The following XML represents a `RequestSecurityTokenResponse` message:

```
<?xml version="1.0" encoding="utf-8"?>
<s:Envelope xmlns:a="http://www.w3.org/2005/08/addressing" ➡
xmlns:s="http://www.w3.org/2003/05/soap-envelope">
  <s:Header>
    <a:Action s:mustUnderstand="1">➡
http://schemas.xmlsoap.org/ws/2005/02/trust/RSTR/Issue</a:Action>
    <a:RelatesTo>urn:uuid:47d34de5-c07e-4efb-8f17-c3c0a404fb10➡
</a:RelatesTo>
  </s:Header>
  <s:Body>
    <t:RequestSecurityTokenResponse Context=➡
"ProcessRequestSecurityToken" xmlns:t=➡
"http://schemas.xmlsoap.org/ws/2005/02/trust">
      <t:TokenType>urn:oasis:names:tc:SAML:1.0:assertion</t:TokenType>
      <t:RequestedSecurityToken>
        <saml:Assertion MajorVersion="1" MinorVersion="1" ➡
AssertionID="uuid-e4f5f610-a5a6-49a3-915b-4560f723fab3" ➡
Issuer="www.fabrikam.com" IssueInstant="2007-06-03T20:43:36.289Z" ➡
xmlns:saml="urn:oasis:names:tc:SAML:1.0:assertion">
          <saml:Conditions NotBefore="2007-06-03T20:43:36.289Z" ➡
NotOnOrAfter="2007-06-04T04:43:36.289Z"></saml:Conditions>
          <saml:AuthenticationStatement ➡
AuthenticationMethod="urn:oasis:namespace:tc:SAML:1.0:am:unspecified"➡
 AuthenticationInstant="2007-06-03T20:43:36.289Z">
            <saml:Subject>
              <saml:SubjectConfirmation>
                <saml:ConfirmationMethod>➡
```

```
urn:oasis:names:tc:SAML:1.0:cm:sender-vouches</saml:ConfirmationMethod>
              </saml:SubjectConfirmation>
            </saml:Subject>
          </saml:AuthenticationStatement>
          <saml:AttributeStatement>
            <saml:Subject>
              <saml:SubjectConfirmation>
                <saml:ConfirmationMethod>➡
urn:oasis:names:tc:SAML:1.0:cm:sender-vouches</saml:ConfirmationMethod>
              </saml:SubjectConfirmation>
            </saml:Subject>
            <saml:Attribute AttributeName=➡
"privatepersonalidentifier"➡
 AttributeNamespace=➡
"http://schemas.xmlsoap.org/ws/2005/05/identity/claims">
              <saml:AttributeValue>*Fill in this field*</saml:AttributeValue>
            </saml:Attribute>
          </saml:AttributeStatement>
          <Signature xmlns="http://www.w3.org/2000/09/xmldsig#">
            <SignedInfo>
              <CanonicalizationMethod Algorithm=➡
"http://www.w3.org/2001/10/xml-exc-c14n#"></CanonicalizationMethod>
              <SignatureMethod Algorithm=➡
"http://www.w3.org/2000/09/xmldsig#rsa-sha1"></SignatureMethod>
              <Reference URI=➡
"#uuid-e4f5f610-a5a6-49a3-915b-4560f723fab3">
                <Transforms>
                  <Transform Algorithm=➡
"http://www.w3.org/2000/09/xmldsig#enveloped-signature"></Transform>
                  <Transform Algorithm=➡
"http://www.w3.org/2001/10/xml-exc-c14n#"></Transform>
                </Transforms>
                <DigestMethod Algorithm=➡
"http://www.w3.org/2000/09/xmldsig#sha1"></DigestMethod>
                <DigestValue>fVjOEGLO6glDGIMZQLKSSLl8ONg=</DigestValue>
              </Reference>
            </SignedInfo>
            <SignatureValue>OiGN1NeXcOS43RDNY2ZZe84904eIEinhumo8➡
yqyRq1S39YCdpBLUM2uJ8kpnpYiNkukPb1RHhtCpg4OU/+UP5aVph24LS7➡
+x1ck/Cm+/55jgYqxFQTvv+WNO7K8cyKj3fc9xYO8ct9CJZ7tzTVZ4/uFIG2V/➡
aPCCVBw96dzHNyu/Jkaiajju1Oh4Q/9i26mfIiYJeETMwcN1mOeOKfFlR9NidIf➡
kPUQ6Nx3jXsTNYG6AEGf+uiCRqYBTOkzYiyz4FEteKjrve4TppfR8dR1vp6jDT➡
DKbXFGFKwcOLoA7EFaSStlnNH+HOO4O6z+OtiilOMIVTJD4BZuxrPzMM24➡
SRA==</SignatureValue>
            <KeyInfo>
              <X509Data>
                <X509Certificate>MIIGRDCCBSygAwIBAgIKKCtCOAAAAAAALz➡
```

ANBgkqhkiG9w0BAQUFADBuMRMwEQYKCZImiZPyLGQBGRYDY29tMRkwF➥
wYKCZImiZPyLGQBGRYJbWljcm9zb2ZOMRQwEgYKCZImiZPyLGQBGRYEY29➥
ycDEVMBMGCgmSJomT8ixkARkWBW50ZGV2MQ8wDQYDVQQDEwZBZGF➥
OdWOwHhcNMDYwNTE5MjMOMjMzWhcNMTEwMzEwMTgyNzU2WjBiMQ➥
swCQYDVQQGEwJVUzETMBEGA1UECBMKV2FzaGluZ3RvbjEQMA4GA1UEB➥
xMHUmVkbW9uZDERMA8GA1UEChMIRmFicmlrYWOxGTAXBgNVBAMTEH➥
d3dy5mYWJyaWthbS5jb2OwggEiMAOGCSqGSIb3DQEBAQUAA4IBDwAwg➥
gEKAoIBAQDAAqeU11oie9Zaf01ua9eW8J3nGqxnYeJ5zE1Y/ltIWlAiIkSnr+➥
TnwUcq43iXxMuIL/QdTBOqSSYLiJX5OoTMseU4rYnGuSf2gVlttQcWg6tOa➥
/U/sGX37J8b6mHMFsOshuv6Bt7A5Pk679v5qRPEjSVYBHKpQ+4b1iD2t6K➥
Y5PADA/IJqNJNx8OoB7fMZpwBLG+e4NMy5hwKPPoi37PrtIvHnwZ34C65➥
NP6wGnre+HOlEuem15hsjb1ORReqxCxBji5Fnx/yyvNhJpU6GpAqHBDpkJh➥
QpDaUIUB8nqcCp3RdAJo1Seez0Yx9BHsDhKZCLijyTEScJ/4LcVvDFoQTAg➥
MBAAGjggLuMIIC6jAOBgNVHQ8BAf8EBAMCBPAwRAYJKoZIhvcNAQkPB➥
DcwNTAOBggqhkiG9w0DAgICAIAwDgYIKoZIhvcNAwQCAgCAMACGBSs➥
OAwIHMAoGCCqGSIb3DQMHMBOGA1UdDgQWBBSX8lpAdmwjX7vbmO➥
lB1JV4wSwkxDATBgNVHSUEDDAKBggrBgEFBQcDATAfBgNVHSMEGDAW➥
gBTsobxGxn8LezMRzpHVQ+nhhv5WujA5BgNVHR8EMjAwMC6gLKAqhih➥
odHRwOi8vd3d3LmFkYXR1bS5jb20ovY3JsZGF0YS9hZGF0dWOuY3JsMIIBC➥
gYIKwYBBQUHAQEEgfOwgfowegYIKwYBBQUHMAKGbmhodHA6Ly90aG9➥
uLXRlc3QxLTIwMDMubnRkZXYuY29ycC5taWNyb3NvZnQuY29tLONlcnRF➥
bnJvbGwvdGhvbi1OZXNOS0yMDAzLm50ZGV2LmNvcnAubWljcm9zb2Z➥
OLmNvbV9BZGF0dWOuY3JOMHwGCCsGAQUFBzAChnBmaaWxlOi8vXFxoa➥
G9uLXRlc3QxLTIwMDMubnRkZXYuY29ycC5taWNyb3NvZnQuY29tXENlcn➥
RFbnJvbGxcdGhvbi1OZXNOS0yMDAzLm50ZGV2LmNvcnAubWljcm9zb➥
2ZOLmNvbV9BZGF0dWOuY3JOMIHaBggrBgEFBQcBDASBzTCByqFhoF8w➥
XTBbMFkwCWltYWdlL2dpZjAhMB8wBwYFKw4DAhoEFAdN4arCOM6hg➥
N20U76UlOixItG8MCkWJ2hodHA6Ly93d3cuYWRhdHVtLmNvbS9pbWFn➥
ZXMvYWRhdHVtLmdpZqJloGMwYTBfMFOWCWltYWdlL2dpZjAhMB8wB➥
wYFKw4DAhoEFPPrgHBqOxRSSDUqLsF874in51RrMCOWK2hodHA6Ly93➥
d3cuZmFicmlrYWOuY29tL2ltYWdlcy9mYWJyaWthbS5naWYwFwYDVROg➥
BBAwDjAMBgorBgEEAYI3PGQBMAOGCSqGSIb3DQEBBQUAA4IBAQBM➥
2LFyAYOxm27hyFG7/v+yhRFsOn97tt5KDgZb8yB1Oolw+uJnYa169RvalN➥
/bROnyscm3wqfOlNNzTG/d0iBObQtibxPwCXDbODqvUheVQhhRjATQF➥
ygQbicrK3ENn4Ar77HGjRPDpsgLVtCAcx6qqUTuq33HcORP5tVMsh7Z7➥
qnQD1AV6ohO8UewRMO4Rwz83OHOxTFPXq7N3IwWfbHMHAS+jSF➥
OOOS/7yqmiM5ZLCCPOOXoEa+ixB9Gk8qM5PSHThC+VvSUHmNl9hJ➥
G9/jLSzSOXwM1JrDJGdNyUbk8XWbDppi2BKnPTnO5Fngud5PrALVuvT➥
aDIyPdflaPzuEd</X509Certificate>
                    </X509Data>
                </KeyInfo>
            </Signature>
        </saml:Assertion>
    </t:RequestedSecurityToken>
    <t:RequestedAttachedReference>
        <o:SecurityTokenReference xmlns:o=➥

```
"http://docs.oasis-open.org/wss/2004/01/oasis-200401-wss-wssecurity-secext-1.0.xsd">
        <o:KeyIdentifier ValueType=➥
"http://docs.oasis-open.org/wss/➥
oasis-wss-saml-token-profile-1.0#SAMLAssertionID">➥
uuid-e4f5f610-a5a6-49a3-915b-4560f723fab3</o:KeyIdentifier>
      </o:SecurityTokenReference>
    </t:RequestedAttachedReference>
    <t:RequestedUnattachedReference>
      <o:SecurityTokenReference xmlns:o=➥
"http://docs.oasis-open.org/wss/2004/01/oasis-200401-wss-wssecurity-secext-1.0.xsd">
        <o:KeyIdentifier ValueType=➥
"http://docs.oasis-open.org/wss/➥
oasis-wss-saml-token-profile-1.0#SAMLAssertionID">➥
uuid-e4f5f610-a5a6-49a3-915b-4560f723fab3</o:KeyIdentifier>
      </o:SecurityTokenReference>
    </t:RequestedUnattachedReference>
  </t:RequestSecurityTokenResponse>
 </s:Body>
</s:Envelope>
```

If you want to write SecurityTokenRequestResponse to a file, you can easily do this with the following code:

```
//The following will write out the outgoing response to a file
System.Xml.XmlDictionaryWriter writer = ➥
System.Xml.XmlDictionaryWriter.CreateDictionaryWriter(➥
System.Xml.XmlWriter.Create("C:\\SecurityTokenRequestResponse" + ➥
Guid.NewGuid().ToString() + ".xml"));
response.WriteMessage(writer);
writer.Flush();
 writer.Close();
```

Extending the Simple-STS Sample

If you look closely at the Simple-STS sample, you'll see that in the RequestSecurityTokenResponse class there's an operation named GetTokenAttributes.

In that class, you'll find the following code:

```
protected List<SamlAttribute> GetTokenAttributes()
{
    List<SamlAttribute> result = new List<SamlAttribute>();


    result.Add(new SamlAttribute(new Claim(ClaimTypes.PPID ,➥
"*Fill in this field*", Rights.PossessProperty)));
    return result;
}
```

Although this is great for a demo, it doesn't provide a lot of value if you want to produce more than one token. Currently, regardless of the request that's received, the Simple-STS sample provides a token with a single claim, a hard-coded PPID.

In this next section, I'll show you how to retrieve information from SecurityTokenRequest and generate tokens based on the claims that were requested; I'll also discuss transforming claims to meet the needs of a relying party.

Creating the InformationCardReference Class

One of the additions you'll be making to the RequestSecurityToken class is adding visibility to the InformationCardReference data provided in the request. As discussed earlier in the chapter, InformationCardReference contains a unique card ID as well as a card version. The STS can use this when retrieving data to populate the token.

1. If you haven't already done so, open the SampleSecurityTokenService project.

2. Right-click the SampleSecurityTokenService project in Solution Explorer, and select Add and then Class.

3. Name the class **InformationCardReference**, and populate it with the following code:

```
using System;
using System.Collections.Generic;
using System.Text;

namespace BeginningCardspace
{
    public class InformationCardReference
    {
        private string cardID = "";
        private string cardVersion = "";

        public string CardID
        {
            get { return cardID; }
            set { cardID = value; }
        }

        public string CardVersion
        {
            get { return cardVersion; }
            set { cardVersion = value; }
        }

    }
}
```

Modifying the RequestSecurityToken Class

Next, you'll modify the RequestSecurityToken class to retrieve key pieces of information from the incoming request and expose it through properties on the class. This information will later be retrieved by the RequestSecurityTokenClassResponse class when generating the token.

1. In Solution Explorer, right-click RequestSecurityToken, and select View Code.

2. You'll want to use the InformationCardReference class that was just created, so add a using statement to the top of file for the BeginningCardspace namespace:

   ```
   using BeginningCardspace;
   ```

   Next, you'll need to create private variables to store the information you'll be exposing on the class. In addition to InformationCardReference, you'll be exposing details on the RequestDisplayToken, ClientPseudonym, and Claims elements in the incoming requests.

3. Add the following private variables to store details from the request:

   ```
   private bool requestDisplayToken = false;
   private string requestDisplayTokenLanguage = "";
   private string clientPseudonym = "";
   private List<string> requestedClaims = new List<string>();
   private InformationCardReference informationCardReference =➡
   new InformationCardReference();
   ```

4. Next, add properties that map to these variables. Add the following properties to the file:

   ```
   public bool RequestDisplayToken
       {
           get { return requestDisplayToken; }
           set { requestDisplayToken = value; }
       }
   public string RequestDisplayTokenLanguage
       {
           get { return requestDisplayTokenLanguage; }
           set { requestDisplayTokenLanguage = value; }


       }
   public string ClientPseudonym
       {
           get { return clientPseudonym; }
           set { clientPseudonym = value; }


       }
   public List<string> RequestedClaims
       {
           get { return requestedClaims; }
           set { requestedClaims = value; }
   ```

```
        }
        public InformationCardReference InformationCardReferenceInRequest
        {
                get {return informationCardReference;}
            set { informationCardReference = value; }
        }
```

With the variables defined, you'll next want to create methods that process these elements. If you examine the InitializeHandlers method, you'll see that handlers are created for Claims, InformationCardReference, RequestDisplayToken, and ClientPseudonym. By default, the Simple-STS sample uses the IgnoreElement handler for each of these.

As you might imagine, this handler ignores the element and continues processing the XML in XmlReader. You'll now add handlers for each of these elements.

In the InitializeHandlers method, you will see the following comment:

```
        // Elements that are accepted, but ignored
```

5. Modify the code so it resembles the following:

```
        // Elements that are accepted, but ignored
        wsTrustElements.Add(Constants.WSTrust.Elements.Claims,➡
  ClaimsHandler);
        wsTrustElements.Add(Constants.WSTrust.Elements.➡
EncryptionAlgorithm, IgnoreElement);
        wsIdentityElements.Add(➡
Constants.WSIdentity.Elements.InformationCardReference, ➡
InformationCardReferenceHandler);
        wsIdentityElements.Add(➡
Constants.WSIdentity.Elements.RequestDisplayToken, RequestDisplayTokenHandler);
        wsIdentityElements.Add(➡
Constants.WSIdentity.Elements.ClientPseudonym, ClientPseudonymHandler);
```

You will next add new methods that map to the names you specified in the InitializeHandlers method.

The wst:Claims element contains a number of elements of ClaimType. Each ClaimType element contains an attribute with the URI of a claim that was requested by the relying party. These claims are stored in a string collection and exposed via the RequestedClaims property. These will be used to dynamically determine which claims should be placed in the generated token.

6. Add the ClaimsHandler method, and populate it with the following code:

```
        private void ClaimsHandler(XmlReader reader)
        {
            while (reader.Read() && !(reader.NodeType ➡
== XmlNodeType.EndElement && reader.Name == "wst:Claims"))
                {
```

```
            if (reader.IsStartElement())
            {
                if (reader.HasAttributes)
                {
                    reader.MoveToFirstAttribute();
                    RequestedClaims.Add(reader.Value);
                }


            }
        }

    }
```

7. Next, you will add a handler to retrieve the information from the InformationCardReference element. This element contains two child elements, CardId and CardVersion, which are captured and placed into the property InformationCardReferenceInRequest.

```
        private void InformationCardReferenceHandler(XmlReader reader)
        {


            while (reader.Read() && !(reader.NodeType ➥
== XmlNodeType.EndElement && reader.Name == "wsid:InformationCardReference"))
            {
                if (reader.IsStartElement())
                {
                 string elementName = reader.Name;
                 elementName = elementName.Substring(5); //remove 'wsid:'
                 reader.Read();
                 string elementValue = reader.Value;
                 if (elementName == "CardId")
                 {
                     informationCardReference.CardID = elementValue;
                 }
                 if (elementName == "CardVersion")
                 {
                     informationCardReference.CardVersion = elementValue;
                 }
                }

            }
```

8. As mentioned earlier in the chapter, the RequestDisplayToken element allows an identity selector to request a token that is used to display the value of the token inside the selector:

```
        }
        private void RequestDisplayTokenHandler(XmlReader reader)
        {
            RequestDisplayToken = true;
            if (reader.HasAttributes)
            {
                reader.MoveToFirstAttribute();

                RequestDisplayTokenLanguage = reader.Value;
            }
            reader.Read();
        }
```

9. The incoming request may contain the element ClientPseudonym. This allows the caller to provide a pseudonym PPID. This is stored in a child element of PPID, which is retrieved and placed in the ClientPseudonym property.

```
        private void ClientPseudonymHandler(XmlReader reader)
        {

            reader.Read();
            reader.Read();
            ClientPseudonym = reader.Value;
            reader.Read();
        }
```

Modifying the RequestSecurityTokenResponse Class

Now that you've exposed these properties in the RequestSecurityToken class, you'll next write code that will consume them in the RequestSecurityTokenResponse class:

1. In Solution Explorer, right-click RequestSecurityTokenResponse.cs, and select View Code.

2. Add a using statement for the BeginningCardspace namespace to the top of the file:

   using BeginningCardspace;

3. Just as you did with the RequestSecurityToken class, add private variables to hold the values that will be passed in:

```
        private bool requestDisplayToken = false;
        private string requestDisplayTokenLanguage = "";
        private string clientPseudonym = "";
        private List<string> requestedClaims = new List<string>();
        private InformationCardReference ➥
informationCardReference = new InformationCardReference();
```

4. Next, modify the constructor for the class, and populate these variables from the values in the incoming RequestSecurityToken variable RST:

```
public RequestSecurityTokenResponse(RST rst)
    :base(false)
{
    this.context = rst.Context;
    this.useKey = rst.UseKey;
    this.keyType = rst.KeyType;
    //Added for Beginning Cardspace
    this.requestDisplayToken = rst.RequestDisplayToken;
    this.requestDisplayTokenLanguage = rst.RequestDisplayTokenLanguage;
    this.clientPseudonym = rst.ClientPseudonym;
    this.requestedClaims = rst.RequestedClaims;
    this.informationCardReference = ➥
rst.InformationCardReferenceInRequest;

}
```

At this point, you've laid all the groundwork to generate tokens that return the requested claims. You've done this in the GetTokenAttributes method of the RenResponse class. It is in this method that a list of SamlAttributes are used in the SAML token.

It is here that you can reference the values of the CardId and CardVersion elements passed in with InformationCardReference and use them to retrieve information for a token from a back-end data store.

Once you have the detail for CardId, you'll want to cycle through the claims in the requestedClaims variable. For each claim, you'll create a new SamlAttribute and add it to the list.

As you examine each claim, you can also determine whether a transformation is required. For example, the relying party may request a claim of Over21, which would be a Boolean value, while in your database you may store the birth date of the cardholder. In this case, you could evaluate the birth date and determine whether the individual is older than 21. Based on the result, you could populate an Over21 claim with a Boolean value and add it to the token.

5. Modify the GetTokenAttributes class to contain the following code. Make edits to this to retrieve data from your particular database and perform any specific claims transformation. (For those looking to simply test this functionality, you can always build conditional logic to populate the claims, handing off to another routine that evaluates the URI of the requested claim and the CardId and returns a fixed value in return.)

```
    protected List<SamlAttribute> GetTokenAttributes()
        {
            List<SamlAttribute> result = new List<SamlAttribute>();

            //Retrieve data for token using CardId and CardVersion


            //Iterate through claims in Claims variable
             foreach(string claimName in requestedClaims)
             {
                 // Generate claim date with transformation, if needed.
                 //  For example a claim of type boolean for 'over21'
                 //  could be generated from a identity provider stored
                 //  datetime field for Birthdate

                 //Add the claim to result
                 result.Add(new SamlAttribute(➥
   new Claim(claimName,"ValueGoesHere", Rights.PossessProperty)));
             }

            return result;
        }
```

Congratulations, you now have an STS that can issue tokens based on your specific claims.

Authorizing Issuance of a Token

One of the items mentioned earlier in the text is that you may want to examine the claims of the party authenticating to the STS to make a request.

The information for the requestor is available within AuthorizationContext. This section serves to provide you with code that can be used to extract that information so that it can be used by your authentication routines.

This code looks at two authentication scenarios—username and password and self-issued SAML. When presenting an information card secured with another self-issued card, you can find the information for the PPID for that card within the claimset that is provided.

If you happen to be using a card authenticated with username and password, you can interrogate AuthorizationContext's Properties collection and examine the Identities property.

By default, username and password will use a Windows identity. By retrieving the Windows identity from the Identities collection, you can get extended information, such as the authentication type, the name, a flag that specifies whether the requestor is authenticated, and the impersonation level.

In the Issue method, the WsTrustResponder class currently has a line of code that populates AuthorizationContext. You can add the following code beneath the variable used to hold AuthorizationContext, called ctx, to retrieve the data for the requestor:

```
                AuthorizationContext ctx = ➥
OperationContext.Current.ServiceSecurityContext.AuthorizationContext;
                Console.Write("ID:" + ctx.Id);
                if (ctx.Properties.Count > 0)
                {
                    System.Collections.Generic.List<System.Security.➥
Principal.IIdentity> identities = ➥
(System.Collections.Generic.List<➥
System.Security.Principal.IIdentity>)ctx.Properties["Identities"];
                    switch (identities[0].GetType().Name)
                    {
                        case "WindowsIdentity":
                            System.Security.Principal.➥
WindowsIdentity identity = (System.Security.Principal.WindowsIdentity)identities[0];
                            Console.WriteLine("-----------------------------");
                            Console.WriteLine("Windows Identity");
                            Console.WriteLine("-----------------------------");
                            Console.WriteLine(➥
"AuthenticationType:" + identity.AuthenticationType);
                            Console.WriteLine("Name:" + identity.Name);
                            Console.WriteLine("IsAuthenticated:" +➥
 identity.IsAuthenticated.ToString ());
                            Console.WriteLine("User:" + identity.User.Value);
                            Console.WriteLine(➥
"ImpersonationLevel:" + identity.ImpersonationLevel);

                            break;

                        default:
                            break;
                    }
                }

                foreach (ClaimSet cs in ctx.ClaimSets)
                {

                    Console.WriteLine(➥
"-----------------------------------------------");
                    Console.WriteLine("ClaimSet");
                    Console.WriteLine(➥
"-----------------------------------------------");
```

```
            foreach (Claim claim in cs)
            {
                Console.WriteLine(➡
"----------------------------------------------");
                Console.WriteLine("Claim");
                Console.WriteLine(~CC
"----------------------------------------------");

                Console.WriteLine("Type:" + claim.ClaimType);
                Console.WriteLine("Resource:" + claim.Resource);
                Console.WriteLine("Right:" + claim.Right);

            }

        }
```

Auditing the Relying Party

By default, the identity provider will not be provided with details about the relying party. This is done to provide a level of anonymity so that the identity provider cannot ascertain the location or context in which you are using your information cards.

In scenarios where an identity provider or the relying party is governed by law or business policy to audit the usage of information cards, this scenario is supported.

For an identity provider, this is done when creating an information card via the RequireAppliesTo element. For the relying party, this can be done with the AppliesTo element in the RequestSecurityTokenTemplate parameter in the token policy.

Note In the next chapter, I discuss managed cards in more detail, including the RequireAppliesTo element.

Summary

In this chapter, you began to focus on the identity provider, specifically the security token servers used to issue tokens for use at relying parties. In the upcoming chapters, you'll learn more about the underlying information cards, how to define templates for them, and how to issue and deliver them.

■■■

CHAPTER 11

Managed Cards

The earlier chapters in this book have focused on using information cards in your applications. They've shown how you can build websites, services, and clients that can accept cards, and in the previous chapter, you built a security token service that can generate tokens for card-carrying individuals. One topic noticeably absent, however, is any in-depth discussion about the cards themselves.

This chapter changes that by turning the lens squarely on cards, with coverage from the conceptual to the logical to the physical. This chapter looks at who you can expect to issue cards and the scenarios where you might want to issue your own. The chapter then puts information cards under the microscope, covering the underlying format of the CRD files that contain information cards. For those who want to generate their own managed cards, the chapter concludes with two exercises that generate functional utilities—the first serves to create templates that will be used in the creation of cards, and the second will generate the cards themselves. This chapter also serves as the prerequisite for Chapter 12, which will evolve these utilities to be used in automated workflows inside Windows Workflow Foundation.

Thinking About Cards

When thinking and writing about cards, I begin by focusing on two factors—card type and card scope. When I refer to *type*, I refer to the major buckets into which a card could be classified. The following paragraphs identify some of the major categories of cards—identity, payment/ financial, membership, and loyalty. When I refer to *scope*, I reference the universe of sites at which a card can be used. This can range from a single site to a federation of specific sites to any other site.

Outside the public sector, which can mandate the possession of cards, a card provider needs to offer benefits—be they real or perceived—for the card owner. But rest assured that cards are issued because they provide a realizable benefit for the *issuer*.

When talking about credit cards, most people immediately think of names such as Master-Card, Visa, and Discover. The attractiveness of these cards is that they are trusted and widely accepted across the globe. Each of these companies runs card programs and benefits directly from per-transaction fees paid by merchants.

Although most major retail outlets will accept these cards, they many times offer their own credit cards as well. In the United States, major department stores such as Sears, JCPenny, Macy's, and Best Buy offer customers their own store-specific credit cards. Like the more ubiquitous cards, these cards also benefit from finance charges and fees paid by the user.

Because these cards are tied to a particular chain, the store can incorporate the card into attractive offerings that will help drive revenue from sales and/or credit. If one examines the weekly advertisements from one of these chains, it's not hard to find an offer like "No payments or interest for 18 months!" or "10% off all purchases made with this card!"

Another type of card is one that identifies the cardholder as a member. Membership, as they say, has its privileges. In this category, membership typically authorizes your consumption of one or more services. Common examples include the ability to rent DVDs from a video store, the ability to use the facilities at a health club, and the ability to get access to emergency road service from an auto club. The issuer gains value from one or more areas (membership dues from cardholders in most scenarios), while in others (such as a video store) it expedites the process by which the issuer conducts business.

Another popular type of card is a loyalty card. The concept of loyalty is relatively straight-forward. In exchange for your loyalty to a merchant, you are provided with a reward of some kind. Seen most often in grocery store chains in the United States, these cards provide the cardholders with the ability to get discounts on items by providing their cards. What's in it for a loyalty card provider? Information.

When you sign up for a loyalty card, you are providing, or *opting in*, information about yourself that will be attached to a card. This can range from your name, age, address, and phone number to an ID number. But this information is combined with your purchase history to provide a profile of you, the consumer. It can provide information about which products you buy and how often you buy them. This data can be used for internal marketing purposes, that is, determining which items could be put on sale to entice you to come into the store. As with most sales and discounts, the merchant typically expects you will not just buy the sale item but a whole basket of items.

In addition, this information can be used in providing marketing access to third parties. If you buy yogurt from Fabrikam Corporation, the grocery store chain could offer Contoso, Inc., the ability to give you a buy-one-get-one-free coupon for Contoso yogurt on your next visit. Are you buying wine and cheese? If so, certain inferences might be made. Based on those inferences, the *Wall Street Journal* might want to give you a special offer for three free issues. Other times, the store can provide a vendor with the ability to provide you with an on-the-spot reward. A few months back I was at the grocery store and was a bit surprised that in addition to my receipt, I was also handed a coupon for three free music downloads. Why? Because I bought a particular brand of salad.

Not only merchants can issue cards, however; individuals can issue their own. I can self-publish business cards that represent who I am, who I work for, my title, and my contact information. The card enables me, the issuer, to readily share contact information with others in an expedited manner. Because there was cost and effort involved in the creation of the card, as long as the card does not say "King of the Universe," the card also provides an additional level of credibility to claims stated in conversation.

Branding and Federation

When talking about value for the issuer, another consideration is branding. Companies spend millions upon millions of dollars advertising their brands and attempting to gain "mind share" with consumers. Sometimes this occurs in obvious forms such as advertisements, but other times this occurs with more subtlety. One such example is the "check presenter," the binder in which a restaurant presents you with the check for a meal. If you look at the check presenter, there is typically a logo for a type of credit card. I've been told that this statistically has improved the chances that the restaurant patron will use a card bearing that same logo. Information cards are represented by an image, and a managed card with your brand embedded on it could be an opportunity to have your brand seen regularly via the identity selector, which could drive additional usage.

In addition to the branding of the card, an issuer may find value in encouraging the use of the card on a number of third-party sites. There are a number of reasons and opportunities to do this.

Let's begin by looking at a real-world example—my auto club card. I can use my auto club card for discounts at a number of places that have nothing to do with my car, such as theme parks and online flower shops. Typically, this is a win-win-win situation. The issuer of the card wins, because their card is seen as more highly valued. In many cases, such as with the auto club, there are actually stickers that bear their brand at many locations. The merchant that provides the discount gets a customer purchasing goods or services, and the new customer acquisition cost is relatively low. And for the cardholder, I'm pleased to be getting a discount. By issuing your own card, you have the opportunity to take a similar approach online and increase your brand visibility and value.

Another scenario is using the card as an identity across multiple sites that you own. A company may own a number of web properties and would like to use a single sign-on mechanism for each of these sites. Imagine a magazine publisher that offers hundreds of magazines, each across all may have its own site online. In addition to offering subscriptions to individual magazines, the publisher could offer subscriptions to magazine genres.

You could, for example, purchase a Sports package or a News and Current Events package, which would allow you to read online content from multiple sources that cover a particular genre. These categories could be broad or narrow, say a Films category or stories about films directed by Alfred Hitchcock. This could open up a number of potential revenue streams from the same content.

Another opportunity would use a card across multiple sites, whereby the cardholder would be given access to particular items, such as online articles, videos, and so on. The card issuer would subsidize the cost of the items viewed in exchange for opt-in information from the consumer.

As you begin thinking about the possibilities, you begin to find new and creative ways that managed information cards could introduce interesting opportunities.

To Issue or Not to Issue

Regardless of the type of card or the scope in which it will be used, issuing cards costs money. Both the card issuance and the associated token issuance will require infrastructure, and that infrastructure brings with it associated costs, management, and maintenance. As you begin to think about whether to issue your own cards, if you are a for-profit business, it's OK to be selfish. The first two questions you should ask yourself when looking at issuing your own cards should be "Do self-issued or existing third-party cards provide functionality that will suit my needs?" and "What are the tangible benefits of issuing my own cards?" If there are benefits commensurate with the value you'll receive, you should consider becoming an issuer. Many times, however, you'll find that accepting third party cards will provide the desired effect, without the costs and responsibilities of being an issuer.

Looking Inside an Information Card

Today, individuals provide and business entities accept a wide variety of cards—bank, credit, and identity. In many cases, the individuals who possess the cards and the businesses that accept them have no real knowledge of the systems, protocols, and workflows required by the underlying network that issues the cards.

Take, for example, your banking and credit cards. Most people have no idea what's encoded on the magnetic strip on the back or how that information is used to validate both their identity and the availability of funds. The same can be said for the individuals who own the businesses that accept them. Does the local diner, gas station, bookshop, or hardware store really spend a lot of time learning the underlying card information and protocols used by the system? I would venture to say no. Consumers receive cards from institutions that they trust, and institutions receive card-processing equipment from people they trust. Through this trust on both their parts, electronic commerce can take place. Sure, a percentage of individuals will investigate the inner workings of the system, but for most of the population, it could be a great technical infrastructure or otherworldly magic that facilitates their transactions. As long as money is dispensed from the cash machine and purchases made with credit cards are approved (and merchants paid), many people are blissfully ignorant of how it actually happens.

Realistically, many people will never need or care to know the underlying technical details for their information cards. This section, however, is for people who *are* actually curious about what's stored in the card and for those who want to create them.

To begin with, it is important to note that information cards do not contain actual details but instead contain metadata about which details are available. They also contain a list of token services that can serve up those details via a token, as well as metadata endpoints for those services that provide information on how to interact with them. The card also identifies what varieties of tokens can be delivered from the service, such as, SAML 1.0.

The card contains information about the card itself, including an identifier for the card, the version of the card, and the date and time the card was issued.

The information card also contains metadata that can be used by the identity selector. This metadata ranges from the default name of the card, the name of the issuer, and the location of the privacy notice.

All of this information is placed in a signed XML document, specifically within an element named InformationCard.

The following XML represents the InformationCard element and its subelements:

```
<InformationCard
xmlns="http://schemas.xmlsoap.org/ws/2005/05/identity"
xmlns:wsa="http://www.w3.org/2005/08/addressing"
xmlns:wst="http://schemas.xmlsoap.org/ws/2005/02/trust"
xml:lang="en-us">
<InformationCardReference>
<CardId>http://www.fabrikam.com/CardId/1234567890</CardId>
<CardVersion>1</CardVersion>
</InformationCardReference>
```

```
<CardName>Fabrikam Loyalty Card</CardName>
<CardImage MimeType="image/gif"> ... </CardImage>
<Issuer>http://www.fabrikam.com</Issuer>
<TimeIssued>2007-01-02T00:00:01Z</TimeIssued>
<TokenServiceList>
<TokenService>
<wsa:EndpointReference>
<wsa:Address>http://www.fabrikam.com/sts</wsa:Address>
<wsa:Metadata>
<wsx:Metadata>
<wsx:MetadataSection
Dialect="http://schemas.xmlsoap.org/ws/2004/09/mex">
<wsx:MetadataReference>
<wsa:Address>https://www.fabrikam.com/sts/mex</wsa:Address>
</wsx:MetadataReference>
</wsx:MetadataSection>
</wsx:Metadata>
</wsa:Metadata>
</wsa:EndpointReference>
<UserCredential>
<UsernamePasswordCredential>
<Username>mmercuri</Username>
</UsernamePasswordCredential>
</UserCredential>
</TokenService>
</TokenServiceList>
<SupportedTokenTypeList>
<wst:TokenType>urn:oasis:names:tc:SAML:1.0:assertion</wst:TokenType>
</SupportedTokenTypeList>
<SupportedClaimTypeList>
<SupportedClaimType Uri=".../ws/2005/05/identity/claims/givenname">
<DisplayTag>Given Name</DisplayTag>
</SupportedClaimType>
<SupportedClaimType Uri=".../ws/2005/05/identity/claims/surname">
<DisplayTag>Last Name</DisplayTag>
</SupportedClaimType>
</SupportedClaimTypeList>
<RequireAppliesTo />
<PrivacyNotice Version="1">
http://www.fabrikam.com/privacynotice
</PrivacyNotice>
</InformationCard>
```

Table 11-1 provides more details on each of the key elements in the XML file.

Table 11-1. *The InformationCard Element*

Element	Description
InformationCard	This is the container element for the information card.
InformationCardReference/CardID	This is an identifier provided by the issuer that is used to identify the card. Sample value: http://www.fabrikam.com/CardId/1234567890
InformationCardReference/CardVersion	This is the version of the card. Sample value: 1
CardName	This is a name that describes the card. This will be the default name used for the card when loaded into the identity selector. Sample value: Fabrikam Loyalty Card
Issuer	This identifies a URI for the issuer. When a relying party has a policy that cards are accepted only from a specific issuer, the value in this field will be used to identify cards from that issuer. Sample value: http://www.fabrikam.com
TimeIssued	This identifies the time when the card was issued. Note: Cards typically do not contain expiry information. The security token server determines whether a card has been expired or revoked.
CardImage	This is an image to be used for the card in Base64. This element contains an attribute named MimeType that identifies the MIME type for the image. Sample MimeType value: image/png Note: The Windows CardSpace identity selector will display this image in two different sizes: 120×80 and 90×60. When developing an image to be displayed on a card, the target size should be 120×80.
TokenServiceList/TokenService	An information card does not actually contain any claim values. It contains information about what claims are associated with the card and where the token services that can provide those claims can be contacted. Within the InformationCard element is TokenServiceList. This contains one or more TokenService elements that identify services that can provide a token. The TokenService elements are prioritized, with the first item in the list receiving top priority.

Table 11-1. *The InformationCard Element (Continued)*

Element	Description
TokenServiceList/TokenService/EndpointReference	Each token service is available at a particular endpoint. The EndpointReference element identifies the URIs for both the STS and the metadata service for the STS. The URI for the STS itself is stored in the Address subelement. Sample value: http://www.fabrikam.com/sts The URI for the mex service is stored in the subelement Metadata\Metadata\MetadataSection\MetadataReference\Address. The relying party will retrieve the WSDL from this endpoint and use the metadata to identify how to connect with the STS. Sample value: https://www.fabrikam.com/mex
TokenServiceList/TokenService/UserCredential	This element identifies the type of credential required for a given TokenService. Sample value for Kerberos:

```
<UserCredential>
<KerberosV5Credential />
</ UserCredential>
```
Sample value for UsernameAndPassword:
```
<UserCredential>
<UsernamePasswordCredential>
<Username>mmercuri</Username>
</UsernamePasswordCredential>
</UserCredential>
```

Sample value for SelfIssuedCredential:
```
<UserCredential>
<SelfIssuedCredential>
<PrivatePersonalIdentifier>
..PPIDGoesHere..
</PrivatePersonalIdentifier>
</SelfIssuedCredential>
</UserCredential>
```
Sample value for Certificate:
```
<UserCredential>
<DisplayCredentialHint>
Please insert your smart card
</DisplayCredentialHint>
<X509V3Credential>
<ds:X509Data>
<wsse:KeyIdentifier
ValueType=http://docs.oasis-open.org/wss/2004/xx/➥
oasis-2004xx-wsssoap-message-➥
security-1.1#ThumbprintSHA1
EncodingType="http://docs.oasis-open.org/wss/2004/
01/oasis200401-wsssoap-
message-security-1.0#Base64Binary">
..CerticateInformation
</wsse:KeyIdentifier>
</ds:X509Data>
</X509V3Credential>
</UserCredential>
```

Table 11-1. *The InformationCard Element (Continued)*

Element	Description
SupportedTokenTypeList	An STS receives a request for a token and responds with a token. This element contains one or more TokenType subelements that identify the types of tokens available from the identity provider.

SupportedTokenTypeList/TokenType	This element defines a type of token that can be provided by the STS, for example SAML 1.0.
	Sample value:
	`<SupportedTokenTypeList>`
	`<wst:TokenType>urn:oasis:names:tc:SAML:1.0`
	`:assertion</wst:TokenType>`
	`</SupportedTokenTypeList>`

RequiresAppliesTo	This element contains a boolean that indicates whether the card will require the identification of the relying party (true) or will not (false). Typically, a security token server will not require information about the relying party. false is the typical value for this element. Some scenarios, particularly those that involve compliance policies and require auditing, will require that the relying party be identified. For those cases, the value for RequiresAppliesTo should be true.
PrivacyNotice	This contains the location of the privacy notice. This element also has a Version attribute that identifies the version of the privacy policy. Sample value: http://www.fabrikam.com/privacynotice

Starting with Information Card Templates

When you've decided you want to issue information cards, the *s* on the end of *cards* implies you want to create more than one. When building a system to generate cards, you'll first want to create one or more templates that define the cards you will issue. A template will identify the key pieces of information that will be static and consistent across all cards of a given type. This can include the token service list, the supported token type list, the card name, the issuer, the privacy notice, and so on. In addition, it can also contain default values for elements.

In the next sections, you'll create an application that you will use to create templates for cards. To begin with, you'll create a series of objects that will allow you to store, save, and load values for your template. You'll use these classes in your managed card template creator. In addition, you'll use these same objects later in this chapter to generate an actual card, as well as in Chapter 12, where you'll incorporate them into an automated issuance solution.

Building a Card Template Creator

To build a card template creator, follow these steps:

1. Open Visual Studio, and create a new Class Library project. Name the project **ManagedInformationCard**, and name the solution **PartI**.

2. Right-click project, and select Add References.

3. Add references to System.IdentityModel, System.Runtime.Serialization, System.Security, System.ServiceModel, and System.Xml.

4. Right-click the project, and select Properties. Set the default namespace to **BeginningCardspace**, and click OK.

   You will now create a set of classes that map to the XML hierarchy for an information card that was reviewed earlier. You'll add the Serialization attribute so that the class can be serialized to and deserialized from the disk.

5. Rename Class1.cs to **InformationCardReference.cs**.

6. Open the newly renamed file, and modify it so that it contains the following code:

```
using System;
using System.Collections.Generic;
using System.Text;

namespace BeginningCardspace
{
    [Serializable]
    public class InformationCardReference
    {
        private string _cardID ="";
        private int _cardVersion =1;

        public string CardID
        {
            get { return _cardID; }
            set { _cardID = value; }
        }

        public int CardVersion
        {
            get { return _cardVersion; }
            set { _cardVersion = value; }
        }

    }

}
```

7. Right-click the project, and add a new class. Name it **CardImage**.

8. Modify the new class so it contains the following code. You'll remember that the XML contained the MIME type for the image format. This class evaluates the filename provided and automatically sets the MIME type for the image.

```csharp
using System;
using System.Collections.Generic;
using System.Text;

namespace BeginningCardspace
{

    [Serializable]
    public class CardImage
    {
        private string _imageName;
        private string _imageMimeType;

        public string ImageMimeType
        {
            get { return _imageMimeType; }

        }

        public string ImageName
        {
            get { return _imageName; }
            set
            {

                _imageName = value;
                switch (_imageName.Substring(_imageName.Length - 3).ToLower())
                {

                    case "bmp":
                        _imageMimeType = "image/bmp";
                        break;

                    case "gif":
                        _imageMimeType = "image/gif";
                        break;

                    case "jpg":
                        _imageMimeType = "image/jpeg";
                        break;
                    case "png":
                        _imageMimeType = "image/png";
                        break;
                    case "tif":

                        _imageMimeType = "image/tiff";
```

```
                        break;
                    case "tiff":

                        _imageMimeType = "image/tiff";
                        break;

            }

        }

    }
  }
}
```

You'll need to sign your XML to ensure it has not been tampered with. To provide information about the certificate that will be used, you will create an object to store information about the certificate that will be used to retrieve it.

9. Right-click the project, and add a new class. Name the class **CertificateInfo**, and populate it with the following code:

```
using System;
using System.Collections.Generic;
using System.Text;

namespace BeginningCardspace
{
    [Serializable]
    public class CertiticateInfo
    {
        private string _store;
        private string _location;
        private string _commonName;


        public string Store
        {
            get { return _store; }
            set { _store = value; }

        }

        public string Location
        {
            get { return _location; }
            set { _location = value;}
```

```
        }

        public string CommonName
        {
            get { return _commonName; }
            set { _commonName = value; }
        }


    }
}
```

Note This assumes that the certificate is in a certificate store. Your scenario may have a certificate located in a file, located on an another server, or accessed via a hardware device. The code for those scenarios is beyond the scope of this sample, but you can extend this class to add support for the fields required for those scenarios.

Next, you'll create a class that will store an EndpointReference. This will be used later in the TokenService class.

10. Right-click the project, and create a new class. Name the class **EndpointReference**, and populate it with the following code:

```
using System;
using System.Collections.Generic;
using System.Text;

namespace BeginningCardspace
{
    [Serializable]
    public class EndpointReference
    {
        private string _address;
        private string _mex;
        private string _identity;

        public string Address
        {
            get { return _address; }
            set { _address = value; }
        }

        public string Mex
        {
            get { return _mex; }
```

```
        set { _mex = value; }
    }

    public string Identity
    {
        get { return _identity; }
        set { _identity = value; }
    }

    }
}
```

11. You'll also need to create a UserCredential class for TokenService. Right-click the project, and add a new class. Name the class **UserCredential**, and populate it with the following code. You'll also include an enumeration in this file that will store the different types of credentials (Kerberos, SelfIssued, SmartCard, and UsernameAndPassword).

```
using System;
using System.Collections.Generic;
using System.Text;

namespace BeginningCardspace
{
    [Serializable]
    public enum CredentialType
    {
        Kerberos=0,
        SelfIssued =1,
        SmartCard=2,
        UsernameAndPassword=3

    }

    [Serializable]
    public class UserCredential
    {
        private string _displayCredentialHint;
        private CredentialType _userCredentialType;
        private string _value;

        public string DisplayCredentialHint
        {
            get {return _displayCredentialHint;}
            set {_displayCredentialHint = value;}
        }
```

```
            public CredentialType UserCredentialType
            {
                get {return _userCredentialType;}
                set {_userCredentialType = value;}
            }


            public string Value
            {
                get {return _value;}
                set {_value = value;}

            }


        }
    }
```

12. With those two classes created, you can now create the TokenService class. Right-click the project, and add a new class. Name it **TokenService.cs**, and populate it with the following code:

```
using System;
using System.Collections.Generic;
using System.Text;

namespace BeginningCardspace
{
    [Serializable]
    public class TokenService
    {
        private EndpointReference _endpointReference;
        private UserCredential _userCredential;


        public TokenService()
        {
            _endpointReference = new EndpointReference();
            _userCredential = new UserCredential();
        }

        public EndpointReference EndpointReference
        {
            get { return _endpointReference; }
            set { _endpointReference = value; }

        }
```

```
        public UserCredential UserCredential
        {
            get { return _userCredential; }
            set { _userCredential = value; }
        }



    }
}
```

13. Right-click the project, and add a new class. Name the class **TokenType**, and populate it with the following code:

```
using System;
using System.Collections.Generic;
using System.Text;

namespace BeginningCardspace
{
    [Serializable]
    public class TokenType
    {
        private string _uri;
        private string _name;
        private bool _accepted;

        public TokenType()
        { }

        public TokenType(string uri, string name, bool accepted)
        {
            _uri = uri;
            _name = name;
            _accepted = accepted;
        }

        public string Uri
        {
            get { return _uri; }
            set { _uri = value; }
        }

    }
```

```
        public string Name
        {
            get { return _name; }
            set { _name = value; }

        }

        public bool Accepted
        {
            get { return _accepted; }
            set { _accepted = value; }

        }

    }
}
```

14. Right-click the project, and add a new class. Name the class **CardClaim**, and populate it with the following code:

```
using System;
using System.Collections.Generic;
using System.Text;

namespace BeginningCardspace
{
    [Serializable]
    public class CardClaim
    {
        private string _uri;
        private string _displayTag;
        private string _description;
        private string _value;

        public string Uri
        {
            get {return _uri;}
            set {_uri = value;}

        }

        public string DisplayTag
        {
            get {return _displayTag;}
            set { _displayTag = value; }
        }
```

```csharp
public string Description
{
    get { return _description; }
    set { _description = value; }
}


public string Value
{
    get { return _value; }
    set { _value = value; }

}


public override string ToString()
{
    return DisplayTag;
}


public CardClaim()
{ }

public CardClaim(string uri, string displayTag, string description)
{
    _uri = uri;
    _displayTag = displayTag;
    _description = description;

}

public CardClaim(string uri, string displayTag, ➥
string description, string value)
{
    _uri = uri;
    _displayTag = displayTag;
    _description = description;
    _value = value;
}


    }
}
```

■**Note** Although the information card and template will not contain an actual value for any claim, this class includes a `Value` property so that it can be used to collect claim values in other applications. In those applications, the data would be collected in this class and later placed in a data store of some kind (database, XML, and so on).

15. You're now ready to create the `InformationCard` class. Right-click the project, and add a new class. Name the class **InformationCard.cs**, and populate it with the following code:

```
using System;
using System.Collections.Generic;
using System.Text;

namespace BeginningCardspace
{


    [Serializable]
    public class InformationCard
    {
        private InformationCardReference _informationCardReference;
        private string _cardName;
        private CardImage _cardImage;
        private string _issuer;
        private DateTime _timeIssued;
        private DateTime _timeExpires;
        private List<TokenService> _tokenServiceList;
        private List<CardClaim> _supportedClaimType;
        private string _privacyNotice;
        private bool _requireRPIdentification;
        private List<TokenType> _acceptedTokenTypes;
        private string _issuerName;

        public string IssuerName
        {
            get { return _issuerName; }
            set { _issuerName = value; }
        }

        public InformationCard()
        {
            _tokenServiceList = new List<TokenService>();
            _supportedClaimType = new List<CardClaim>();
            _acceptedTokenTypes = new List<TokenType>();
            _informationCardReference = new InformationCardReference();
            _cardImage = new CardImage();
```

```csharp
}

public InformationCardReference CardReference
{
    get { return _informationCardReference; }
    set { _informationCardReference = value; }
}

public string CardName
{
    get { return _cardName; }
    set { _cardName = value; }
}


public CardImage CardImage
{
    get { return _cardImage; }
    set { _cardImage = value; }

}

public string Issuer
{
    get { return _issuer; }
    set { _issuer = value; }
}

public DateTime TimeIssued
{
    get { return _timeIssued; }
    set { _timeIssued = value; }

}

public DateTime TimeExpires
{
    get { return _timeExpires; }
    set { _timeExpires = value; }
}

public List<TokenService> TokenServiceList
{
    get { return _tokenServiceList; }
    set { _tokenServiceList = value; }

}
```

```
        public List<CardClaim> SupportedClaimTypeList
        {
            get { return _supportedClaimType; }
            set { _supportedClaimType = value; }

        }

        public string PrivacyNotice
        {
            get { return _privacyNotice; }
            set { _privacyNotice = value; }

        }


        public bool RequireRPIdentification
        {

            get { return _requireRPIdentification; }
            set { _requireRPIdentification = value;}

        }


        public List<TokenType> AcceptedTokenTypes
        {
            get { return _acceptedTokenTypes; }
            set { _acceptedTokenTypes = value; }


        }

    }
}
```

Next, you'll create the top-level class for the template. The template will contain properties for an information card as well as information about the certificate that should be
used to sign it.

16. Right-click the project, and add a new class. Name the class **InformationCardTemplate**.
    Populate the class with the following code:

```
using System;
using System.Collections.Generic;
using System.Text;
```

```
namespace BeginningCardspace
{
    [Serializable]
    public class InformationCardTemplate
    {
        private InformationCard _informationCard;
        private CertificateInfo _certificateInfo;

        public InformationCard InformationCardDefinition
        {
            get { return _informationCard; }
            set { _informationCard = value; }
        }

        public CertificateInfo SigningCertificateInfo
        {
            get { return _certificateInfo; }
            set { _certificateInfo = value; }
        }

        public InformationCardTemplate()
        {
            _informationCard = new InformationCard();
            _certificateInfo = new CertificateInfo();

        }


    }
}
```

Up to this point, you've created the classes necessary to define a card template and identify the signing certificate. You may have noticed that the classes created for the template also include properties where values for the actual cards could be assigned. This provides the ability for you to create both default values. In addition, it allows you to create base values for things such as the card ID so at runtime you can add just the identifier.

Next, you'll create a class that contains a number of helper functions. These functions handle everything including returning a list of "standard" claims for a user interface, retrieving certificates from the certificate store, creating the information card XML, and signing the card.

Note As you look at the operations, you may ask yourself why everything related to the creation of the card isn't in the same operation. Although this would make sense if you were creating cards one at a time, when you're looking at creating cards in volume, this can be less than ideal. The specific rationale for splitting out operations will become apparent in the next chapter, because you'll use this same code to power the automated creation of cards. The code will be wrapped in custom activities for Windows Workflow Foundation.

---

17. Right-click the project, and add a new class. Name the class **ManagedCardHelper**.

18. Open ManagedCardHelper, and add the following using statements and the constructor for the class:

```
using System;
using System.Collections.Generic;
using System.Text;
using System.IdentityModel.Claims;
using System.ServiceModel.Description;
using System.ServiceModel;
using System.Xml;
using System.IO;
using System.Drawing;
using System.ServiceModel.Channels;
using System.Runtime.Serialization;
using System.Security.Cryptography.Xml;
using System.Security.Cryptography.X509Certificates;

namespace BeginningCardspace
{
    public class ManagedCardHelper
    {

        public ManagedCardHelper()
        {
        }
```

Next, you'll create two operations that will query the certificate store and return an X.509 certificate. The two operations actually have the same name, RetrieveCertificate. One instance accepts an instance of a CertificateInfo class that was created earlier. The other will take a slash-delimited text string and parse the location, store, and common name. Those values are then used to populate a CertificateInfo class, which is then passed into the former operation.

As you'll see when creating the UI, you'll need to have flexibility when accepting the value that will be used in the Identity element of EndpointReference. The most straightforward approach for collecting this information from the UI is to use a delimited text field when representing a certificate. That delimited string value would appear as LOCATION/STORE/COMMONNAME.

19. Add the following code to the ManagedCardHelper class:

```
public static X509Certificate2 RetrieveCertificate(string certDetails)
    {
        CertificateInfo certInfo = new CertificateInfo();
        string[] splitCertDetails = certDetails.Split("/".ToCharArray(),➥
StringSplitOptions.RemoveEmptyEntries);
        certInfo.Location = splitCertDetails[0];
        certInfo.Store = splitCertDetails[1];
        certInfo.CommonName = splitCertDetails[2];
        return RetrieveCertificate(certInfo);



    }

    public static X509Certificate2 RetrieveCertificate(CertificateInfo ➥
certInfo)
    {
        StoreName storeName = StoreName.My;
        StoreLocation storeLocation = StoreLocation.LocalMachine;
        X509Certificate2 certificate = new X509Certificate2();

        try
        {
            storeLocation = (StoreLocation)Enum.Parse(➥
typeof(StoreLocation), certInfo.Location, true);
        }
        catch (Exception)
        {
            throw new Exception("No Certificate Location: " + ➥
certInfo.Location);
        }
        try
        {
            storeName = (StoreName)Enum.Parse(➥
typeof(StoreName), certInfo.Location, true);
        }
        catch (Exception)
        {
            throw new Exception("No Certificate Store: " + ➥
certInfo.Location + " in " + certInfo.Store);
        }
```

```
                    X509Store s = new X509Store(storeName, storeLocation);
                    s.Open(OpenFlags.MaxAllowed);
                    foreach (X509Certificate2 thisCert in s.Certificates)
                    {
                        if (thisCert.Subject.StartsWith("CN=" + certInfo.CommonName))
                        {
                            certificate = thisCert;
                            break;
                        }


                    }
                    return certificate;



                }
```

20. Next you'll create two more operations. The first will serialize a template and save it to a file; the second will do the opposite, deserializing the template stored in a file and returning an InformationCardTemplate object:

```
    public static void SaveCardTemplate(InformationCardTemplate card➥
, string templateFilename)
        {
            System.Xml.Serialization.XmlSerializer xmlSerializer = new➥
    System.Xml.Serialization.XmlSerializer(card.GetType());
            XmlTextWriter xmlTextWriter = ➥
new XmlTextWriter(templateFilename, Encoding.UTF8);
            xmlSerializer.Serialize(xmlTextWriter, card);
            xmlTextWriter.Flush();
            xmlTextWriter.Close();


        }
        public static InformationCardTemplate LoadCardTemplate(➥
string templateFileName)
        {
            System.Xml.Serialization.XmlSerializer x = ➥
new System.Xml.Serialization.XmlSerializer(typeof(➥
InformationCardTemplate));

            XmlTextReader fileReader = new XmlTextReader(templateFileName);
            InformationCardTemplate ict = (InformationCardTemplate)➥
x.Deserialize(fileReader);
            return ict;

        }
```

21. Next, you'll write the routine that will take an InformationCard object and create the InformationCard XML for the CRD file. When the actual information card is created, you'll sign the file. This creates the unsigned XML, and another operation will perform the actual signing.

```
public XmlDocument CreateInformationCardXML(InformationCard card)
    {
        MemoryStream stream = new MemoryStream();
        XmlWriter writer = XmlWriter.Create(stream);

        writer.WriteStartElement("InformationCard", ➥
"http://schemas.xmlsoap.org/ws/2005/05/identity");


        writer.WriteAttributeString("lang", ➥
"http://www.w3.org/XML/1998/namespace", "en-US");
        writer.WriteStartElement("InformationCardReference",➥
 "http://schemas.xmlsoap.org/ws/2005/05/identity");
        writer.WriteElementString("CardId",➥
 "http://schemas.xmlsoap.org/ws/2005/05/identity", card.CardReference.CardID);
        writer.WriteElementString("CardVersion",➥
 "http://schemas.xmlsoap.org/ws/2005/05/identity", ➥
card.CardReference.CardVersion.ToString());
        writer.WriteEndElement();

        if (card.CardName != null && card.CardName.Length > 0)
        {
            writer.WriteStartElement("CardName",➥
 "http://schemas.xmlsoap.org/ws/2005/05/identity");
            writer.WriteString(card.CardName);
            writer.WriteEndElement();
        }


        if (card.CardImage != null && card.CardImage.ImageName.Length > 0)
        {
            writer.WriteStartElement("CardImage", ➥
"http://schemas.xmlsoap.org/ws/2005/05/identity");
            if (card.CardImage != null && ➥
card.CardImage.ImageMimeType != null && ➥
card.CardImage.ImageMimeType.Length > 0)
            {
                writer.WriteAttributeString("MimeType", ➥
card.CardImage.ImageMimeType);
            }
```

```
                    FileInfo cardImage = new FileInfo(card.CardImage.ImageName);
                    if (cardImage.Exists)
                    {
                        byte[] cardImageBytes = new byte[cardImage.Length];
                        using (FileStream imageFS = cardImage.OpenRead())
                        {
                            imageFS.Read(cardImageBytes, 0, ➥
cardImageBytes.Length);
                        }


                        string imageBase64 = ➥
Convert.ToBase64String(cardImageBytes);
                        writer.WriteString(imageBase64);
                        writer.WriteEndElement();
                    }
                }


            writer.WriteStartElement("Issuer", ➥
"http://schemas.xmlsoap.org/ws/2005/05/identity");
            writer.WriteString(card.Issuer);
            writer.WriteEndElement();

            //writer.WriteStartElement("IssuerName",➥
 "http://schemas.xmlsoap.org/ws/2005/05/identity");
            //writer.WriteString(card.IssuerName);
            //writer.WriteEndElement();

            writer.WriteStartElement("TimeIssued", ➥
"http://schemas.xmlsoap.org/ws/2005/05/identity");
            writer.WriteString(➥
XmlConvert.ToString(card.TimeIssued, ➥
XmlDateTimeSerializationMode.Utc));
            writer.WriteEndElement();


            writer.WriteStartElement("TimeExpires", ➥
"http://schemas.xmlsoap.org/ws/2005/05/identity");
            writer.WriteString(➥
XmlConvert.ToString(card.TimeExpires, ➥
XmlDateTimeSerializationMode.Utc));
            writer.WriteEndElement();
```

```
            writer.WriteStartElement("TokenServiceList", ➥
    "http://schemas.xmlsoap.org/ws/2005/05/identity");


            foreach (TokenService ts in card.TokenServiceList)
            {
                EndpointAddressBuilder endpointBuilder = ➥
    new EndpointAddressBuilder();

                endpointBuilder.Uri = new Uri(ts.EndpointReference.Address);

                endpointBuilder.Identity = ➥
    new X509CertificateEndpointIdentity(➥
    RetrieveCertificate(ts.EndpointReference.Identity));

                if (null != ts.EndpointReference.Mex)
                {

                    MetadataReference mexReference = new MetadataReference();
                    mexReference.Address = ➥
    new EndpointAddress(ts.EndpointReference.Mex);
                    mexReference.AddressVersion =
    AddressingVersion.WSAddressing10;

                    MetadataSection mexSection = new MetadataSection();
                    mexSection.Metadata = mexReference;

                    MetadataSet mexSet = new MetadataSet();
                    mexSet.MetadataSections.Add(mexSection);


                    MemoryStream mexMemoryStream = new MemoryStream();

                    XmlTextWriter mexWriter = ➥
    new XmlTextWriter(mexMemoryStream, ➥
    System.Text.Encoding.UTF8);

                    mexSet.WriteTo(mexWriter);

                    mexWriter.Flush();

                    mexMemoryStream.Seek(0, SeekOrigin.Begin);

                    XmlDictionaryReader reader = ➥
```

```
        XmlDictionaryReader.CreateTextReader(mexMemoryStream,
XmlDictionaryReaderQuotas.Max);

                    endpointBuilder.SetMetadataReader(reader);


                    writer.WriteStartElement("TokenService", ➥
    "http://schemas.xmlsoap.org/ws/2005/05/identity");
                    EndpointAddress endpoint = ➥
    endpointBuilder.ToEndpointAddress();
                    endpoint.WriteTo(➥
    AddressingVersion.WSAddressing10, writer);

                    writer.WriteStartElement("UserCredential", ➥
    "http://schemas.xmlsoap.org/ws/2005/05/identity");


                    if (ts.UserCredential.DisplayCredentialHint != null && ➥
    ts.UserCredential.DisplayCredentialHint.Length > 0)
                    {
                        if (ts.UserCredential.UserCredentialType == ➥
    CredentialType.SelfIssued)
                        {
                        //Override the user value as this
                        //should be false for types of SelfIssued
                            ts.UserCredential.DisplayCredentialHint="false";
                        }
                        writer.WriteStartElement("DisplayCredentialHint",➥
     "http://schemas.xmlsoap.org/ws/2005/05/identity");
                        writer.WriteString(➥
    ts.UserCredential.DisplayCredentialHint);
                        writer.WriteEndElement();
                    }

                    switch (ts.UserCredential.UserCredentialType)
                    {
                      case CredentialType.SelfIssued:


                        writer.WriteStartElement(➥
    "SelfIssuedCredential", ➥
    "http://schemas.xmlsoap.org/ws/2005/05/identity");
                        if (!string.IsNullOrEmpty(➥
    ts.UserCredential.Value))
                        {
                            writer.WriteStartElement(➥
```

```
"PrivatePersonalIdentifier", ➥
"http://schemas.xmlsoap.org/ws/2005/05/identity");
                              writer.WriteString(➥
ts.UserCredential.Value);
                              writer.WriteEndElement();
                         }
                         writer.WriteEndElement();
                         break;
                    case CredentialType.UsernameAndPassword:
                         writer.WriteStartElement(➥
"UsernamePasswordCredential", ➥
"http://schemas.xmlsoap.org/ws/2005/05/identity");
                              if (ts.UserCredential.Value.GetType() == ➥
typeof(string) && !string.IsNullOrEmpty((string)ts.UserCredential.Value))
                              {
                                   writer.WriteStartElement("Username",➥
 "http://schemas.xmlsoap.org/ws/2005/05/identity");
                                   writer.WriteString(➥
(string)ts.UserCredential.Value);
                                   writer.WriteEndElement();
                              }
                         writer.WriteEndElement();
                         break;
                    case CredentialType.Kerberos:
                         writer.WriteStartElement("KerberosV5Credential",➥
 "http://schemas.xmlsoap.org/ws/2005/05/identity");
                         writer.WriteEndElement();
                         break;

                    case CredentialType.SmartCard:
                         writer.WriteStartElement("X509V3Credential", ➥
"http://schemas.xmlsoap.org/ws/2005/05/identity");

                         writer.WriteStartElement("X509Data",➥
 "http://www.w3.org/2000/09/xmldsig#");
                              if ((ts.UserCredential.Value.GetType() == ➥
typeof(CertificateInfo) && ts.UserCredential.Value != null))
                              {
                                   writer.WriteStartElement("KeyIdentifier", ➥
"http://docs.oasis-open.org/wss/2004/01/➥
oasis-200401-wss-wssecurity-secext-1.0.xsd");
                                   writer.WriteAttributeString("ValueType",
                                        null,
                                        "http://docs.oasis-open.org/➥
wss/2004/xx/oasis-2004xx-wss-soap-message-security-1.1#➥
ThumbprintSHA1");
                                   writer.WriteString(➥
```

```
            RetrieveCertificate((CertificateInfo)➡
            ts.UserCredential.Value).Thumbprint);
                                    writer.WriteEndElement();
                            }
                            else
                            {
                                throw new ➡
            InvalidDataException("No thumbprint was specified");
                            }
                            writer.WriteEndElement();
                            writer.WriteEndElement();
                            break;
                        default:
                            break;
                    }
                    writer.WriteEndElement();
                    writer.WriteEndElement();
                }
            }
            writer.WriteEndElement(); //end of tokenservice list

            writer.WriteStartElement("SupportedTokenTypeList",➡
        "http://schemas.xmlsoap.org/ws/2005/05/identity");
            foreach (TokenType tokenType in card.AcceptedTokenTypes)
            {
                writer.WriteElementString("TokenType",
                  "http://schemas.xmlsoap.org/ws/2005/02/trust",
                                            tokenType.Uri);
            }
            writer.WriteEndElement();

            writer.WriteStartElement("SupportedClaimTypeList",➡
        "http://schemas.xmlsoap.org/ws/2005/05/identity");
            foreach (CardClaim claim in card.SupportedClaimTypeList)
            {

                writer.WriteStartElement("SupportedClaimType",➡
        "http://schemas.xmlsoap.org/ws/2005/05/identity");
                writer.WriteAttributeString("Uri", claim.Uri);


                if (!String.IsNullOrEmpty(claim.DisplayTag))
                {
                    writer.WriteElementString("DisplayTag", ➡
        "http://schemas.xmlsoap.org/ws/2005/05/identity",
                                                claim.DisplayTag);
                }
```

```
            if (!String.IsNullOrEmpty(claim.Description))
            {
                writer.WriteElementString("Description",➼
    "http://schemas.xmlsoap.org/ws/2005/05/identity",
                                            claim.Description);
            }
            writer.WriteEndElement();

        }
        writer.WriteEndElement();


        if (card.RequireRPIdentification)
        {
            writer.WriteElementString("RequireAppliesTo",➼
    "http://schemas.xmlsoap.org/ws/2005/05/identity", ➼
card.RequireRPIdentification.ToString());
        }


        if (!String.IsNullOrEmpty(card.PrivacyNotice))
        {
            writer.WriteStartElement("PrivacyNotice", ➼
"http://schemas.xmlsoap.org/ws/2005/05/identity");
            writer.WriteString(card.PrivacyNotice);
            writer.WriteEndElement();
        }
        writer.WriteEndElement();

        writer.Close();



        stream.Position = 0;

        XmlDocument doc = new XmlDocument();
        doc.PreserveWhitespace = false;
        doc.Load(stream);

        return doc;
    }
```

22. Next, you'll add a method that will perform the signing. Add the following code to the class:

```
    public XmlElement SignInformationCardXML(XmlDocument ➥
doc, X509Certificate2 cert)
        {
            SignedXml signed = new SignedXml();
            signed.SigningKey = cert.PrivateKey;
            signed.Signature.SignedInfo.➥
CanonicalizationMethod = ➥
SignedXml.XmlDsigExcC14NTransformUrl;

            Reference reference = new Reference();
            reference.Uri = "#_Object_InfoCard";
            reference.AddTransform(
                        new XmlDsigExcC14NTransform());
            signed.AddReference(reference);


            KeyInfo info = new KeyInfo();
            KeyInfoX509Data certData = ➥
new KeyInfoX509Data(cert, X509IncludeOption.WholeChain);
            info.AddClause(certData);

            signed.KeyInfo = info;
            DataObject cardData = ➥
new DataObject("_Object_InfoCard", null, null, doc.DocumentElement);
            signed.AddObject(cardData);

            signed.ComputeSignature();

            XmlElement e = signed.GetXml();

            return e;


        }
```

23. Next, you'll create an operation to save the card to a file. Add the following code:

```
        public void SaveInformationCard(XmlElement ➥
signedInformationCard, string filename)
        {

            XmlTextWriter textWriter = ➥
new XmlTextWriter(filename, Encoding.UTF8);
            signedInformationCard.WriteTo(textWriter);

            textWriter.Flush();
            textWriter.Close();

        }
```

24. If you'd like to have a consolidated operation that will create the XML, sign the card, and save it to a file, you can add the following operation:

```
      public void SaveCard( InformationCard card, ➥
X509Certificate2 cert, string filename)
      {

          XmlDocument doc = CreateInformationCardXML(card);
          XmlElement e = SignInformationCardXML(doc, cert);
          SaveInformationCard(e, filename);
      }
```

25. The last thing you'll add is a helper function that will return a list of "standard claims." This list will be used in the user interface for the template creator.

■**Note** This example defines standard claims as those provided in the `ClaimTypes` enumeration. You can modify this to add any of your organization's specific claims that will be used.

```
public static List<CardClaim> GetStandardClaims()
       {

          List<CardClaim> StandardClaims = new List<CardClaim>();
          StandardClaims.Add(new CardClaim(ClaimTypes.GivenName,➥
 "Given Name", "Given Name"));
          StandardClaims.Add(new CardClaim(ClaimTypes.Surname, ➥
"SurName", "SurName"));
          StandardClaims.Add(new CardClaim(ClaimTypes.Email,➥
 "Email Address", "Email Address"));
          StandardClaims.Add(new CardClaim(ClaimTypes.StreetAddress,➥
 "Street Address", "Street Address"));
          StandardClaims.Add(new CardClaim(ClaimTypes.Locality,➥
 "Locality", "Locality"));
          StandardClaims.Add(new CardClaim(ClaimTypes.StateOrProvince,➥
 "State or Province", "State or Province"));
          StandardClaims.Add(new CardClaim(ClaimTypes.PostalCode,➥
 "Postal Code", "Postal Code"));
          StandardClaims.Add(new CardClaim(ClaimTypes.Country,➥
 "Country", "Country"));
          StandardClaims.Add(new CardClaim(ClaimTypes.HomePhone,➥
 "Home Phone", "Home Phone"));
          StandardClaims.Add(new CardClaim(ClaimTypes.OtherPhone, ➥
```

```
"Other Phone", "Other Phone"));
            StandardClaims.Add(new CardClaim(ClaimTypes.MobilePhone, ➥
"Mobile Phone", "Mobile Phone"));
            StandardClaims.Add(new CardClaim(ClaimTypes.Gender, ➥
"Gender", "Gender"));
            StandardClaims.Add(new CardClaim(ClaimTypes.DateOfBirth, ➥
"Date of Birth", "Date of Birth"));
            StandardClaims.Add(new CardClaim(ClaimTypes.PPID, ➥
"Site Specific ID", "Site Specific ID"));
            StandardClaims.Add(new CardClaim(ClaimTypes.Webpage, ➥
"Webpage", "Webpage"));
            return StandardClaims;

    }
```

You've now created all the classes that you'll need for the managed card template creator.

26. Right-click the solution, and add a new project. Name the project **ManagedCardTemplateCreator**, and click OK.

27. Rename Form1 to **DefineCardTemplate**.

28. Right-click the project, and add a new form. Name the form **AddClaim**.

29. On the AddClaim form, add a radio button. Name the radio button **rbStandardClaim**.

30. Change the text for the radio button to **Standard Claim**.

31. Add a combo box, and name it **cboStandardClaims**.

32. Add another radio button, and name it **rbCustomClaim**.

33. Change the text for the radio button to **Custom Claim**.

34. Under this radio button, add three labels. For the Text value of the labels, assign **Uri**, **Display Tag**, and **Description**.

35. Next to each of these labels, add a textbox.

36. Rename the textboxes to **tbUri**, **tbDisplayTag**, and **tbDescription**.

37. At the bottom of the form, add a button named **btnAdd**, with a Text value set to **Add**.

38. Next to that button, add a new button named **btnCancel**, with a Text value of **Cancel**.

The layout of these controls should look like Figure 11-1.

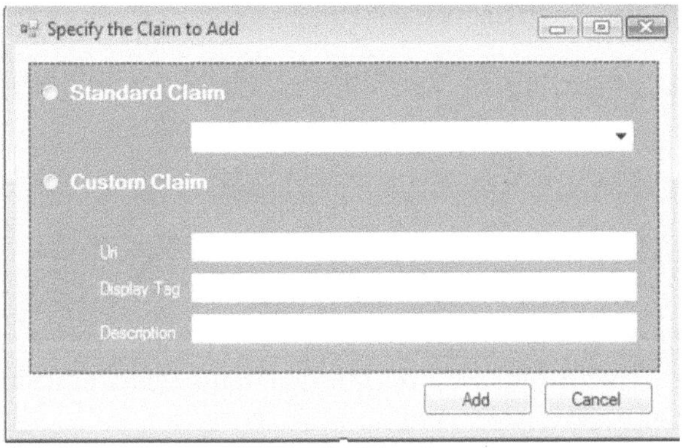

Figure 11-1. *Adding a claim*

This form will display as a dialog box in the template creator program and serve the purpose of identifying a claim that will be supported in the information card. The user will be able to select from a standard claim or add support for a custom claim. Clicking the Add or Cancel button closes the dialog box. If a claim was specified, it is returned as a CardClaim object, courtesy of a new ShowDialog method.

To enable this, you'll add a private member variable named _claim of type CardClaim to the form. You'll also modify the constructor to set DisplayMember for the combo box to DisplayTag and then populate the combo box with the GetStandardClaims operation in the ManagedCardHelper class.

39. View the code for the form.

40. Modify the code so it resembles the following:

```
private CardClaim _claim;

public AddClaim()
{
    InitializeComponent();
    cboStandardClaims.DisplayMember = "DisplayTag";
    List<CardClaim> standardClaims = ➥
ManagedCardHelper.GetStandardClaims();

    foreach (CardClaim claim in standardClaims)
    {

        cboStandardClaims.Items.Add(claim);

    }

}
```

```
public new CardClaim ShowDialog()
{
    base.ShowDialog();


    return _claim;

}
```

Next, you'll add code to handle the button clicks. If the user selects Add, the information will be collected from the form, placed in a CardClaim, and returned to the caller. If the user selects Cancel, the claim will be set to null.

41. In the designer view, double-click the Cancel button, and btnCancel_Click will be created for you.

42. Modify this code to look like this:

```
private void btnCancel_Click(object sender, EventArgs e)
    {
        _claim = null;
        Close();
    }
```

43. In the designer view, double-click the Add button, and btnAdd_Click will be created for you. Modify this code to look like this:

```
private void btnAdd_Click(object sender, EventArgs e)
{

    if (rbStandardClaim.Checked)
    {
        _claim = (CardClaim)cboStandardClaims.SelectedItem;
        _claim.Value = tbClaimValue.Text;
    }
    else
    {

        _claim = new CardClaim();
        _claim.Description = tbDescription.Text;
        _claim.DisplayTag = tbDisplayTag.Text;
        _claim.Uri = tbUri.Text;
        _claim.Value = tbClaimValue.Text;


    }
    Close();
}
}
```

That form is now complete, and you'll create a second dialog box to add new token services to the template.

44. Right-click the project, and add a new form. Name the form **AddTokenService**.

45. Add a label, and set the Text value to **Endpoint Address**.

46. Add three labels, and set the Text values to **Address**, **Mex**, and **Identity**.

47. Next to these labels, add textboxes named **tbAddress**, **tbMex**, and **tbIdentity**.

48. Below these, add a new label, and set the Text value to **User Credential**.

49. Add three labels, and set the Text values to **Type**, **Value**, and **Display Credential Hint**.

50. Next to the Type label, add a combo box named **cboType**.

51. Next to the Value and Display Credential Hint labels, add corresponding textboxes named **tbValue** and **tbDisplayCredentialHint**.

52. At the bottom of the form, add a button named **btnAdd**, with a Text value set to **Add**.

53. Next to that button, add a new button named **btnCancel**, with a Text value to **Cancel**.

The placement of the controls should resemble Figure 11-2.

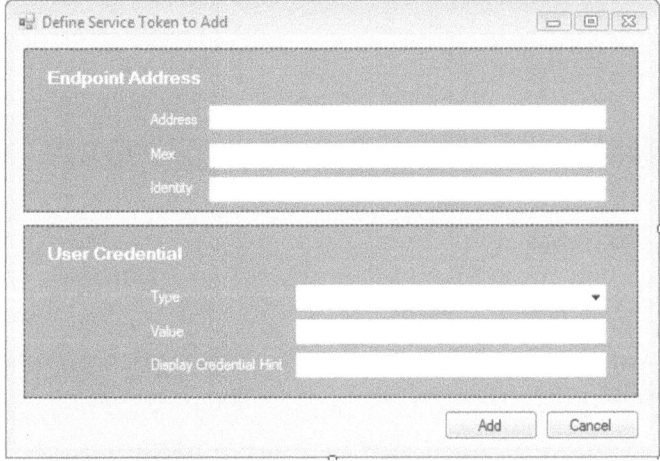

Figure 11-2. *The proper layout for the dialog box*

54. View the code for the form.

As was the case with the AddClaim form, this form will use a member variable and new ShowDialog operation to collect and return the definition of a new token service. In addition, you'll populate the combo box with the names of the four types of tokens—Kerberos, Self-Issued, SmartCard, and UserName and Password.

55. Add the following code to the form:

```
private TokenService ts;

    public AddTokenService()
    {
        InitializeComponent();

        cboType.Items.Add("Kerberos");
        cboType.Items.Add("Self-Issued");
        cboType.Items.Add("SmartCard");
        cboType.Items.Add("Username and Password");
    }


    public new TokenService ShowDialog()
    {
        base.ShowDialog();


        return ts;

    }
```

56. In the designer view, double-click the Cancel button, and btnCancel_Click will be created for you.

57. Modify this code to look like this:

```
private void btnCancel_Click(object sender, EventArgs e)
    {
        ts = null;
        Close();
    }
```

58. In the designer view, double-click the Add button, and btnAdd_Click will be created for you.

59. Modify the code to look like this:

```
    private void btnAdd_Click(object sender, EventArgs e)
    {

        ts = new TokenService();
        ts.UserCredential.DisplayCredentialHint = ➥
tbDisplayCredentialHint.Text;
        ts.UserCredential.UserCredentialType = ➥
(CredentialType)cboType.SelectedIndex;
        ts.UserCredential.Value = tbValue.Text;
```

```
            ts.EndpointReference.Address = tbAddress.Text;


            ts.EndpointReference.Identity = tbIdentity.Text;
            ts.EndpointReference.Mex = tbMex.Text;
            Close();
        }
```

The definition of what the Value is for a credential is dependent on the type of token. For example, with Kerberos, you won't need to specify a value at all, while for certificates you'd want to provide information on where the certificate could be found. For usernames and passwords, you might prompt for a default username.

60. Add a SelectedIndexChanged event for cboType that makes the UI display the appropriate prompts for the token value:

```
private void cboType_SelectedIndexChanged(object sender, EventArgs e)
    {
        switch (cboType.SelectedIndex)
        {
            case 0:
                //Kerberos - No Value Specified
                tbValue.Visible = false;
                lblValue.Visible = false;
                break;
            case 1:
                //Self-Issued - PPID
                tbValue.Visible = true;
                lblValue.Text = "PPID";
                lblValue.Visible = true;
                break;
            case 2:
                //SmartCard/Certificate
                tbValue.Visible = true;
                lblValue.Text = "Cert Path(Location/Store/CN)";
                lblValue.Visible = true;
                break;
            case 3:
                //Username and Password
                tbValue.Visible = true;
                lblValue.Text = "Username";
                lblValue.Visible = true;
                break;

        }
    }
```

61. You're now ready to create the template manager form. Open the DefineCardTemplate form in the designer.

You'll begin by creating the user interface; Figure 11-3 shows the completed UI. Use this as a guide when adding controls to the form.

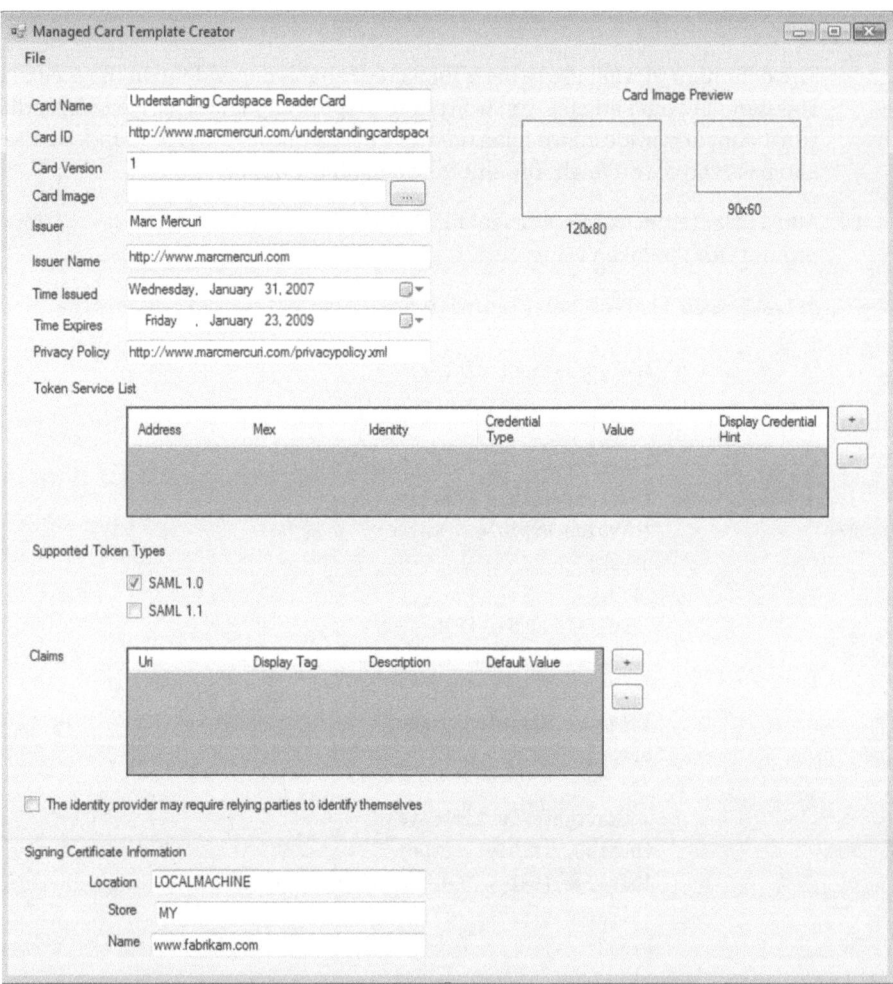

Figure 11-3. *The layout of the template creator form*

62. Add nine labels on the form, and set the Text values to **Card Name**, **Card ID**, **Card Version**, **Card Image**, **Issuer**, **Time Issued**, **Time Expires**, and **Privacy Policy**.

63. Next to the first six labels, add textboxes, and name them **tbCardName**, **tbCardID**, **tbCardVersion**, **tbCardImage**, and **tbIssuer**.

64. Next to the labels set to Time Issued and Time Expired, add date time picker controls named **dtpTimeIssued** and **dtpTimeExpires**.

65. Add a textbox next to the label set to Privacy Policy, and name it **tbPrivacyPolicy**.

66. To the right of tbCardImage, add a button named **btnCardImage**, and set the text to **....**

67. To the right of these, add a label with the text set to **Card Image Preview.**

68. Beneath this label, add two picture boxes. The first should be set to a width of 120 and a height of 80. The second should be set to a width of 90 and a height of 60.

69. Underneath each of these picture boxes, add labels, and set the text property to reflect the size of each image (120×80 and 90×60).

70. Below the Privacy Policy text box, add a label with the Text property set to **Token Service List**.

71. Underneath that, add a DataGridView control, and name it **dgvTokenServiceList**.

72. In the properties for dgvTokenServiceList, set the RowHeaderVisible property to **False**.

73. In the properties for dgvTokenServiceList, set the SelectionMode property to **FullRowSelect**.

74. In the properties for dgvTokenServiceList, set the AllowUserToAddRows property to **False**.

75. In the properties for dgvTokenServiceList, set the Columns property, adding the columns shown in Table 11-2 to the DataGridView control.

Table 11-2. *Column Definitions for dgvTokenServiceList*

Name	HeaderText	ColumnType
Address	Address	TextBoxColumn
Mex	Mex	TextBoxColumn
Identity	Identity	TextBoxColumn
CredentialType	Credential Type	TextBoxColumn
Value	Value	TextBoxColumn
DisplayCredentialHint	Display Credential Hint	TextBoxColumn

76. To the right of dgvTokenServiceList, add a button named **btnAddTokenService**, and set the text to +.

77. To the right of dgvTokenServiceList, add a button named **btnRemoveTokenService**, and set the text to -.

78. Beneath the DataGridView control, add a label. Set the Text value for the label to **Supported Token Types**.

79. Add a checkbox underneath the label. Name the checkbox **cbSAML10**, and set the Text value to **SAML 1.0**.

80. Add another checkbox. Name the checkbox **cbSAML11**, and set the Text value to **SAML 1.1**.

81. Below that checkbox, add a label, and set the Text value to **Claims**.

82. Underneath that, add a DataGridView, and name it **dgvClaims**.

83. In the properties for dgvClaims, set the RowHeaderVisible property to **False**.

84. In the properties for dgvClaims, set the SelectionMode property to **FullRowSelect**.

85. In the properties for dgvClaims, set the AllowUserToAddRows property to **false**.

86. In the properties for dgvClaims, set the Columns property, adding the columns shown in Table 11-3 to the DataGridView control.

Table 11-3. *Column Definitions for dgvClaims*

Name	HeaderText	ColumnType
Uri	Uri	TextBoxColumn
DisplayTag	Display Tag	TextBoxColumn
Description	Description	TextBoxColumn
DefaultValue	Default Value	TextBoxColumn

87. To the right of dgvClaims, add a button named **btnAddClaim**, and set the text to +.

88. To the right of dgvClaims, add a button named **btnRemoveClaim**, and set the text to -.

89. Add an OpenFileDialog component to the form.

90. Add a SaveFileDialog component to the form.

91. Add a MenuStrip component to the form.

92. Populate the menu strip so that it resembles the one shown in Figure 11-4.

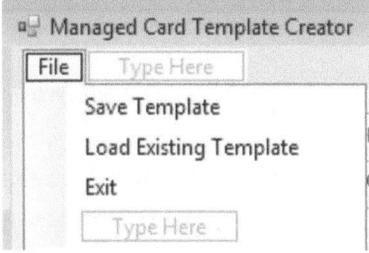

Figure 11-4. *The File menu*

93. Double-click btnCardImage to create the btnCardImage_Click event.

94. Populate the event with the following code. After selecting an image, the file type is evaluated to determine whether it is one of the supported types.

```
private void btnCardImage_Click(object sender, EventArgs e)
{
    DialogResult result = openFileDialog1.ShowDialog();
    if (result == DialogResult.OK)
    {
        string filename = openFileDialog1.FileName;
        string fileExtension = ➥
filename.Substring(filename.Length - 3).ToUpper();

        if (fileExtension == "BMP" || fileExtension == "GIF" ➥
|| fileExtension == "JPG" || fileExtension == "PNG" || ➥
fileExtension == "TIF")
        {
            tbCardImage.Text = filename;
            picCardImagePreview.ImageLocation = filename;
            picCardImagePreviewSmall.BackgroundImage = ➥
picCardImagePreview.Image;
        }
        else
        {
            if (fileExtension == "IFF")
            {
                if (filename.Substring(filename.Length - 4).ToUpper() ➥
== "TIFF")
                {
                    tbCardImage.Text = filename;
                    picCardImagePreview.ImageLocation = filename;
                    picCardImagePreviewSmall.BackgroundImage = ➥
picCardImagePreview.Image;
                }
                else
                {
                    MessageBox.Show("The file extension for file " ➥
+ filename + " is not supported. Please select another file.", ➥
"Unsupported Image Format");

                }
            }
            else
            {
                MessageBox.Show("The file extension for file "➥
+ filename + ➥
" is not supported. Please select another file.", ➥
"Unsupported Image Format");
```

```
                }
            }
        }
    }
```

95. Add a click event for btnAddTokenService.

96. Populate the event with the following code. This will display the AddTokenService form
and then take the returned TokenService object and use it to populate a new row in the
DataGridView control.

```
private void btnAddTokenService_Click(object sender, EventArgs e)
        {
            AddTokenService dialog = new AddTokenService();
            TokenService ts = dialog.ShowDialog();
            if (ts != null)
            {
                //Add the token service
                DataGridViewTextBoxCell address = ➥
new DataGridViewTextBoxCell();
                DataGridViewTextBoxCell mex = new DataGridViewTextBoxCell();
                DataGridViewTextBoxCell identity = ➥
new DataGridViewTextBoxCell();
                DataGridViewTextBoxCell credentialType =➥
 new DataGridViewTextBoxCell();
                DataGridViewTextBoxCell value = new DataGridViewTextBoxCell();
                DataGridViewTextBoxCell displayCredentialHint = ➥
new DataGridViewTextBoxCell();

                DataGridViewRow row = new DataGridViewRow();

                address.Value = ts.EndpointReference.Address;
                mex.Value = ts.EndpointReference.Mex;
                identity.Value = ts.EndpointReference.Identity;


                credentialType.Value = ➥
ts.UserCredential.UserCredentialType.ToString();
                credentialType.Tag = ts.UserCredential.UserCredentialType;
                value.Value = ts.UserCredential.Value;
                displayCredentialHint.Value = ➥
ts.UserCredential.DisplayCredentialHint;
```

```
            row.Cells.Add(address);
            row.Cells.Add(mex);
            row.Cells.Add(identity);
            row.Cells.Add(credentialType);
            row.Cells.Add(value);
            row.Cells.Add(displayCredentialHint);

            dgvTokenServiceList.Rows.Add(row);

        }
    }
```

97. Add a click event for btnRemoveTokenService.

98. Populate the event with the following code:

```
        private void btnRemoveTokenService_Click(object sender, EventArgs e)
          {

                foreach (DataGridViewRow r in dgvTokenServiceList.SelectedRows)
                {
                    dgvTokenServiceList.Rows.Remove(r);
                }
            }
```

99. Add a click event for btnAddClaim.

100. Populate the event with the following code:

```
    private void btnAddClaim_Click(object sender, EventArgs e)
          {
                AddClaim addClaim = new AddClaim();
                CardClaim cardClaim = addClaim.ShowDialog();

                DataGridViewRow row = new DataGridViewRow();

                DataGridViewTextBoxCell uri = new DataGridViewTextBoxCell();
                DataGridViewTextBoxCell displayTag = ➥
    new DataGridViewTextBoxCell();
                DataGridViewTextBoxCell description = ➥
    new DataGridViewTextBoxCell();
                DataGridViewTextBoxCell claimValue = ➥
    new DataGridViewTextBoxCell();

                uri.Value = cardClaim.Uri;
                displayTag.Value = cardClaim.DisplayTag;
                description.Value = cardClaim.Description;
                claimValue.Value = cardClaim.Value;
```

```
                        row.Cells.Add(uri);
                        row.Cells.Add(displayTag);
                        row.Cells.Add(description);
                        row.Cells.Add(claimValue);

                        dgvClaims.Rows.Add(row);

                    }
```

101. Add a click event for btnRemoveClaim.

102. Populate the event with the following code:

```
            private void btnRemoveClaim_Click(object sender, EventArgs e)
            {
                foreach (DataGridViewRow r in dgvClaims.SelectedRows)
                {
                    dgvClaims.Rows.Remove(r);
                }
            }
```

103. You'll next add two operations. One will populate a new InformationCardTemplate from what has been entered in the user interface. The other will read an InformationCardTemplate and populate the user interface with the template values. Add the following code to the class:

```
private InformationCardTemplate PopulateCardTemplateFromUI()
        {
            InformationCard ic = new InformationCard();

            ic.CardImage.ImageName = tbCardImage.Text;
            ic.CardName = tbCardName.Text;
            ic.CardReference.CardID = tbCardID.Text;
            ic.CardReference.CardVersion = ➥
Convert.ToInt32(tbCardVersion.Text);
            ic.Issuer = tbIssuer.Text;
            ic.IssuerName = tbIssuerName.Text;
            ic.PrivacyNotice = tbPrivacyPolicy.Text;
            ic.RequireRPIdentification = cbRequireAppliesTo.Checked;
            ic.TimeExpires = dtpTimeExpires.Value;
            ic.TimeIssued = dtpTimeIssued.Value;

            foreach (DataGridViewRow row in dgvClaims.Rows)
            {
```

```
            CardClaim claim = new CardClaim();
            claim.Description = row.Cells["Description"].Value.ToString();
            claim.DisplayTag = row.Cells["DisplayTag"].Value.ToString();
            claim.Uri = row.Cells["Uri"].Value.ToString();
            claim.Value = row.Cells["ClaimValue"].Value.ToString();
            ic.SupportedClaimTypeList.Add(claim);


        }

        if (cbSAML10.Checked)
        {
            TokenType SAML10 = new TokenType();
            SAML10.Name = "SAML10";
            SAML10.Uri = "urn:oasis:names:tc:SAML:1.0:assertion";
            SAML10.Accepted = true;
            ic.AcceptedTokenTypes.Add(SAML10);
         }
        if (cbSAML11.Checked)
        {
            TokenType SAML11 = new TokenType();
            SAML11.Name = "SAML11";
            SAML11.Uri = "http://docs.oasis-open.org/wss/➥
oasis-wss-saml-token-profile-1.1#SAMLV1.1";
            ic.AcceptedTokenTypes.Add(SAML11);
        }

        foreach (DataGridViewRow tsRow in dgvTokenServiceList.Rows)
        {
            TokenService ts = new TokenService();
            ts.EndpointReference.Address = ➥
tsRow.Cells["Address"].Value.ToString();
            ts.EndpointReference.Identity = ➥
tsRow.Cells["Identity"].Value.ToString();
            ts.EndpointReference.Mex = tsRow.Cells["Mex"].Value.ToString();
            ts.UserCredential.DisplayCredentialHint =➥
 tsRow.Cells["DisplayCredentialHint"].Value.ToString();
            ts.UserCredential.UserCredentialType = (CredentialType)➥
 (tsRow.Cells["CredentialType"].Tag);
            ts.UserCredential.Value = tsRow.Cells["Value"].Value.ToString();
            ic.TokenServiceList.Add(ts);
        }
```

```
                    InformationCardTemplate ict = new InformationCardTemplate();
                    ict.InformationCardDefinition = ic;
                    ict.SigningCertificateInfo.CommonName = ➡
        tbCertificateCommonName.Text;
                    ict.SigningCertificateInfo.Location = tbCertificateLocation.Text;
                    ict.SigningCertificateInfo.Store = tbCertificateStore.Text;




                    return ict;
                }


            private void PopulateUIFromCardTemplate(string filename)
                {
                    InformationCardTemplate ict = ➡
        ManagedCardHelper.LoadCardTemplate(filename);

                    InformationCard ic = ict.InformationCardDefinition;

                    tbCardImage.Text = ic.CardImage.ImageName;
                    tbCardName.Text = ic.CardName;
                    tbCardID.Text = ic.CardReference.CardID;
                    tbCardVersion.Text = ic.CardReference.CardVersion.ToString();
                    tbIssuer.Text = ic.Issuer;
                    tbIssuerName.Text = ic.IssuerName;
                    tbPrivacyPolicy.Text = ic.PrivacyNotice;
                    cbRequireAppliesTo.Checked = ic.RequireRPIdentification;
                    dtpTimeExpires.Value = ic.TimeExpires;
                    dtpTimeIssued.Value = ic.TimeIssued;

                    foreach (CardClaim cardClaim in ic.SupportedClaimTypeList)
                    {
                        DataGridViewRow row = new DataGridViewRow();

                        DataGridViewTextBoxCell uri = new DataGridViewTextBoxCell();
                        DataGridViewTextBoxCell displayTag = ➡
        new DataGridViewTextBoxCell();
                        DataGridViewTextBoxCell description = ➡
        new DataGridViewTextBoxCell();
                        DataGridViewTextBoxCell claimValue = ➡
        new DataGridViewTextBoxCell();

                        uri.Value = cardClaim.Uri;
                        displayTag.Value = cardClaim.DisplayTag;
                        description.Value = cardClaim.Description;
                        claimValue.Value = cardClaim.Value;
```

```
            row.Cells.Add(uri);
            row.Cells.Add(displayTag);
            row.Cells.Add(description);
            row.Cells.Add(claimValue);

            dgvClaims.Rows.Add(row);

        }

        cbSAML10.Checked = false;
        cbSAML11.Checked = false;

        foreach (TokenType tokenType in ic.AcceptedTokenTypes)
        {
            if (tokenType.Name == "SAML10")
                cbSAML10.Checked = true;

            if (tokenType.Name == "SAML11")
                cbSAML11.Checked = true;


        }

        foreach (TokenService ts in ic.TokenServiceList)
        {
            //Add the token service
            DataGridViewTextBoxCell address = ➡
new DataGridViewTextBoxCell();
            DataGridViewTextBoxCell mex = new DataGridViewTextBoxCell();
            DataGridViewTextBoxCell identity = ➡
new DataGridViewTextBoxCell();
            DataGridViewTextBoxCell credentialType = ➡
new DataGridViewTextBoxCell();
            DataGridViewTextBoxCell value = new DataGridViewTextBoxCell();
            DataGridViewTextBoxCell displayCredentialHint = ➡
new DataGridViewTextBoxCell();

            DataGridViewRow row = new DataGridViewRow();

            address.Value = ts.EndpointReference.Address;
            mex.Value = ts.EndpointReference.Mex;
            identity.Value = ts.EndpointReference.Identity;
```

```
                    credentialType.Value = ➡
    ts.UserCredential.UserCredentialType.ToString();
                    credentialType.Tag = ts.UserCredential.UserCredentialType;
                    value.Value = ts.UserCredential.Value;
                    displayCredentialHint.Value = ➡
    ts.UserCredential.DisplayCredentialHint;


                    row.Cells.Add(address);
                    row.Cells.Add(mex);
                    row.Cells.Add(identity);
                    row.Cells.Add(credentialType);
                    row.Cells.Add(value);
                    row.Cells.Add(displayCredentialHint);

                    dgvTokenServiceList.Rows.Add(row);


                }

                cbRequireAppliesTo.Checked = ic.RequireRPIdentification;


            }
```

104. Next, add events for each of the items in your menu strip.

105. Populate the resulting click events for those menu items as follows:

```
        private void saveTemplateToolStripMenuItem_Click(object sender, EventArgs e)
            {
                InformationCardTemplate ict = PopulateCardTemplateFromUI();
                saveFileDialog1.Filter = "Card Templates|*.crdtemplate";
                DialogResult dr = saveFileDialog1.ShowDialog();

                string filename = saveFileDialog1.FileName;
                ManagedCardHelper.SaveCardTemplate(ict, filename);

            }

            private void loadExistingTemplateToolStripMenuItem_Click(➡
        object sender, EventArgs e)
            {
                openFileDialog1.Filter = "Card Templates|*.crdtemplate";
                DialogResult dr = openFileDialog1.ShowDialog();
                string filename = openFileDialog1.FileName;
                System.IO.FileInfo f = new System.IO.FileInfo(filename);
```

```
        if (f.Exists)
        {
            PopulateUIFromCardTemplate(filename);

        }
        else
        {
            MessageBox.Show("A file by that name does not exist.");
        }

    }

    private void exitToolStripMenuItem_Click(object sender, EventArgs e)
    {
        this.Close();
    }
```

106. Finally, add the following using statement to the top of the file:

```
using System.Security.Cryptography.X509Certificates;
```

Congratulations, you've just created a utility to easily create information card templates.

Creating an Information Card Template

Your managed card template creator is now complete and ready for testing. You'll create a card template. Start the application, and then follow these steps:

1. Specify the card name as **ReaderCard (Username and Password)**.

2. Specify the card ID as **http://www.fabrikam.com/readercard/**.

Note This is used as the base ID in the template. When creating actual cards, you will specify a card-specific ID.

---

3. Specify the card version as **1**.

4. Click the button labeled **....** This will display the file open dialog box. Using the dialog box, navigate to ReaderCardImage.jpg, and click OK. You can find this file in the source files for this chapter, which are located at the Apress website.

5. Specify the issuer as **http://www.fabrikam.com:6700/unap/sts**.

6. Specify the time issued as today's date.

7. Specify the privacy policy as **http://www.fabrikam.com/privacy/PrivacyPolicy.xml**.

8. Click the button labeled + next to the Token Service List data grid view.

9. Specify the address as **http://www.fabrikam.com:7000/usernamdandpassword/sts**.

10. Specify the mex as **https://www.fabrikam.com:7001/usernameandpassword/mex**.

11. Specify the identity as **LOCALMACHINE/MY/www.fabrikam.com**.

12. Specify the user credential type as **Username and Password**.

13. Specify **Please enter your username and password** in the Display Credential Hint textbox. The dialog should resemble the one shown in Figure 11-5.

14. Click Add.

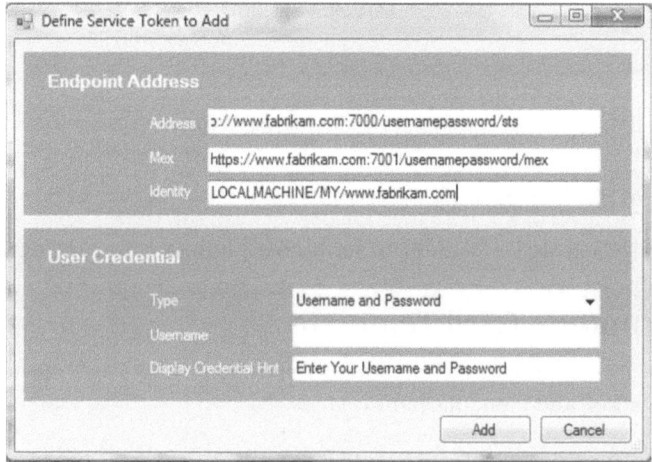

Figure 11-5. *The populated data for the endpoint and user credential*

15. Check the SAML 1.0 checkbox.

16. Click the button labeled + next to the Claims data grid view.

17. Select Site Specific ID in the drop-down list for Standardized Claims, and click OK.

18. Click the button labeled + next to the Claims data grid view.

19. Select Given Name in the drop-down list for Standardized Claims, and click OK.

20. Click the button labeled + next to the Claims data grid view.

21. Select Last Name in the drop-down list for Standardized Claims, and click OK.

22. For the Signing Certificate Information, specify the location as **LOCALMACHINE**, the store as **MY**, and the name as **www.fabrikam.com**.

The application should resemble Figure 11-6.

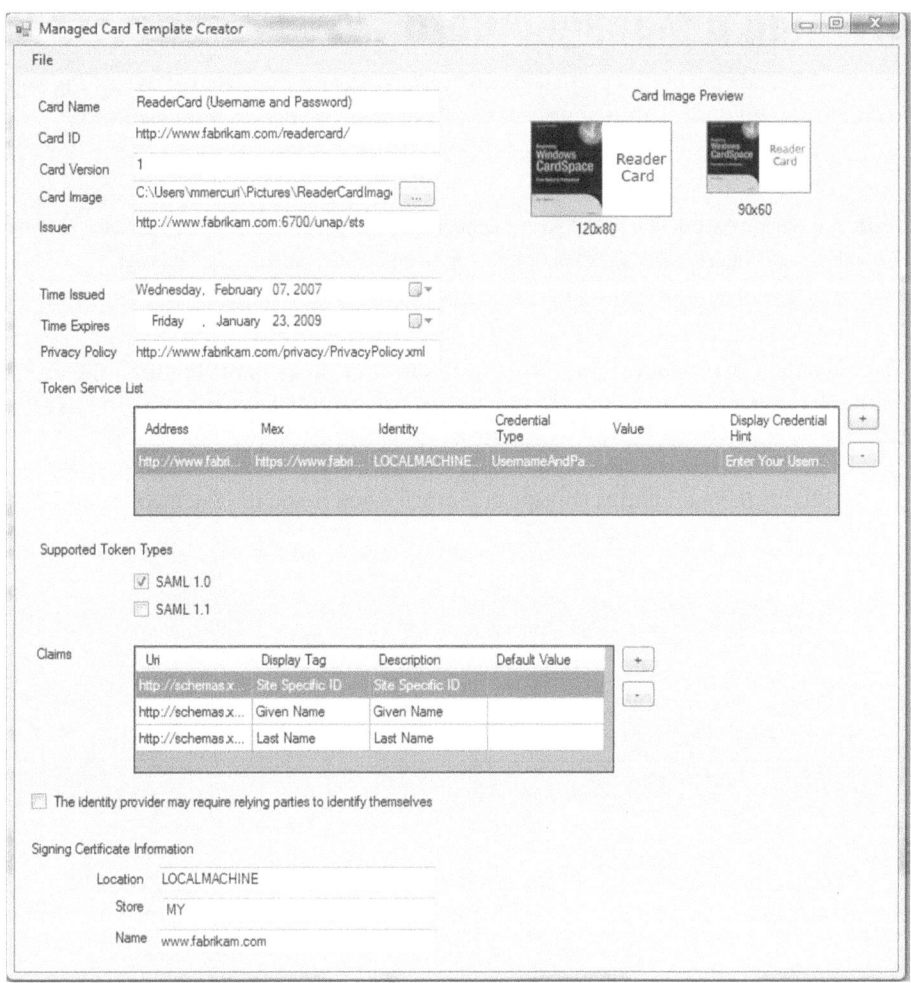

Figure 11-6. *The fully populated template*

23. Click the File menu item, and select Save Template.

24. Name the file **readercard_template**, and click OK.

25. Click the File menu, and select Exit.

26. Start the application again.

27. Click the File menu, and click Load Existing Template.

28. Navigate to the template you just created, and click OK.

Your template should now be displayed in the application.

Creating a Managed Card

You're now ready to create a managed card. In this example, you'll use the existing application to create a single card. This is simply to show you how to create a managed card.

Note If you are considering becoming an identity provider, you will want to read Chapter 12, which shows how to leverage Windows Workflow Foundation for an automated card creation process.

As you may have noticed, some of the classes and UI elements in the earlier exercises of this book provided an opportunity to include a value. You'll leverage those in this section and enhance the existing application to create a managed card here:

1. Modify the menuStrip1 control, and insert a new menu item named **Create Information Card**, as shown in Figure 11-7.

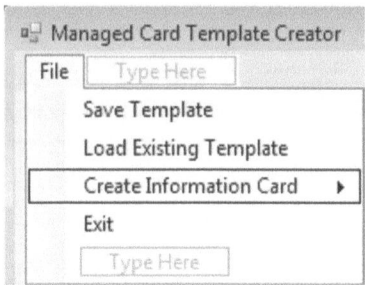

Figure 11-7. *Adding Create Information Card to the menu*

2. Name the new menu item **CreateICToolStripMenuItem**.

3. Double-click the item to open the click event.

4. Populate the event with the following code:

```
InformationCardTemplate ict = PopulateCardTemplateFromUI();
        saveFileDialog1.Filter = "Managed Card (*.crd)|*.crd";
        DialogResult dr = saveFileDialog1.ShowDialog();

        string filename = saveFileDialog1.FileName;

        CertificateInfo certInfo = new CertificateInfo();
        certInfo.CommonName = tbCertificateCommonName.Text;
        certInfo.Location = tbCertificateLocation.Text;
        certInfo.Store = tbCertificateStore.Text;
        X509Certificate2 certificate = ➥
ManagedCardHelper.RetrieveCertificate(certInfo);
```

```
ManagedCardHelper helper = new ManagedCardHelper();

helper.SaveCard(ict.InformationCardDefinition, certificate,
filename);
```

This code will read the information in from the user interface, retrieve the signing certificate, and request the filename for the card. With those three pieces of information, it will utilize the ManagedCardHelper class, which will save the card.

5. Run the application.

6. Click the File menu, and click Load Existing Template.

7. Navigate to the template you just created, and click OK. Your template should now be displayed in the application.

8. Append **12345** to the end of the card ID. It should now read http://www.fabrikam.com/readercard/12345.

9. In the data grid view for the token service list, populate the value field with a username, such as **mmercuri**.

10. In the Claims data grid view, in the last column, specify values for both Given Name and Last Name (such as **Marc** and **Mercuri**).

11. Click the File menu item, and click Create Information Card.

12. Enter the name for your card, and click OK.

You've just created a card. You can test that the card was created successfully by doing the following:

1. Open the Control Panel.

2. Click Windows CardSpace.

3. Click Add a Card, and follow the instructions.

If your card was created properly, it will show in the identity selector. If there was an issue creating your card, you'll want to check the event logs. They're helpful in identifying which part of the card is causing challenges for the identity selector.

Summary

This chapter covered a fair amount on the topic of issuing cards. The chapter began with a review of who issues cards in the real world today and what the benefits are to both the issuer and the cardholder. I also covered two key topics to think about when deciding whether to become an issuer and the benefits of branding and federation.

The chapter concluded with hands-on exercises in which you created a series of information card and information card helper classes, as well as an application that created both the templates and the cards.

CHAPTER 12

Automating Card Issuance with WF

In the previous chapter, you learned the details of what was required to create an information card. You also created a helper class that facilitated several key functions, including saving and loading a card template and creating and signing an information card.

Although the previous chapter walked you through how to create an information card, the exercise was fairly academic because it focused on creating a single card. What you've not yet learned is how to handle issuing information cards in a scalable way. This chapter focuses on how you might automate the creation of cards, specifically by developing a card creation workflow that can be automated. The technology you'll use to do this will be the .NET Framework's Windows Workflow Foundation (WF).

Note WF is a fantastic technology, and it could be a perfect fit for your organization. If, however, your company has a commitment and investment in another workflow product or technology, you shouldn't stop reading here. The baseline code and the underlying approach to automated card issuance presented here should be readily translatable to other workflow/orchestration technology platforms.

Introducing Workflow

Before we start talking about WF and how to implement the solution, let's begin with a baseline discussion of what workflow is:

A workflow is a set of activities that coordinate people and/or software.

So, what is an activity? Think of *activities* as logical units of work. In an expense-reporting workflow, for example, submitting an expense report, comparing the expenses on that report against corporate policies, and approving the expense report would all be considered activities.

Types of Workflow

Workflows fall into two commonly agreed upon categories. Workflows that involve people, such as a document review process, are referred to as *human-based workflows*, and workflows that involve interaction between applications, services, and other workflows, such as in supply-chain management, are referred to as *system workflows*.

Based on the participants in the workflow, these types of workflows have certain characteristics. For example, for system-to-system communication, the flow and underlying data are much more structured. In human-based workflows, you're performing workflows that require human intervention. Many times this involves unstructured data such as documents.

Human-based workflows, on the other hand, can often require more flexibility and can be more dynamic. In a human-based workflow, an individual may be empowered to add steps to a workflow to accommodate a given situation.

The reality is that although there are two distinct categories, it is not uncommon to have hybrid workflows that encompass the two styles. You can see this in everything from line-of-business applications (that is, quote to cash) to IT scenarios (that is, help desk or provisioning) where there is both human interaction and system-to-system interaction.

Long-Running Workflows

If you think about a number of workflows, they don't fit a synchronous request-response pattern. These are workflows that require manual interaction or are triggered by a future event. These workflows do not last seconds but instead last minutes, hours, days, weeks, months, or even years. You can see long-running workflows both in the consumer space and in the enterprise space. Whether it's an ongoing request for season tickets for your favorite football team, a request for notification on the release of a new product, the processing of a permit from a local/state/federal government, a relocation process, and so on, long-running workflows are fairly common.

Introducing Windows Workflow Foundation

CardSpace was released as part of the .NET Framework 3.0. This upgrade to the framework includes four technologies. In addition to Windows CardSpace and Windows Communication Foundation, which you've worked with already, it also includes Windows Presentation Foundation and Windows Workflow Foundation.

This chapter focuses on leveraging Windows Workflow Foundation to automate issuing information cards. Before I cover how to create the workflows, I'll quickly review Windows Workflow Foundation.

Note This chapter provides a high-level background of Windows Workflow Foundation to provide some context. It is not a definitive reference on the technology. If you are new to Windows Workflow Foundation, I encourage you to reference the tutorials provided by the product group. You can find these online at `http://msdn2.microsoft.com/en-us/library/ms735967.aspx`.

Activities

A *workflow* is a set of activities that coordinate people and/or software. In WF, workflows are designed using *activities*, functional units of work packaged into a component. WF provides a base activity library that covers the core functionality you would expect with support for if/else statements, while loops, transactions, and compensation. In addition, it includes activities that provide the ability to interact with and raise events to the workflow host.

Custom Code and Activities

The base activity library is what its name implies, basic. Without question, at some point you will need to write a workflow that incorporates your own custom code. You can do this by using a Code activity or by creating your own custom activities.

The easiest approach is to use the generic Code activity provided by the base activity library. This provides a mechanism through which you can execute .NET code at a certain point(s) in the workflow. This makes sense when the code you're adding is workflow-specific and not complex, reusable, or any combination thereof.

Although you may use Code activities to perform some basic functions or to serve as the glue between other activities in a workflow, for anything of significance you'll want to create your own custom activities. The good news is that this is very straightforward to do.

With the creation and use of custom activities, you can also gain value in packaging your business logic into a reusable form that can be independently compiled, modified, and versioned. You can then share these activities for use in creating other workflows, including SharePoint Services 3.0 and Office 2007 SharePoint Server.

By the end of this chapter, you will have written a number of custom activities used for issuing information cards.

Workflow and Web Services

In the previous section, I mentioned you can leverage your code in Windows Workflow Foundation in three ways. The third is to invoke a web service that contains your code.

In WF 1.0, the base activity library includes an InvokeWebService activity. This makes it easy to consume web services within your workflow. The current version of this control has some limitations, however, because it can utilize only those services that implement Basic Profile 1.0 (BP 1.0).

But by using technologies such as WCF, you can extend that functionality by writing custom activities that can consume WS-* services. For that matter, you can also write activities that consume POX and REST services.

Through this functionality, WF provides the ability to consume services, as well as coordinate multiple services in a workflow. But in addition to consumption, workflows can also be exposed as web services. As mentioned earlier, workflows can be triggered by external events, and those events can take the form of a web service call.

Workflow Types in Windows Workflow Foundation

Earlier I discussed two types of workflows: system-to-system workflows and human-based workflows. When mapping these workflows on paper, people have traditionally used a flowchart diagram or a state machine diagram, respectively.

A flowchart is probably the most common, and the flow for these types of charts is sequential. Several steps connect in a sequence, with potentially some branching based on certain conditions. In WF, this type of workflow is referred to as a *sequential workflow* (see Figure 12-1).

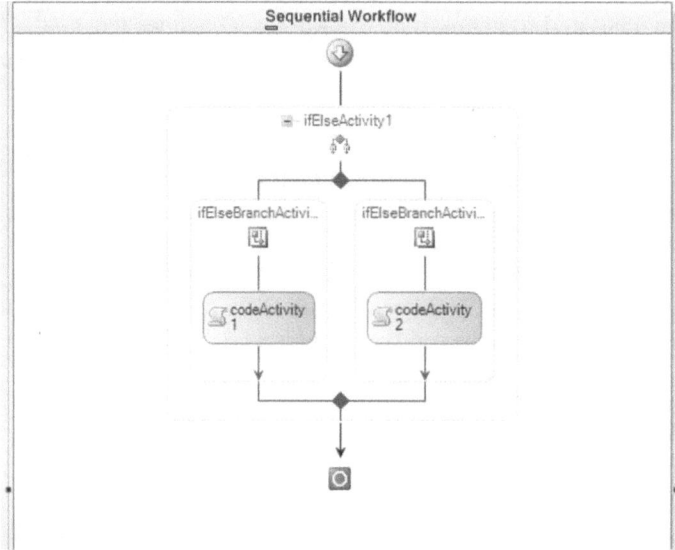

Figure 12-1. *A sequential workflow in workflow designer view in Visual Studio*

Windows Workflow Foundation also provides the ability to model state machines. Here, a workflow can be in a number of states. In an order-processing scenario, those states could include WaitingForOrder, OrderOpen, OrderProcessed, and OrderCompleted. Figure 12-2 shows simple state machine workflow that contains three states.

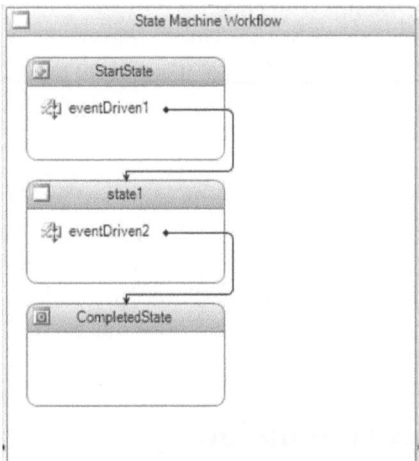

Figure 12-2. *A state machine workflow in Visual Studio designer view*

Workflow Hosting

Workflows don't run on their own; they require a host process to instantiate them.

A host process first creates an instance of the workflow runtime engine, which is found in the appropriately named WorkflowRuntime class. Once created, the workflow runtime can create new instances of a workflow via the runtime's CreateWorkflow operation.

In addition to providing the ability to create new workflows, the WorkflowRuntime class also exposes events that occur during different points in the lifetime of a workflow, such as when the workflow instance is created, completed, idled, or aborted.

Any .NET application can host the workflow runtime. This provides a number of possibilities, allowing you to host workflows in services, in IIS, in desktop applications, and even in console applications!

As shown in the following code, the actual instantiation of the runtime and the creation of a workflow are very straightforward. Here, the workflow runtime is created, and a new instance of Workflow is created via the runtime's CreateWorkflow method.

```
using System;
using System.Threading;
using System.Workflow.Runtime;
using System.Workflow.Runtime.Hosting;

class Program
{
    static void Main(string[] args)
    {
        using (WorkflowRuntime workflowRuntime = new WorkflowRuntime())
        {
WorkflowInstance instance = ➥
workflowRuntime.CreateWorkflow(➥
typeof(WorkflowConsoleApplication1.Workflow1));
        }
    }
}
```

The workflow runtime also provides a number of events that can be triggered at certain points in the lifetime of a workflow instance.

The provided events include the following:

- WorkflowAborted

- WorkflowCompleted

- WorkflowCreated

- WorkflowIdled

- WorkflowLoaded

- WorkflowPersisted

- WorkflowSuspended

- WorkflowResumed

- WorkflowStarted

- WorkflowTerminated

- WorkflowUnloaded

Runtime Services

The runtime also supports the ability to implement services. There are a core set of services focused on controlling how the runtime handles threads, transactions, persistence, and the generation of monitoring data. If the included services don't meet your needs, you can create your own.

Scheduling Services

Scheduling services control the scheduling of workflow instances by the workflow runtime. Windows Workflow Foundation includes two scheduling services, DefaultWorkflowSchedulerService and ManualWorkflowSchedulerService.

DefaultWorkflowSchedulerService creates a new thread for each new workflow. As a result, the workflows are executed asynchronously, and there is no blocking on the application thread.

With ManualWorkflowSchedulerService, the host donates a thread to execute the workflow. In cases where you're running a website or web service, your server will already be managing threads to process each request. Rather than create an additional thread for each workflow, the host can utilize existing threads. ManualWorkflowSchedulerService should be used in ASP.NET-hosted workflows.

Persistence Services

Sometimes in the lifetime of a workflow you will want its state persisted to a durable store. With long-running workflows, for example, if you were forced to keep all your workflows in memory, you'd run into scalability challenges. With persistence services, you have the ability to persist inactive workflows to a store.

WF ships with SqlWorkflowPersistenceService, which works with MSDE, SQL Server 2000, and SQL Server 2005.

■**Note** If you're looking to persist your workflow someplace other than SQL, the workflow team has made available a file-based persistence service that provides a good overview of how to create your own persistence service.

Tracking Services

Tracking services provide the ability to collect information about your workflow instances. The specific information to collect is specified in a tracking profile. When creating new workflow instances, for those workflows that specify a tracking profile, the runtime requests a tracking channel from the tracking service. The tracking service then tracks all the information from the service.

A sample tracking service ships with Windows Workflow Foundation and provides the ability to store tracking details in SQL Server.

CommitWorkBatch Services

There is another service that persists information about a workflow to a durable store, CommitWorkBatch services. While persistence services persist idled workflows to a durable store, CommitWorkBatch services manage the persistence of work batches that occur during a workflow. When a work batch commits, a call is made into the CommitWorkBatch service, which will commit the batch.

Transactions are an area where you will want to persist the state of a workflow at varying points. When beginning a transaction, you will want to create a persistence point to roll back to, and you also want to persist information once a transaction has been completed.

Windows Workflow Foundation ships with two CommitWorkBatch services: DefaultWorkflowCommitWorkBatchService and SharedConnectionWorkflowCommitWorkBatchService. SharedConnectionWorkflowCommitWorkBatchService is used for database transactions using a shared connection, such as when you're using SQL Server for both persistence and tracking. As you might imagine, DefaultWorkflowCommitWorkBatchService is what's loaded by the runtime if no CommitWorkBatchService is specified.

Adding a Service to the Runtime

You add a service to the runtime via the AddService method. The following code shows the addition of SqlWorkflowPersistenceService to the runtime:

```
workflowRuntime.AddService(new SqlWorkflowPersistenceService(connectionString));
```

Creating a Simple Workflow

To get you more familiar with Windows Workflow Foundation, this exercise will lead you through creating a simple workflow:

1. Open Visual Studio 2005.

2. Select File ➤ New Project.

3. Select the workflow type, as shown in Figure 12-3, and select the Sequential Workflow Console Application template.

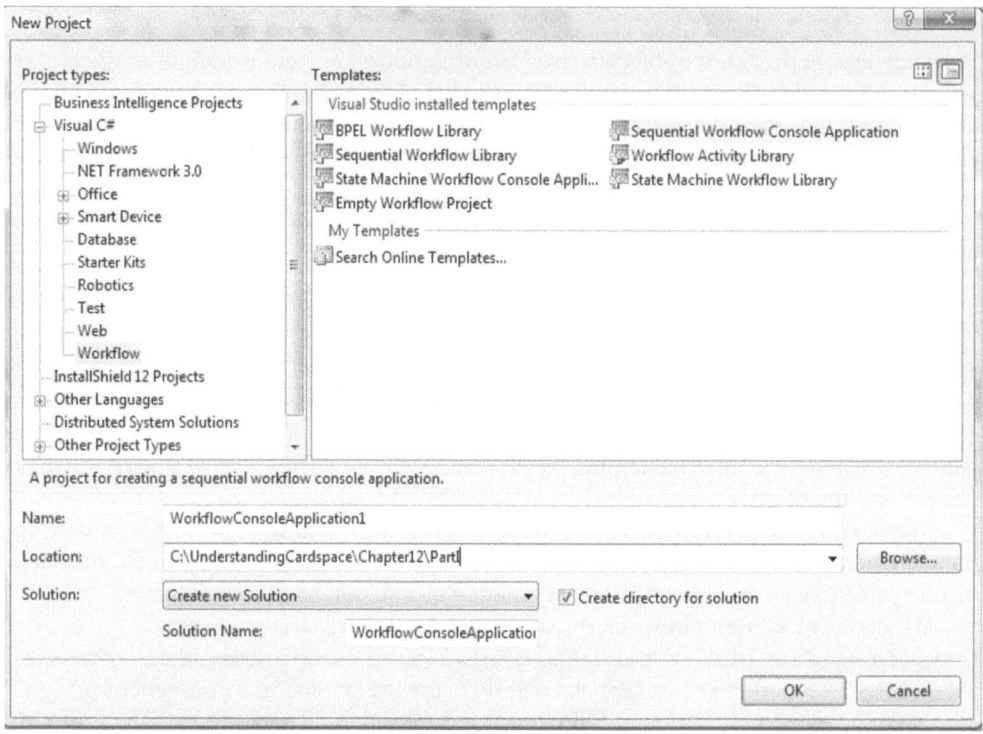

Figure 12-3. *Creating the project*

4. Name the project **SimpleWorkflow**, and save it in C:\BeginningCardspace\ Chapter12\PartI. This will create a new workflow project and display the sequential workflow designer. In this exercise, you'll have the workflow write the obligatory "Hello, World" program.

5. From the Toolbox, drag and drop a Code activity onto the designer view. The Code activity allows for the execution of .NET code within a workflow. The activity is associated with a code function, and that function is associated via the Properties window in the designer view.

6. With the Code activity selected in the designer view, open the Properties window.

7. In the properties for codeActivity1, set the ExecuteCode property to **codeActivity1_Execute**. This will create a new function named codeActivity1_Execute.

8. In that function, add the following code:

```
Console.WriteLine("Hello World, the current time is "➥
  + System.DateTime.Now.ToLongTimeString());
```

9. With the workflow created, you now need to make sure there is a host that can create instances of it. Fortunately, this project template provides code to create a basic console host for the workflow runtime. Open Program.cs, and you'll see the code used to create the runtime:

```
static void Main(string[] args)
    {
        using(WorkflowRuntime workflowRuntime = new WorkflowRuntime())
        {
            AutoResetEvent waitHandle = new AutoResetEvent(false);
            workflowRuntime.WorkflowCompleted ➥
+= delegate(object sender, WorkflowCompletedEventArgs e)➥
 {waitHandle.Set();};
            workflowRuntime.WorkflowTerminated +=➥
 delegate(object sender, WorkflowTerminatedEventArgs e)
            {
                Console.WriteLine(e.Exception.Message);
                waitHandle.Set();
            };

            WorkflowInstance instance =➥
 workflowRuntime.CreateWorkflow(typeof(➥
 SimpleWorkflow.Workflow1));
            instance.Start();

            waitHandle.WaitOne();
        }
    }
```

10. Just below `waitHandle.WaitOne()`, add the following code:

```
            Console.WriteLine("Press any key to exit");
            Console.ReadLine();
```

This code is added solely to stop the console from exiting after executing the workflow.

Creating a Basic Custom Activity

As mentioned earlier, Windows Workflow Foundation provides a base activity library, but sometimes you'll want to wrap your own code or services as custom activities.

Because this chapter focuses on creating custom activities used with the issuance of information cards, this exercise will step you through creating a basic custom activity:

1. Right-click your existing project, and select Add New Item.

2. Specify Activity as the type of item, and name it **TimeAwareHelloWorld.cs**. This will result in the display of the activity designer, and your screen should resemble the one shown in Figure 12-4.

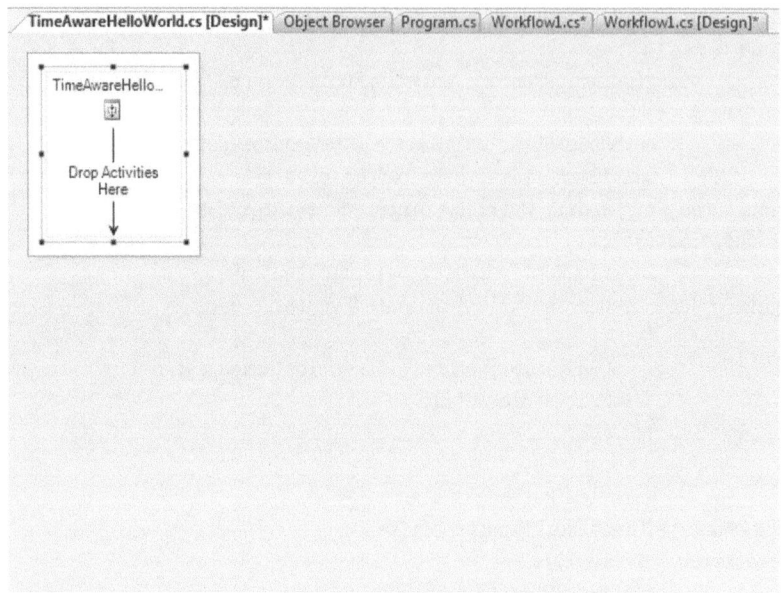

Figure 12-4. *Creating the* `TimeAwareHelloWorld` *activity*

By default, activities will look very much like sequential workflows, and all the activities and visual connections between the activities appear. This is great for creating composite activities, where you will have an activity that is in reality the recurring execution of a number of existing activities in a sequential flow.

In this chapter, you are not creating composite activities; you're creating our activities using custom code. Although you could do this through adding multiple Code activities, the visualization is neither helpful nor attractive.

As a result, the view shown in the activity designer is not desirable. Let's change it.

3. Right-click the designer, and select View Code.

   Looking at the code, you'll see the reason for the sequential workflow-like visualization in the activity designer. The template for activities, by default, inherits from SequenceActivity:

   ```
   public partial class TimeAwareHelloWorld: SequenceActivity
   ```

4. In the class definition, replace SequenceActivity with Activity:

   ```
   public partial class TimeAwareHelloWorld: Activity
   ```

If you now open the designer for the activity, you'll see that the visualization has changed to the one shown in Figure 12-5.

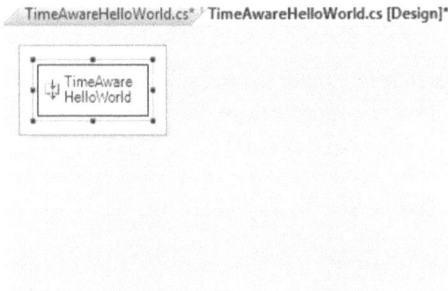

Figure 12-5. *The* TimeAwareHelloWorld *activity after changing to* Activity *(from* SequenceActivity*)*

■ **Note** If you're aesthetically minded and you'd like something beyond black text on a white box, not to worry. Although not covered in this chapter, Windows Workflow Foundation does provide the ability to change the appearance of the activity to include graphics, shapes, color schemes, and so on.

The next step is to create the implementation of your activity. In this chapter, I'll cover three areas of functionality in regard to custom activities: setting properties, creating events, and implementing the execution.

Creating Properties for the Activity

When creating activities, you'll want to think about what the activity inputs and outputs are. If your activity will need to take values as input, you'll need to create corresponding properties to accept them.

In the case of the TimeAwareHelloWorld activity, you'll be taking one input that specifies the name of the person to whom to say "Hello." The name of this property will be PersonToGreet and be of type string.

Right-click the designer, and select View Code. Then follow these steps:

1. Right-click the code window, and select Insert Snippet ➤ Workflow ➤ Dependency Property-Property.

   This will create a snippet of a dependency property. For those unfamiliar with snippets, there is text on the screen with a background color of green. This text is part of the snippet template and should be changed to your specific implementation.

   This activity will contain a single property, PersonToGreet, of type string.

2. Modify the code generated by the snippet to resemble the following:

```
public static DependencyProperty PersonToGreetProperty =➥
System.Workflow.ComponentModel.DependencyProperty.Register(➥
"PersonToGreet", typeof(string), typeof(TimeAwareHelloWorld));

        [Description("This is the name of the person to say hello to.")]
        [Category("Input Parameters")]
        [Browsable(true)]
        [DesignerSerializationVisibility(➥
DesignerSerializationVisibility.Visible)]
        public string PersonToGreet
        {
            get
            {
                return ((string)(base.GetValue(➥
TimeAwareHelloWorld.PersonToGreetProperty)));
            }
            set
            {
                base.SetValue(➥
TimeAwareHelloWorld.PersonToGreetProperty, value);
            }
        }
```

This simple activity will write its message to the console window and as a result does not need to provide a property that contains the result of the execution. It should be noted that this is more the exception than the rule. When creating information card–related activities later in the chapter, the activities will also have a property named Result that contains the result of the activity execution.

Creating Events

At some points in the activity's life, you may want to fire events to the workflow that contains it. This is commonly desired at two times: when the activity is first invoked and when the activity execution has been completed.

In the former scenario, you may need to determine a property value at runtime. Having an event named invoke or invoking can provide a hook that you can assign in a just-in-time fashion.

In addition, after an activity has completed its work, you may want to call an invoked event. This will allow you to take the result of the activity and perform some functionality before going on to the execution of the next activity in the workflow.

In this exercise, you'll be creating an `Invoke` event and assigning the name of PersonToGreet at runtime.

Just as with properties, there is a snippet for creating events:

1. Right-click the designer, and select View Code.

2. Right-click the code window, and select Insert Snippet ➤ Workflow ➤ Dependency Property-Event Handler.

3. In the case of the event, you'll change very little code. Modify the `Description` and `Category` attributes as shown here:

```
public static DependencyProperty InvokeEvent = ➥
DependencyProperty.Register("Invoke", ➥
typeof(EventHandler), typeof(TimeAwareHelloWorld));

  [Description("This is the event fired when the activity is invoked.")]
  [Category("PreExecution")]
        [Browsable(true)]
        [DesignerSerializationVisibility(➥
DesignerSerializationVisibility.Visible)]
        public event EventHandler Invoke
        {
            add
            {
                base.AddHandler(TimeAwareHelloWorld.InvokeEvent, value);
            }
            remove
            {
                base.RemoveHandler(TimeAwareHelloWorld.InvokeEvent, value);
            }
        }
```

Creating the Actual Activity Code

With the property and event assigned, you'll next define what the activity will do when it is executed. You do this by overriding the `Execute` method of the `Activity` class.

This activity is a simple one. It is aware of the time, and based on time of day, it will respond with "Good morning" or "Good afternoon" and with the value of the PersonToGreet property, as in "Good morning, Marc."

1. Enter the following code:

```
protected override ActivityExecutionStatus➡
Execute(ActivityExecutionContext executionContext)
    {


        base.RaiseEvent(TimeAwareHelloWorld.InvokeEvent,➡
this, EventArgs.Empty);

        string greeting = "";
        if (System.DateTime.Now.Hour < 12)
        { greeting += "Good morning, "; }
        else
        { greeting += "Good afternoon, "; }

        greeting += PersonToGreet + ➡
". The current time is " + ➡
System.DateTime.Now.ToLongTimeString();

        Console.WriteLine(greeting);

        return ActivityExecutionStatus.Closed;
    }
```

At the start of the method, you invoke your event using base.RaiseEvent. This will fire an event that can be received by the containing workflow. This will give you, as you'll see in a moment, the ability to set properties of the control just before it is executed.

You'll also note that the operation returns ActivityExecutionStatus. In this case, it is returning the status of Closed, which indicates that the activity has completed.

2. Build your project.

3. Open the designer for the workflow, and you will see that the TimeAwareHelloWorld activity now is visible in your Toolbox.

4. Drag a TimeAwareHelloWorld activity to the workflow.

5. Set the value of the PersonToGreet property to **Marc**.

6. Drag another TimeAwareHelloWorld activity to the workflow, and place it beneath the activity you just added. Your designer should resemble Figure 12-6.

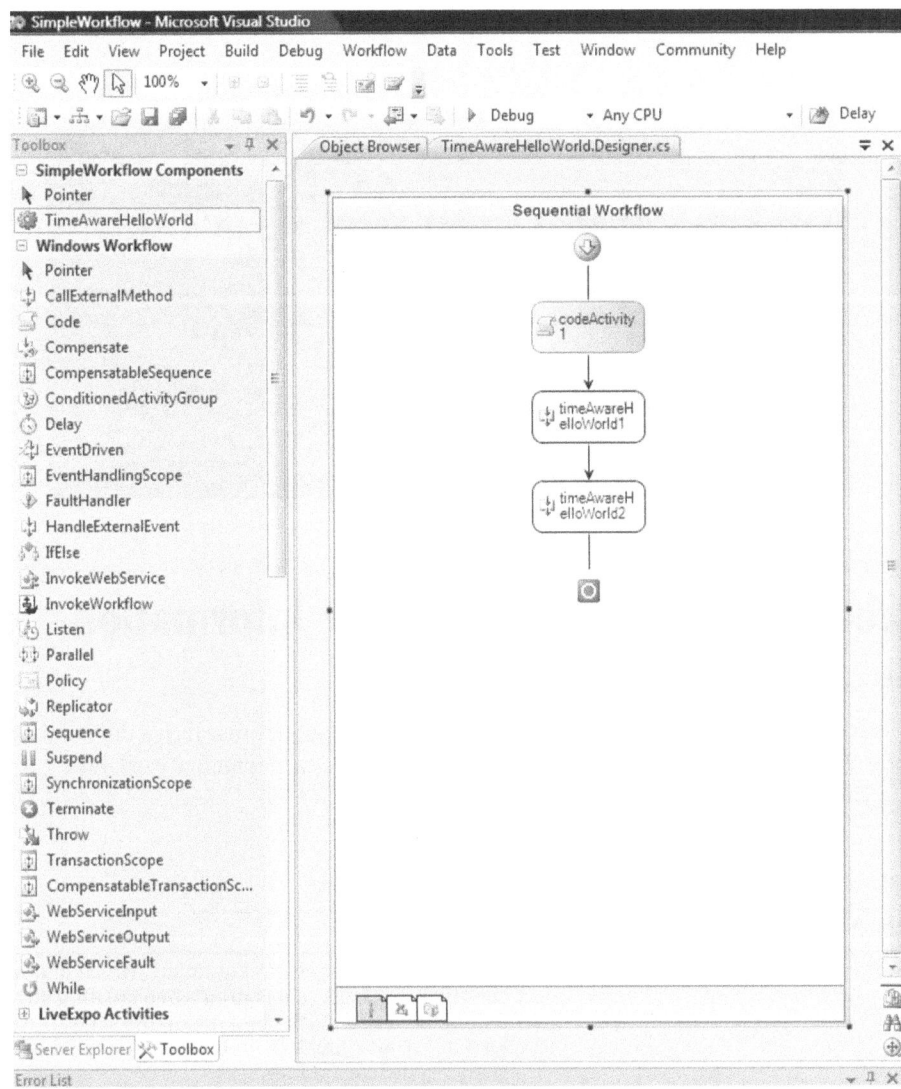

Figure 12-6. *The workflow in the workflow designer within Visual Studio*

7. In the properties for this activity, called timeAwareHelloWorld2, set the Invoke property to **timeAwareHelloWorld2_Invoke**.

8. This will create a new method named timeAwareHelloWorld2_Invoke. Populate it with the following code:

```
private void timeAwareHelloWorld2_Execute(object sender, EventArgs e)
    {
        timeAwareHelloWorld2.PersonToGreet = "Katie";
    }
```

9. Now, you're ready to run the application. This will generate a console window that should resemble Figure 12-7.

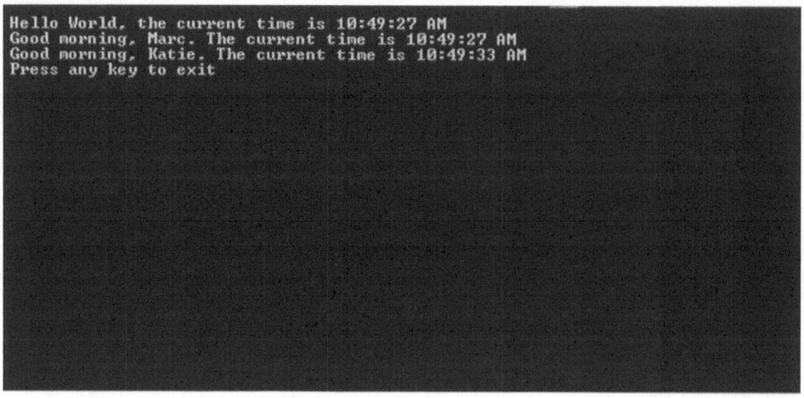

```
Hello World, the current time is 10:49:27 AM
Good morning, Marc. The current time is 10:49:27 AM
Good morning, Katie. The current time is 10:49:33 AM
Press any key to exit
```

Figure 12-7. *The output of the running workflow*

Creating Custom Activities for Information Card Issuance

With a quick primer on Windows Workflow Foundation out of the way, it's time to write some code. You'll begin by creating the activities required for a card issuance workflow.

Table 12-1 defines the activities you'll be creating.

Table 12-1. *Custom Activities for Information Card Issuance*

Activity Name	Description
LoadManagedCardTemplate	This loads a managed card template, which defines the claims and default values used when creating an information card of a particular type. In the sample, we'll load this from a file. In a production system, this would likely reside in a database.
RetrieveX509CertificateFromStore	This will retrieve the X.509 certificate to be used in conjunction with creating the information card. This assumes that the certificate is in the local store, which is the case for this sample.
CreateAndSignInformationCard	This creates and signs the information card and will return the signed XML.
SaveInformationCardToFile	This saves the information card to a file. In the workflow that will be subsequently created with this activity, the information card is written to a file and then attached to an outgoing email.

Table 12-1. *Custom Activities for Information Card Issuance*

Activity Name	Description
SaveManagedCardTemplate	If you are creating multiple types of cards or multiple versions of a type of card, you may want to create a separate workflow for the creation and update of card templates. This is a simple control that will receive template information and save it to a file.
SendEmail	This activity provides the ability to create an email, optionally include attachments, and send the email via SMTP.

The good news is that each of these activities will use the ManagedCardHelper class from the previous chapter.

Begin by creating a new activity library project that will contain your activities.

1. Create a new activity library project.

2. Name the project **InformationCardActivities**, and create it in the folder C:\BeginningCardspace\Chapter12\PartII.

3. Delete Activity1.cs from the project.

Creating the CreateAndSignInformationCard Activity

To create the CreateAndSignInformationCard activity, follow these steps:

1. Right-click the project, and select Add New File.

2. Select Activity, and name the activity **CreateAndSignInformationCard**.

3. View the code for the activity, and populate it with the following code:

```
using System;
using System.ComponentModel;
using System.ComponentModel.Design;
using System.Collections;
using System.Drawing;
using System.Workflow.ComponentModel;
using System.Workflow.ComponentModel.Design;
using System.Workflow.ComponentModel.Compiler;
using System.Workflow.ComponentModel.Serialization;
using System.Workflow.Runtime;
using System.Workflow.Activities;
using System.Workflow.Activities.Rules;
using BeginningCardspace;
using System.Security.Cryptography.X509Certificates;
using System.Xml;
```

```
namespace InformationCardActivities
{
    public partial class CreateAndSignInformationCard: Activity
    {
        public CreateAndSignInformationCard()
        {
            InitializeComponent();
        }


        public static DependencyProperty ➥
InformationCardProperty = ➥
System.Workflow.ComponentModel.DependencyProperty. ➥
Register("InformationCard", typeof(InformationCard), ➥
typeof(CreateAndSignInformationCard));

        [Description("This is the Information Card ➥
information that will be generated into the .CRD file")]
        [Category("Miscellaneous")]
        [Browsable(true)]
        [DesignerSerializationVisibility(➥
DesignerSerializationVisibility.Visible)]
        public InformationCard InformationCard
        {
            get
            {
                return ((InformationCard)(base.GetValue(➥
CreateAndSignInformationCard.InformationCardProperty)));
            }
            set
            {
                base.SetValue(➥
CreateAndSignInformationCard.InformationCardProperty, value);
            }
        }


        public static DependencyProperty ➥
SigningCertificateProperty =➥
 System.Workflow.ComponentModel.DependencyProperty. ➥
Register("SigningCertificate", typeof(X509Certificate2), ➥
 typeof(CreateAndSignInformationCard));
```

```
        [Description(➥
"This is the X509 certificate to sign the Information Card with")]
        [Category("Miscellaneous")]
        [Browsable(true)]
        [DesignerSerializationVisibility(➥
DesignerSerializationVisibility.Visible)]
        public X509Certificate2 SigningCertificate
        {
            get
            {
                return ((X509Certificate2) ➥
(base.GetValue(CreateAndSignInformationCard. ➥
SigningCertificateProperty)));
            }
            set
            {
                base.SetValue(CreateAndSignInformationCard. ➥
SigningCertificateProperty, value);
            }
        }


        public static DependencyProperty ResultProperty =➥
 System.Workflow.ComponentModel.DependencyProperty. ➥
Register("Result", typeof(System.Xml.XmlElement), ➥
 typeof(CreateAndSignInformationCard));


        [Description("This is the signed Information Card in XML form.")]
        [Category("Result")]
        [Browsable(true)]
        [DesignerSerializationVisibility(➥
DesignerSerializationVisibility.Visible)]
        public System.Xml.XmlElement Result
        {
            get
            {
                return ((System.Xml.XmlElement) ➥
(base.GetValue(CreateAndSignInformationCard.ResultProperty)));
            }
            set
            {
                base.SetValue(➥
CreateAndSignInformationCard.ResultProperty, value);
            }
        }
```

```
                    protected override ActivityExecutionStatus➡
            Execute(ActivityExecutionContext executionContext)
                {
                    ManagedCardHelper helper = new ManagedCardHelper();
                    System.Xml.XmlDocument doc = ➡
            helper.CreateInformationCardXML(InformationCard);
                    XmlElement e = ➡
            helper.SignInformationCardXML(doc, SigningCertificate);
                    Result = e;

                    return base.Execute(executionContext);
                }


            }
        }
```

Creating the LoadManagedCardTemplate Activity

To create the LoadManagedCardTemplate activity, follow these steps:

1. Right-click the project, and select Add New File.

2. Select Activity, and name the activity **LoadManagedCardTemplate**.

3. View the code for the activity, and populate it with the following code:

```
using System;
using System.ComponentModel;
using System.ComponentModel.Design;
using System.Collections;
using System.Drawing;
using System.Workflow.ComponentModel;
using System.Workflow.ComponentModel.Design;
using System.Workflow.ComponentModel.Compiler;
using System.Workflow.ComponentModel.Serialization;
using System.Workflow.Runtime;
using System.Workflow.Activities;
using System.Workflow.Activities.Rules;
using BeginningCardspace;

namespace InformationCardActivities
{
    public partial class LoadManagedCardTemplate: Activity
    {
        public LoadManagedCardTemplate()
        {
            InitializeComponent();
        }
```

```
        public static DependencyProperty ➥
TemplateDirectoryProperty = ➥
System.Workflow.ComponentModel.DependencyProperty. ➥
Register("TemplateDirectory", typeof(string), ➥
 typeof(LoadManagedCardTemplate));

        [Description("This is the directory where templates are stored")]
        [Category("Miscellaneous")]
        [Browsable(true)]
        [DesignerSerializationVisibility(➥
DesignerSerializationVisibility.Visible)]
        public string TemplateDirectory
        {
            get
            {
                return ((string) ➥
(base.GetValue(➥
LoadManagedCardTemplate.TemplateDirectoryProperty)));
            }
            set
            {
                base.SetValue(➥
 LoadManagedCardTemplate.TemplateDirectoryProperty, value);
            }
        }

        public static DependencyProperty ➥
TemplateNameProperty =➥
 System.Workflow.ComponentModel.DependencyProperty. ➥
Register("TemplateName", typeof(string), ➥
 typeof(LoadManagedCardTemplate));

        [Description("The name of the template")]
        [Category("Miscellaneous")]
        [Browsable(true)]
        [DesignerSerializationVisibility(➥
DesignerSerializationVisibility.Visible)]
        public string TemplateName
        {
            get
            {
                return ((string) ➥
(base.GetValue(LoadManagedCardTemplate.TemplateNameProperty)➥
));
            }
            set
            {
```

```
                        base.SetValue(LoadManagedCardTemplate.TemplateNameProperty,➡
        value);
                }
        }

        public static DependencyProperty ResultProperty =➡
    System.Workflow.ComponentModel.DependencyProperty.➡
    Register("Result", typeof(InformationCardTemplate),➡
    typeof(LoadManagedCardTemplate));

        [Description("The template for an Information Card")]
        [Category("Result")]
        [Browsable(true)]
        [DesignerSerializationVisibility(➡
    DesignerSerializationVisibility.Visible)]
        public InformationCardTemplate Result
        {
            get
            {
                return ((InformationCardTemplate)➡
    (base.GetValue(LoadManagedCardTemplate.ResultProperty)));
            }
            set
            {
                base.SetValue(LoadManagedCardTemplate.ResultProperty, value);
            }
        }

        protected override ActivityExecutionStatus ➡
    Execute(ActivityExecutionContext executionContext)
        {


            if (TemplateDirectory.Substring(➡
    TemplateDirectory.Length-1) != "/" ||➡
    TemplateDirectory.Substring(TemplateDirectory.Length-1)➡
    != "\\")
                TemplateDirectory += "\\";
            string fileName = TemplateDirectory + TemplateName + ".template";
            InformationCardTemplate ict =➡
    ManagedCardHelper.LoadCardTemplate(fileName);

            Result = ict;
            return base.Execute(executionContext);
        }

    }
}
```

Note This activity adds a property named TemplateDirectory. This is a base folder in the file system where template files are stored.

Creating the RetrieveX509CertificateFromStore Activity

To create the `RetrieveX509CertificateFromStore` activity, follow these steps:

1. Right-click the project, and select Add New File.

2. Select Activity, and name the activity **RetrieveX509CertificateFromStore**.

3. View the code for the activity, and populate it with the following code:

```
using System;
using System.ComponentModel;
using System.ComponentModel.Design;
using System.Collections;
using System.Drawing;
using System.Workflow.ComponentModel;
using System.Workflow.ComponentModel.Design;
using System.Workflow.ComponentModel.Compiler;
using System.Workflow.ComponentModel.Serialization;
using System.Workflow.Runtime;
using System.Workflow.Activities;
using System.Workflow.Activities.Rules;
using System.Security.Cryptography.Xml;
using System.Security.Cryptography.X509Certificates;

namespace InformationCardActivities
{
    public partial class RetrieveX509CertificateFromStore: Activity
    {
        public RetrieveX509CertificateFromStore()
        {
            InitializeComponent();
        }
        public static DependencyProperty➡
CertificateStoreLocationProperty =➡
System.Workflow.ComponentModel.DependencyProperty.➡
Register("CertificateStoreLocation", typeof(string),➡
 typeof(RetrieveX509CertificateFromStore));

        [Description("The certificate store location.")]
        [Category("Search Criteria")]
        [Browsable(true)]
        [DesignerSerializationVisibility(➡
```

```
DesignerSerializationVisibility.Visible)]
        public string CertificateStoreLocation
        {
            get
            {
                return ((string)(base.GetValue(➡
RetrieveX509CertificateFromStore.➡
CertificateStoreLocationProperty)));
            }
            set
            {
                base.SetValue(RetrieveX509CertificateFromStore.➡
CertificateStoreLocationProperty, value);
            }
        }

        public static DependencyProperty ➡
CertificateStoreNameProperty =➡
 System.Workflow.ComponentModel.DependencyProperty.➡
Register("CertificateStoreName", typeof(string),➡
 typeof(RetrieveX509CertificateFromStore));

        [Description("The certificate store name.")]
        [Category("Search Criteria")]
        [Browsable(true)]
        [DesignerSerializationVisibility(➡
DesignerSerializationVisibility.Visible)]
        public string CertificateStoreName
        {
            get
            {
                return ((string)➡
(base.GetValue(➡
RetrieveX509CertificateFromStore.CertificateStoreNameProperty)));
            }
            set
            {
                base.SetValue(➡
RetrieveX509CertificateFromStore.CertificateStoreNameProperty,➡
 value);
            }
        }
        public static DependencyProperty ➡
CertificateCommonNameProperty =➡
 System.Workflow.ComponentModel.DependencyProperty.➡
Register("CertificateCommonName", typeof(string),➡
 typeof(RetrieveX509CertificateFromStore));
```

```
        [Description("The Common Name (CN) of the Certificate")]
        [Category("Search Criteria")]
        [Browsable(true)]
        [DesignerSerializationVisibility(➥
DesignerSerializationVisibility.Visible)]
        public string CertificateCommonName
        {
            get
            {
                return ((string)(base.GetValue(➥
RetrieveX509CertificateFromStore.➥
CertificateCommonNameProperty)));
            }
            set
            {
                base.SetValue(➥
RetrieveX509CertificateFromStore.➥
CertificateCommonNameProperty, value);
            }
        }
        public static DependencyProperty ➥
ResultProperty = System.Workflow.ComponentModel.DependencyProperty. ➥
Register("Result", typeof(X509Certificate2), ➥
 typeof(RetrieveX509CertificateFromStore));

        [Description("This is the certificate requested")]
        [Category("Result")]
        [Browsable(true)]
        [DesignerSerializationVisibility(➥
DesignerSerializationVisibility.Visible)]
        public X509Certificate2 Result
        {
            get
            {
                return ((X509Certificate2) ➥
(base.GetValue(RetrieveX509CertificateFromStore. ➥
ResultProperty)));
            }
            set
            {
                base.SetValue(RetrieveX509CertificateFromStore. ➥
ResultProperty, value);
            }
        }
        protected override ActivityExecutionStatus➥
 Execute(ActivityExecutionContext executionContext)
        {
```

```
            StoreName storeName = StoreName.My;
            StoreLocation storeLocation = StoreLocation.LocalMachine;
            X509Certificate2 certificate = new X509Certificate2();

            try
            {
                storeLocation = (StoreLocation) ➥
Enum.Parse(typeof(StoreLocation), ➥
CertificateStoreLocation, true);
            }
            catch (Exception)
            {
                throw new Exception(➥
"No Certificate Location: " + CertificateStoreLocation);
            }
            try
            {
                storeName = (StoreName)➥
Enum.Parse(typeof(StoreName), CertificateStoreName, true);
            }
            catch (Exception)
            {
                throw new Exception(➥
"No Certificate Store: " + ➥
CertificateStoreName + " in " + ➥
CertificateStoreLocation);
            }

            X509Store s = new X509Store(storeName, storeLocation);
            s.Open(OpenFlags.MaxAllowed);
            foreach (X509Certificate2 xCert in s.Certificates)
            {
                if (xCert.Subject.StartsWith("CN=" + CertificateCommonName))
                {
                    certificate = xCert;
                    break;
                }


            }
            Result =  certificate;

            return base.Execute(executionContext);
        }

    }
}
```

Creating the SaveInformationCardToFile Activity

To create the SaveInformationCardToFile activity, follow these steps:

1. Right-click the project, and select Add New File.

2. Select Activity, and name the activity **SaveInformationCardToFile**.

3. View the code for the activity, and populate it with the following code:

```
using System;
using System.ComponentModel;
using System.ComponentModel.Design;
using System.Collections;
using System.Drawing;
using System.Workflow.ComponentModel;
using System.Workflow.ComponentModel.Design;
using System.Workflow.ComponentModel.Compiler;
using System.Workflow.ComponentModel.Serialization;
using System.Workflow.Runtime;
using System.Workflow.Activities;
using System.Workflow.Activities.Rules;
using BeginningCardspace;
using System.Xml;
namespace InformationCardActivities
{
    public partial class SaveInformationCardToFile: Activity
    {
        public SaveInformationCardToFile()
        {
            InitializeComponent();
        }

        public static DependencyProperty ➥
SignedInformationCardProperty =➥
 System.Workflow.ComponentModel.DependencyProperty.➥
Register("SignedInformationCard", typeof(XmlElement),➥
 typeof(SaveInformationCardToFile));

        [Description(➥
"This is the signed information card to be saved to a file.")]
        [Category("Miscellaneous")]
        [Browsable(true)]
        [DesignerSerializationVisibility(➥
DesignerSerializationVisibility.Visible)]
        public XmlElement SignedInformationCard
        {
            get
            {
```

```csharp
                return ((XmlElement)➡
(base.GetValue(➡
SaveInformationCardToFile.SignedInformationCardProperty)));
            }
            set
            {
                base.SetValue(➡
SaveInformationCardToFile.SignedInformationCardProperty,➡
 value);
            }
        }

        public static DependencyProperty ➡
InformationCardPathProperty =➡
 System.Workflow.ComponentModel.DependencyProperty.➡
Register("InformationCardPath", typeof(string),➡
 typeof(SaveInformationCardToFile));

        [Description(➡
"This is the path where Information Cards should be stored.")]
        [Category("Miscellaneous")]
        [Browsable(true)]
        [DesignerSerializationVisibility(➡
DesignerSerializationVisibility.Visible)]
        public string InformationCardPath
        {
            get
            {
                return ((string)➡
(base.GetValue(➡
SaveInformationCardToFile.InformationCardPathProperty)));
            }
            set
            {
                base.SetValue(SaveInformationCardToFile.➡
InformationCardPathProperty, value);
            }
        }

        public static DependencyProperty➡
 InformationCardFileNameProperty =➡
 System.Workflow.ComponentModel.DependencyProperty.➡
Register("InformationCardFileName", typeof(string),➡
 typeof(SaveInformationCardToFile));

        [Description("This is the name to be used for the CRD file.")]
        [Category("Miscellaneous")]
```

```
        [Browsable(true)]
        [DesignerSerializationVisibility(➥
DesignerSerializationVisibility.Visible)]
        public string InformationCardFileName
        {
            get
            {
                return ((string)➥
(base.GetValue(➥
SaveInformationCardToFile.InformationCardFileNameProperty)));
            }
            set
            {
                base.SetValue(➥
SaveInformationCardToFile.InformationCardFileNameProperty, ➥
value);
            }
        }


        protected override ActivityExecutionStatus ➥
Execute(ActivityExecutionContext executionContext)
        {
            if (InformationCardPath.Substring(➥
InformationCardPath.Length - 1) != "\\")
                InformationCardPath += "\\";
            string filename = InformationCardPath + InformationCardFileName;

            ManagedCardHelper helper = new ManagedCardHelper();
            helper.SaveInformationCard(SignedInformationCard, filename);

            return base.Execute(executionContext);
        }

    }
}
```

The InformationCardPath property will determine the directory in the file system where information cards should be stored.

Creating the SaveManagedCardTemplate Activity

To create the SaveManagedCardTemplate activity, follow these steps:

1. Right-click the project, and select Add New File.

2. Select Activity, and name the activity **SaveManagedCardTemplate**.

3. View the code for the activity, and populate it with the following code:

```
using System;
using System.ComponentModel;
using System.ComponentModel.Design;
using System.Collections;
using System.Drawing;
using System.Workflow.ComponentModel;
using System.Workflow.ComponentModel.Design;
using System.Workflow.ComponentModel.Compiler;
using System.Workflow.ComponentModel.Serialization;
using System.Workflow.Runtime;
using System.Workflow.Activities;
using System.Workflow.Activities.Rules;
using BeginningCardspace;

namespace InformationCardActivities
{
    public partial class SaveManagedCardTemplate: Activity
    {
        public SaveManagedCardTemplate()
        {
            InitializeComponent();
        }

        public static DependencyProperty ➥
TemplateDirectoryProperty =➥
 System.Workflow.ComponentModel.DependencyProperty.➥
Register("TemplateDirectory", typeof(string),➥
 typeof(SaveManagedCardTemplate));

        [Description("This is the directory where templates are stored")]
        [Category("Miscellaneous")]
        [Browsable(true)]
        [DesignerSerializationVisibility(➥
DesignerSerializationVisibility.Visible)]
        public string TemplateDirectory
        {
            get
            {
                return ((string)➥
(base.GetValue(➥
SaveManagedCardTemplate.TemplateDirectoryProperty)));
            }
            set
            {
                base.SetValue(➥
SaveManagedCardTemplate.TemplateDirectoryProperty, ➥
value);
```

```
        }
    }

    public static DependencyProperty ➥
TemplateNameProperty =➥
 System.Workflow.ComponentModel.DependencyProperty.➥
Register("TemplateName", typeof(string),➥
 typeof(SaveManagedCardTemplate));

    [Description("The name of the template")]
    [Category("Miscellaneous")]
    [Browsable(true)]
    [DesignerSerializationVisibility(➥
DesignerSerializationVisibility.Visible)]
    public string TemplateName
    {
        get
        {
            return ((string)➥
(base.GetValue(➥
SaveManagedCardTemplate.TemplateNameProperty)));
        }
        set
        {
            base.SetValue(➥
SaveManagedCardTemplate.TemplateNameProperty, value);
        }
    }

    public static DependencyProperty ➥
TemplateProperty = System.Workflow.ComponentModel.DependencyProperty.➥
Register("Template", typeof(InformationCardTemplate),➥
 typeof(SaveManagedCardTemplate));

    [Description("This is the Information Card Template to Save")]
    [Category("Miscellaneous")]
    [Browsable(true)]
    [DesignerSerializationVisibility(➥
DesignerSerializationVisibility.Visible)]
    public InformationCardTemplate Template
    {
        get
        {
            return ((InformationCardTemplate)➥
(base.GetValue(SaveManagedCardTemplate.TemplateProperty)));
        }
        set
```

```
            {
                base.SetValue(➡
        SaveManagedCardTemplate.TemplateProperty, value);
            }
        }

        protected override ActivityExecutionStatus ➡
        Execute(ActivityExecutionContext executionContext)
        {
            if (TemplateDirectory.Substring(➡
        TemplateDirectory.Length - 1) == "/" ||➡
         TemplateDirectory.Substring(TemplateDirectory.Length - 1)➡
         == "\\")
                TemplateDirectory += "\\";
            string fileName = TemplateDirectory + TemplateName;
            ManagedCardHelper.SaveCardTemplate(Template, fileName);


            return base.Execute(executionContext);
        }



    }
}
```

Note This activity adds a property named TemplateDirectory. This is a base folder in the file system where template files are stored.

Creating the SendEmail Activity

To create the SendEmail activity, follow these steps:

1. Right-click the project, and select Add New File.

2. Select Activity, and name the activity **SendEmail**.

3. View the code for the activity, and populate it with the following code:

```
using System;
using System.ComponentModel;
using System.ComponentModel.Design;
using System.Collections;
using System.Drawing;
using System.Workflow.ComponentModel;
using System.Workflow.ComponentModel.Design;
```

```
using System.Workflow.ComponentModel.Compiler;
using System.Workflow.ComponentModel.Serialization;
using System.Workflow.Runtime;
using System.Workflow.Activities;
using System.Workflow.Activities.Rules;
using System.Net.Mail;
using System.Net.Security;
using System.Collections.Generic;
using System.Net;

namespace InformationCardActivities
{
    public partial class SendEmail: Activity
    {
        public SendEmail()
        {
            InitializeComponent();
          Attachments = new List<Attachment>();
        }
      public static DependencyProperty SubjectProperty ➡
= System.Workflow.ComponentModel.DependencyProperty.➡
Register("Subject", typeof(string), typeof(SendEmail));

  [Description("This is the subject of the email message.")]
  [Category("Email")]
  [Browsable(true)]
  [DesignerSerializationVisibility(DesignerSerializationVisibility.Visible)]
  public string Subject
  {
      get
    {
      return ((string)(base.GetValue(SendEmail.SubjectProperty)));
    }
    set
    {
      base.SetValue(SendEmail.SubjectProperty, value);
    }
  }
}
public static DependencyProperty FromProperty = ➡
System.Workflow.ComponentModel.DependencyProperty.➡
Register("From", typeof(string), typeof(SendEmail));

  [Description("This is whom the message will be sent from.")]
  [Category("Email")]
  [Browsable(true)]
  [DesignerSerializationVisibility(DesignerSerializationVisibility.Visible)]
  public string From
```

```
    {
        get
      {
        return ((string)(base.GetValue(SendEmail.FromProperty)));
      }
      set
      {
        base.SetValue(SendEmail.FromProperty, value);
      }
    }
public static DependencyProperty ToProperty =➡
 System.Workflow.ComponentModel.DependencyProperty.➡
Register("To", typeof(string), typeof(SendEmail));

    [Description("This is who the email is being sent to.")]
    [Category("Email")]
    [Browsable(true)]
    [DesignerSerializationVisibility(DesignerSerializationVisibility.Visible)]
    public string To
    {
        get
      {
        return ((string)(base.GetValue(SendEmail.ToProperty)));
      }
      set
      {
        base.SetValue(SendEmail.ToProperty, value);
      }
    }
  public static DependencyProperty SMTPHostProperty =➡
  System.Workflow.ComponentModel.DependencyProperty.Register(➡
"SMTPHost", typeof(string), typeof(SendEmail));

    [Description("This is the SMTP Host to use to send the email.")]
    [Category("Email")]
    [Browsable(true)]
    [DesignerSerializationVisibility(DesignerSerializationVisibility.Visible)]
    public string SMTPHost
    {
        get
      {
        return ((string)(base.GetValue(SendEmail.SMTPHostProperty)));
      }
      set
      {
        base.SetValue(SendEmail.SMTPHostProperty, value);
      }
    }
```

```
public static DependencyProperty ➡
MessageBodyProperty = System.Workflow.ComponentModel.DependencyProperty.➡
Register("MessageBody", typeof(string), typeof(SendEmail));

    [Description("This is the body of the message.")]
    [Category("Email")]
    [Browsable(true)]
    [DesignerSerializationVisibility(DesignerSerializationVisibility.Visible)]
    public string MessageBody
    {
        get
      {
        return ((string)(base.GetValue(SendEmail.MessageBodyProperty)));
      }
      set
      {
        base.SetValue(SendEmail.MessageBodyProperty, value);
      }
    }

public static DependencyProperty AttachmentsProperty =➡
 System.Workflow.ComponentModel.DependencyProperty.➡
Register("Attachments", typeof(List<Attachment>),➡
 typeof(SendEmail));

    [Description("This is a list of attachments to send with the email.")]
    [Category("Email")]
    [Browsable(true)]
    [DesignerSerializationVisibility(DesignerSerializationVisibility.Visible)]
    public List<Attachment> Attachments
    {
        get
      {
        return ((List<Attachment>)➡
(base.GetValue(SendEmail.AttachmentsProperty)));
      }
      set
      {
        base.SetValue(SendEmail.AttachmentsProperty, value);
      }
    }

public static DependencyProperty EmailUsernameProperty =➡
 System.Workflow.ComponentModel.DependencyProperty.➡
Register("EmailUsername", typeof(string), ➡
typeof(SendEmail));
```

```csharp
[Description("This is the username for the SMTP host.")]
[Category("Email")]
[Browsable(true)]
[DesignerSerializationVisibility(DesignerSerializationVisibility.Visible)]
public string EmailUsername
{
    get
  {
    return ((string)(base.GetValue(SendEmail.EmailUsernameProperty)));
  }
  set
  {
    base.SetValue(SendEmail.EmailUsernameProperty, value);
  }
}

  public static DependencyProperty EmailPasswordProperty =➥
 System.Workflow.ComponentModel.DependencyProperty.➥
Register("EmailPassword", typeof(string), ➥
typeof(SendEmail));

[Description("This is the password to use with the SMTP server.")]
[Category("Email")]
[Browsable(true)]
[DesignerSerializationVisibility(DesignerSerializationVisibility.Visible)]
public string EmailPassword
{
  set
  {
    base.SetValue(SendEmail.EmailPasswordProperty, value);
  }
  get
  {
      return ((string)(base.GetValue(SendEmail.EmailPasswordProperty)));
  }


}
        protected override ActivityExecutionStatus ➥
Execute(➥
ActivityExecutionContext executionContext)
        {
            MailAddress toAddress = new MailAddress(To);
            MailAddress fromAddress = new MailAddress(From);
```

```
            MailAddressCollection addresses = new MailAddressCollection();
            addresses.Add(toAddress);

            MailMessage msg = new MailMessage(fromAddress, toAddress);

            msg.Subject = Subject;
            msg.Body = MessageBody;
            if (Attachments != null)
            {
                foreach (Attachment a in Attachments)
                {
                    msg.Attachments.Add(a);
                };

            }

            SmtpClient mail = new SmtpClient(SMTPHost);
            mail.Credentials = ➡
    new NetworkCredential(EmailUsername, EmailPassword);
            mail.Send(msg);


            return base.Execute(executionContext);
        }




    }
}
```

You've completed the last of the activities you'll need in order to automate the issuance of information cards. At this point, build the project, and after a successful build, you're ready to create your workflow.

Creating a Sequential Workflow to Issue Information Cards

This workflow, as shown in Figure 12-8, will be simple in nature; it shows you how you can automate the creation of information cards:

1. Right-click the current solution, and select Add New Project.

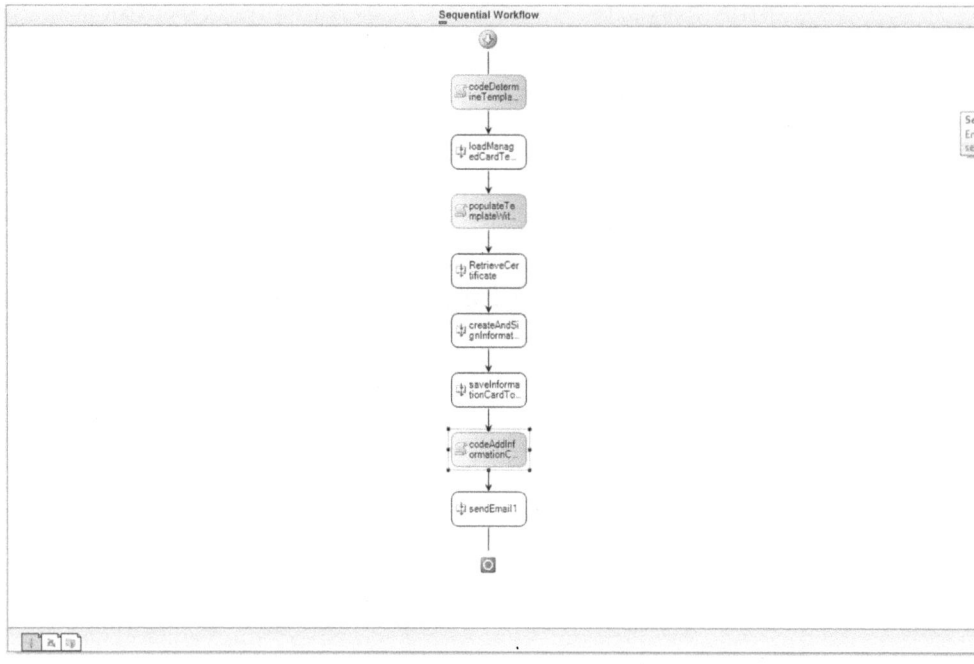

Figure 12-8. *An example workflow that will issue information cards*

2. Select a project of type Sequential Workflow Console Application, and name it
   ConsoleCardIssuanceWorkflow.

3. Right-click the project, and select Add New Item.

4. Select Class, and name it **ManagedCardCreationRequest**. This is a class that will be
   populated and then provided to the workflow for each card to be created. It contains the
   claim values for the card, as well as the email address to which the card should be sent.

5. View the code for the project, and add the following code:

```
using System;
using System.Collections.Generic;
using System.Text;
using BeginningCardspace;

namespace ConsoleCardIssuanceWorkflow
{
    public class ManagedCardCreationRequest
    {

        private Dictionary<string, string> _claimValues;
        private string _templateName;
        private string _emailDeliveryAddressForCard;
        public string TemplateName
```

```
        {
            get { return _templateName; }
            set { _templateName = value; }


        }
        public string EmailDeliveryAddressForCard
        {
            get { return _emailDeliveryAddressForCard; }
            set { _emailDeliveryAddressForCard = value; }


        }
        public Dictionary<string, string> ClaimValues
        {
            get { return _claimValues; }
            set { _claimValues = value; }


        }

        public ManagedCardCreationRequest()
        {
            _claimValues = new Dictionary<string, string>();

        }

    }
}
```

6. Right-click the project, and select Add New Item.

7. Select Sequential Workflow, and name it **CardIssuanceByEmailWorkflow**.

8. As mentioned earlier, one ManagedCardCreationRequest will be created and passed into the workflow for every card that should be created. You'll next add a list of ManagedCardCreationRequest objects to the class and add code to initialize it in the constructor. So, view the code for the workflow, and modify it to resemble the following code:

```
        private List<ManagedCardCreationRequest>
_managedCardCreationRequests;

        public List<ManagedCardCreationRequest> ManagedCardCreationRequests
        {
            get { return _managedCardCreationRequests; }
            set { _managedCardCreationRequests = value; }


        }
        public CardIssuanceByEmailWorkflow()
        {
            InitializeComponent();
```

```
            ManagedCardCreationRequests = ➧
    new List<ManagedCardCreationRequest>();
        }
```

9. Add a Code activity to the workflow.

10. Name the activity **codeDetermineTemplateName**, and specify the ExecuteCode property as populateTemplateWithClaimValues_Execute:

    ```
        private void codeDetermineTemplateName_➧
    ExecuteCode(object sender, EventArgs e)
        {
            this.loadManagedCardTemplate1.TemplateName➧
    = ManagedCardCreationRequests[0].TemplateName;
        }
    ```

11. Add a LoadManagedCardTemplate activity, and set the TemplateDirectory property to **C:\BeginningCardspace\Chapter12\Templates**.

12. Click the blue circle next to the TemplateName property, and bind the property to **ManagedCardCreationRequests[0].TemplateName**. The properties for this activity should resemble Figure 12-9.

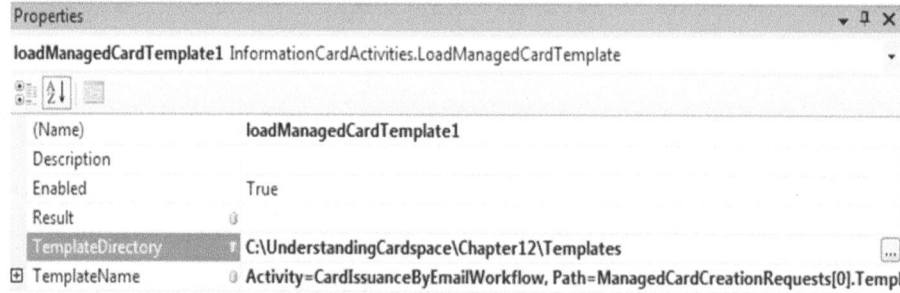

Figure 12-9. *Setting the properties on the LoadManagedCardTemplate activity*

Note In this demo, you will be creating only one card, and you will use the path from the first request. If you are using templates stored in multiple directories, you can add an Invoke event to the activity and assign it dynamically each time it is run.

---

13. Add another Code activity to the workflow.

14. Name the activity **codePopulateTemplateWithClaimValues**, and specify the ExecuteCode property as **codePopulateTemplateWithClaimValues_Execute**:

```
            private void codePopulateTemplateWithClaimValues_➡
    Execute(object sender, EventArgs e)
            {
                foreach (CardClaim cardClaim in➡
      this.loadManagedCardTemplate1.Result.➡
    InformationCardDefinition.SupportedClaimTypeList)
                {
                    cardClaim.Value = ➡
    ManagedCardCreationRequests[0].➡
    ClaimValues[cardClaim.Uri];
                }
                this.saveInformationCardToFile1.➡
    InformationCardFileName = this.loadManagedCardTemplate1.➡
    Result.InformationCardDefinition.CardName + "_" +➡
     Guid.NewGuid().ToString() + ".CRD";



            }
```

15. Add a `RetrieveX509CertificateFromStore` activity to the workflow.

16. Click the blue circle next to CertificateCommonName, and through the user interface that is displayed, navigate to the `loadManagedCardTemplate1` activity. On the Result property of the activity, navigate to SigningCertificateInfo.CommonName, and click OK.

17. Click the blue circle next to the CertificateStoreLocation, and follow the same process, this time mapping to SigningCertificateInfo.Location.

18. Click the blue circle next to the CertificateStoreName, and follow the same process, this time mapping to SigningCertificateInfo.Store. The properties for this activity should resemble Figure 12-10.

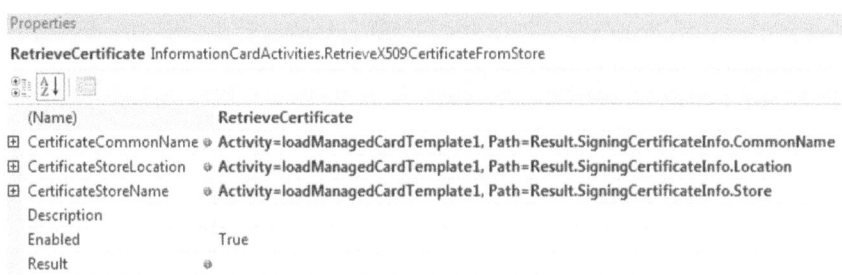

Figure 12-10. *Setting the properties on the* `RetrieveCertificate` *activity*

19. Add a `CreateAndSignInformationCard` activity to the workflow.

20. For the InformationCard property, click the blue circle next to the property name. Using the UI, navigate to loadManagedCardTemplate1.Result.InformationCardDefinition, and click OK.

21. For the Signing Certificate, click the blue circle next to the SigningCertificate property, and navigate to RetrieveCertificate.Result, as shown in Figure 12-11.

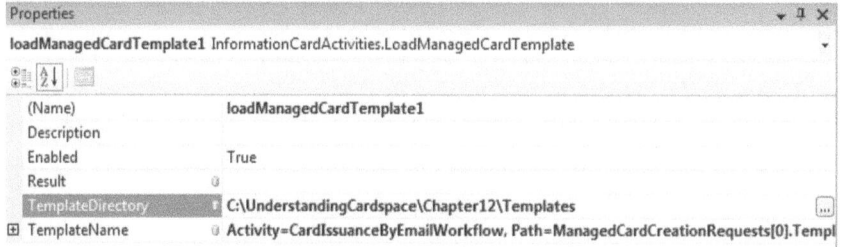

Figure 12-11. *Setting the properties on the* CreateAndSignInformationCard *activity*

22. Next, add a SaveInformationCardToFile activity to the workflow.

23. Specify InformationCardPath as **C:\BeginningCardspace\Chapter12\Templates**.

24. For SignedInformationCard, click the blue circle next to the property, and navigate to createAndSignInformationCard1.Result. Your Properties window should resemble Figure 12-12.

Figure 12-12. *Setting the properties on the* SaveInformationCardToFile *activity*

25. Add a Code activity to the workflow.

26. Name the activity **codeAddInformationCardAsAttachment**, and specify the ExecuteCode property as **codeAddInformationCardAsAttachment_Execute**:

```
        private void codeAddInformationCardAsAttachment➥
_Execute(object sender, EventArgs e)
        {
            sendEmail1.To = ➥
ManagedCardCreationRequests[0].EmailDeliveryAddressForCard;

            if (saveInformationCardToFile1.➥
InformationCardPath.Substring(saveInformationCardToFile1.➥
InformationCardPath.Length - 1) != "\\")
```

```
            saveInformationCardToFile1.InformationCardPath += "\\";
        string filename =➡
saveInformationCardToFile1.InformationCardPath +➡
saveInformationCardToFile1.InformationCardFileName;
            if (sendEmail1.Attachments == null)
                sendEmail1.Attachments = ➡
new List<System.Net.Mail.Attachment>();
            sendEmail1.Attachments.Add(➡
new System.Net.Mail.Attachment(filename));
        }
```

27. Next, add a SendEmail activity to the workflow.

28. In the Properties window, specify the information for your email server, including the email username, password, and SMTP host.

29. Next, specify the properties for the message itself, including the MessageBody and From properties.

30. Next, add a binding for the To property. Click the blue circle next to the To property, and navigate to ManagedCardCreationRequests[0].EmailDeliveryAddressForCard, as shown in Figure 12-13.

To	● Activity=CardIssuanceByEmailWorkflow, Path=ManagedCardCreationRequests[0].EmailDeliveryAddressForCard
Name	CardIssuanceByEmailWorkflow
Path	ManagedCardCreationRequests[0].EmailDeliveryAddressForCard

Figure 12-13. *Setting the activity properties*

Note When handling multiple requests, this is another instance where the property would be assigned to the current ManagedCardCreationRequest in the loop.

---

31. Next, you'll modify Program.cs, adding code to create a ManagedCardRequest that will be sent into the workflow. So, open Program.cs, and populate it with the following code:

```
#region Using directives

using System;
using System.Collections.Generic;
using System.Text;
using System.Threading;
using System.Workflow.Runtime;
using System.Workflow.Runtime.Hosting;
using BeginningCardspace;
#endregion
```

```
namespace ConsoleCardIssuanceWorkflow
{
    class Program
    {
        static void Main(string[] args)
        {
            using(WorkflowRuntime workflowRuntime = new WorkflowRuntime())
            {
                AutoResetEvent waitHandle = new AutoResetEvent(false);
                workflowRuntime.WorkflowCompleted += ➥
delegate(object sender, WorkflowCompletedEventArgs e)➥
 {waitHandle.Set();};
                workflowRuntime.WorkflowTerminated += ➥
delegate(object sender, WorkflowTerminatedEventArgs e)
                {
                    Console.WriteLine(e.Exception.Message);
                    waitHandle.Set();
                };

                ManagedCardCreationRequest request =➥
 new ManagedCardCreationRequest();
                request.EmailDeliveryAddressForCard =➥
 "mmercuri@microsoft.com";
                request.TemplateName = "ReaderCard";
                CardClaim claim = new CardClaim();


                request.ClaimValues.Add(➥
"http://schemas.xmlsoap.org/ws/2005/05/identity/claims/➥
privatepersonalidentifier",
                                        "1234567889");
                request.ClaimValues.Add(➥
"http://schemas.xmlsoap.org/ws/2005/05/identity/claims/➥
postalcode",
                                            "98011");
                request.ClaimValues.Add(➥
"http://schemas.xmlsoap.org/ws/2005/05/identity/claims/➥
gender",
                                            "Male");


                List<ManagedCardCreationRequest> requests➥
 = new List<ManagedCardCreationRequest>();
                requests.Add(request);
```

```
            Dictionary<string, object> parameters ➥
    = new Dictionary<string,object>();
            parameters.Add("ManagedCardCreationRequests", requests);


            WorkflowInstance instance =➥
  workflowRuntime.CreateWorkflow(➥
  typeof(➥
  ConsoleCardIssuanceWorkflow.CardIssuanceByEmailWorkflow)➥
  ,parameters);
            instance.Start();

            waitHandle.WaitOne();
        }
      }
    }
  }
```

Here, you've created a single request, containing three claims—PPID, postal code, and gender—and sent it into the workflow for processing. This assumes you've created a card template in the previous chapter; if you created a template with different claims, modify this code accordingly.

You're now ready to run the application. Executing the program should result in the creation of an information card and the delivery of that card to the email account that was specified.

Figure 12-14 shows an example screen from Outlook Web Access (OWA) with the received card.

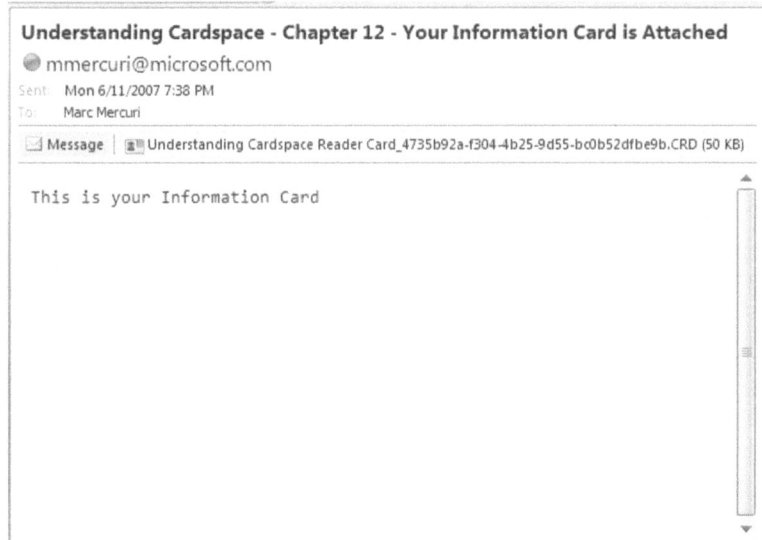

Figure 12-14. *The information card delivered via email, as shown in Microsoft Outlook*

Summary

In this chapter, you learned about workflow; Microsoft's workflow technology, Windows Workflow Foundation; and how to implement workflows that generate information cards.

Along the way, you also learned how to create a simple workflow and a simple custom activity for workflow, and then you dove in and created six custom activities specific to creating information cards.

At this point, you have all the tools to generate information cards in a scalable fashion. You can now incorporate the activities you've created into different types of workflows (that is, state machines) and incorporate more complex workflows that implement policy, that tie into your own back-end systems, and so on.

■ ■ ■

CHAPTER 13

Resources for Supporting Information Cards in PHP, Java, Ruby, and Perl-Based Relying Parties

Although the core focus of this book is on using information cards in conjunction with Microsoft technologies, this is not your only choice. Information cards have no affinity to platform or vendor, so in this chapter you'll explore the resources that are available for other development platforms. This chapter will begin with a look at how to use two of the available relying party code libraries, one Java-based and one PHP-based. This will be followed by a review of other relying parties that are available and how to find them.

It is important to note that the content for this chapter is different from the other chapters of this book. This is primarily because of the multitude of development environments and web servers for these other languages.

C# and ASP.NET have a single tool that is used by most developers, Visual Studio. They also have a single web server that is used by the vast majority of developers, IIS.

For Java, PHP, and Ruby, on the other hand, there is not a single development tool or web server. As a result, the format of this chapter will be different from what you've seen elsewhere in the book. Although other chapters have taken you step by step through configuring your server, creating projects in the IDE, and identifying menu locations and where to right-click, this chapter will focus squarely on overviews and code and not on IDE-specific steps or server configuration.

If you have not read the prior 12 chapters because of the Microsoft technology focus, the chapter will begin with a quick refresher on how the relying party requests and later processes a token.

The Sequence of an Information Card Exchange

Before getting to the code, I'll review the steps involved in the request, presentation, and acceptance of an information card at a relying party (see Figure 13-1).

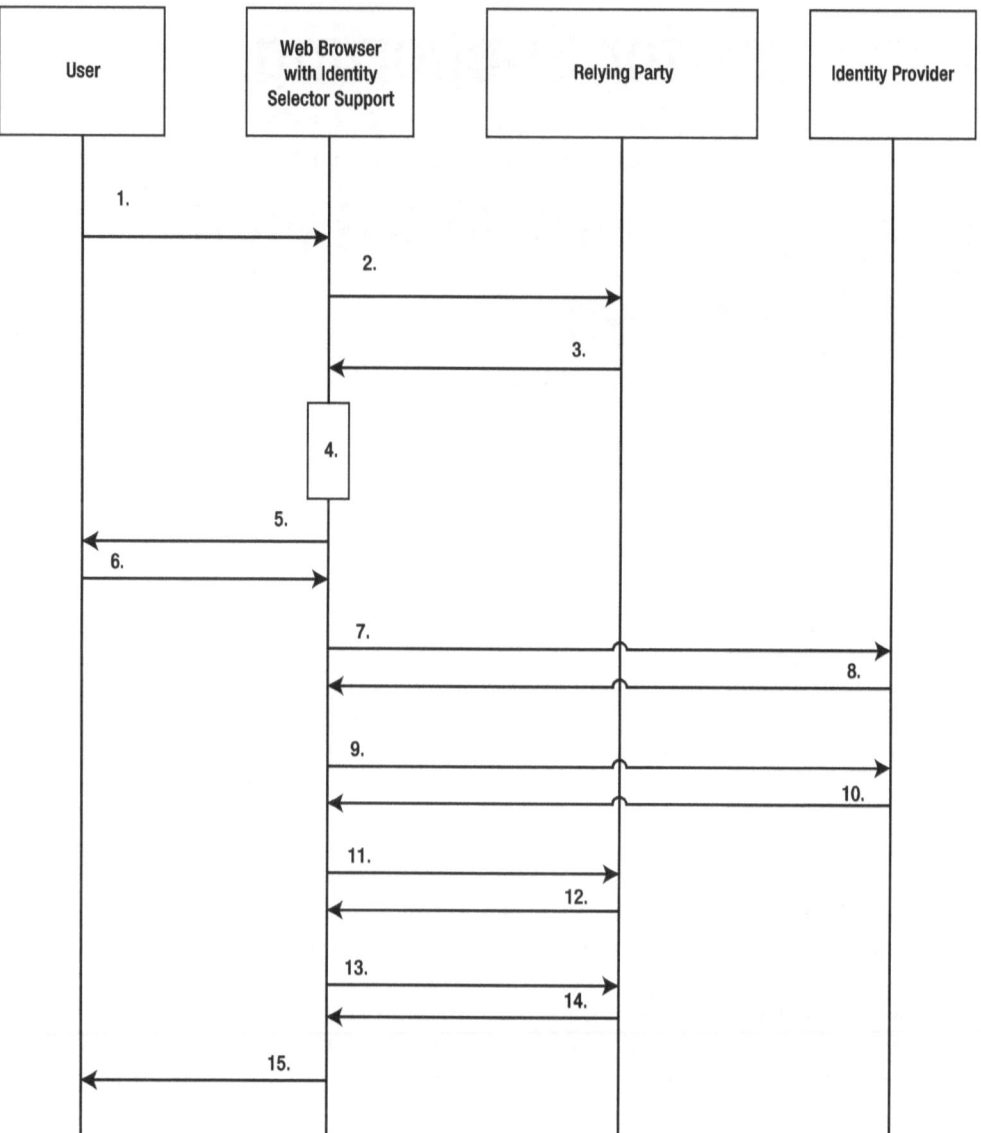

Figure 13-1. *Sequence for logging into a website with an information card*

Each of the steps in Figure 13-1 is described in the following list:

1. The user goes to the login page for a website.

2. An HTTP GET is sent to the relying party for the login page.

3. An HTML login page with the OBJECT tag is returned to the browser.

4. The user clicks a Log In with Information Card button, which triggers the identity selector to evaluate the policy of the relying party, as specified in the OBJECT tag. The selector then finds the subset of information cards that fit the policy.

5. The identity selector displays the subset of cards.

6. The user selects an information card to use.

7. The identity selector makes a request to the card issuer (identity provider) to retrieve the security policy.

8. The security policy is returned.

9. The user authenticates themselves to the identity provider and a request is sent to the identity provider for a security token, identifying the required claims.

10. The security token is returned.

11. There is an HTTPS POST of the login page (with security token) to the relying party.

12. An HTTP redirect to the home page with a cookie is returned.

13. An HTTP GET is sent to the relying party for the home page URL.

14. The HTML page is returned to the browser.

15. The user is now authenticated and able to access the website.

Creating a Login Page

The first step for the relying party is to create a login page. The purpose of this page is for the relying party to specify the claims it expects and the type of token it expects to be delivered.

The page contains an OBJECT element of type "application/x-informationCard." This element will contain PARAM subelements named tokenType, requiredClaims, and optionalClaims. Table 13-1 describes each of these elements.

Table 13-1. *PARAM Subelements Used When Requesting an Information Card*

Parameter	Definition
tokenType	Specifies the type of token being requested by the relying party
requiredClaims	Specifies the claims that are required by the relying party
optionalClaims	Specifies the optional claims that can be used by the relying party

This OBJECT tag resides within a form element. The form will populate the method attribute with the value of post and the action attribute with a pointer to the page that will process the token containing the claims.

The following is an example HTML page that specifies a SAML 1.0 token, the required claims as a private personal identifier (PPID), a given name, a surname, and an email address.

It also includes a number of additional claims (the street address, locality, state or province, postal code, country, home phone, mobile phone, other phone, date of birth, and gender) that are optional. The processing page in this case is powered by a Java servlet.

```
<html>
<head>
    <title>Sample Relying Party</title>
    <style>BODY {color:#000;font-family: verdana, ➥
arial, sans-serif;}</style>
</head>
<body>

    <h2>Log In with Information Card</h2>

    <form name='infocard' method='post' ➥
action='./infocard' enctype='application/x-www-form-urlencoded'>
        <img src="img/card_off.png"
            onMouseOver="this.src='img/card_on.png';"
            onMouseOut="this.src='img/card_off.png';"
            onClick="infocard.submit()"/>

        <OBJECT type="application/x-informationCard" name="xmlToken">
            <PARAM Name="tokenType" ➥
Value="urn:oasis:names:tc:SAML:1.0:assertion">
            <PARAM Name="requiredClaims" ➥
Value="http://schemas.xmlsoap.org/ws/2005/05/identity/claims/➥
privatepersonalidentifier ➥
http://schemas.xmlsoap.org/ws/2005/05/identity/claims/➥
givenname ➥
http://schemas.xmlsoap.org/ws/2005/05/identity/claims/surname➥
 http://schemas.xmlsoap.org/ws/2005/05/identity/claims/➥
emailaddress">
            <PARAM Name="optionalClaims"
        Value=➥
"http://schemas.xmlsoap.org/ws/2005/05/identity/claims/➥
streetaddress ➥
http://schemas.xmlsoap.org/ws/2005/05/identity/claims/➥
locality ➥
http://schemas.xmlsoap.org/ws/2005/05/identity/claims/➥
stateorprovince ➥
http://schemas.xmlsoap.org/ws/2005/05/identity/claims/➥
postalcode ➥
http://schemas.xmlsoap.org/ws/2005/05/identity/claims/➥
country ➥
http://schemas.xmlsoap.org/ws/2005/05/identity/claims/➥
homephone ➥
http://schemas.xmlsoap.org/ws/2005/05/identity/claims/➥
otherphone ➥
```

```
http://schemas.xmlsoap.org/ws/2005/05/identity/claims/➡
mobilephone ➡
http://schemas.xmlsoap.org/ws/2005/05/identity/claims/➡
dateofbirth ➡
http://schemas.xmlsoap.org/ws/2005/05/identity/claims/➡
gender">
        </OBJECT>
    </form>

    <br>Click the image above to log in with an information card.<br>
</body>
</html>
```

The following is an example of a PHP script that will generate a similar login page, placing the content in a div. Here, a PHP script named informationcard-processing.php on the server will process the token.

```
<div id="login" style="font-family: arial; font-size: 2em;">

<h2> Log In with an InfoCard</h2>

 <left>
   <form name="infocard" id="infocard" method="post" ➡
action="informationcard-processing.php">
        <img src="img/card_off.png"
           onMouseOver="this.src='img/card_on.png';"
           onMouseOut="this.src='img/card_off.png';"
           onClick="infocard.submit()"/>
        <OBJECT type="application/x-informationCard" name="xmlToken">
              <PARAM Name="tokenType" ➡
Value="urn:oasis:names:tc:SAML:1.0:assertion">
              <PARAM Name="requiredClaims" ➡
Value="http://schemas.xmlsoap.org/ws/2005/05/identity/claims/➡
privatepersonalidentifier ➡
http://schemas.xmlsoap.org/ws/2005/05/identity/claims/➡
givenname ➡
http://schemas.xmlsoap.org/ws/2005/05/identity/claims/surname➡
 http://schemas.xmlsoap.org/ws/2005/05/identity/claims/➡
emailaddress">
              <PARAM Name="optionalClaims"
       Value=➡
"http://schemas.xmlsoap.org/ws/2005/05/identity/claims/➡
streetaddress ➡
http://schemas.xmlsoap.org/ws/2005/05/identity/claims/➡
locality ➡
http://schemas.xmlsoap.org/ws/2005/05/identity/claims/➡
stateorprovince ➡
http://schemas.xmlsoap.org/ws/2005/05/identity/claims/➡
```

```
postalcode ➥
http://schemas.xmlsoap.org/ws/2005/05/identity/claims/➥
country ➥
http://schemas.xmlsoap.org/ws/2005/05/identity/claims/➥
homephone ➥
http://schemas.xmlsoap.org/ws/2005/05/identity/claims/➥
otherphone ➥
http://schemas.xmlsoap.org/ws/2005/05/identity/claims/➥
mobilephone ➥
http://schemas.xmlsoap.org/ws/2005/05/identity/claims/➥
dateofbirth ➥
http://schemas.xmlsoap.org/ws/2005/05/identity/claims/➥
gender">
            </OBJECT>
      </form>
    </left>
</div>
```

As specified in the diagram earlier in the chapter, when the user clicks the submit button, it kicks off steps 4 through 11 in Figure 13-1:

4. The user clicks a Log In with Information Card button, which triggers the identity selector to evaluate the policy of the relying party, as specified in the OBJECT tag. The selector then finds the subset of information cards that fit the policy.

5. The identity selector displays the subset of cards.

6. The user selects an information card to use.

7. The identity selector makes a request to the card issuer (identity provider) to retrieve the security policy.

8. The security policy is returned.

9. The user authenticates themselves to the identity provider and a request is sent to the identity provider for a security token, identifying the required claims.

10. The security token is returned.

11. There is an HTTPS POST of the login page (with security token) to the relying party.

In step 11, the browser does a post of the form, including the security token. At this point, the relying party server code begins its work to decrypt the token and extract the claims.

Java Relying Party Spotlight: xmldap.org's Java-Based Relying Party

Chuck Mortimore is well known in the identity community for his contributions to the identity metasystem. In addition to creating a Java-based identity selector for Firefox (covered in Chapter 2), he has also created a Java-based relying party.

During the process of writing the book, I contacted Chuck to talk about his information card–related work, and he graciously contributed a .java file with code for a sample Java servlet. The code, shown later in this chapter, leverages his xmldap.org relying party. Figure 13-2 shows a sample UI built on top of that relying party code.

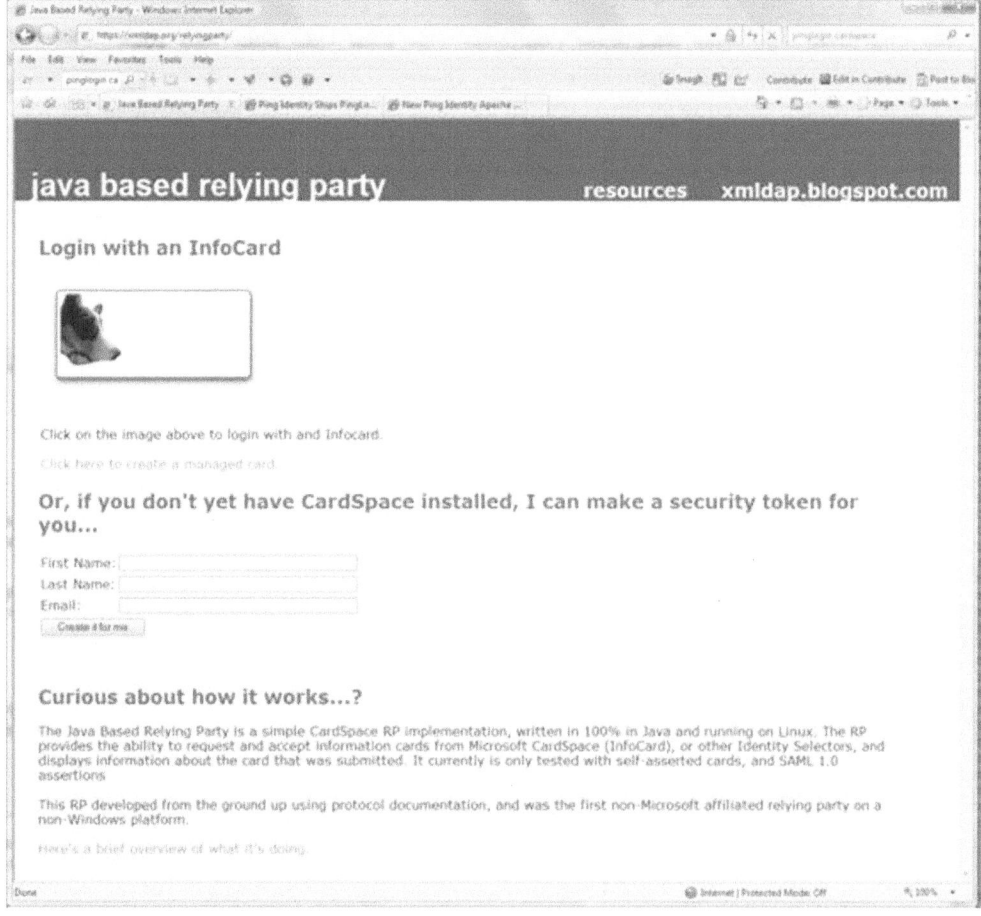

Figure 13-2. *xmldap.org's relying party site*

Getting the Bits

To begin, you'll want to download the bits for the xmldap.org relying party. The code has been posted to a project on the Google Code site. The direct link to the code for the project is http://code.google.com/p/openinfocard/source.

Note Google Code uses the Subversion version control system. If you do not have a Subversion client, you can find links to a number of clients at http://subversion.tigris.org/links.html#clients.

Creating the Java Servlet

The xmldap.org relying party provides a straightforward wrapper, making it easy to add information card support to your existing site.

The following is the code for the servlet in its entirety. The next section provides an overview of the functionality, examining specific sections of the code.

```
package org.xmldap.rp.servlet;

import org.xmldap.exceptions.InfoCardProcessingException;
import org.xmldap.exceptions.KeyStoreException;
import org.xmldap.rp.Token;
import org.xmldap.util.KeystoreUtil;

import javax.servlet.ServletConfig;
import javax.servlet.ServletException;
import javax.servlet.http.HttpServlet;
import javax.servlet.http.HttpServletRequest;
import javax.servlet.http.HttpServletResponse;
import java.io.IOException;
import java.io.PrintWriter;
import java.security.PrivateKey;
import java.util.Iterator;
import java.util.Map;
import java.util.Set;

public class SampleRelyingParty extends HttpServlet {

    private PrivateKey privateKey = null;

    public void init(ServletConfig config) ➥
throws ServletException {

        try {
```

```java
            //Get the private key used for decryption ➥
- must correspond to the server's SSL cert
            KeystoreUtil keystore = new KeystoreUtil(➥
"xmldap.jks", "storepassword");
            privateKey = keystore.getPrivateKey("certalias",➥
 "keypassword");

        } catch (KeyStoreException e) {
            throw new ServletException(➥
"Error accessing PrivateKey", e);
        }

    }


    public void doPost(HttpServletRequest request, ➥
HttpServletResponse response) throws ServletException, IOException {


        try {

            //Get the encrypted token from the request
            String encryptedXML = request.getParameter("xmlToken");
            if ((encryptedXML == null) || ➥
(encryptedXML.equals("")))➥
 throw new ServletException("No token provided");

            //Decryt the token
            Token token = new Token(encryptedXML, privateKey);

            //Check the token's validity
            if ((token.isSignatureValid()) && ➥
 (token.isConditionsValid()) && (token.isCertificateValid())) {

                //Print out the provided claims
                PrintWriter out = response.getWriter();
                Map claims = token.getClaims();
                out.println("<h2>You provided the ➥
following claims:</h2>");
                Set keys = claims.keySet();
                Iterator keyIter = keys.iterator();
                while (keyIter.hasNext()) {
                    String name = (String) keyIter.next();
                    String value = (String) claims.get(name);
                    out.println(name + ": " + value + "<br>");
                }
                out.close();
```

```
            }

        } catch (InfoCardProcessingException e) {
            throw new ServletException(e);
        }

    }


}
```

Reviewing the Servlet Code

In addition to namespaces provided with Java, the servlet references four namespaces from xmldap.org:

```
import org.xmldap.exceptions.InfoCardProcessingException;
import org.xmldap.exceptions.KeyStoreException;
import org.xmldap.rp.Token;
import org.xmldap.util.KeystoreUtil;
```

You can find details on each namespace in Table 13-2.

Table 13-2. *xmldap.org Namespaces and Their Contents*

Namespace	Contains
org.xmldap.util.KeyStoreUtil	The KeystoreUtil class that is used to create a keystore
org.xmldap.exceptions.KeyStoreException	The KeyStoreException exception that can be triggered from within KeyStoreUtil
org.xmldap.rp.Token	The Token used at the relying party to create and query a decrypted token
org.xmldap.util.exceptions.➥ InfoCardProcessingException	The InfoCardProcessingException exception that can be triggered while processing an information card at the relying party

When the token is delivered to the relying party, it will be encrypted. As you can see at the top of the class, the init method populates a new keystore using the KeystoreUtil class. The private key used for decryption is then retrieved from the keystore and assigned to the member variable privatekey.

```
public void init(ServletConfig config) throws ServletException {

    try {

        //Get the private key used for decryption - ➥
must correspond to the server's SSL cert
```

```
        KeystoreUtil keystore = new KeystoreUtil("xmldap.jks", "storepassword");
        privateKey = keystore.getPrivateKey("certalias", "keypassword");

    } catch (KeyStoreException e) {
        throw new ServletException("Error accessing PrivateKey", e);
    }

}
```

When a form is submitted to the relying party via a post, it is processed by the doPost method of the class.

The code first retrieves the xmlToken element from the incoming request and assigns it to a String named encryptedXml.

```
public void doPost(HttpServletRequest request, ➥
HttpServletResponse response) throws ServletException, IOException {


    try {

        //Get the encrypted token from the request
        String encryptedXML = request.getParameter("xmlToken");
        if ((encryptedXML == null) || ➥
(encryptedXML.equals("")))➥
 throw new ServletException("No token provided");
```

The code validates that the token was actually provided and, if it was, creates a new Token object. The Token class is part of the xmldap.org relying party, and it takes both the encrypted XML for the token and the private key as parameters in its constructor. The constructor will decrypt the token provided in the form.

```
        //Decrypt the token
        Token token = new Token(encryptedXML, privateKey);
```

With the token populated, the code then checks the validity of the token by checking three methods on the Token class: isSignatureValid, isConditionsValid, and isCertificateValid:

```
        //Check the token's validity
        if ((token.isSignatureValid()) && ➥
 (token.isConditionsValid()) && (token.isCertificateValid())) {
```

If all the methods are valid, a new Map object is created, and it is populated with the claims held within the token. Claims are retrieved by using the Token class' getClaims method:

```
            //Print out the provided claims
            PrintWriter out = response.getWriter();
            Map claims = token.getClaims();
```

The claims are then iterated through, and the claim name and claim value are written to the page that will be returned to the client:

```
                out.println("<h2>You provided the ➡
following claims:</h2>");
                Set keys = claims.keySet();
                Iterator keyIter = keys.iterator();
                while (keyIter.hasNext()) {
                    String name = (String) keyIter.next();
                    String value = (String) claims.get(name);
                    out.println(name + ": " + value + "<br>");
                }
                out.close();

            }

        } catch (InfoCardProcessingException e) {
            throw new ServletException(e);
        }

    }

}
```

PHP Relying Party Spotlight: Kim Cameron's Simple Information Card Demo for PHP

Kim Cameron is the father of the identity metasystem, and he created some PHP sample code to showcase how you can accept information cards on your PHP-based site.

Cameron states on his website, "My only goal is to share information as widely as possible" (http://www.identityblog.com/?page_id=430). This code has been embraced by those in the PHP community, and it serves as the core for the first version of the PamelaWare plug-in for WordPress, which provides information card support to that popular PHP-based blogging engine.

Getting the Bits

You can find the source code for Kim Cameron's sample on his website at the following address: http://www.identityblog.com/wp-content/resources/simple-infocard-demo/simple-infocard-demo-v3.zip.

If you have not already done so, unzip it to a directory that is accessible by your web server.

■ **Note** This sample code is written for PHP 5 and is dependent on the mcrypt and OpenSSL libraries. Please validate that these are part of your PHP installation. You can download OpenSSL from `http://www.openssl.org/`. For use with PHP 5, you will need version 0.9.6 or higher. You can download mcrypt from `http://sourceforge.net/projects/mcrypt`.

Requesting a Card

If you examine the file `infocard-demo.php`, you will see that it closely resembles the login page shown at the start of the chapter. In this sample, the relying party specifies that four claims—givenname, surname, emailaddress, and privatepersonalidentifier—are required and that a SAML 1.0 token is expected:

```
<div id="login" style="font-family: arial; font-size: 2em;">

<p>Simple Login Demo</p>

 <left>
   <form name="ctl00" id="ctl00" method="post" ➥
action="infocard-demo-processing.php">
      <img src='wp-images/card.jpg' onClick='ctl00.submit()'/>
      <OBJECT type="application/x-informationCard" name="xmlToken">
        <PARAM Name="tokenType" Value="urn:oasis:names:tc:SAML:1.0:assertion">
                 <PARAM Name="requiredClaims"
value="http://schemas.xmlsoap.org/ws/2005/05/identity/claims/givenname~CC
 http://schemas.xmlsoap.org/ws/2005/05/identity/claims/surname➥
 http://schemas.xmlsoap.org/ws/2005/05/identity/claims/emailaddress➥
 http://schemas.xmlsoap.org/ws/2005/05/identity/claims/➥
privatepersonalidentifier">
      </OBJECT>
   </form>
  </left>
</div>
```

Processing the Token at the Relying Party

The form specifies the file `infocard-demo-processing.php` for its `action` property. When the form is submitted, the form contents (which will contain the token provided by the identity provider) will be delivered to this page for processing.

If you open `infocard-demo-processing.php`, you'll see at the top of the file that `infocard-print-binary.php`, `infocard-post-decrypt.php`, and `infocard-post-get-claims.php` are all included references. It's in these files that the heavy lifting is done. Specifically, this is where the decryption of tokens and the retrieval of the claims from within that token occur.

```php
include_once("infocard-print-binary.php");
include_once("infocard-post-decrypt.php");
include_once("infocard-post-get-claims.php");
```

Three string variables are then created. `$token` contains the token received as part of the form post. `$claims` is an array that will contain the claims from the token. `$error`, as you might imagine, is used to store an error message.

```php
$claims = array();
$token = "";
$error = "";
```

The code then performs some validation logic on the incoming request. It checks first to see whether the incoming request has both an HTTP referrer and that the referrer sent the information securely via an SSL connection (HTTPS.) If either of these is not true, the code will populate `$error`.

```php
        // Checking that there is a referrer
        if (TRUE != array_key_exists('HTTP_REFERER', $_SERVER)){
            $error = "infocard-demo-processing.php cannot be accessed directly";
            break;
        }

        // Checking for people who don't know you need to use HTTPS at this point
        if (strncmp("https:", $_SERVER["HTTP_REFERER"], 5) != 0){
            $error = "infocards currently must be invoked from ➥
an https protected page";
            break;
        }
```

Next, the code validates that a token was provided as part of the request. This happens by checking for the existence of the `xmlToken`. This was the name of the `OBJECT` embedded in `infocard-demo.php`. If the token is not provided, the code populates `$error`.

■**Note** For those unfamiliar with `$_POST`, this variable is used to store the values contained within a form that is sent via a POST.

```
// Checking to see whether a token was produced
if (!array_key_exists("xmlToken", $_POST)){
    $error = "InfoCard not present";
     break;
}
```

Next, the `stripslashes` command is applied against the provided token:

```
if (!$tokenContent=stripslashes($_POST["xmlToken"]))
{
    $error = "No xml token";
     break;
}
```

The next `if` statement will decrypt the token, if not already decrypted. This happens via the `infocard_post_decrypt` function provided in the included file `infocard-post-decrypt.php`. If there is an error in decryption, the code populates $error.

```
if (array_key_exists("decrypted", $_POST) == FALSE){
    // Decrypting the token
    $error=infocard_post_decrypt($tokenContent, $token);
    if ($error != NULL)
    {
        $error = "infocard_post_decrypt returns $error";
        break;
    }
}
else{
    $token = $tokenContent;
}
```

Next, the function `infocard_post_get_claims` is called to check the signature and retrieve the claims:

```
// Checking the signature of what's inside - and getting the claims
if ($error = infocard_post_get_claims($token, $claims))
{
    break;
}
```

The claims are then iterated through and printed to the page that is returned to the browser:

```
    // Printing the claims
    print "<div style=\"font-family: arial; font-size: 1.2em;\">";
    foreach ($claims as $name => $value) {
        if ($name == "modulusHash")
            continue;
        print "claim:  $name -- $value <br>";
    }
    print "</div>";
```

You'll notice at the bottom of the file a function named get_settings. As you can see in the following code, if the key passed in is infocard_key, the function will return the private key used to decrypt the incoming token.

The private key in the code is an example. When using this with your website, this should map to the private key for the SSL certificate used to secure your site.

```
function get_settings($key)
{
    if ($key == "infocard_key") {

$retVal = "-----BEGIN RSA PRIVATE KEY-----
Proc-Type: 4,ENCRYPTED
DEK-Info: DES-EDE3-CBC,9266952B733BFBE0

Z4WmpirV4dXvYjNmfSN99Iu4iYzUWa4/CPZGONParYSVHMOhb4lsS6iISjgniGG9
zhA862KDwsYUjgoyAIXfJAd5Z3hXiyJYdkygF/DUgeQFcwQjsWmkguq27EDHW6nS
TVq7lTGsSxKPzc6HmcR5jEupq9xFLcqrSbC3Jn3lmiRlQYOw1BLcuv3o1WUoQsqb
.........................
+j4OvRpPzY6ngd1QNOfd5jkin7sjW1YlsEsRPV8OzEJvNmBZF274Cw==
-----END RSA PRIVATE KEY-----";
    }
    else if ($key == "infocard_opener"){
        $retVal = "1234567";
    }
    else {
        $retVal = NULL;
    }
    return($retVal);
}
```

Additional Relying Parties

Although I've spotlighted two relying party projects, a number of other relying parties are available, with more becoming available as time progresses.

The following sections look at some of these other relying party projects and provide details on where to find them.

Java-Based Relying Parties

In addition to the xmldap.org relying party reviewed earlier in the chapter, other implementations are available.

JInformationCard

One of the Java implementations is the JInformationCard project. You can find the main website for the project at http://informationcard.sourceforge.net. The project was developed by the Fraunhofer Institute FOKUS in Germany and is published under the BSD license.

According to that site, the purpose of the project "is to demonstrate information card interoperability on heterogeneous platforms written using Java language to support Apache Tomcat, Sun Java web servers, and WebSphere Application Server platforms running on Linux or Windows."

The project provides a sample relying party application called Bio Mini Shop, which you can find at https://zeno.fokus.fraunhofer.de/BioMiniShop/home.jsp. Figure 13-3 shows the login page for that test site.

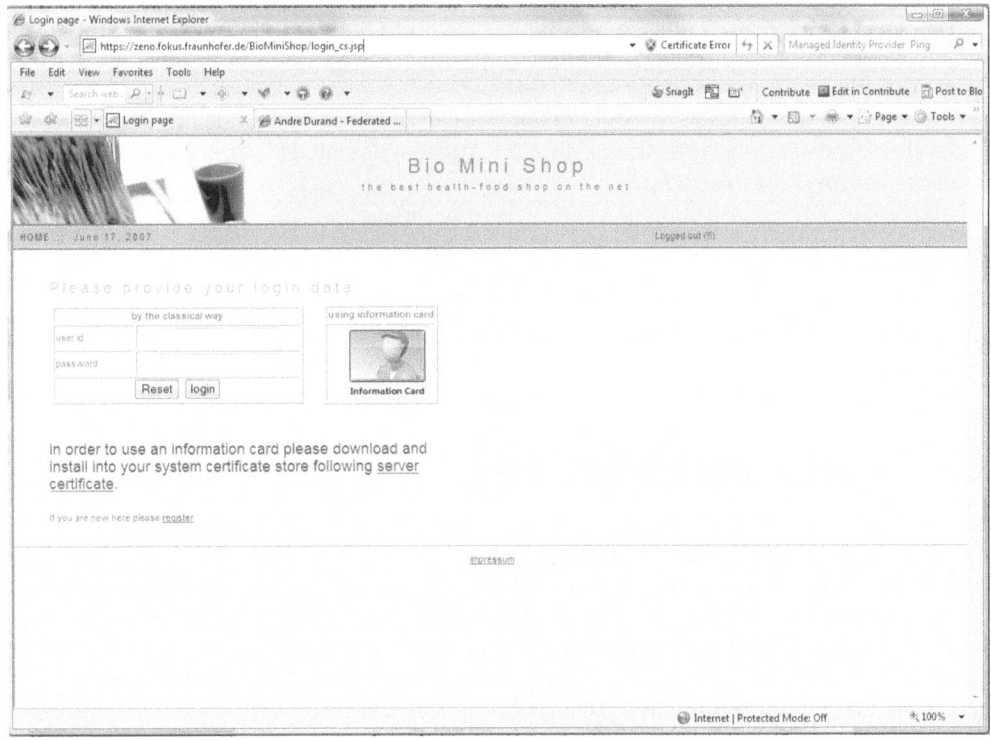

Figure 13-3. *The login page of the JInformationCard test application, Bio Mini Shop*

cardspaceauthn Project

This project provides a snap-in module for OpenSSO and Sun Access Manager for information card authentication. You can find this project on the Java website, and it is published under the Common Development and Distribution License.

The home page for this project is `https://cardspaceauthn.dev.java.net/`.

PHP-Based Relying Parties

In addition to Kim Cameron's PHP sample code, other projects exist that focus on facilitating PHP-enabled relying parties. Two projects of note include the Apache Authentication Module for CardSpace and the PamelaWare add-in for WordPress.

Apache Authentication Module for CardSpace

In 2007, PingIdentity released the Apache Authentication Module for CardSpace.

As stated on the project website, "the Apache Authentication Module for CardSpace is an open source module that allows applications using an Apache server for hosting or proxy to use information cards as an additional authentication mechanism. It allows the Apache applications to act as CardSpace relying parties (RP) by means of simple configuration. The module is responsible for decrypting the tokens submitted by CardSpace, retrieving the claims, and making them available for the application's use."

The Apache Authentication Module for CardSpace was written by PingIdentity and published under the SourceID Open Software License 2.1. You can download it from `http://www.sourceid.org/download/list`.

PamelaWare Add-In for WordPress

The PamelaWare add-in for WordPress provides information card support to the popular blogging engine WordPress. Pamela Dingle is the sponsor of the code, and it is built upon the PHP sample developed by Kim Cameron reviewed earlier in the chapter.

The home page for the project is `http://pamelaproject.com/pwwp/`.

Ruby on Rails-Based Relying Party

At the time of this writing, there is a single Ruby on Rails–based relying party, called Information Card Ruby. The home page is located at `http://www.codeplex.com/informationcardruby/`, as shown in Figure 13-4. The project is sponsored by Microsoft and ThoughtWorks and is published under the BSD license.

The project website states that the project "aims to provide a Rails plug-in and supporting library for integrating personal information cards to your Ruby on Rails relying party web application. In the identity metasystem, an application that requests and consumes digital identities about an individual is called a *relying party*. As we develop and learn from this project, Information Card Ruby will generate a developer guideline for integrating information cards to your Rails website, much in the spirit of accepting information cards to your ASP.NET site."

You can find the latest code for the project on RubyForge at the following URL: `http://rubyforge.org/projects/informationcard/`.

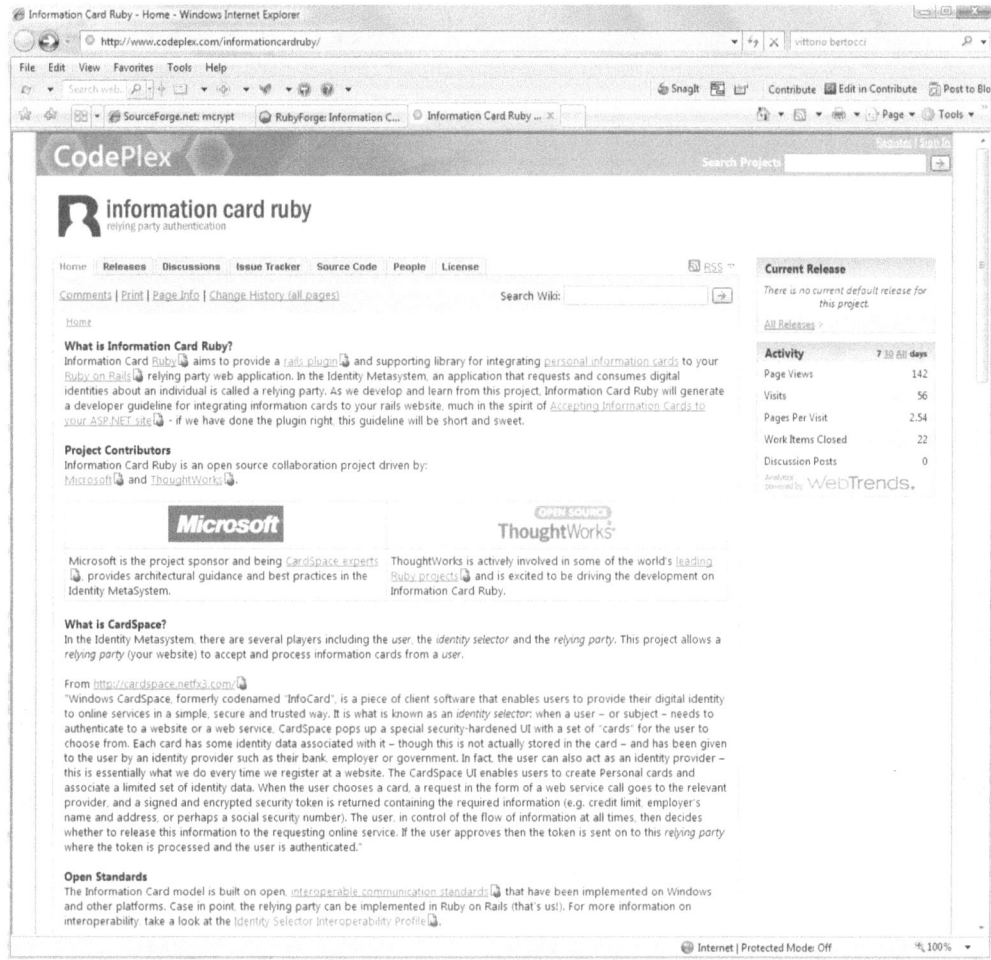

Figure 13-4. *The Information Card Ruby project home page*

Summary

This chapter introduced how to implement relying parties in languages outside of those provided as part of Visual Studio .NET. The chapter provided specific coverage of two relying parties, one Java-based and one PHP-based, as well as provided details on several others.

CHAPTER 14

■ ■ ■

Personalization

In this chapter, I'll cover the topic of personalization. I'll begin with an introduction, examine personalization and the "long tail," and review some sites that do personalization well today. I'll also discuss how the claims on an information card could allow you to do personalization beginning with a consumer's first visit and continuing throughout the life cycle.

Introduction to Personalization

In 1999 I was living in England, working on a joint venture project between my company and a British firm. I lived in the northwest of the country in a town called Chester. Chester was an old Roman town, and the town had a very welcoming, very friendly village area.

Each weekend I would walk over the bridge into the village and do my grocery shopping. Two major, modern grocery stores were near my flat (apartment). From a convenience perspective, and in most cases a cost perspective, it would have made sense to do all of my grocery shopping at those modern stores.

But for a number of my items, I shopped in the village. In fact, I looked forward to stopping in at the bakery and the butcher shop on Saturday mornings. Although the products in these shops were definitely fresher and arguably higher quality, that's not why I chose them over a grocery megastore. The reason I went was because of the experience.

The retailers knew me. They remembered what I had purchased in the past, and they would make recommendations based on what they "knew" about me from earlier purchases or from things I had told them. On more than one occasion I ended up walking out with a different set of items than I had intended on purchasing when I had walked in the door. The unplanned additions to my purchases were based solely on the retailers' recommendations.

That's not to say that the larger grocery chains couldn't provide similar types of advice, but it wasn't part of their standard workflow. Their standard workflow is a much less personal experience. And if you do have a positive experience, it's likely going to be an exception rather than the rule for your ongoing relationship with the store. Why? Well, in addition to the workflow being nonstandard, your interaction with the staff is almost surely stateless. The grocery stores have a much larger staff, and there is no guarantee that the people who have knowledge of "you" would be on shift when you were there. Their business models are likely based on volume with enticements based on lower prices. In my case, however, the butcher and the baker had higher-priced items but also a high focus on service and personalization.

I felt that the butcher and the baker knew me and that they had a good idea of what I would like. It was always nice to be pleasantly surprised by unexpected—but well-received—recommendations. For me, and for many other people, the experience and customized service are intangible qualities that lead to higher sales, higher rates of loyalty, and higher rates of referral.

I felt they knew me, but what did they really know? They knew I was American by my accent, and they knew about my buying habits, but anything else they "knew" about me was either directly from my purchases or by what I chose to tell them. So, even though they didn't know everything about me, with the information they did have, they were able to deliver a highly personalized experience, and they "knew me" in my context as a customer. This was not a significant amount of information, and it was not difficult or intrusive to collect, but when utilized, it made a fundamental difference in my store of choice. Not only did I have a good experience, but I also bought more—and close to a decade later I still remember it and am telling people about it.

Beyond retail, think about personalization in the hospitality vertical market. Wine is one of the highest-markup items sold in a restaurant. A bottle of wine that might cost $10 at a retail store can easily sell for $30 in a restaurant. When looking at items such as champagne, the markup can be even more significant.

If I was out for an anniversary dinner with my wife and I was looking at the wine list, I might select a particular bottle of wine. I might make this purchase based on any number of characteristics, but likely it's based on familiarity and/or price. If the waiter were to come to the table and ask, "Have you made a selection from our wine list?" I could tell him confidently that I wanted Brand Y of a particular vintage.

However, if the waiter or sommelier stops by to say, "Mr. Mercuri, when you were last with us, you had a bottle of Brand X. Did you enjoy that?" If the answer is no, he can ask about what I didn't like about Brand X. At that point, he can use the information I've provided him and recommend a wine he thinks I might enjoy. More often than not, the item is a higher-priced item. If the staff has a good memory and recalls the name of the rosé champagne I had on the night we were engaged, there's a strong chance I might order that as well. Again, at a higher price.

Regardless of which bottle of wine I might purchase, I would leave the restaurant with a positive feeling. They remembered me, and they made a suggestion based on what I was interested in. If the wine they recommended was particularly good, I would feel they were knowledgeable about both wine and what I like. Depending on the level of personalization in this environment, I could walk away feeling like a VIP. I'm going to remember the experience, and I'm going to be a return customer and a generator of referrals.

In the previous several paragraphs, when I said this is a personalized experience, I chose the word *experience* very specifically. In addition to providing a higher quality of service, which is valuable in its own right, the personal nature of the service generates feelings about the restaurant or shop. It is a connection on an emotional level.

Why is that important? If I get a great buy at an electronics store, I feel like I got a great price, but I do not have an experience. My relationship with that vendor is based in large part on their discount of goods. I may be a key referrer to that business, but it will be based on the lower cost of consumer items. My relationship with that vendor is then based on price. If the relationship is based solely on price, there is a clear opportunity for other businesses to steal customers away, also based on price.

Cost is almost always a factor, but when I have an experience, cost is not weighted as highly. If I have a positive, personal experience with a business, I'm likely to continue to do business with them, buy more from them, be open to recommendations, and—and this is important—tell other people about the experience. The cost of goods might actually be higher, but as a consumer I place enough value on the personal nature of the relationship that I willingly pay more.

Personalization and the Long Tail

In his book *The Long Tail: Why the Future of Business Is Selling Less of More* (Hyperion, 2006), Chris Anderson goes into great detail talking about the "long tail." In that book, he talks about how retail outlets have determined their inventories based on hits. Regardless of the types of items in a retail store—be they CDs, DVDs, books, and so on—the items take up physical space on a shelf. That shelf space is real estate, and like all real estate, it has a value. For the business to be successful, a certain number of units must be sold to justify their existence on the store shelf.

Because space in a retail store is finite, the focus is on items that sell in large volumes—the hits. If you go to a retail store, you'll see that there are sections dedicated to the hits, whether it's the Billboard Hot 100 for music, the New York Times Best Sellers list for books, or a particular store's hit list, with the focus being that what has sold is what sells the most. You'll be hard-pressed to find a large volume of niche albums in a typical music store.

Although there are a small number of hits, if you look at the sales of all of the items available for purchase, you'll see something interesting, as shown in Figure 14-1. Although the hits sell in large volume, the curve has a long tail. A large number of items, although not hits, have an audience willing to purchase them. If the obstacles of shelf space and distribution are resolved, there is an opportunity to service the long tail.

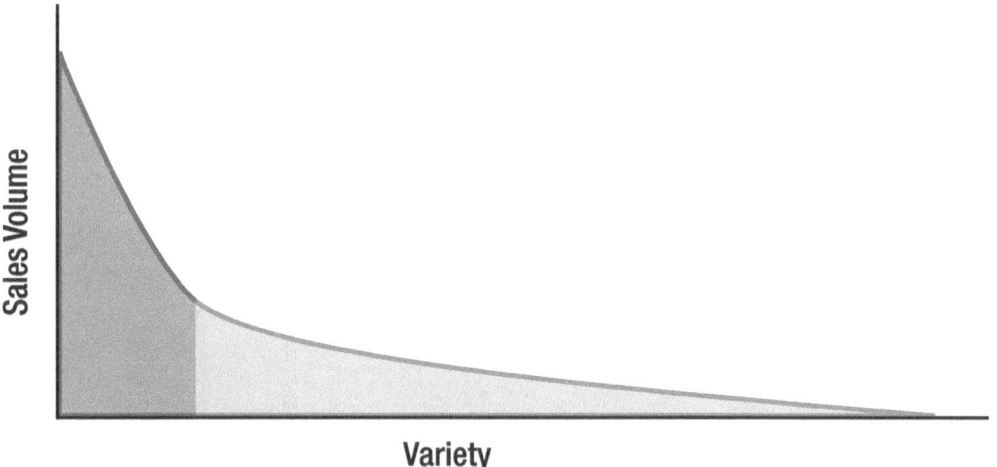

Figure 14-1. *The long tail visualized*

With the ability to have virtual storefronts that span a business's inventory as well as the inventory of their partners, combined with the very reasonable price of storage, it becomes reasonable to consider servicing the long tail online. But the key to success isn't to offer every book, CD, and/or DVD ever made but instead help highlight items in the tail that are of interest to *me*. By knowing key demographics and potentially my purchase history, a system can make recommendations on what I might be interested in. Personalization can help drive customer experiences and potentially move higher margin items, but it can also help business profitability and consistently connect customers with items in the tail.

In addition to helping the business expand into niche markets, getting more customers, and making higher sales, a personalized view of the tail can also connect customers with excess inventory.

Netflix is a business that has an extensive inventory of films. It offers rental plans where for a flat fee a customer can "check out" a certain number of DVDs at a given time. As you might imagine, that business has a large inventory of films. As you might also imagine, the demand for new releases would be, by default, much higher than the demand for films in the existing inventory.

As is documented in Anderson's book, Netflix uses a personalized approach to help manage demand. By understanding the interests of their customers, they can make quality recommendations that are not necessarily comprised of the most recently arrived inventory.

As you can see in Figure 14-2, recommendations targeted for me include the films *Double Indemnity* and *GoodFellas: Special Edition*. Because I like thrillers and Martin Scorsese films, these are both great recommendations. Now if I were left to my own devices and came across these items only as a result of wandering the virtual aisles of Netflix's online video store, I might have never been inspired to check out these titles. Without these personalized recommendations, I'd be focusing primarily on new inventory. With these quality recommendations, my rentals consist primarily of their historical catalog, and I continue to be a happy customer.

Figure 14-2. *Netflix recommendations*

Personalization with CardSpace

So, where does CardSpace fit in? CardSpace—through both self-issued and managed cards—makes it easy for individuals to communicate information about themselves to businesses and to do so in a controlled way.

This information by itself can provide a level of personalization and overall ease of navigation of a site by presenting those areas most relevant to me. If this is a retail site, it could present items and/or offers that might be relevant based on that information.

If I have a new relationship with a business, this information can be coupled with information I provide in an opt-in profile questionnaire provided by the business. Based on my selections, the business can attempt to further discern what items and services may be of interest to me and provide a more targeted, personalized experience.

If I have a purchasing history with a site, my opt-in information can be combined with my purchase history and purchase behavior, and this can drive an even deeper, more targeted level of personalization.

In the remainder of this chapter, we'll review these three different approaches and then go through the code of a simple example that shows how one could leverage CardSpace to retrieve information to drive a personalized experience.

Basic Personalization with a Self-Issued or Third-Party Card

The first scenario to examine is the one that has the broadest applicability and easiest implementation—personalization using self-issued or third-party cards. Rather than use a retail site as an example, let's instead look to one of the least personalized categories of websites—the public sector.

Government is big. In the United States, there are agencies, committees, senators, and congressman at the federal, state, and local level. A citizen may be interested in numerous pieces of legislation, regulation, services, entitlements, and forms. In general, the government is very good at posting this information. The challenge lies in the discoverability of the information. Finding the appropriate websites, tolerating multiple levels of navigation to receive a single data element, and so on, can be frustrating, and many citizens aren't fully aware of pending legislation of interest or fully taking advantage of the benefits and services.

If you go to the website for the U.S. Senate today, you are presented with an introductory screen and a drop-down list that presents all the U.S. states, as shown in Figure 14-3. Selecting the state will effectively perform a query and return the results, as shown in Figure 14-4. This is a common form of interface—go to any large multinational corporation in any vertical market, and you'll see this.

Figure 14-3. *Senate.gov website asks for U.S. state*

On the U.S. Senate site, the result is a list of senators. I then must click the link to visit that senator's own website. There, I begin my search for information again, in a different user experience.

This is done out of necessity today. Some sites will offer to "remember" you by placing the information provided in a cookie that will be used on subsequent visits. With CardSpace, this information likely already exists in the form of a self-issued card or in a managed card. By requesting claims such as city, state/province, country, and/or postal code, the site has the potential to gather multiple pieces of information from multiple data stores to provide a My Government view. In this case, this is based solely on geography, with no additional preferences.

Imagine if, by using simple geographic data, the site could tailor the information specifically for me. On my initial entry page, I could be shown who my representatives are and legislation that may be of interest because it affects my state or city. I could see which day garbage collection occurs in my area, which location I would go to in order to vote, and the status of a water ban for my postal code. This is all on the first page I reach on the site. This is a much better experience.

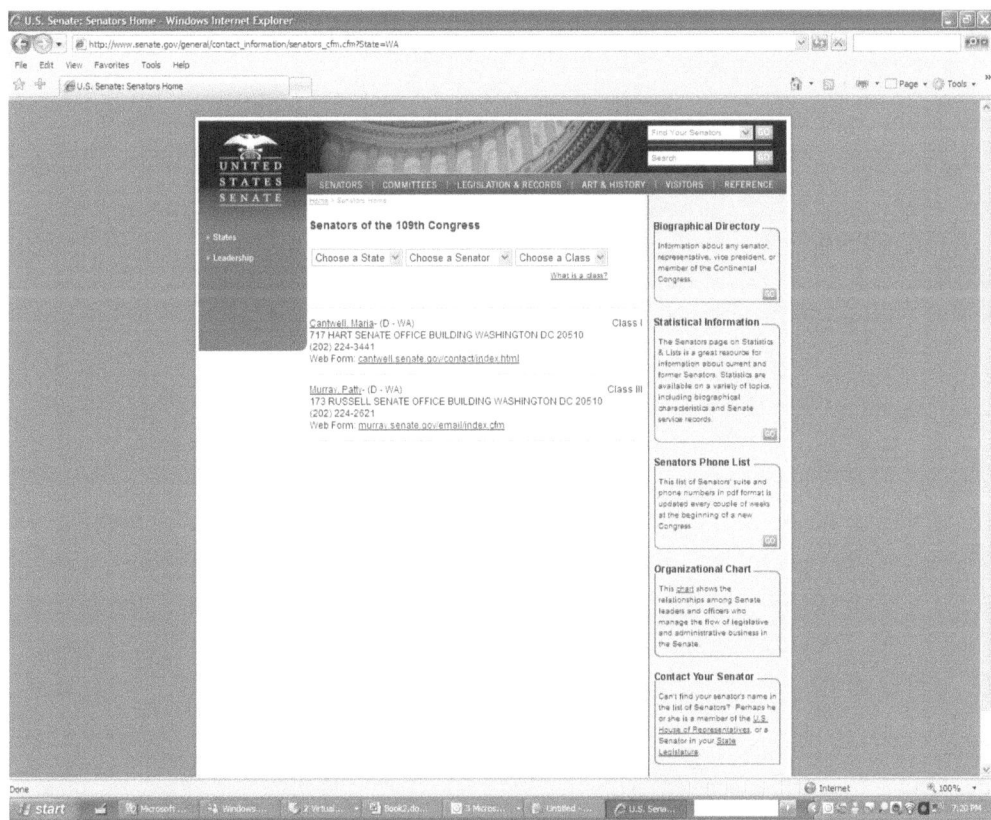

Figure14-4. *The result of picking a site*

■ **Note** Although this chapter provides a high-level introduction to personalization and how information cards can be used for personalization, the next chapter will step you through creating an actual "My Government" site.

Again, I would *feel* like they knew me, but as was the case before, they would know very little about me. They know what I chose to share, which included only city, state, and postal code. As mentioned earlier, the interface on the U.S. Senate site is extremely common. Every site from McDonald's to FedEx uses a similar interface. Nearly every retail store offers a "store finder" feature that also requests geographical information. Some sites, such as Mitsubishi, will go so far as to ask you to select your preferred language for the site, as shown in Figure 14-5.

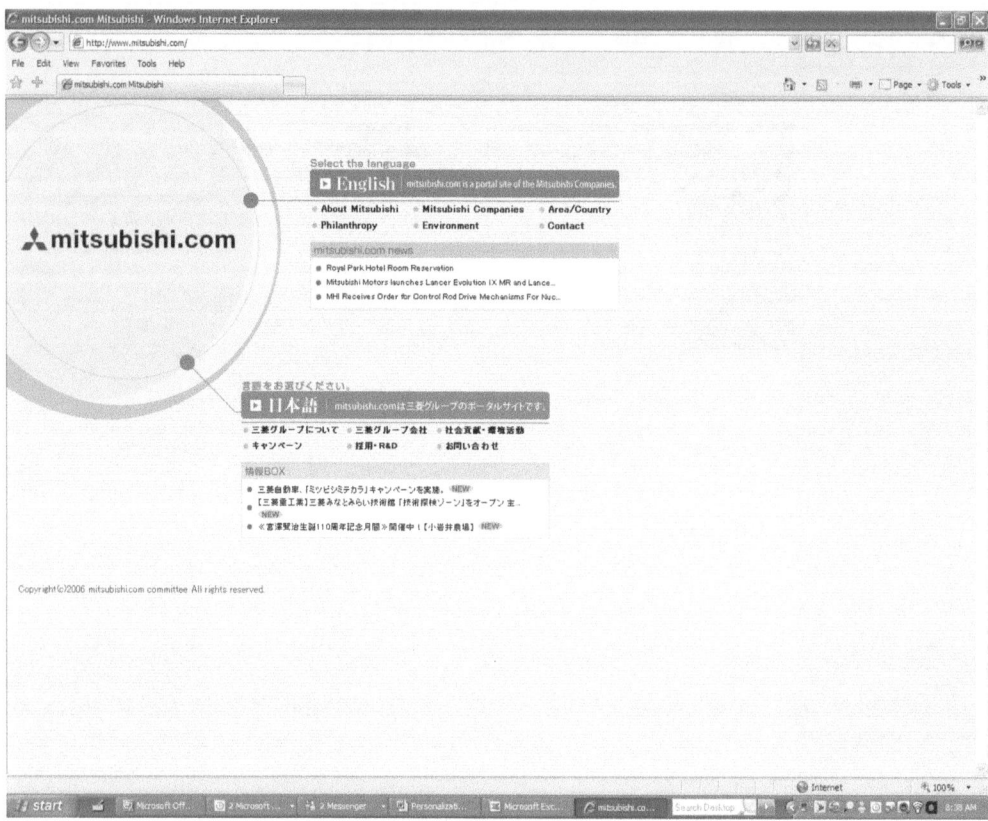

Figure 14-5. *Mitsubishi.com asks you to select a language.*

In this scenario, you could make each of the geographic requests required and add optional requests for information such as age, gender, and so on. In a public sector scenario, this could be used to richen the experience with more relevant information. For example, if I were a senior citizen, it could identify services, programs, discounts, and activities available to seniors in my area. In a retail-clothing site, it could use my gender to present the Men's section. The beauty with CardSpace is that I have control and consent to release the information I feel comfortable sharing. My level of personalization can match my interest level in sharing, which in most cases will change over time.

In providing personalization for the consumer, there are definite benefits to the business. Personalization makes the site more enjoyable for the consumer and thus brings them back to the site. In addition to personalizing the experience for the user, you can do targeted marketing for a geography. At U.S. department store Best Buy, sale items vary based on geography. At Bestbuy.com, I'm asked to provide my postal code to determine what the weekly sale items are for my area. If my geography was known, it could also be used for targeted marketing. The items on sale in my area could be shown by default. In addition, local stores could offer sales based on excess inventory to individuals in their areas—or as an incentive to individuals who may be farther away from the store.

Personalization with a Card and Purchase History

Once a user is associated with a site, personalization can be coupled with information based on purchase history, viewed items, and so on. Amazon does this particularly well.

Amazon knows which items I purchase, knows which items I view, and generates a list of items that it thinks I would be interested in. It places these items in "Marc's Store" and makes that available on the main page of the site.

Marc's Store, as shown in Figure 14-6, is a virtual store with pointers to items across a number of different categories. Although I have no insight into how Amazon specifically goes about the selection of the items in my store, I know of some straightforward approaches that can be used to help generate the personalized store.

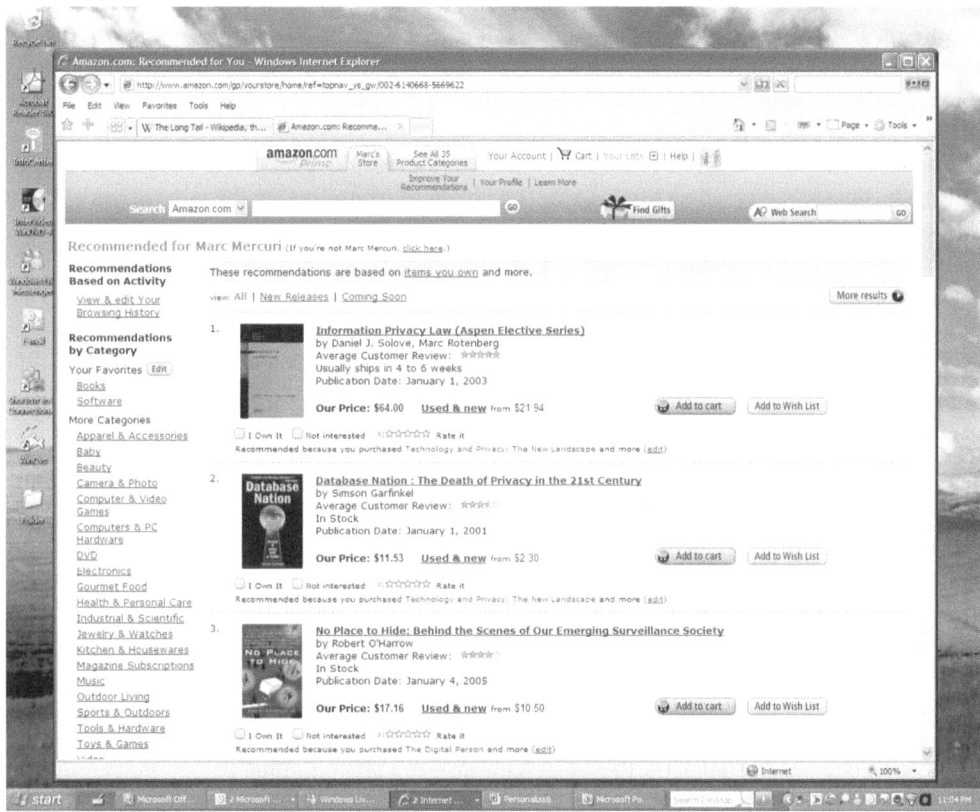

Figure 14-6. *Amazon's Marc's Store*

Each item purchased should be in a category. If the items are films, the categories could be Action/Adventure, Thriller, Comedy, and so on. Ideally, you would have a lower level of categorization. In films, this could be the subgenre, such as Romantic Comedy. Your initial subset of items for a personalized store could start by examining the categories where I made a purchase most recently, the categories where I buy most frequently, and the categories where I spend the most money.

■**Note** Although outside the scope of this book, there is a lot of research on the segmentation of customers by these criteria, and it is referred to as *recency, frequency, and monetary* (RFM).

But that alone will not provide a valuable personalized experience. If there are 50,000 films in the Comedy category, which of those 50,000 would your customer most likely buy? Here you could look at characteristics of the items I've purchased. If looking again at films, are there clusters of films that were directed by a particular director? Did they star a particular actor? Were they on a particular topic—say, World War II?

Every item has characteristics. For example, there is a band named Van Halen. That band has had several lead singers—David Lee Roth, Sammy Hagar, and Gary Cherone. If I recently bought an album from the Van Halen back catalog, who was the lead singer at that time? If it was David Lee Roth, there's a good chance I'd be interested in another album where David Lee Roth was the lead singer. If you offered me an album where Gary Cherone was the lead singer, I'd likely be less interested.

When you start looking at personalization and combine it with your existing domain expertise for your business, you can begin to identify the characteristics that are the most applicable. Whether it's news items that focus on the Iraq war, a particular politician or celebrity, or certain businesses or technologies, you can provide a customized magazine/newspaper/information agent.

This information can be further combined with demographics such as age, gender, and geography available on information cards to increase the relevance of the items placed in the personalized store.

Although some items are popular for people of all ages, a great number of products are most popular with people in particular age brackets. Identifying items in a category and with characteristics that are popular by age bracket will add value to the selections placed in your personalized store.

As with age, some product categories definitely appeal more to men than women, and vice versa. When determining your subset, consider the gender of the customer for whom the store is being personalized. By identifying items that are popular with others of the same gender, you increase the likelihood again that what is presented to the user is going to be a closer match to their interests.

Geography comes back as another key asset in personalization. In my career, I've had the good fortune and opportunity to live and work in the United States, the United Kingdom, and Puerto Rico. My various positions have taken me across a great number of U.S. states, as well as to a number of countries in Europe and Latin America. Geography becomes a key asset, because there are cultural and language differences as one moves across borders. As such, certain products don't "translate well" to other markets.

The one example that comes to mind most prominently is comedy. There are certain things that most people, regardless of geography, find funny. These are the hits. But when looking at the long tail, you must look at a number of nuances and cultural aspects. American friends who have a similar taste as mine in comedy films have watched British shows I find hilarious and "don't get" the humor. The reality is that I find these shows hilarious because I'm familiar with the culture, the language, the places, or the local celebrities involved in the program. Clustering of items by location of origin and/or locations of popularity will help deliver a better set of items to a personalized store.

Finally, look at the inclusion of allowing consumers to rate items. This provides an opportunity for personalization on several fronts. First, it allows you to identify what items the customer not only bought but also found valuable. This allows you to identify items with similar characteristics of the highly rated items. In addition, this information can be used with the ratings of other customers to identify "people like me." By looking at items popular with "people like me," you can look at the items that I haven't purchased but that others in my peer group have purchased and rated highly. Finally, it provides the ability to highlight the hits when displaying information by categories for a nonpersonalized site.

When you examine all of these factors, you have the potential to provide a very rich experience—rich in personalization for the user and rich in business opportunity for the site.

Personalization with a Card and Opt-in Profile Information

Personalization based on real purchase history is ideal, because it provides insight into the customer on an ongoing basis. There is one catch, however—it requires purchases.

How can you go deeper into personalization beyond what claims are available on a customer's information cards? You can allow the customer to tell you. You can provide a survey so customers can tell you what their interests are.

Netflix, the film rental site, does this, and the end result is very positive. Earlier in this chapter, I suggested the first step was to look at items by category. As you can see in Figure 14-7, Netflix begins its opt-in personalization with a ranking. The user is presented with a list of film categories and is asked to rate the film on a scale of 1 to 5.

This is a great approach to collecting information, because it is easy to understand and complete. The user clicks the appropriate number of stars. It's intuitive and easy to complete, and the user doesn't feel like they're answering 17 questions (which they are).

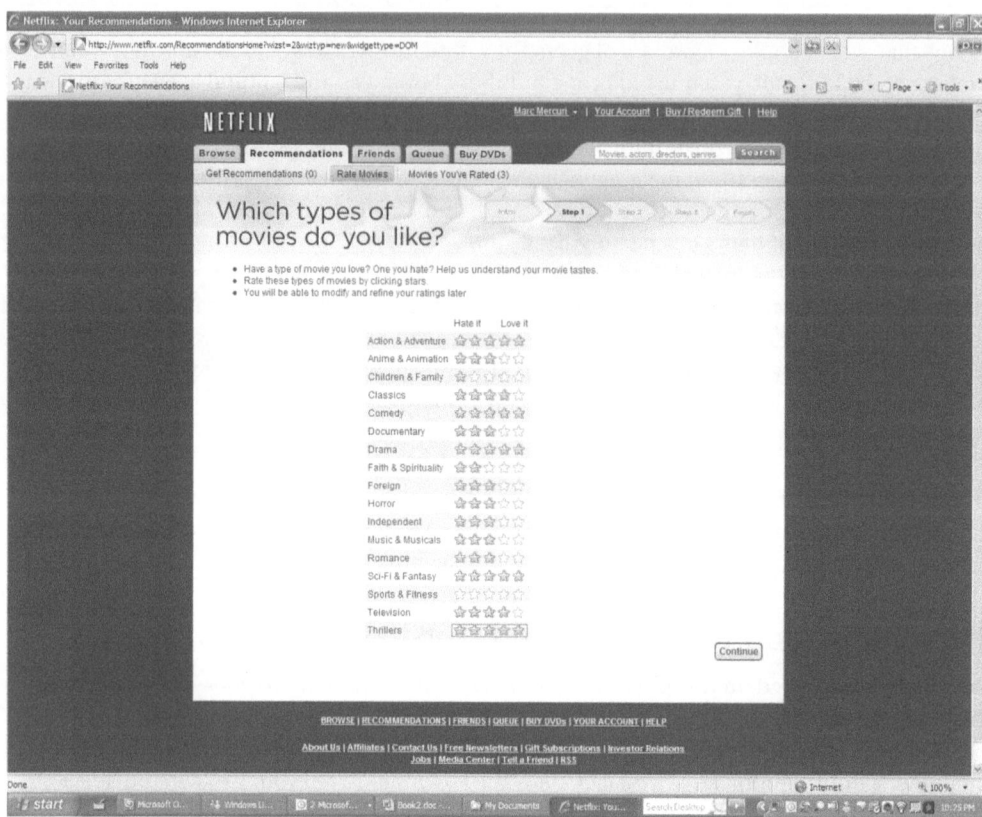

Figure 14-7. *Identifying the categories I'm interested in*

After identifying the categories that are of the most interest, a cross-section of films from the higher rated categories is presented, as shown in Figure 14-8. The user is then asked to rank those. Here you continue to simulate the data that would be gathered through actual purchases.

Note that these films are primarily hit films and major studio releases. As such, it is likely that I've seen these films. Also, a number of other people have seen these films, which can aid in further personalization.

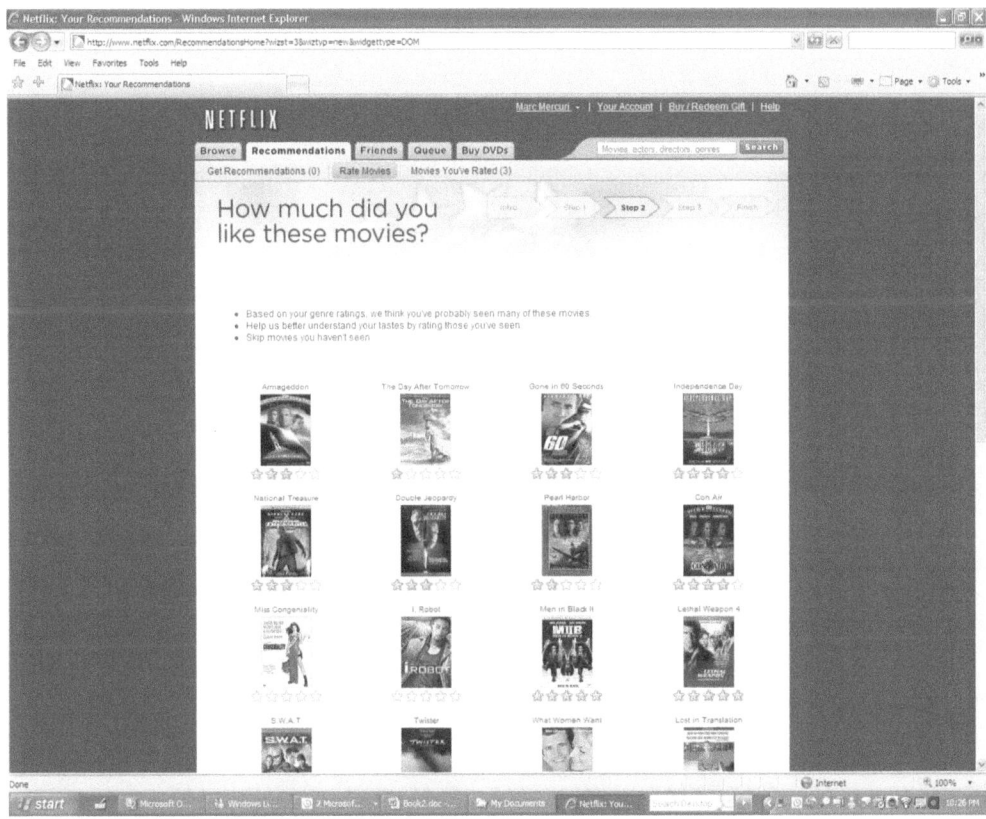

Figure 14-8. *Rating the hits*

In Figure 14-9, Netflix then returns a list of first-pass suggestions. Notice that the choices that are brought back are placed into two buckets—"We think you'll like these" and "We're not sure about these." In the "We think you'll like these" category, you have primarily hits. These are broadly received films, and based on my ratings in the prior screens, it's likely that I'll like these films.

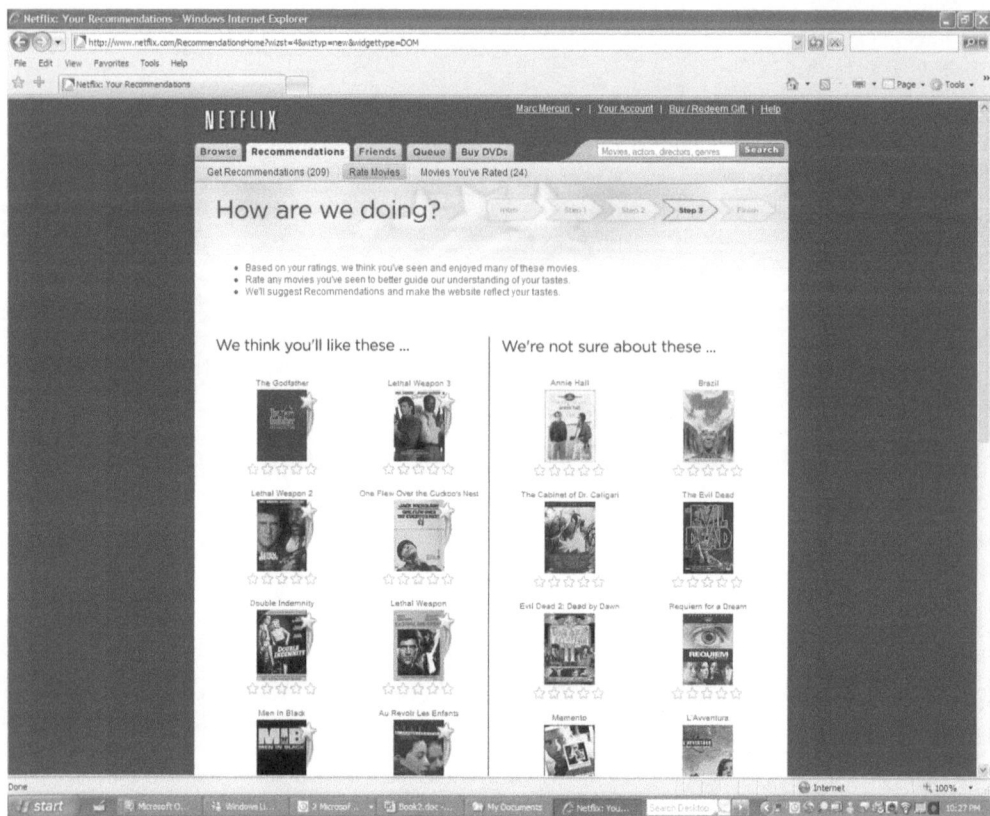

Figure 14-9. *The initial suggestions*

In the "We're note sure about these" films, note that these movies are not quite as mainstream. There's a Woody Allen comedy, a Terry Gilliam comedy, an old Vincent Price horror film, and an *Evil Dead* zombie horror film. They're showing me subgenre films with certain characteristics. Based on my choices here, the site can begin to generate a profile for me without a transaction history.

In the end, Netflix makes some recommendations, as shown in Figure 14-10. Of the films I've seen on this page, I've liked them. I'll add these movies to my rental queue.

This process collects the same information mentioned in the previous section but does it without purchase history.

You should note several points about Netflix's approach. The most striking is that this is a rating survey. This is not a list of questions, where I need to make significant decisions or invest a lot of thought. There are easily identifiable graphics, descriptions, and a universally understood mechanism for ranking with stars.

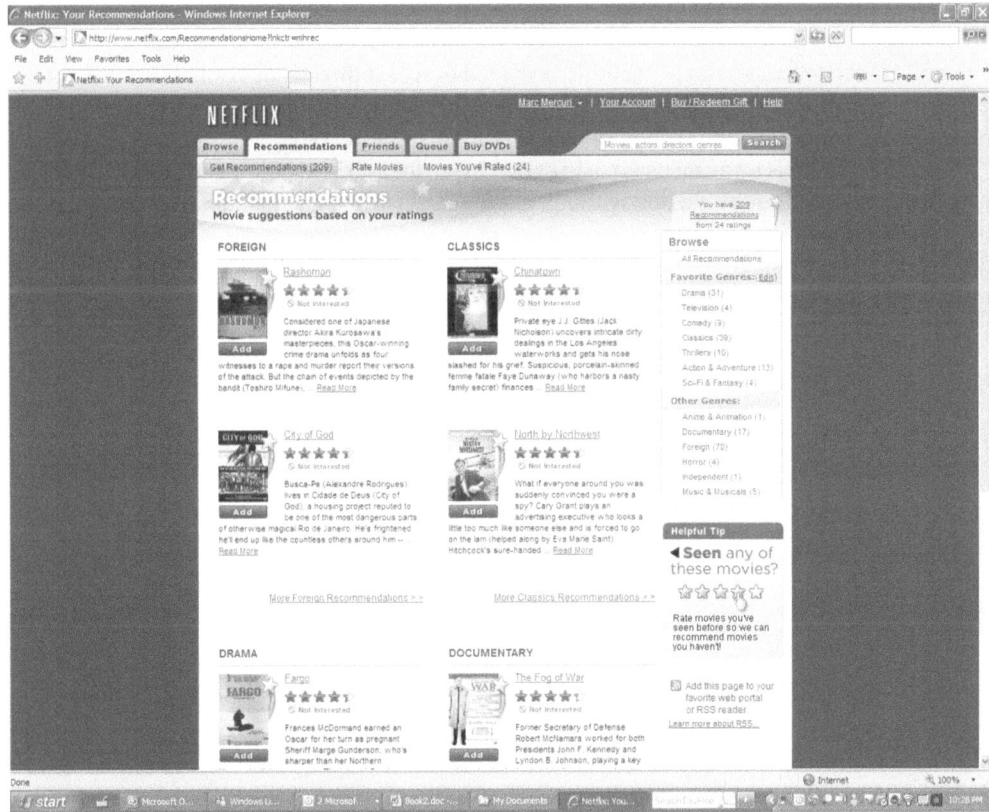

Figure 14-10. *The recommendations*

Note that *none* of the recommendations is for a new release. I am getting a personalized experience with recommendations of movies I'll likely enjoy. For someone who has seen more than his fair share of films, this is a greatly appreciated piece of personalization. For Netflix, not only does it retain a happy customer, but it also offers better inventory management with more rentals of older titles.

What I didn't mention in this chapter is that for me to get to a point on Netflix where I could provide the opt-in information, I needed to create an account. Effectively, there needed to be a customer record for me in the database, created with some base demographics and billing information. This would require me to populate a number of fields such as name, address, and so on. Although this is not a horrible burden by any means, it could be greatly simplified by simply using details from one of my information cards.

Summary

Personalization leverages data—whether provided by a user directly or via their transactions—to create a richer, more valuable user experience. This chapter focused on personalization and reviewed the concepts, approaches, and sites that personalize well.

Although there is a key focus on using CardSpace for authentication and authorization in your applications, one should not overlook its value in creating a personalized experience.

CardSpace is a mechanism through which you can allow users to easily provide information for personalization. In the next chapter, you'll see how with just one piece of information—a postal code—you can provide a rich level of personalization.

CHAPTER 15

■■■

Information Cards and Personalization

In the previous chapter, I talked about the benefits that personalization can bring to your websites and applications. I pointed out some of the companies that do personalization very well, such as Amazon and Netflix, and I pointed out a few that had room for improvement.

Most people think of e-commerce sites when they think of personalization. With e-commerce sites typically come purchase histories, where metadata about the products that the user purchased can be aggregated and mined to provide recommendations for future purchases.

But what about the first time someone comes to your site? Even if you sell items on your site, you won't have a purchase history for that user yet, so you don't have any robust data stores behind the scenes to generate targeted recommendations. Before information cards, doing personalization at many websites required an individual to enter information about themselves. Users don't necessarily want to give away a lot of information about themselves when they've first arrived at a site, so this type of personalization is limited.

With information cards, the effort to provide data is trivial and makes first-visit personalization easier to achieve. In this chapter, I will show you how with just a single data element from an information card—in conjunction with some back-end data services—you can provide a personalized experience on a user's first visit.

Earlier in the book, I pointed out some opportunities for enhancement on the U.S. Senate website. The exercises in this chapter focus on addressing the issue I presented earlier and going even further to create a personalized government page. This page will take one claim—a U.S. postal code—and interact with six back-end data services to retrieve government information at the federal, state, county, city, and ZIP code level.

These back-end services are provided free of charge by StrikeIron. StrikeIron is an online marketplace for web services, and one of its offerings includes a free set of data services. Known as the Super Data Pack, this set of services contains data for a number of different subject areas, including the government-related information that will be used in this chapter.

Registering for the StrikeIron Data Services

To begin, you will need to register for the StrikeIron Super Data Pack service:

1. Navigate to the StrikeIron products page at `http://www.strikeiron.com/tools/ tools_overview.aspx`.

2. Under the Free APIs section, select Super Data Pack.

3. Click the Get It! button.

4. Review and, if you accept the license agreement, click Subscribe.

5. If you're not already registered, register for an account and complete the Super Data Pack registration.

When you've completed the wizard, click Your Account. Your screen should look similar to the one in Figure 15-1.

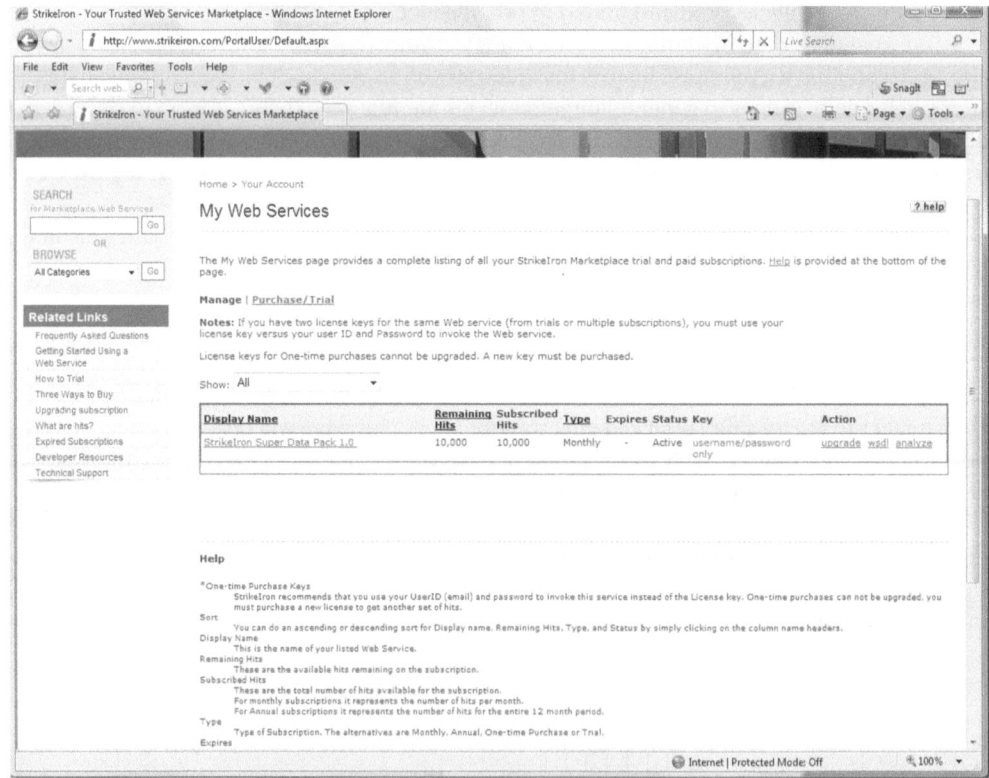

Figure 15-1. *The Your Account screen on StrikeIron*

Make a note of your username and password, because you will need them later in the chapter.

Creating the Website

Now that you're registered, it's time to use the services in a website. To create the website, follow these steps:

1. Open Visual Studio.

2. Within Visual Studio, create a new website by selecting File ➤ New ➤ Website.

3. In the New Web Site dialog box, select ASP.NET Web Site, and set the location to **C:\BeginningCardspace\Chapter15\PersonalGovernment**, as shown in Figure 15-2. Then click OK.

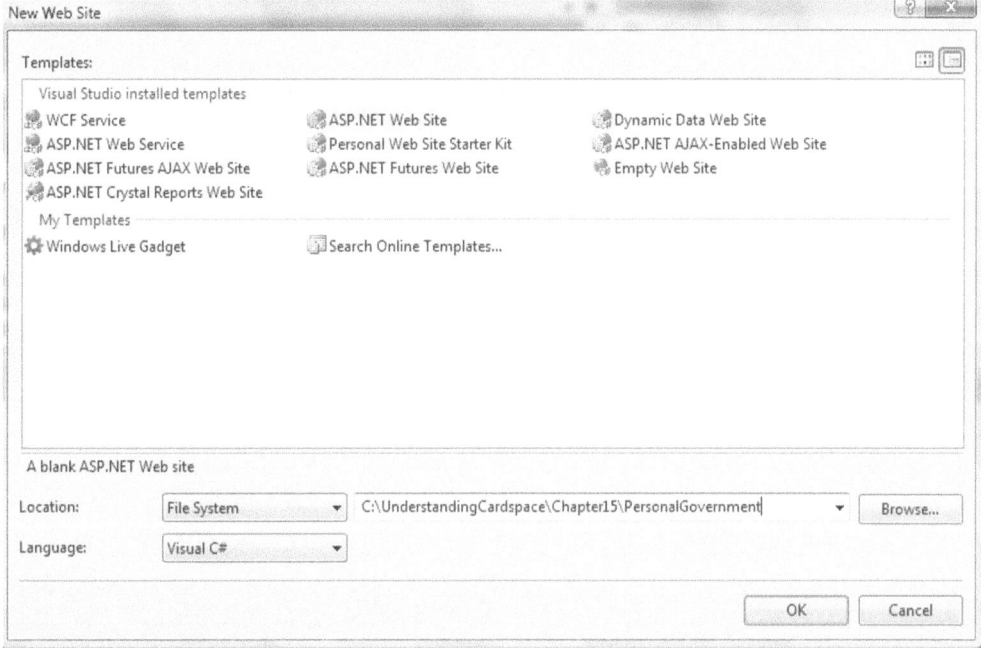

Figure 15-2. *Creating the project*

Referencing the Services in the Personal Government Website

With the base website created, you will add references to each of the StrikeIron web services that you will use to power the personal government site.

Adding a Reference to the ZipCodeInformation Service

The first service to be added will be the ZipCodeInformation service. This service will retrieve the city, state, and county for any U.S. ZIP code.

1. Right-click the project, and select Add Web Reference.

2. In the URL field, enter **http://sdpws.strikeiron.com/sdpZIPCodeInfo?WSDL**, and click
   the Go button.

3. In the Web Reference Name field, change the name to **ZipCodeInformation**, as shown
   in Figure 15-3.

4. Click Add Reference.

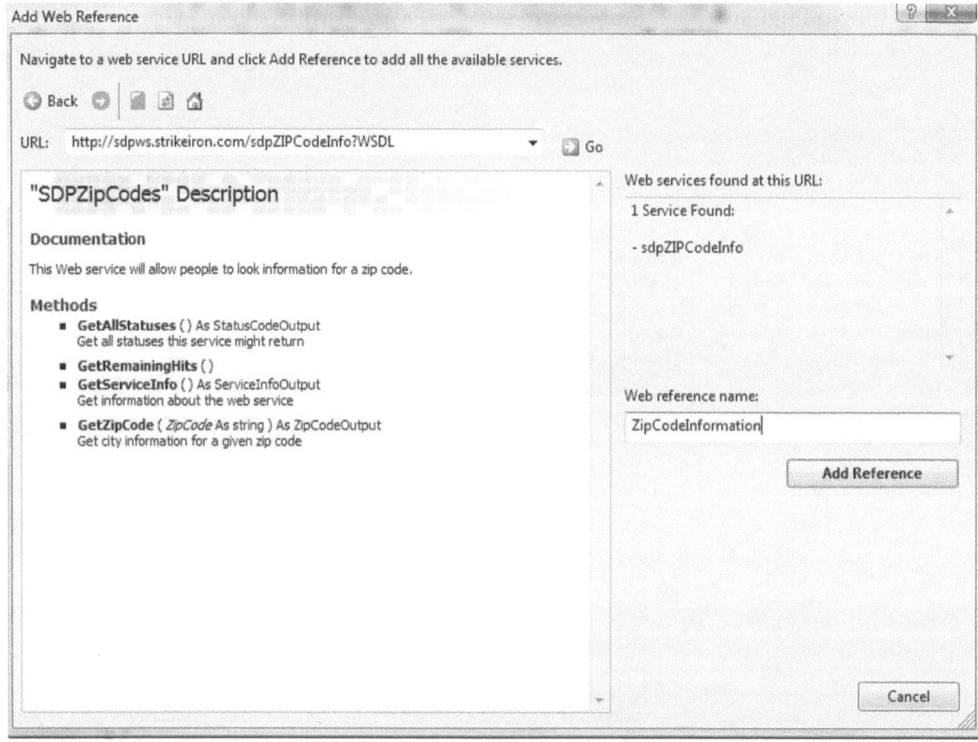

Figure 15-3. *Adding a web reference for the ZipCodeInformation service*

Adding a Reference to the StateInformation Service

Next you'll add the StateInformation service. This service will return information for a given
U.S. state, such as population, website, governor, and time zone.

1. Right-click the project, and select Add Web Reference.

2. In the URL field, enter **http://sdpws.strikeiron.com/sdpStateInformation?WSDL**, and
   click the Go button.

3. In the Web Reference Name field, change the name to **StateInformation**, as shown in
   Figure 15-4.

4. Click Add Reference.

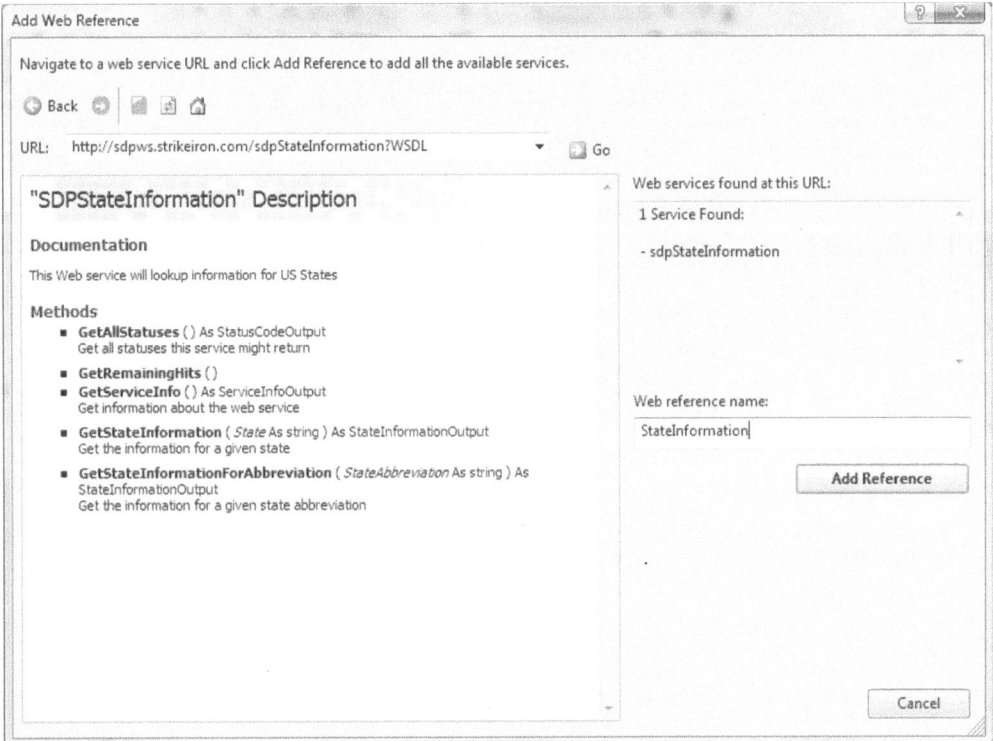

Figure 15-4. *Adding a web reference for the StateInformation service*

Adding a Reference to the SenatorInformation Service

The next service you'll add will be the SenatorInformation service. This service will return senator information for a given U.S. state, including senator name, party, and office contact information.

1. Right-click the project, and select Add Web Reference.

2. In the URL field, enter **http://sdpws.strikeiron.com/sdpUSSenators?WSDL**, and click the Go button.

3. In the Web Reference Name field, change the name to **SenatorInformation**, as shown in Figure 15-5.

4. Click Add Reference.

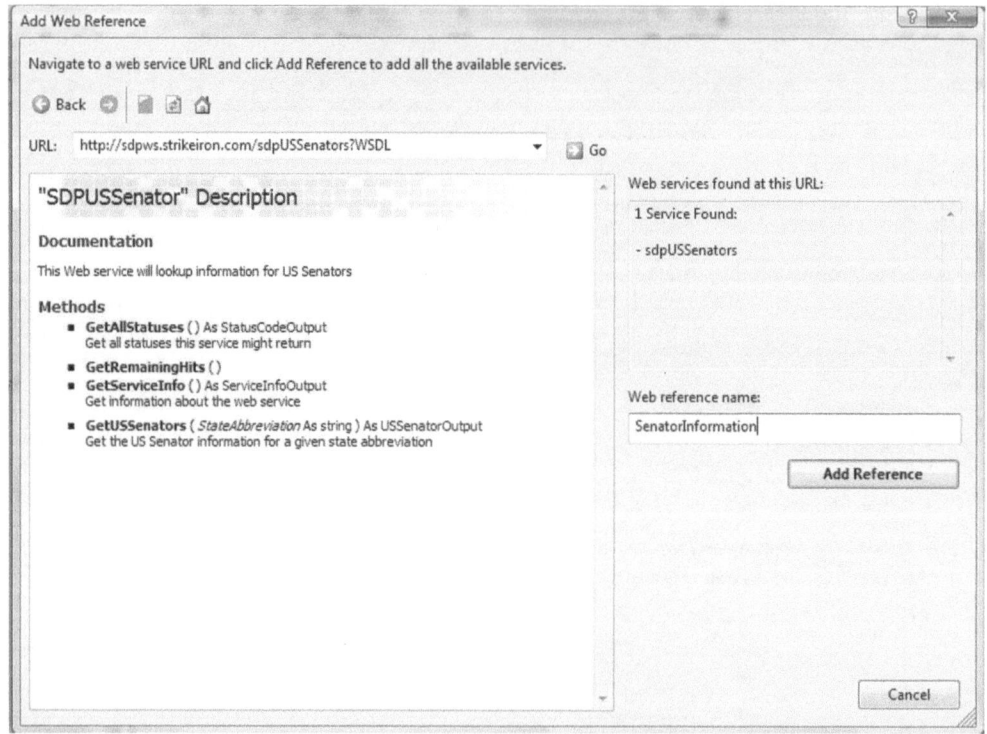

Figure 15-5. *Adding a web reference for the SenatorInformation service*

Adding a Reference to the CountyWebSites Service

The next service you'll add will be the CountyWebSites service. If a website exists for a given county, this service will return the URL for it.

1. Right-click the project, and select Add Web Reference.

2. In the URL field, enter **http://sdpws.strikeiron.com/sdpUSCountyWebsites?WSDL**, and click the Go button.

3. In the Web Reference Name field, change the name to **CountyWebsites**, as shown in Figure 15-6.

4. Click Add Reference.

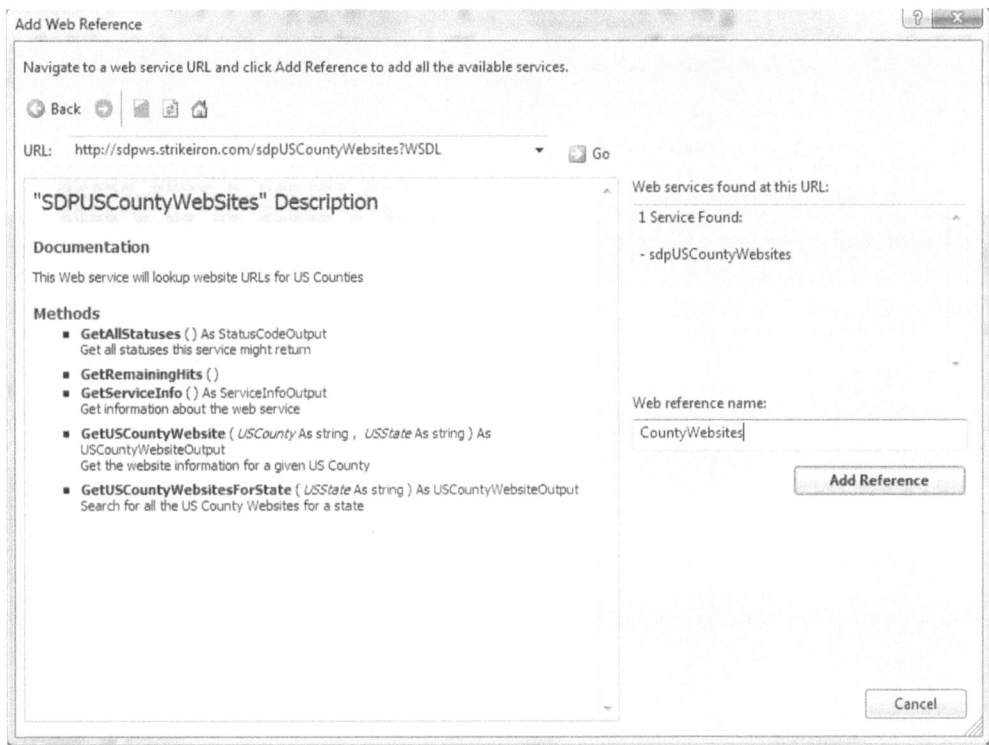

Figure 15-6. *Adding a web reference for the CountyWebSites service*

Adding a Reference to the CityWebSites Service

The next service you'll add will be the CityWebSites service. If a website exists for a given city, this service will return the URL for it.

1. Right-click the project, and select Add Web Reference.

2. In the URL field, enter **http://sdpws.strikeiron.com/sdpUSCityWebsites?WSDL**, and click the Go button.

3. In the Web Reference Name field, change the name to **CityWebSites**, as shown in Figure 15-7.

4. Click Add Reference.

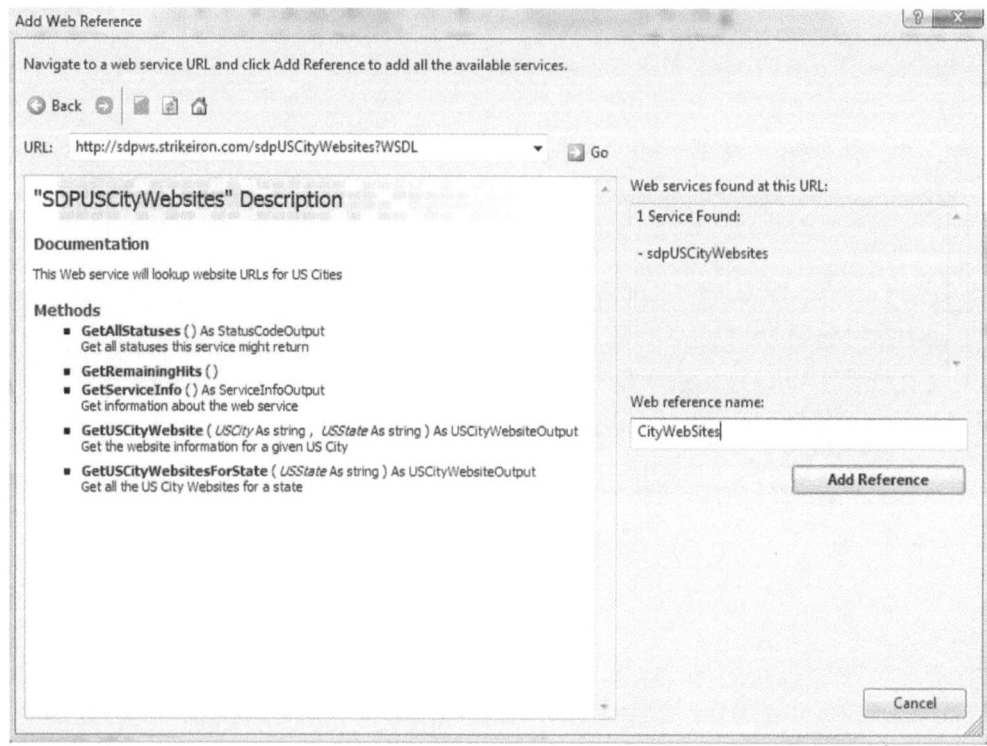

Figure 15-7. *Adding a web reference for the CityWebSites service*

Adding a Reference to the CensusInformationForZipCode Service

The next service you'll add will be the CensusInformationForZipCode service. For a given ZIP code, this service will return a wealth of data collected during the U.S. Census.

1. Right-click the project, and select Add Web Reference.

2. In the URL field, enter **http://sdpws.strikeiron.com/sdpCensus?WSDL**, and click the Go button.

3. In the Web Reference Name field, change the name to **CensusInformationForZipCode**, as shown in Figure 15-8.

4. Click Add Reference.

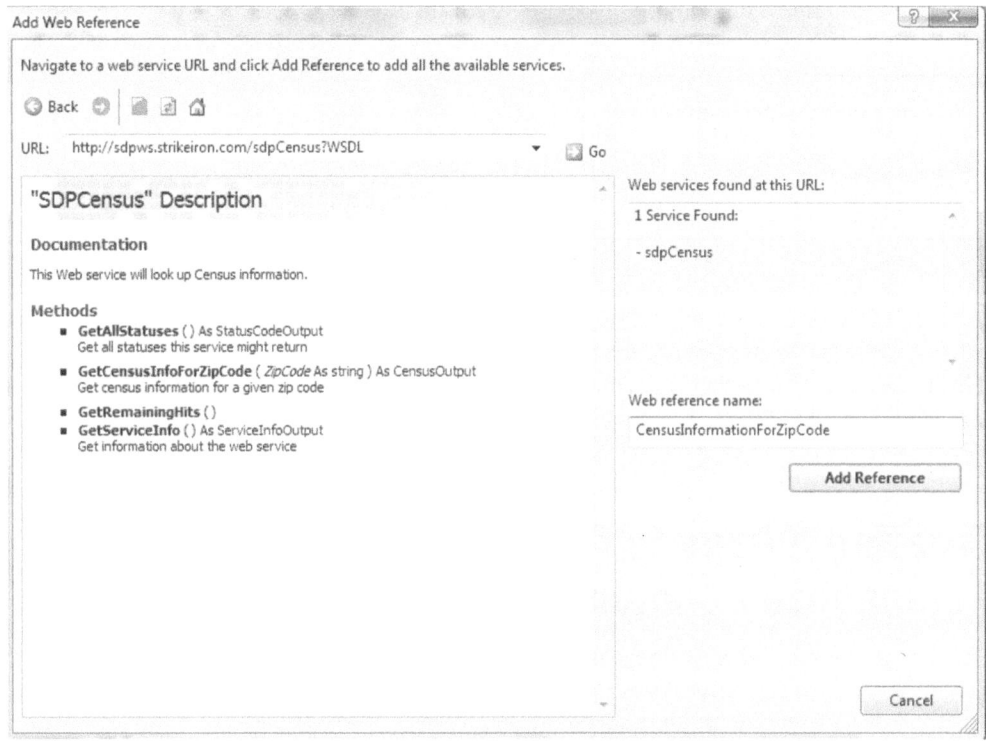

Figure 15-8. *Adding a web reference for the CensusInformationForZipCode service*

Creating a Page to Collect the ZIP Code

When you created the project, Visual Studio created a single web form, named Default.aspx. You will use this page to collect the postal code information from the citizen:

1. Click the Design button to enter the design mode for this page.

2. Add a Label control to the form, and set the Text property to **Welcome to Personal Government**.

3. Add a Label control to the form, and set the Text property to **Please enter your U.S. ZIP Code**.

4. Add a TextBox control to the form, and name it **tbZipCode**.

5. Add a Button control to the form, and name it **btnNext**.

6. Set PostBackUrl for the btnNext property to **PersonalizedHome.aspx**.

Figure 15-9 shows an example layout of the controls.

Welcome to Personal Government

Please enter your U.S. ZIP Code

[   ] [Next]

Figure 15-9. *The control layout of* Default.aspx

■**Note** Because of the number of services involved, you're first creating a test page to collect the postal code information. Once the services have been tested, you will add support for information cards.

Creating a Page to Display the Personalized Content

The page you've created will retrieve the postal code for a citizen and pass that information to a secondary page, PersonalGovernment.aspx. This secondary page will take the ZIP code and use it as a parameter into multiple back-end web services. It will display a personalized, aggregated view of data from these services.

1. Right-click the project, and select Add New Item.

2. In the Add New Item dialog box, select Web Form, and name the form **PersonalizedHome.aspx**, as shown in Figure 15-10.

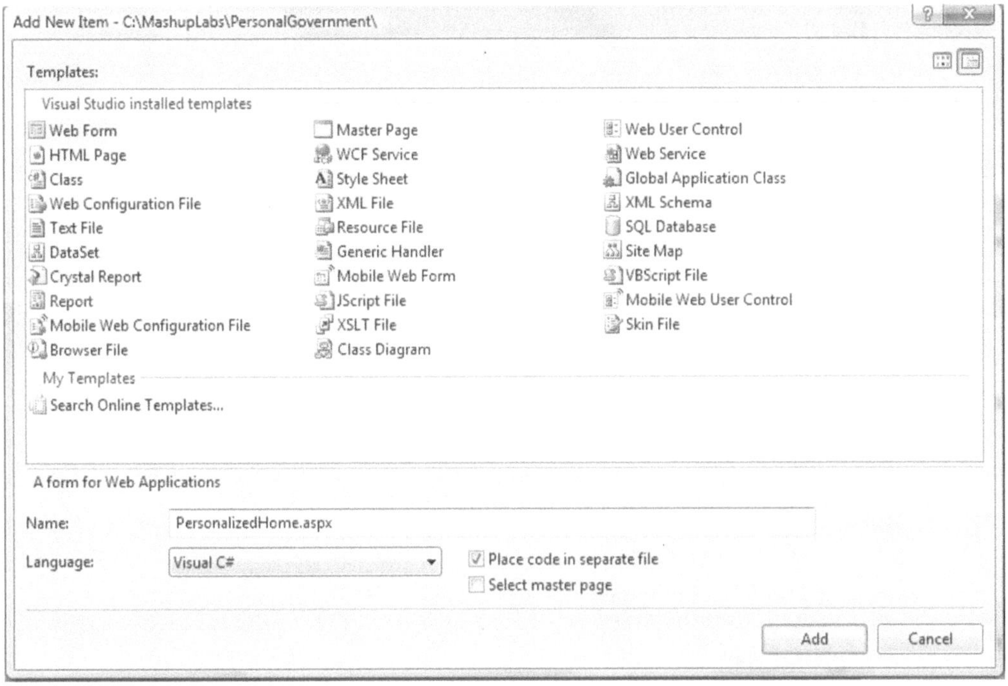

Figure 15-10. *Creating the personalized home page*

The approach that you'll take for this page is to create a number of ASP.NET panels that map to the different types of content, such as state information, US Census data, and so on. Later in this section, you will add code that will dynamically write the results of each web service call to the body of these panels.

1. View the source for the page, and modify it to match the content shown here:

```
<%@ Page Language="C#" AutoEventWireup="true"➥
 CodeFile="PersonalizedHome.aspx.cs" ➥
Inherits="PersonalizedHome" ValidateRequest="false" %>

<!DOCTYPE html PUBLIC ➥
"-//W3C//DTD XHTML 1.0 Transitional//EN"➥
 "http://www.w3.org/TR/xhtml1/DTD/xhtml1-transitional.dtd">

<html xmlns="http://www.w3.org/1999/xhtml" >
<head id="Head1" runat="server">
    <title>Home</title>
</head>
```

```
<body style="font-size: 10pt; color: black; font-family: Arial">
    <form id="form1" runat="server">
         <table style="width: 491px">
            <tr>
                <td colspan="3">
                    <asp:Panel ID="pnlHeader" ➥
runat="server" Height="50px" Width="450px">
                    </asp:Panel>
                    </td>
            </tr>
        </table>
        <asp:Panel ID="pnlStateInfo" runat="server"➥
 Height="189px" Width="490px">
        </asp:Panel>
        <hr />
        <asp:Panel ID="pnlCityInfo" runat="server"➥
Height="103px" Width="487px">
        </asp:Panel><hr />
        <asp:Panel ID="pnlSenatorInfo" runat="server"➥
 Height="196px" Width="488px">
        </asp:Panel>
        <hr />
        <asp:Panel ID="pnlCensusInformation" runat="server"➥
 Height="154px" Width="487px">
        </asp:Panel>


    </form>
</body>
</html>
```

2. Right-click PersonalizedHome.aspx, and select View Code.

3. At the top of the file, add two variables, userID and password, as shown in the following code. For each of these variables, provide the appropriate variable (user ID or password) for your StrikeIron account created earlier.

```
public partial class PersonalizedHome : System.Web.UI.Page
{

    //TODO: Add your userID and password here.

    //if you don't have a userid and password, sign up here:
    //http://www.strikeiron.com/ProductDetail.aspx?p=257
string userID = "username@hotmail.com ";
string password = "password";
```

Next, you will modify the Page_Load event.

You will make additions to the code for this event that will do the following:

- Retrieve the postal code provided from the previous page

- Use that postal code to retrieve city, county, and state information from StrikeIron

- Populate session variables with those values

- Specify render delegates for each of the panels

4. Modify the Page_Load event to resemble the following:

```
protected void Page_Load(object sender, EventArgs e)
   {
       string postalCode = Request.Params["tbZipCode"];

       if (!String.IsNullOrEmpty(postalCode))
       {
           Session["postalCode"] = postalCode;
           ZipCodeInformation.RegisteredUser ➥
zcUser = new ZipCodeInformation.RegisteredUser();
           zcUser.UserID = userID;
           zcUser.Password = password;
           ZipCodeInformation.LicenseInfo zcLicenseIfo ➥
= new ZipCodeInformation.LicenseInfo();
           zcLicenseIfo.RegisteredUser = zcUser;

           ZipCodeInformation.SDPZipCodes ➥
zipCodeService = new ZipCodeInformation.SDPZipCodes();
           zipCodeService.LicenseInfoValue = ➥
new ZipCodeInformation.LicenseInfo();
           zipCodeService.LicenseInfoValue = zcLicenseIfo;
           ZipCodeInformation.ZipCodeOutput ➥
zipCodeInfo = zipCodeService.GetZipCode(postalCode);

           // Use the ZIP code to retrieve city, state, and county.
           // These will be used with the other services.

           Session["city"] =➥
 zipCodeInfo.ServiceResult.ZipCodes[0].PreferredCityName;
           Session["state"] = zipCodeInfo.ServiceResult.ZipCodes[0].State;
           Session["county"] = zipCodeInfo.ServiceResult.ZipCodes[0].County;

           pnlStateInfo.SetRenderMethodDelegate(➥
new System.Web.UI.RenderMethod(RenderStateInfo));
           pnlCityInfo.SetRenderMethodDelegate(➥
```

```
new System.Web.UI.RenderMethod(➥
RenderCountyAndCityInfo));
            pnlCensusInformation.SetRenderMethodDelegate(➥
new System.Web.UI.RenderMethod(RenderCensusInfo));
            pnlSenatorInfo.SetRenderMethodDelegate(➥
new System.Web.UI.RenderMethod(RenderSenatorInfo));
            pnlHeader.SetRenderMethodDelegate(➥
new System.Web.UI.RenderMethod(RenderHeader));
        }
    }
```

> **Note** If you're unfamiliar with render delegates, they allow you to specify a method that will be called when rendering a particular control. In this sample, this is used to render the panels with content resulting from the web service calls.

5. Add the RenderHeader method using the following code. This is a simple example of how the render delegate is writing content to a panel in the page. As you can see, this is using an HtmlTextWriter and writing the phrase "Your Government Information" in the Heading 2 style.

```
public void RenderHeader(HtmlTextWriter writer,➥
System.Web.UI.Control control)
    {
        writer.Write("<h2>Your Government Information" + "</h2>");

    }
```

6. Add the RenderStateInfo method using the following code. This method calls the StateInformation service and then renders the results in a panel using HTML tables.

```
public void RenderStateInfo(HtmlTextWriter writer,➥
System.Web.UI.Control control)
    {

                StateInformation.SDPStateInformation ➥
stateService = new StateInformation.SDPStateInformation();
                StateInformation.StateInformationOutput stateInfo;
                StateInformation.LicenseInfo ➥
stateLicenseInfo = new StateInformation.LicenseInfo();
                StateInformation.RegisteredUser stateUser ➥
= new StateInformation.RegisteredUser();
                stateUser.UserID = userID;
                stateUser.Password = password;
                stateLicenseInfo.RegisteredUser = stateUser;
                 stateService.LicenseInfoValue = stateLicenseInfo;
```

```
            string state = (string)Session["state"];
            if (state.Length == 2)
            {
                stateInfo =➥
stateService.GetStateInformationForAbbreviation(state);
            }
            else
            {
                stateInfo = stateService.GetStateInformation(state);
            }

            writer.WriteLine("<h1><b>" +➥
 stateInfo.ServiceResult.StateInformation[0].State + ➥
"</b></h1>");
            writer.WriteLine("<a href=\"http://" +➥
 stateInfo.ServiceResult.StateInformation[0].Website +➥
 "\">http://" + ➥
stateInfo.ServiceResult.StateInformation[0].Website +➥
 "</a>");
            writer.WriteLine("<br>");
            writer.Write("<table>");
            writer.Write("<tr>");
            writer.Write("<td>Governor</td>");
            writer.Write("<td>" +➥
 stateInfo.ServiceResult.StateInformation[0].Governor +➥
 "</td>");
            writer.WriteLine("</tr>");

            writer.Write("<tr>");
            writer.Write("<td>State Capital</td>");
            writer.Write("<td>" +➥
 stateInfo.ServiceResult.StateInformation[0].Capital +➥
 "</td>");
            writer.WriteLine("</tr>");

            writer.Write("<tr>");
            writer.Write("<td>Population</td>");
            writer.Write("<td>" +➥
 stateInfo.ServiceResult.StateInformation[0].➥
Population.ToString() + "</td>");
            writer.WriteLine("</tr>");

            writer.Write("<tr>");
            writer.Write("<td>Area</td>");
            writer.Write("<td>" +➥
 stateInfo.ServiceResult.StateInformation[0].➥
```

```
Area.ToString() + "</td>");
                writer.WriteLine("</tr>");
                writer.Write("<tr>");
                writer.Write("<td>Time Zone</td>");
                writer.Write("<td>" +➥
stateInfo.ServiceResult.StateInformation[0].Timezone➥
+ "</td>");
                writer.WriteLine("</tr>");
                writer.WriteLine("</table>");



}
```

7. Add the RenderSenatorInfo method using the following code. This method calls the SenatorInformation service and then renders the results in a panel using HTML tables.

```
public void RenderSenatorInfo(HtmlTextWriter writer,➥
System.Web.UI.Control control)
   {


            SenatorInformation.SDPUSSenator senatorService =➥
new SenatorInformation.SDPUSSenator();
            SenatorInformation.RegisteredUser senatorUser = ➥
new SenatorInformation.RegisteredUser();
            senatorUser.UserID = userID;
            senatorUser.Password = password;
            SenatorInformation.LicenseInfo senatorLicenseInfo➥
= new SenatorInformation.LicenseInfo();
            senatorLicenseInfo.RegisteredUser = senatorUser;
            senatorService.LicenseInfoValue = senatorLicenseInfo;
            string stateAbbreviation = (string)Session["state"];
            SenatorInformation.USSenatorOutput senatorInfo =➥
senatorService.GetUSSenators(stateAbbreviation);
            writer.WriteLine("<table>");
            writer.WriteLine("<tr>");
            foreach(SenatorInformation.USSenatorInfo ➥
senatorDetail in senatorInfo.ServiceResult.USSenators)
            {
                writer.WriteLine("<td>");
                writer.WriteLine("<b>Senator " +➥
senatorDetail.FirstName + " " + senatorDetail.LastName +➥
"</b><br/>");
                writer.WriteLine(senatorDetail.Party+ "<br/>");
                writer.WriteLine("Term expires:" +➥
senatorDetail.TermExpires + "<br/><br/>");
```

```
                    writer.WriteLine("<table>");
                    writer.Write("<tr>");
                    writer.Write("<td>Website</td>");
                    writer.Write("<td><a href=\"http://" +➥
senatorDetail.Website + "\">http://" + senatorDetail.Website +➥
"</a></td>");
                    writer.WriteLine("</tr>");

                    writer.Write("<tr>");
                    writer.Write("<td>Address</td><td></td>");
                    writer.Write("</tr>");
                    writer.Write("<tr>");
                    writer.Write("<td><td>" + senatorDetail.Address + "<br/>");
                    writer.Write(senatorDetail.CityState + "<br/>");
                    writer.Write("</td>");
                    writer.WriteLine("</tr>");

                    writer.Write("<tr>");
                    writer.Write("<td>Phone</td>");
                    writer.Write("<td>" + senatorDetail.Phone + "</td>");
                    writer.WriteLine("</tr>");
                    writer.WriteLine("</table>");

                    writer.WriteLine("</td>");
                }
                writer.WriteLine("</tr>");
                writer.WriteLine("</table>");
        }
```

8. Add the RenderCountyAndCityInfo method using the following code. This method calls both the CountyWebSites service and the CityWebSites service and then renders the results in a panel. Because not every city and county has a website; the code also checks to see whether a website was returned. If no website was returned, the control will not be displayed.

```
    public void RenderCountyAndCityInfo(HtmlTextWriter writer,➥
    System.Web.UI.Control control)
        {

            CountyWebsites.SDPUSCountyWebSites countyService =➥
    new CountyWebsites.SDPUSCountyWebSites();
            CountyWebsites.RegisteredUser countyUser = new➥
    CountyWebsites.RegisteredUser();
            countyUser.UserID = userID;
            countyUser.Password = password;
            CountyWebsites.LicenseInfo countyLicenseInfo = ➥
```

```
new CountyWebsites.LicenseInfo();
        countyLicenseInfo.RegisteredUser = countyUser;
        string county = (string)Session["county"];
        string state = (string)Session["state"];
        countyService.LicenseInfoValue = countyLicenseInfo;

        CountyWebsites.USCountyWebsiteOutput countyInfo = ➡
countyService.GetUSCountyWebsite(county, state);
        if (countyInfo.ServiceResult.Websites.Length > 0)
        {
            writer.Write("<b>" +➡
 countyInfo.ServiceResult.Websites[0].County + ➡
" County</b></br>");
            writer.WriteLine("<a href=\"http://" +➡
 countyInfo.ServiceResult.Websites[0].Website +➡
 "\">http://" + ➡
countyInfo.ServiceResult.Websites[0].Website + "</a>");
            writer.WriteLine("<br/>");
            writer.WriteLine("<br/>");
        }
            CityWebSites.SDPUSCityWebsites cityService ➡
= new CityWebSites.SDPUSCityWebsites();
            CityWebSites.RegisteredUser cityUser = ➡
new CityWebSites.RegisteredUser();
            cityUser.UserID = userID;
            cityUser.Password = password;
            CityWebSites.LicenseInfo cityLicenseInfo ➡
= new CityWebSites.LicenseInfo();
            cityLicenseInfo.RegisteredUser = cityUser;
            cityService.LicenseInfoValue = cityLicenseInfo;

            string city = (string)Session["city"];

            CityWebSites.USCityWebsiteOutput ➡
cityInfo =  cityService.GetUSCityWebsite(city,state);

            if (cityInfo.ServiceResult.USCityWebsites.Length > 0)
            {
                writer.Write("<b>" + city + "</b></br>");
                writer.WriteLine("<a href=\"http://" +➡
 cityInfo.ServiceResult.USCityWebsites[0].Website + ➡
"\">http://" + cityInfo.ServiceResult.USCityWebsites[0].Website➡
 + "</a>");

            }


    }
```

9. Add the RenderCensusInfo method using the following code. This method calls the CensusInformationForZipCode service and then renders the results in a panel using HTML tables.

```
public void RenderCensusInfo(HtmlTextWriter writer,➡
  System.Web.UI.Control control)
    {
        string postalCode = (string)Session["postalCode"];

        CensusInformationForZipCode.SDPCensus censusService = new➡
  CensusInformationForZipCode.SDPCensus();
        CensusInformationForZipCode.RegisteredUser censusUser = ➡
new CensusInformationForZipCode.RegisteredUser();
        censusUser.UserID = userID;
        censusUser.Password = password;
        CensusInformationForZipCode.LicenseInfo ➡
censusLicenseInfo = ➡
new CensusInformationForZipCode.LicenseInfo();
        censusLicenseInfo.RegisteredUser = censusUser;
        censusService.LicenseInfoValue = censusLicenseInfo;
        CensusInformationForZipCode.CensusOutput ➡
censusInfo = ➡
censusService.GetCensusInfoForZipCode(postalCode);
        if (censusInfo.ServiceResult.CensusInfo.Length > 0)
        {
            writer.WriteLine(➡
"<h4>US Census Information for Zip Code " +➡
  (string)Session["PostalCode"] + "</h4>");
            writer.WriteLine("<table>");
            writer.Write("<tr>");
            writer.Write("<td>Total Population</td>");
            writer.Write("<td>" +➡
  censusInfo.ServiceResult.CensusInfo[0].Total_pop.ToString() +➡
  "</td>");
            writer.Write("</tr>");

            writer.Write("<tr>");
            writer.Write("<td>Median Age</td>");
            writer.Write("<td>" +➡
  censusInfo.ServiceResult.CensusInfo[0].Median_age.ToString()➡
+ "</td>");
            writer.Write("</tr>");

            writer.Write("<tr>");
            writer.Write("<td>Gender Composition</td>");
            writer.Write("<td >");
            writer.WriteLine("<table><tr>");
            writer.WriteLine("<td> Male:" +➡
```

```
              censusInfo.ServiceResult.CensusInfo[0].Male_pop + ➡
        "<td>");
                    writer.WriteLine("<td> Female:" +➡
          censusInfo.ServiceResult.CensusInfo[0].Female_pop + "<td>");
                    writer.WriteLine("</tr></table>");
                    writer.Write("</td>");
                    writer.Write("</tr>");

                    writer.Write("<tr>");
                    writer.Write("<td>Total Housing Units</td>");
                    writer.Write("<td>" +➡
          censusInfo.ServiceResult.CensusInfo[0].➡
        Total_housing_units.ToString() + "</td>");
                    writer.Write("</tr>");

                    writer.Write("<tr>");
                    writer.Write("<td>Owner/Renter Composition</td>");
                    writer.Write("<td >");
                    writer.WriteLine("<table><tr>");
                    writer.WriteLine("<td> Owner:" +➡
          censusInfo.ServiceResult.CensusInfo[0].➡
        Owner_occupied_housing_units + "<td>");
                    writer.WriteLine("<td> Renter:" +➡
          censusInfo.ServiceResult.CensusInfo[0].➡
        Renter_occupied_housing_units + "<td>");
                    writer.WriteLine("</tr></table>");
                    writer.Write("</td>");
                    writer.Write("</tr>");

                    writer.Write("<tr>");
                    writer.Write("<td>Rental vacancy percent</td>");
                    writer.Write("<td>" +➡
        censusInfo.ServiceResult.CensusInfo[0].➡
        Rental_vacancy_rate_percent.ToString() + "</td>");
                    writer.Write("</tr>");
```

```
            writer.Write("<tr>");
            writer.Write("<td>Number of households</td>");
            writer.Write("<td>" +➥
  censusInfo.ServiceResult.CensusInfo[0].➥
Householder_pop.ToString() + "</td>");
            writer.Write("</tr>");

            writer.Write("<tr>");
            writer.Write("<td>Average household size</td>");
            writer.Write("<td>" +➥
  censusInfo.ServiceResult.CensusInfo[0].➥
Avg_household_size.ToString() + "</td>");
            writer.Write("</tr>");

            writer.Write("<tr>");
            writer.Write("<td>Number of family households</td>");
            writer.Write("<td>" +➥
  censusInfo.ServiceResult.CensusInfo[0].Family_households.ToString()➥
+ "</td>");
            writer.Write("</tr>");

            writer.Write("<tr>");
            writer.Write("<td>Average family size</td>");
            writer.Write("<td>" +➥
  censusInfo.ServiceResult.CensusInfo[0].➥
Avg_family_size.ToString() + "</td>");
            writer.Write("</tr>");



            writer.Write("</table>");
        }

    }
```

Testing the Solution

You are now ready to test the solution:

1. Press F5 to start the website. You will be presented with the screen shown in Figure 15-11.

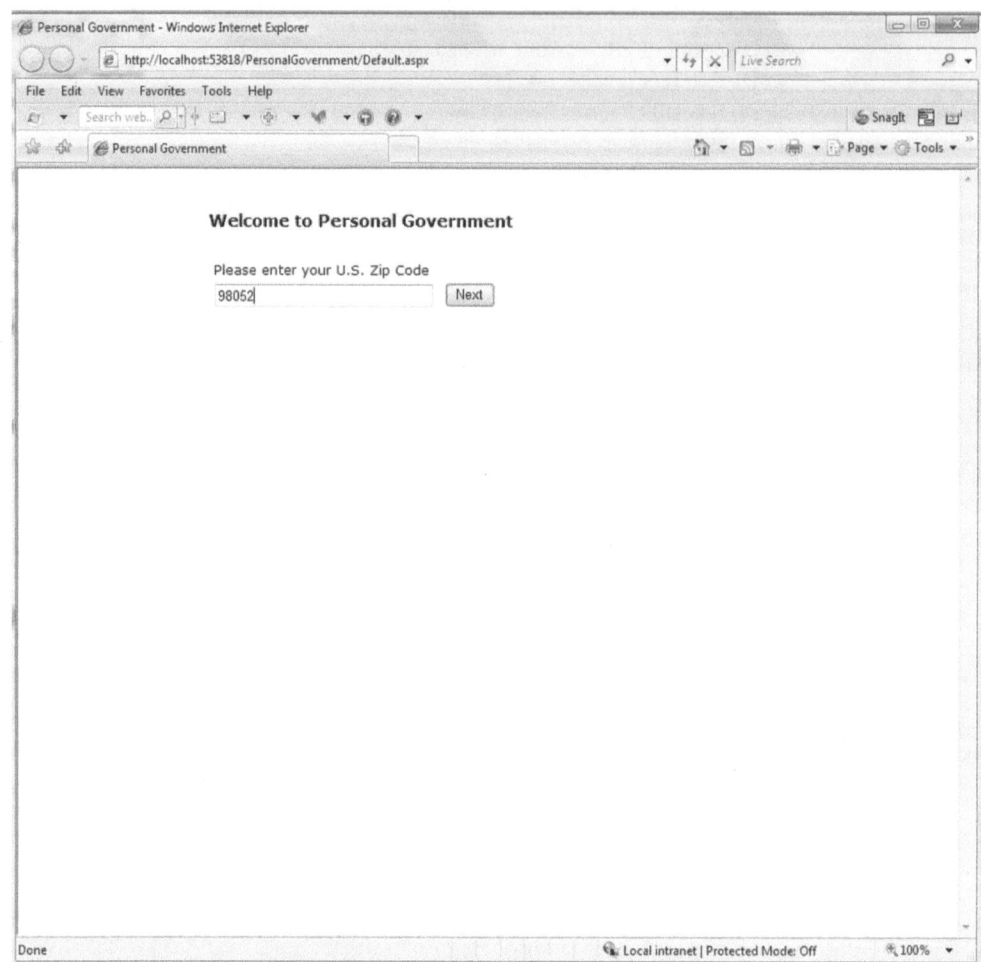

Figure 15-11. *Entering the ZIP code*

2. Enter a U.S. ZIP code in the text box, and click the Next button.

Note If you are outside the United States, you can test this with the ZIP code 98052.

This will call the StrikeIron data services and display all the available information for that ZIP code, as shown in Figure 15-12.

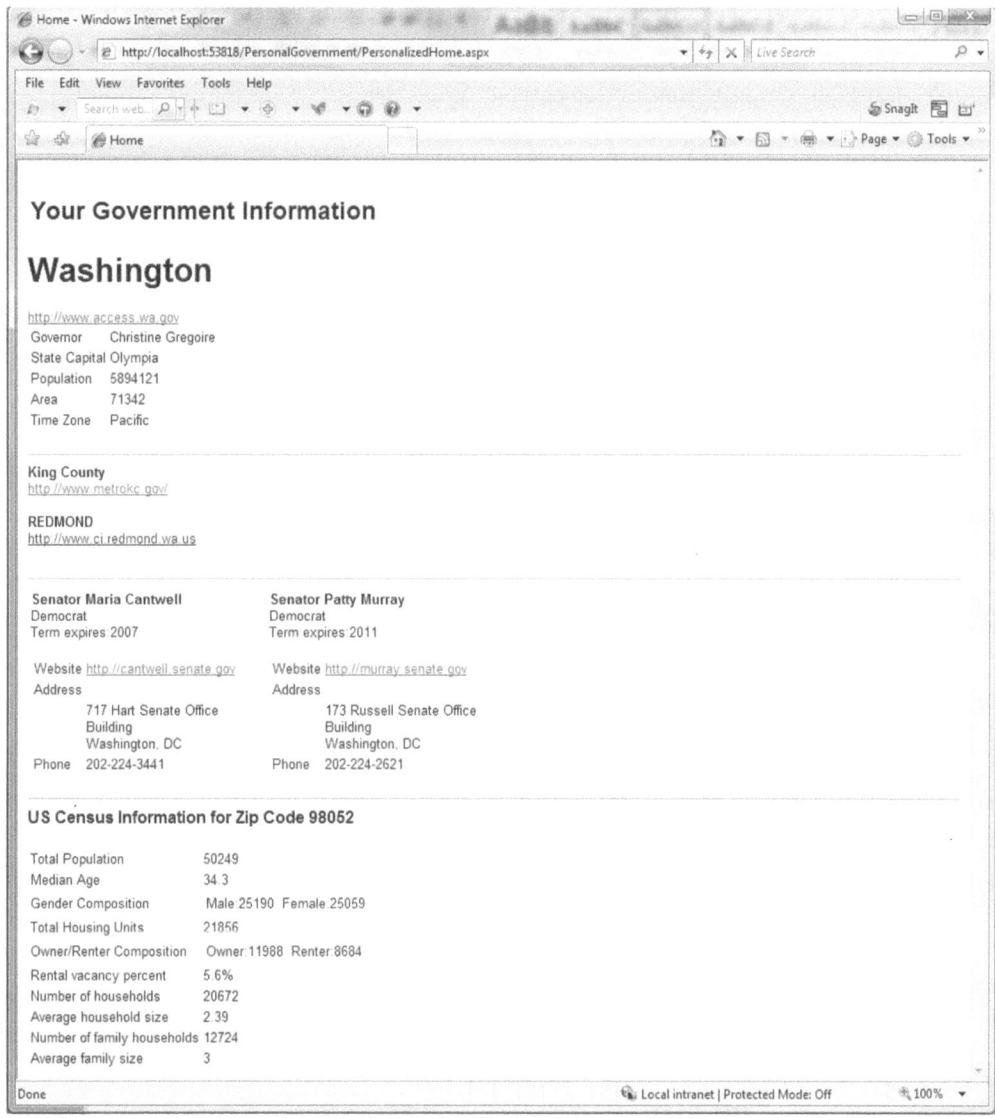

Figure 15-12. *The personalized page*

Adding Information Card Support

In the website you just created, the user was prompted to enter a ZIP code. You will now modify the site to retrieve the details from an information card:

1. Open Default.aspx, and look at the markup.

2. Modify the page directive, setting the `validateRequest` parameter to `false`, as shown here:

```
<%@ Page Language="C#" AutoEventWireup="true"➥
 CodeFile="Default.aspx.cs" Inherits="_Default"➥
  validateRequest="false"%>
```

3. Modify the `html` element to resemble the following:

```
<html xmlns="http://www.w3.org/1999/xhtml" xmlns:ic >
```

4. Right-click the project, and select New Folder. Name the folder **images**.

5. Right-click the new folder, and select Add Existing Item.

6. Navigate to the `login.png` file found in the completed project, and add it to the Images folder.

7. Modify the body of the page to request the `postalcode` claim, and add elements to the UI to request the information card from the user. The complete markup for this is as follows:

```
<body>
    <form id="form1" runat="server" action="PersonalizedHome.aspx" >
    <ic:informationcard
    name='xmlToken'
    style='behavior: url(#default#informationCard)'
    issuer='http://schemas.xmlsoap.org/ws/2005/05/identity/issuer/self'
    tokenType='urn:oasis:names:tc:SAML:1.0:assertion'>
    <ic:add claimType=➥
'http://schemas.xmlsoap.org/ws/2005/05/identity/➥
claims/postalcode' optional='false' />

    </ic:informationcard><div>
                 <table style="width: 491px">
                    <tr>
                        <td style="width: 159px">
                        </td>
                        <td>
                            <asp:Label ID="Label1" ➥
runat="server" Font-Bold="True" Font-Names="Verdana" ➥
Font-Size="Medium"
                                Style="z-index: 100; ➥
left: 189px; position: absolute; top: 41px" ➥
Text="Welcome to Personal Government"
                                Width="305px"></asp:Label>
                            <asp:Label ID="Label3" ➥
```

```
runat="server" Font-Names="Verdana" Font-Size="Smaller" ➥
Style="z-index: 100;
                                       left: 195px; ➥
position: absolute; top: 78px" ➥
Text="Login with your information card" Width="264px"></asp:Label>
                                   
                           <asp:Label ID="Label2" ➥
runat="server" Font-Names="Verdana" Font-Size="Smaller" ➥
Style="z-index: 101;
                                       left: 196px; position: absolute;➥
 top: 176px" Text="Or Enter Your U.S. Zip Code"
                                  Width="219px"></asp:Label>
                           <asp:TextBox ID="tbZipCode" ➥
runat="server" Style="z-index: 102; left: 192px; position: absolute;
                                  top: 204px" Width="209px"></asp:TextBox>
                           <asp:Button ID="btnNext" ➥
runat="server" PostBackUrl="PersonalizedHome.aspx" ➥
Style="z-index: 104;
                                       left: 414px; ➥
position: absolute; top: 202px" Text="Next" Width="50px" />
                           </td>
                      </tr>
                  </table>
              </div>
        <asp:ImageButton ID="ImageButton1" ➥
runat="server" ImageUrl="~/Images/login.png"➥
 PostBackUrl="PersonalizedHome.aspx"
            Style="z-index: 102; left: 214px; position: absolute; top: 108px" />
    </form>
</body>
```

If you switch to design mode, the form should resemble Figure 15-13.

8. Right-click the project, select Add ASP.NET Folder, and then select App_Code.

9. Add the TokenHelper.cs class used earlier in the book. You can find a copy of this class in the App_Code directory of the completed version of the exercise, available only at the Apress website.

10. Right-click PersonalizedHome.aspx, and select View Code.

11. Add the following using lines at the top of the file:

```
using System.IdentityModel.Claims;
using Microsoft.IdentityModel.Samples;
```

Figure 15-13. *The updated start page*

12. Modify the Page_Load event to process a token, if provided. The complete code for the event is as follows, with the required changes in bold:

```
protected void Page_Load(object sender, EventArgs e)
{

string xmlToken;
xmlToken = Request.Params["xmlToken"];

if (xmlToken == null || xmlToken == "")
{
    Session["postalCode"] = Request.Params["tbZipCode"];
}

else
{
    TokenHelper tokenHelper = new TokenHelper(xmlToken);
    RetrieveTokenClaims(tokenHelper.IdentityClaims);
}
```

```
string postalCode = (string)Session["postalCode"];
if (!String.IsNullOrEmpty(postalCode))
{

        ZipCodeInformation.RegisteredUser zcUser ➥
= new ZipCodeInformation.RegisteredUser();
        zcUser.UserID = userID;
        zcUser.Password = password;
        ZipCodeInformation.LicenseInfo zcLicenseIfo ➥
= new ZipCodeInformation.LicenseInfo();
        zcLicenseIfo.RegisteredUser = zcUser;

        ZipCodeInformation.SDPZipCodes zipCodeService ➥
= new ZipCodeInformation.SDPZipCodes();
        zipCodeService.LicenseInfoValue = ➥
new ZipCodeInformation.LicenseInfo();
        zipCodeService.LicenseInfoValue = zcLicenseIfo;
        ZipCodeInformation.ZipCodeOutput zipCodeInfo ➥
= zipCodeService.GetZipCode(postalCode);

        // Use the ZIP code to retrieve city, state, and county.
        // These will be used with the other services.

        Session["city"] = ➥
zipCodeInfo.ServiceResult.ZipCodes[0].PreferredCityName;
        Session["state"] = zipCodeInfo.ServiceResult.ZipCodes[0].State;
        Session["county"] = zipCodeInfo.ServiceResult.ZipCodes[0].County;

        pnlStateInfo.SetRenderMethodDelegate(➥
new System.Web.UI.RenderMethod(RenderStateInfo));
        pnlCityInfo.SetRenderMethodDelegate(➥
new System.Web.UI.RenderMethod(RenderCountyAndCityInfo));
        pnlCensusInformation.SetRenderMethodDelegate(➥
new System.Web.UI.RenderMethod(RenderCensusInfo));
        pnlSenatorInfo.SetRenderMethodDelegate(➥
new System.Web.UI.RenderMethod(RenderSenatorInfo));
        pnlHeader.SetRenderMethodDelegate(➥
new System.Web.UI.RenderMethod(RenderHeader));
    }
}
```

13. Add the RetrieveTokenClaims method to the file. This will query the claimset retrieved from the token and assign the provided claim to a session variable of the same name.

Note Although this chapter uses only one claim, postalcode, you can see how you could use these additional fields to further personalize the experience on the website.

```
private void RetrieveTokenClaims(ClaimSet claims)
{
    foreach (Claim claim in claims)
    {

        switch (claim.ClaimType)
        {
            case "http://schemas.xmlsoap.org/ws/2005/05/identity/claims/➥
givenname":
                Session["givenName"] = claim.Resource.ToString();
                break;
            case "http://schemas.xmlsoap.org/ws/2005/05/identity/claims/➥
surname":
                Session["surName"] = claim.Resource.ToString();
                break;
            case "http://schemas.xmlsoap.org/ws/2005/05/identity/claims/➥
privatepersonalidentifier":
                Session["ppid"] = claim.Resource.ToString();
                break;
            case "http://schemas.xmlsoap.org/ws/2005/05/identity/claims/➥
emailaddress":
                Session["email"] = claim.Resource.ToString();
                break;

            case "http://schemas.xmlsoap.org/ws/2005/05/identity/claims/➥
locality":
                Session["city"] = claim.Resource.ToString();
                break;

            case "http://schemas.xmlsoap.org/ws/2005/05/identity/claims/➥
country":
                Session["country"] = claim.Resource.ToString();
                break;
            case "http://schemas.xmlsoap.org/ws/2005/05/identity/claims/➥
postalcode":
                Session["postalCode"] = claim.Resource.ToString();
                break;

            case "http://schemas.xmlsoap.org/ws/2005/05/identity/claims/➥
stateorprovince":
                Session["state"] = claim.Resource.ToString();
                break;
            case "http://schemas.xmlsoap.org/ws/2005/05/identity/claims/➥
mobilephone":
                Session["mobile"] = claim.Resource.ToString();
                break;
```

```
                case "http://schemas.xmlsoap.org/ws/2005/05/identity/claims/➡
    streetaddress":
                    Session["street"] = claim.Resource.ToString();
                    break;

            }

        }
    }
```

14. Next, add the following elements to the appSettings element in the web.config file. You'll recall that the TokenHelper.cs class uses these elements.

```
    <add key="CertificateSubject" value="www.fabrikam.com"/>
    <add key="StoreName" value="My"/>
    <add key="StoreLocation" value="LocalMachine"/>
    <add key="IdentityClaimType"➡
  value="http://schemas.xmlsoap.org/ws/2005/05/identity/claims/➡
  postalcode"/>
    <add key="MaximumClockSkew" value="60"/>
    </appSettings>
```

> **Note** Because you're not interested in setting up an account or tracking the individual user in this chapter, you do not use privatepersonalidentifier for IdentityClaimType but instead use the one claim you are retrieving, which is postalcode.

15. Next, add a new virtual directory (IIS 6) or application (IIS 7) named personalgovernment that points at this website.

16. Enable SSL for the newly created virtual directory/application.

> **Note** You can find details on how to set up a site in IIS and enable SSL in Chapter 5.

17. Open Internet Explorer, and browse to https://www.fabrikam.com/personalgovernment. You should be presented with the login screen.

18. Click the Sign In with Your Information Card button. You will be prompted for an information card that contains a populated postal code.

19. If you have an existing card, select it. If not, create a card, and populate it with a ZIP code.

> **Note** If you are outside the United States, you can use the ZIP code 98052.

Once your information card has been provided, the website will call the six services from StrikeIron, creating your personal government page, as shown in Figure 15-14.

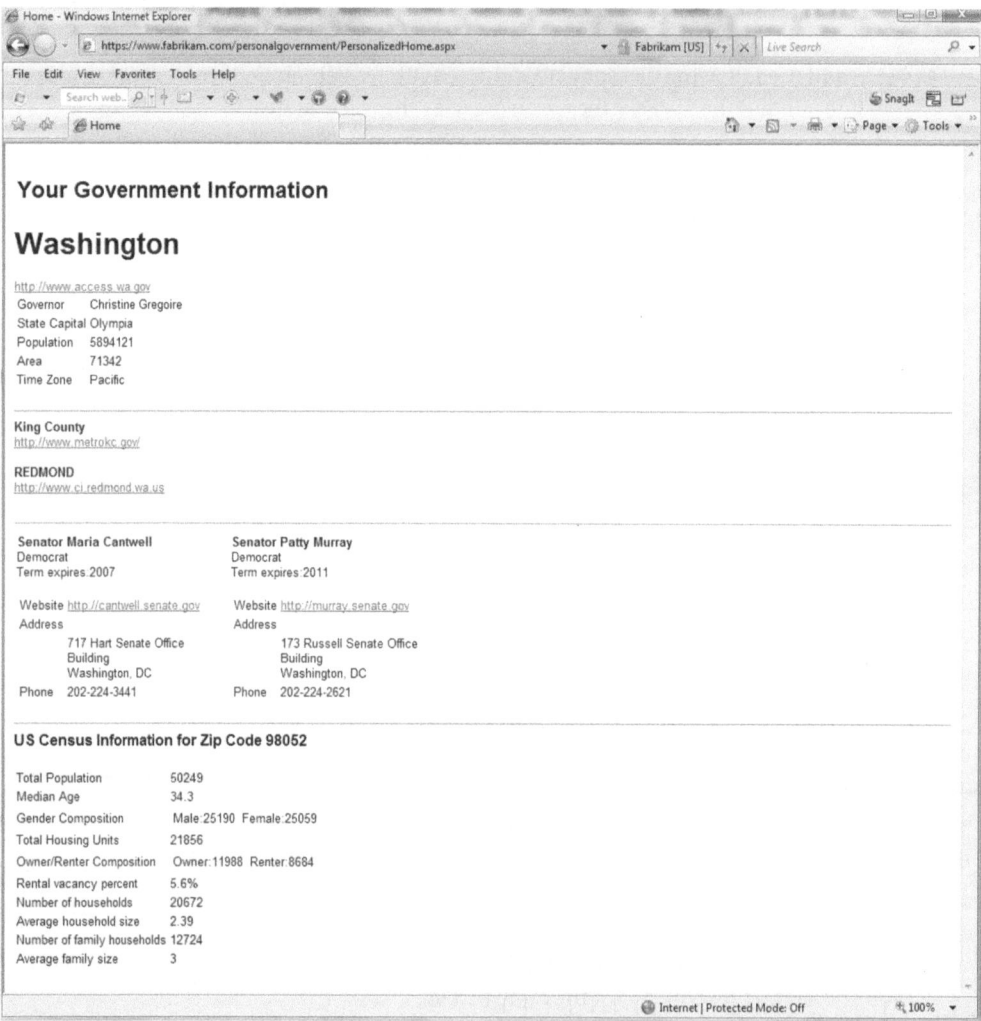

Figure 15-14. *The page personalized using the ZIP code from the information card*

Summary

In Chapter 14, you saw examples of personalization done right and areas where personalization could enhance the experience. This chapter covered how to do personalization without a user account and without historical information on user activity. You learned how to use an information card and just one piece of information, a ZIP code, to create a customized experience on a user's first trip to the site.

Index

You Need the Companion eBook

Your purchase of this book entitles you to buy the companion PDF-version eBook for only $10. Take the weightless companion with you anywhere.

We believe this Apress title will prove so indispensable that you'll want to carry it with you everywhere, which is why we are offering the companion eBook (in PDF format) for $10 to customers who purchase this book now. Convenient and fully searchable, the PDF version of any content-rich, page-heavy Apress book makes a valuable addition to your programming library. You can easily find and copy code—or perform examples by quickly toggling between instructions and the application. Even simultaneously tackling a donut, diet soda, and complex code becomes simplified with hands-free eBooks!

Once you purchase your book, getting the $10 companion eBook is simple:

❶ Visit **www.apress.com/promo/tendollars/**.

❷ Complete a basic registration form to receive a randomly generated question about this title.

❸ Answer the question correctly in 60 seconds, and you will receive a promotional code to redeem for the $10.00 eBook.

2560 Ninth Street • Suite 219 • Berkeley, CA 94710

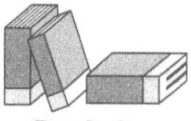

eBookshop

THE EXPERT'S VOICE™

Offer valid through 2/20/08.